THE POWER TO TAX IN EUROPE

This open access book is the sixteenth volume in the Swedish Studies in European Law series. It reflects the series' aim to explore the variety of issues and dilemmas that European law faces in specific areas of EU law and policy, as well as overarching questions of EU institutional and constitutional law. In this volume, experts explore the development of the role of Europe and European law in the field of taxation.

The Power to Tax in Europe

Swedish Studies in European Law
Volume 16

Edited by
Johan Lindholm
and
Anders Hultqvist

•HART•
OXFORD • LONDON • NEW YORK • NEW DELHI • SYDNEY

HART PUBLISHING

Bloomsbury Publishing Plc

Kemp House, Chawley Park, Cumnor Hill, Oxford, OX2 9PH, UK

1385 Broadway, New York, NY 10018, USA

29 Earlsfort Terrace, Dublin 2, Ireland

First published in Great Britain 2023

A catalogue record for this book is available from the British Library.

A catalogue record for this book is available from the Library of Congress.

Library of Congress Control Number: 2022948049

ISBN: HB: 978-1-50996-401-7
ePDF: 978-1-50996-403-1
ePub: 978-1-50996-402-4

Typeset by Compuscript Ltd, Shannon

Contents

1

Introduction

ANDERS HULTQVIST* AND JOHAN LINDHOLM**

DURING 2021, THE Swedish Network for European Legal Studies (SNELS) discussed the importance of understanding how tax law is developing in a European legal context. For centuries, taxation was viewed as being primarily of national importance, the power to tax as 'essential to the very existence of government' and a power that rested with the sovereign and the nation state. This is the principle on which the legal and financial framework of the European Union (EU) is based. However, this system is being challenged by international cooperation, resulting in the unification of many tax rules (ie, the OECD/G20 Base Erosion Profit Shifting project, BEPS), as well as by European law and ambitions in the fiscal field. The European Commission has shown an increasing interest in the unification of the implementation by the Member States of agreements reached on the international arena, as was recently the case after the finalisation of the BEPS project.

EU law requires the removal of discriminatory national tax rules and the Commission has proposed measures aiming to further unify national tax systems, for example, a Common Consolidated Corporate Tax Base (CCCTB). Also, the uniform implementation of the OECD BEPS project through the Anti-Tax Avoidance Directive (ATAD) is now coming into force. Finally, the Commission recently proposed strengthening the EU's so-called own resources through taxes on digital services, major companies and environmentally harmful products and activities, effectively transferring part of the tax base from the Member States to the EU. This dramatic and complex development challenges national tax sovereignty and should be carefully considered with a view to constitutional, international and European law, and what it means for taxation powers.

These developments, in combination with the international coordination of tax law more generally, affect the processes used for deciding taxes and the actors that are involved in those processes. In most modern democratic states, taxes are decided by the elected legislative body, the Parliament, Congress, Reichstag etc. However, international tax coordination is achieved through negotiations

* Professor of Tax Law, Karlstad University. Email: anders.hultqvist@kau.se.
** Professor of Law, Umeå University, Department of Law. Email: johan.lindholm@umu.se.

and compromises by governments. This may lead to a distance and tensions between the formal lawmakers and the negotiating bodies. It also raises democratic concerns and some fear a technocracy where taxes are decided by experts outside the political arena, a development that national politicians may resist and oppose.

The relationship between national tax sovereignty, European union law, the need for international cooperation and international law, tax competition among states, internal national rules and procedures for negotiations, and the creation of international and European tax law provides an interesting field of discussion including the question of where taxing powers ultimately lie: who is behind the wheels of taxation?

In the light of these and similar considerations, SNELS invited legal researchers to discuss related issues at a conference that took place from 25 to 26 November 2021. Due to uncertainties about Covid restrictions, the participants were allowed to choose whether to participate in the conference in person in Stockholm, or digitally. Many contributions were submitted and presented at the conference, some of which have been developed into written contributions presented as chapters in this volume. We hope that both participants and others will enjoy the contributions and that they may inspire and support further discussion and research on this interesting and important topic.

2

Squaring the Constitutional Circle: An Overview of EU Fiscal Powers

JOHAN LINDHOLM[1]

I. A LEGAL PATH TOWARDS GENUINE EU FISCAL POWERS?

TO WHAT EXTENT does or should the European Union (EU) have fiscal powers, in particular 'genuine' taxation powers in the sense that it can levy taxes? The traditional and well-established answer would be 'very limited'. As pointed out by García Antón not long ago even to consider this a possibility would have been cause for ridicule.[2] The explanation for this is simple and straightforward: for a long time there was practically universal agreement that the Treaties on which the Union is based do not provide it with such powers.[3] As a recent European Parliament report so plainly and clearly states, '[a]ccording to the treaties, the EU has no right to levy taxes'[4] and until recently the Commission's position was that 'the EU cannot borrow to finance its budget'.[5] Although the Member States can, and on multiple occasions have, amended the Treaties to increase the EU's powers, there has not been sufficient support among the Member States for granting the EU taxation power. In particular, they have found the significant transfer of sovereignty involved in making this possible, discussed further below,[6] unacceptable.[7]

This may seem to suggest that an inquiry into EU taxation powers is unnecessary. However, recent and ongoing events justify revisiting and reconsidering

[1] Professor of Law, Umeå University, Department of Law.

[2] Ricardo García Antón, 'Does the EU Have a Legitimate Power to Enact Direct Taxes?', ch 3, section I in this volume.

[3] M Ruffert and P Leino-Sandberg, 'Next Generation EU and its Constitutional Ramifications: A Critical Assessment' (2022) 59 *Common Market Law Review* 433, 433–34.

[4] European Parliament, Policy Department for Budgetary Affairs, Directorate-General for Internal Policies, *Reform of the EU own resources*, PE 690.963, March 2021, 10.

[5] Commission's website, quoted in Ruffert and Leino-Sandberg (n 2) 451.

[6] See below section III.

[7] TP Woźniakowski, 'Why the Sovereign Debt Crisis Could Lead to a Federal Fiscal Union: The Paradoxical Origins of Fiscalization in the United States and Insights for the European Union' (2018) 25 *Journal of European Public Policy* 630, 631.

the traditional answer and the theoretical framework on which it relies, as this volume seeks to do. For the EU and its Member States, the last 15 years have consisted of a series of nearly uninterrupted crises, including the global financial crisis, the Euro crisis, the migration crisis, Brexit Covid-19, and most recently the war in Ukraine. These crises highlight that there are many problems facing the Member States that benefit from being resolved through common action at the EU level, that such actions require resources, and that such an approach by extension involves an increased harmonisation, coordination and centralisation in the fiscal area. A well-known example of this development, and of the intra-Union tension that may result from it, can be found in the European Stability Mechanism (ESM), established after the Euro crisis. In May 2020, following a number of challenges of the legality of the ESM and related measures before the Court of Justice of the European Union (CJEU),[8] the Federal Constitutional Court of Germany (BVG) famously refused to accept the proportionality of the European Central Bank's (ECB) public sector purpose programme (PSPP), declaring it ultra vires.[9]

However, it was the Covid-19 crisis that prompted the most dramatic steps in this field, and not only because it prompted the introduction of a new Pandemic Emergency Purchase Programme (PEPP)[10] that is similar and therefore vulnerable to some of the same criticism as the PSPP.[11] In the words of the Council, '[t]he exceptional situation caused by COVID-19 … calls for a coherent and unified approach at Union level'.[12] At the heart of this approach, referred to as Next Generation EU (NGEU), lies the establishment of the EU Recovery Instrument (EURI) that involves the EU borrowing €750 billion, half of which is transferred to the Member States as 'non-repayable support'.[13] Olaf Schultz, at the time Germany's Finance Minister, now its Chancellor, compared the EURI to when the federal government of the United States was first allowed to issue

[8] See, eg, Case C-370/12 *Pringle v Ireland*, ECLI:EU:C:2012:756; Case C-62/14 *Gauweiler et al v German Bundestag*, ECLI:EU:C:2015:400; Case C-493/17 *Weiss et al*, ECLI:EU:C:2018:1000.

[9] BVG, Judgment of 5 May 2020, 2 BvR 859/15, 1651/15, 2006/15, 980/16. The PSPP judgment has been heavily criticised: see, eg, J Basedow et al, 'European Integration: *Quo Vadis*? A Critical Commentary on the *PSPP* Judgment of the German Federal Constitutional Court of May 5, 2020' (2021) 19 *International Journal of Constitutional Law* 188; M Dawson and A Bobic, 'Making Sense of the "Incomprehensible": The PSPP Judgment of the German Federal Constitutional Court' (2020) 57 *Common Market Law Review* 1953.

[10] Decision (EU) 2020/440 of the European Central Bank of 24 March 2020 on a temporary pandemic emergency purchase programme (ECB/2020/17).

[11] Dawson and Bobic (n 8) 1991–94; A Viterbo, 'The PSPP Judgment of the German Federal Constitutional Court: Throwing Sand in the Wheels of the European Central Bank' (2020) 5 *European Papers* 671. However, the BVG has rejected an application for a preliminary injunction against the PEPP. BVG, Order of the Second Senate of 15 April 2021, 2 BvR 547/21.

[12] Council Regulation (EU) 2020/2094 of 14 December 2020 establishing a European Union Recovery Instrument to support the recovery in the aftermath of the COVID-19 crisis [2020] OJ L433 I/23 (EURI Regulation) point 5 of the Preamble.

[13] EURI Regulation, Art 2. For a more detailed overview of events, see B De Witte, 'The European Union's COVID-19 Recovery Plan: The Legal Engineering of an Economic Policy Shift' (2021) 58 *Common Market Law Review* 635.

centrally held federal debt.[14] In the United States, the introduction of this debt significantly strengthened the position of the federal government and was a pivotal moment for the establishment of the United States as we currently know it. With that in mind, Schultz's comparison unavoidably raises the question of whether Europe is witnessing a similar transformation of the EU.[15]

The central raising of debt constitutes an important development in its own right, but arguably even more interesting is the question of how this debt will be repaid. As part of the negotiations on the 2021–2027 Multiannual Financial Framework (MFF), the EU institutions and the Member States through their representations in those institutions have agreed to reform how the EU is financed. In particular, this includes a reform of the system of own resources presented in a new Own Resources Decision[16] and further outlined in the Own Resources Roadmap.[17] By granting the EU new own resources, the Member States would enable the Union to repay the EURI debt.[18] One of the reasons why this approach may be (sufficiently) attractive to the Member States is that it avoids a full, formal debt mutualisation.[19] Also, the new own resources to be assigned to the EU will predominantly be 'fresh' in the sense that the targeted activities do not generally constitute part of the Member States' existing tax base.[20] While it is easy to see how this helps make the reform more appetising to the Member States, by creating those new own resources, the Member States are granting the EU increased taxation powers, including tax-levying powers.[21]

Some proposed new own resources are particularly noteworthy. Already in place is the so-called EU Plastic Tax, a fee of €0.80 per kilogram of non-recyclable plastic that the Member States pay to the EU but which the Member States may and often do pass on to manufacturers, importers, reseller etc.[22] Also,

[14] Peter Dausend and Mark Schieritz, 'Jemand Muss Vorangehen' *Die Zeit* (20 May 2020) 5.

[15] ibid. But see E Jones, 'COVID-19 and the EU Economy: Try Again, Fail Better' (2020) 62 *Survival* 81, 95.

[16] Council Decision (EU, Euratom) 2020/2053 of 14 December 2020 on the system of own resources of the European Union and repealing Decision 2014/335/EU, Euratom [2020] OJ L424/1 (Own Resources Decision).

[17] Interinstitutional Agreement between the European Parliament, the Council of the European Union and the European Commission on budgetary discipline, on cooperation in budgetary matters and on sound financial management, as well as on new own resources, including a roadmap towards the introduction of new own resources [2020] OJ L433I/28.

[18] Own Resources Decision, art 5.

[19] See N da Costa Cabral, 'Borrowing in the European Union: From a Pure National Model to the Antechamber of a European Fiscal Federal Solution' (2021) 43 *Journal of European Integration* 939 (characterising it as a hybrid model).

[20] Own Resources Roadmap, para 2(g).

[21] See Jussi Jaakkola, 'From the Governance of National Tax Systems to Governing Through European Taxation: A Justification for the European Union's Power to Levy Taxes', ch 5, section I in this volume.

[22] Council Regulation (EU, Euratom) 2021/770 of 30 April 2021 on the calculation of the own resource based on plastic packaging waste that is not recycled, on the methods and procedure for making available that own resource, on the measures to meet cash requirements, and on certain aspects of the own resource based on gross national income [2021] OJ L165/15.

starting in January 2023, the plan is that part of the revenues that are generated when emission allowances are auctioned as part of the EU Emissions Trading System (ETS), and which are currently transferred to the Member States, will be redirected straight to the EU and its budget.[23] Similarly, a significant part of the revenues from the proposed Carbon Border Adjustment Mechanism (CBAM) would be transferred to the EU. Under the CBAM, which is aimed to be introduced by January 2023, importers of goods produced outside the EU would need to buy CBAM certificates based on the amount of 'embedded emissions' associated with producing the goods at the average price of emission allowances under the ETS. In this manner, the CBAM seeks to place externally produced goods on an equal footing with goods produced inside the internal market for the purposes of carbon costs.[24]

Looking further into the future, the Own Resources Roadmap envisages the revival of previously introduced but abandoned initiatives now recast as EU Own Resources to be used for the repayment of the EURI debt. This includes the establishment of a Digital Levy,[25] reminiscent of the Digital Service Tax proposed by the Commission in 2018.[26] Since there is as yet no concrete proposal, the exact details of a future Digital Levy are unknown. However, it appears likely that it would take the form of either a direct or indirect tax on social media, online market places, and other digital services and platforms operating in the EU, regardless of where they are established.[27] Finally, the other EU institutions are encouraging the Commission to propose a 'Financial Transaction Tax and a financial contribution linked to the corporate sector or a new common corporate tax base'.[28]

These measures have by some been characterised as 'new, genuine EU taxes'.[29] As discussed in section IV below, it is debatable whether they constitute EU-levied taxes in a formal sense. However, this distinction is largely of a technical nature as the measures serve the same function as taxes and largely affect payers in the same way.

[23] Own Resources Roadmap, para 6. See also Commission, 'Proposal for a Directive of the European Parliament and of the Council amending Directive 2003/87/EC establishing a system for greenhouse gas emission allowance trading within the Union, Decision (EU) 2015/1814 concerning the establishment and operation of a market stability reserve for the Union greenhouse gas emission trading scheme and Regulation (EU) 2015/757' COM(2021) 551 final. At the time of writing the proposal is being considered by the Council.

[24] Commission, 'Proposal for a Regulation of the European Parliament and of the Council establishing a carbon border adjustment mechanism' COM(2021) 564 final.

[25] Own Resources Roadmap, para 5.

[26] Commission, 'Proposal for a Council Directive on the common system of a digital services tax on revenues resulting from the provision of certain digital services' COM(2018) 148 final.

[27] Commission, Ref Ares(2021)312667.

[28] Own Resources Roadmap, para 10.

[29] F Fabbrini, 'The Legal Architecture of the Economic Responses to COVID-19: EMU beyond the Pandemic' (2022) 60 *Journal of Common Market Studies* 186, 193.

The development that has occurred and is proposed for the future can be referred to as fiscalisation, that is to say a process through which the EU level extends its powers to raise its own sources of revenue and, in so doing, decrease its financial dependence on the Member States.[30] The current EU development is in several regards similar to the one of the United States following the Revolutionary War: in both systems, crises-related debt pressures inspired previously reluctant constituent states to allow the central entity to draw common debt and, in order to pay off that debt, granted the central entity increased taxation powers.[31] In light of such fiscalisation, you may ask whether the map of the power to tax in Europe accurately represents the territory and, if not, if it is the territory that needs remodelling or the map that needs redrawing. This volume seeks to shed some light on these salient questions.

An accurate understanding of these questions requires considering a multitude of perspectives, one of which is the budgetary-policy perspective. Which resource-requiring tasks and expenses should be run through the EU and how should the burden of paying for these tasks and expenses be distributed among the Member States? These questions turn on complex political and constitutional concerns and how we answer them depends on our view of what the Union is, can be and should be in relation to the Member States. You might be sceptical whether Europeans will be able to agree on such difficult and divisive questions.[32] Even if you assume that there is sufficient institutional and popular support for granting the EU genuine taxation powers, doing so raises complex legal questions. As the contributions to this volume demonstrate, the EU legal framework governing fiscal powers in general and taxation powers in particular is a highly complex legal environment that is both technically and theoretically challenging. In the end, no clear understanding of these matters can be produced without taking into consideration at once legal, budgetary and policy perspectives. It also requires viewing the EU legal framework governing taxation through a lens of constitutional and taxation principles.

To make this complex task a little more manageable, a distinction can a priori be made between, on the one hand, the rules and principles that make up the EU legal framework governing EU powers, including in the area of taxation (see section II) and, on the other, the constitutional and taxation principles of relevance regarding whether EU taxation powers can be properly justified (see section III).

[30] *cf* Woźniakowski (n 6) 633.

[31] See Woźniakowski (n 6); TP Woźniakowski and M Poiares Maduro, 'Why Fiscal Justice Should Be Reinstalled Through European Taxes That the Citizens Will Support: A Proposal' (December 2020).

[32] See, eg, Frans Vanistendael and others, 'European Solidarity Requires EU Taxes' (*TaxProf Blog*, 30 April 2020), available at: taxprof.typepad.com/taxprof_blog/2020/04/european-solidarity-requires-eu-taxes.html.

II. THE LEGAL REGULATION OF THE EU'S (POTENTIAL) TAXATION POWERS

The EU legal framework governing taxes and taxation is no doubt familiar to the reader and numerous contributors to this volume present and discuss it in greater detail. However, a brief overview of the general structure is in order. The structure of the EU legal framework can be understood and explained using the familiar concepts of negative and positive integration, which in turn are governed by rules that are distinguishable from the rules governing EU fiscal affairs.[33]

Negative harmonisation refers to the harmonising effect of EU law by forbidding Member States to take certain actions, in particular impeding the fundamental freedoms relating to the internal market. This obligation applies to all areas irrespective of and extending beyond the EU's competences. As the European Court of Justice (ECJ) has pointed out on numerous occasions,

> even though, in the areas in which the Community does not have competence, the Member States remain, in principle, free to lay down the conditions for the existence and exercise of the rights at issue, they must nevertheless exercise that competence consistently with Community law.[34]

Consequently, EU Member States may, for example, not exercise their taxation powers in a way that discriminates against goods, persons, or services from other Member States or otherwise hinders market access,[35] or that benefits domestic actors in a way that distorts competition.[36] While negative integration may have a significant impact on Member States' exercise of their fiscal powers, it does not and cannot serve as the basis of EU fiscal powers.

More relevant for the topic discussed here is positive harmonisation, a concept that refers to the 'Europeanisation' of law in certain areas and on certain subjects through the adoption of common Union normative standards using EU legislation. It is undisputed that the EU is a political entity of limited powers, that it only has the enumerated powers conferred upon it by the Member States through the Treaties, and that any measure taken by the Union must consequently rest on a legal basis that can be found in the Treaties.[37]

It is frequently argued that the Union's competence in the area of taxation is weak and it is common to claim that the EU does not enjoy taxation powers.

[33] *cf* E Traversa and G Bizioli, 'Solidarity in the European Union in the Time of COVID-19: Paving the Way for a Genuine EU Tax?' (2020) 48 *Intertax* 743, 743. See also Claudio Sciancalepore, 'The Reform of EU Own Resources under the Next Generation EU Programme: A Suitable Moment for the Introduction of a European Tax?, ch 7, section II in this volume.

[34] Case C-341/05 *Laval un Partneri Ltd v Svenska Byggnadsarbetareförbundet et al*, ECLI:EU:C:2007:809, para 87.

[35] See, eg, Case 270/83 *Commission v France (avoir fiscale)*, ECLI:EU:C:1986:37, para 13; Case C-334/02 *Commission v France*, ECLI:EU:C:2004:129, para 21; Case C-446/03 *Marks & Spencer*, ECLI:EU:C:2005:763, para 29.

[36] Art 107(1) TFEU.

[37] Art 5(2) Treaty on European Union (TEU).

However, even a cursory investigation reveals that it is neither non-existent nor negligible as the EU has harmonised a number of indirect taxes, including custom duties and value-added tax (VAT).[38] Ascertaining the extent to which the Treaties provide a legal basis for Union measures in the area of taxation is, however, not easy. The Treaties do not explicitly state that the Member States have exclusive competence in the area of taxation, nor would this be expected since the Treaties are constructed based on the principle that 'competences not conferred upon the Union in the Treaties remain with the Member States'.[39] In other words, the competences of the Member States thus make up the 'negative space' left after determining what the competences of the EU are.[40] In order to ascertain what competences the Union has in the area of taxation thus requires considering all competence-conferring Treaty provisions, but this is not an easy task since many of these provisions do not have a clearly defined scope and experience – including relating to measures taken and proposed within NGEU – illustrate that it is highly amendable.

Articles 113–15 of the Treaty on the Functioning of the European Union (TFEU) provides the Union with a broad competence to 'approximate' national law to ensure a well-functioning internal market, including in the area of taxation. Whereas Article 113 TFEU specifically targets indirect taxation, Article 115 TFEU allows for the adoption of directives for the purpose of harmonising fiscal provisions, including in the area of direct taxation,[41] to the extent that it 'directly affect the establishment or functioning of the internal market'. It would seem that Article 115 TFEU exclusively provides the EU with the power of legislation for the purpose of harmonising national law, specifically to ensure a well-functioning internal market.[42] However, as it is connected to the internal market, this provision has a potentially broad scope and has, for example, served as the legal basis for the Interest Royalties Directive (IRD),[43] the Parent-Subsidiary Directive (PSD),[44] and the Anti-Tax Avoidance Directives (ATAD).[45] These Articles would likely also serve as the legal basis for the aforementioned Digital Levy.

[38] See, eg, AJ Menéndez, 'Another View of the Democratic Deficit: No Taxation without Representation' in C Joerges, Y Mény and JHH Weiler (eds), *What Kind of Constitution for What Kind of Polity? Responses to Joschka Fischer* (European University Institute 2000) 133.

[39] Art 4(1) TEU.

[40] Plus, with regard to shared competences, to what extent the EU has exercised them.

[41] See, eg, Traversa and Bizioli (n 32) 743.

[42] *cf* François Barreau, 'The Legitimacy of the European Union's Tax-Based Own Resources', ch 4, section III.A.i in this volume.

[43] Council Directive 2003/49/EC of 3 June 2003 on a common system of taxation applicable to interest and royalty payments made between associated companies of different Member States [2003] OJ L157/49.

[44] Council Directive 2011/96/EU of 30 November 2011 on the common system of taxation applicable in the case of parent companies and subsidiaries of different Member States [2011] OJ L345/8.

[45] Council Directive (EU) 2016/1164 of 12 July 2016 laying down rules against tax avoidance practices that directly affect the functioning of the internal market [2016] OJ L193/1 (ATAD 1); Council Directive 2017/952 of 29 May 2017 amending Directive (EU) 2016/1164 as regards hybrid

Article 192(2) TFEU provides the Union with competence to adopt measures of a 'fiscal nature' that seek to protect the environment. The provision plays a prominent role in the fiscalisation process. For example, both the EU ETS and the CBAM, discussed above, rely on Article 192(2) for their legal basis. Related to this, Article 194(3) TFEU provides the Union with the power to act at the intersection of a well-functioning internal market and the preservation of the environment.

Separately from the Treaty provisions that serve as the basis for positive and negative harmonisation, part six of the TFEU regulates the internal fiscal affairs of the EU. A key concept in those rules is the EU's own resources. For example, Article 311 TFEU provides that '[t]he Union shall provide itself with the means necessary to attain its objectives and carry through its policies [and that, w]ithout prejudice to other revenue, the budget shall be financed wholly from *own resources*'.[46] The Treaties do not define what these own resources are and it is, according to the same provision, up to the Council to define, create and abolish these through the Own Resources Decision, which as discussed above, was recently revised as part of NGEU.[47] Although many of those measures have their legal basis in a competence-conferring Treaty provision rather than the budgetary rules, the EU Plastic Tax is an example of an exception that shows that fiscal provisions can serve as the basis of EU taxation measures.

Finally, it is worth mentioning some additional Treaty provisions of relevance in the specific context of EURI. The legal basis for EU borrowing funds is not obvious. On the contrary, Article 310(1) TFEU suggests that the EU may not use borrowing to finance its expenditure.[48] However, in what has been described as a feat of legal engineering,[49] the Commission found a solution by combining two Treaty provisions. The first is Article 122 TFEU which is part of the Treaty section on economic policy and provides for 'emergency powers' in exceptional circumstances and allows the Union to take 'measures appropriate to the economic situation'. This allowed for the raising of funds through borrowing.[50] The second part of the measure, that is the distribution of those funds to the Member States through the Recovery and Resilience Facility (RRF), is based on Article 175(3) TFEU on specific actions necessary for strengthening economic, social, and territorial cohesion.[51]

mismatches with third countries [2017] OJ L144/1 (ATAD 2); Commission, 'Proposal for a Council directive laying down rules to prevent the misuse of shell entities for tax purposes and amending Directive 2011/16/EU' COM(2021) 565 final (proposed ATAD 3).

[46] Emphasis added.

[47] Council Decision (EU, Euratom) 2020/2053 (n 15).

[48] See also Ruffert and Leino-Sandberg (n 2) 450–51.

[49] De Witte (n 12) 679–81.

[50] EURI Decision.

[51] Regulation (EU) 2021/241 of the European Parliament and of the Council of 12 February 2021 establishing the Recovery and Resilience Facility [2021] OJ L57/17–75.

III. JUSTIFYING EU TAXATION POWERS

The measures adopted and proposed under the EU legal framework show that the EU is committed to a significant extension of its tax-levying capacity. Although the creative reinterpretation of the EU legal framework that makes such measures possible can be and rightfully has been criticised,[52] and forced interpretations of its competences hardly helps the EU build legitimacy,[53] it appears unlikely that the fiscalisation process will come to a complete stop 'just' because it violates the traditional interpretation of EU's competence under the Treaties.

As it has become doubtful whether the EU lacks taxation powers, it is natural to turn to the normative question of whether the EU ought to enjoy taxation powers, 'reviewing the legitimacy of the European Union's could-be power to levy taxes'.[54] To borrow Brokelind's analogy, there is a need to identify the 'driving licence' that justifies the holding and exercise of taxation power.[55] Many of the contributions to this volume engage in this complex normative question from different perspectives. While it is true that the EU, like other political entities, needs resources to carry out its obligations,[56] it does not follow that the EU must attain those resources by directly levying taxes. At the same time, it is also not a given that the division of power between the Member States and the Union is fixed along traditional lines.[57]

The different perspectives and arguments raised and discussed by the contributors broadly fall into two categories, where the first category departs from and focuses on constitutional law and theory. A natural point of departure for this discussion is the concept of sovereignty, including more specifically tax sovereignty, and the connection between sovereignty and taxation powers.[58] The concept of sovereignty was instrumental for the formation of the modern notion of states and came to define relations between states. The fundamental idea is, in summary, that each state is sovereign to govern and tax activities taking place in the territory it controls, enjoys a right to do so without interference from other states, and has a corollary obligation not to interfere with other states' right to exercise these powers in the territories they control.[59] As a consequence,

[52] See, eg, Ruffert and Leino-Sandberg (n 2) 472 ('We hold that the Treaties should matter; they are not just an impediment to be circumvented by creative legal drafting, updating an inconvenient webpage or through tweeting whatever suits a particular constituency').

[53] See Francesco Farri, 'Between Form and Substance: At the Root of the Limits of the EU Taxing Powers', ch 6, section IV.B in this volume.

[54] See Jaakkola, ch 5, section IV in this volume.

[55] See Cécile Brokelind, 'The Power to Tax in International and EU Tax Law: Who Is Sitting Behind the Wheel?', ch 10, section II in this volume.

[56] Thomas Hobbes, *Leviathan* (Oxford University Press 1996) 229.

[57] See Jaakkola, ch 5, section V in this volume.

[58] See, eg, Farri, ch 6, sections I–II in this volume.

[59] See Brokelind, ch 10, section II; Mariya Senyk, 'A New System of Tax-Based EU Own Resources: How does it Affect the Fiscal Sovereignty of the Member States?', ch 8, section II; and García Antón, ch 3, section II.B in this volume.

one problem has traditionally been how to allocate the right to tax multinational economic activity between states.[60] As each state is sovereign, traditional thinking dictates that any international obligation among states is voluntary and can be revoked. As demonstrated by Brexit, this thinking and the principles that follow from it ultimately apply to the legal obligations of the Member States under EU law.[61]

Using this as the point of departure, the obvious questions are whether the EU enjoys (tax) sovereignty and, if not, whether it could and, if so, under what conditions. It should be pointed out that these questions do not necessarily involve replacing exclusive national tax sovereignty with exclusive European tax sovereignty,[62] but largely turn on whether and to what extent the EU and the Member States shall exercise parallel or 'shared' taxation powers.[63] At the same time, there is no denying that from the perspective of the Member States, sharing taxation powers with the EU inevitably involves forsaking some taxation powers.

To address these questions, you may return to the origin of the sovereignty of states and the core constitutional ideas that sovereignty ultimately rests with the people (popular sovereignty), that it is the consent of the people that serves as the constituent power (*pouvoir constituant*) that gives a sovereign entity its authority,[64] and that it is the people who decide how to allocate and reallocate sovereignty.[65]

The consent of the people constituting a condition for the EU legitimately levying taxes is also represented in the maxim 'no taxation without representation' that encapsulates one of the fundamental principles of taxation.[66] Using this line of thinking, the questions of where taxation power lies and how taxation power can be legitimately exercised connect to broader issues regarding sovereignty and the legitimate exercise of power via the concept of popular self-governance. As explained by Lindseth, 'the legitimate capacity to extract and redirect fiscal and human resources on a societal scale' lies at the heart of 'the modern notion of democratic self-government'.[67] In his view, this means that the capacity to tax depends on the existence of a 'demos-consciousness' that is

[60] See Brokelind, ch 10, section II in this volume.

[61] Case C-621/18 *Wightman et al v Secretary of State for Exiting the European Union*, ECLI:EU:C:2018:999, paras 56–58.

[62] Which perhaps is where the doctrine on states' tax sovereignty may lead us.

[63] See Jaakkola, ch 5, section IV in this volume.

[64] John Locke, *Two Treatises of Government and a Letter Concerning Toleration* (Yale University Press 2003) paras 95–99.

[65] ibid 240.

[66] See Barreau, ch 4, section III.A in this volume.

[67] PL Lindseth, 'The Perils of "As If" European Constitutionalism' (2016) 22 *European Law Journal* 696, 707.

historically and culturally based.[68] A key question, which multiple contributions to this volume discuss, is whether such a European 'demos' exists and, if not, whether and how it could come about.[69]

When approached from this angle, it is not surprising that the idea of the EU having a genuine power to tax raises the familiar spectre of the EU's 'democratic deficit'. Do the 'Peoples of Europe' enjoy such representation in the EU that they can (and do) consent to the Union taxing them? In democracies, such consent is expressed through democratically elected political institutions. Ignoring for the moment that NGEU relies on approaches that include particularly limited influence by the European Parliament and the national parliaments,[70] you could be inclined to think that an increased involvement of the directly elected European Parliament can both justify and motivate increased powers of taxation at the EU level.[71]

It should in this context be noted that the scope of the Union's taxation powers is largely determined by the Member States. Even under the Commission's creative post-NGEU interpretation of the Treaties, almost all of the Treaty provisions that are likely to serve as the basis for EU measures in the taxation field require the unanimous consent of the Member States' governments.[72] However, the Member States agreeing on the EU having, taking, or exercising certain powers does not necessarily constitute popular consent. While valuable in some regards, a compromise can also 'compromise democracy',[73] and the use of the unanimity principle may in fact enhance the democratic deficit.[74]

Another important aspect of the EU being granted taxation powers is how it affects the relationship between the Union and the Member States. Expanded EU fiscal powers can be seen as an inroad into the autonomy of the Member States and a transfer of power from the national level to the Union level. Although expansion of Union competences generally involves some transfer of power, this one is arguably particularly significant, at least if you agree that taxation powers are particularly important to the Member States and their sovereignty. While this is clearly important to the Member States, their loss of power is not 'merely'

[68] ibid. Art 58 of the Swedish Act of Government of 1809 ('Regeringsformen') echoes this idea by referring to the 'ancient right of the Swedish people to tax itself' (my translation).

[69] See, eg, Barreau, ch 4, section III.B; Farri, ch 6, section V; and García Antón, ch 3, section III in this volume.

[70] Ruffert and Leino-Sandberg (n 2) 446–47, 455–56.

[71] *cf* AJ Menéndez, 'Taxing Europe: Two Cases for a European Power to Tax (with Some Comparative Observations)' (2004) 10 *Columbia Journal of European Law* 297, 308. But see Farri, ch 6, section III.A.ii.c ('if there cannot, in a democratic system, be taxation without representation, there can still be representation without taxation power').

[72] See, eg, Art 115 TFEU.

[73] A von Bogdandy, 'European Democracy: A Reconstruction through Dismantling Misconceptions' (2022) 7, available at: www.ssrn.com/abstract=4014445.

[74] See Claudio Sciancalepore, 'The Reform of EU Own Resources under the Next Generation EU Programme: A Suitable Moment for the Introduction of a European Tax?', ch 7, section VI in this volume.

limited to a transfer of competences in certain areas. The new measures will also endow the EU with 'a fiscal capacity independent from state transfers … akin to those of federal regimes',[75] what can be referred to as the '[f]iscal autonomy by the EU'.[76] The creation of tax-based new own resources, which will probably be made permanent to some extent even after the repayment of the EURI debt, will make the EU less dependent on the Member States for its funding. This represents a fundamental shift in their relationship, the consequences of which are difficult to forecast.

The second category of arguments focuses on tax principles, combined with arguments regarding why the Union ought to enjoy taxation powers. These arguments can also be used to improve the social and political legitimacy of European taxes and help serve as the foundation for a European fiscal contract.[77] One reason for states to federalise is to achieve the scale necessary to tackle problems that each state is too small to address by itself.[78] A similar argument can be made for fiscal federalisation, including specifically in the context of the EU where the Member States are facing a number of great (largely global) challenges that cannot (well) be resolved by the individual states. Using the Covid-19 crisis – and the other crises discussed above – to justify NGEU are examples of a functionalist approach to taxation power.[79] An argument can be made that the EU ought to have the competence to take action against challenges that it, but not the Member States, can resolve. It then naturally follows that the Union should also have the resources necessary to take such action. To the extent that new tax-based own resources are designed in such a way that they, in addition to raising funding for legitimate measures, shape behaviour in a way that helps resolve these problems,[80] they can be justified on dual grounds.[81]

Along similar lines, providing the Union with taxation power can be justified on the basis that there are activities that ought to be taxed and which only the Union can tax. This argument connects to the long-standing global discussion on how to resolve the problem that multinational enterprises (MNEs) exploit the present state-and-territoriality-based tax order to effectively avoid being taxed anywhere.[82] That the EU's proposed new own resources are 'fresh', in the sense that they draw on tax bases not previously tapped by the Member States,

[75] F Fabbrini, 'The EU Economic Constitution after COVID-19 and "Next Generation EU"' (1 April 2022) 24–25, available at: www.ssrn.com/abstract=4101979.

[76] AP Dourado and M Poiares Maduro, 'A Plead for the European Union Fiscal Autonomy' (2020) 48 *Intertax* 695, 697.

[77] See Barreau, ch 4, section III.B.ii in this volume.

[78] R Schütze, 'Political Philosophy of Federalism' (Oxford University Press, June 2016) 5–6, available at: oxcon.ouplaw.com/view/10.1093/law:mpeccol/law-mpeccol-e289.

[79] See Farri, ch 6, section IV.A; and Sciancalepore, ch 7, section V in this volume. Justifying new tax-based EU own resources with the need to resolve the climate crises is in much the same vein. ibid.

[80] At the same time, the ability of taxes to shape tax-payers' behaviour can be discussed.

[81] See, eg, Senyk, ch 8, section V in this volume.

[82] See Brokelind, ch 10, section IV in this volume; Jaakkola, ch 5, section III in this volume. Some form of international, transnational or supernational coordination appears necessary to prevent such behaviour.

means that the development will seem like less of a loss of (tax) sovereignty to the Member States, thereby also making it more palatable. If these new own resources are based on revenue sources that Member States do not currently tax and also cannot effectively tax, NGEU would be broadening the total tax base while seemingly marginally infringing on the Member States' tax sovereignty.[83] However, additionally and equally important, it would also help ensure that MNEs pay an equitable share of their profits in taxes, thereby increasing the legitimacy of the tax system as a whole. New own resources that target MNEs and revenue streams that avoid national taxation, such as the Digital Levy or a potential financial transaction tax, can be justified on these grounds.[84] Finally, by focusing its taxation powers on activities that involve numerous Member States, the EU can help reduce intrastate conflict.[85] At the same time, it should not be ignored that these types of extraterritorial measures challenge well-established tax principles and it is difficult to foresee the consequences that may result from undermining them.

This line of reasoning shares some elements with the theory or principle of benefit taxation according to which the state that provided an enterprise with the resources used to conduct its business should have the right to tax the enterprise. This principle has been invoked in the context of resolving states' competing international tax claims, preventing tax evasion in an increasingly globalised world and, by extension, enhancing the legitimacy of the tax system.[86] By applying this thinking to the context of the EU, a strong claim can be made that the Union has helped generate value and wealth that would otherwise not exist, for example, by creating and maintaining the internal market and by investing in activities. On that basis, a normative argument can be made that the Union should be allowed to tax those who have benefited from the system, who will thereby also contribute economically to uphold it.[87]

An orientation towards EU taxation of centrally created wealth can also help shift the view of the fiscal dimension of EU affairs. The current system, under which the EU's budget is made up of Member State contributions, leads to a focus on how much each Member State pays to and gets back from the Union, a view of EU fiscal affairs as a transfer of wealth between Member States, and MFF negotiations that have been described as an 'embarrassing spectacle'.[88] By comparison, a fiscal system that focuses on and is built around the wealth and value generated by integration and the EU can strengthen and legitimise

[83] Jean Pisani-Ferry, 'European Union Recovery Funds: Strings Attached, but Not Tied up in Knots' (2020) 3, available at: www.bruegel.org/policy-brief/european-union-recovery-funds-strings-attached-not-tied-knots.

[84] See Brokelind, ch 10, section IV in this volume.

[85] See Jaakkola, ch 5, section IV in this volume.

[86] See, eg, C Brokelind, 'EU Tax Law and the Return of the Nation-State' in A Bakardjieva Engelbrekt et al (eds), *The European Union and the Return of the Nation State* (Springer International Publishing 2020) 146–147, available at: link.springer.com/10.1007/978-3-030-35005-5_6.

[87] See Jaakkola, ch 5, section IV; and Sciancalepore, ch 7, section V in this volume.

[88] Fabbrini, 'The Legal Architecture of the Economic Responses to COVID-19' (n 28) 193.

financial solidarity.[89] Finally, you can discuss, as the contributions do, the extent to which a system of taxation that strengthens solidarity within the EU also helps to legitimise itself through solidarity as a democratic ethos.[90]

IV. CONCLUSIONS

NGEU poses an interesting and potentially disruptive case regarding EU taxation powers. Are the measures currently in place and planned to be adopted as part of the NGEU expressions of the exercise of genuine EU taxation powers? Many are probably technically not. For example, the EU Plastic Tax is not a 'genuine' EU tax in the sense that the compulsory transfers involved are most immediately imposed and collected by the Member States. Although these transfers ultimately end up with the EU, the taxes themselves can thus best be characterised as indirectly imposed and collected by the EU.[91] Unlike the EU Plastic Tax, the EU would directly collect the ETS revenues. However, it is also questionable whether ETS auction revenues can be considered a 'tax' imposed by the EU, even though the ETS is functionally similar to a carbon tax. The CBAM system would be enforced by the Member States: it would be the national authorities that would sell the certificates, and the Member States that would transfer a portion of the income from these sales to the EU. In this manner, CBAM is not a tax directly imposed or directly collected by the EU. A Digital Levy or financial transaction tax may possibly be closer to genuine EU taxes, depending on their design, but this is still too uncertain.

At the same time, by providing for the borrowing of funds (EURI), distributing of those funds to the Member States (RRF), and repaying those funds through the creation of new tax-based EU own resources, NGEU clearly leads to fiscalisation in Europe and can be seen as 'an antechamber of a European fiscal federal solution'.[92] To what extent is there a significant and relevant difference between the potential powers of the EU in the area of taxation and 'genuine' taxation powers? Regardless of their formal designation, the type of transfers resulting from the Plastic Tax, ETS, CBAM, a Digital Levy and other similar measures, will largely appear to constitute taxes to the individuals and corporations that are to make the transfers. For example, while the ETS and CBAM are formally distinctively different from a carbon tax, they are functionally similar and affect the 'taxpayers' equally. Moreover, a cursory examination will reveal that these transfers that stem from the EU are regulated through EU legislation

[89] *cf* M Poiares Maduro, 'A New Governance for the European Union and the Euro: Democracy and Justice' (2013) 16 *Yearbook of Polish European Studies* 111, 118.

[90] Compare García Antón, ch 3, section III and Farri, ch 6, section V.B. See also Sciancalepore, ch 7, section V in this volume.

[91] See García Antón, ch 3, section III; and Sciancalepore, ch 7, section IV in this volume.

[92] Costa Cabral (n 18) 4.

and make a substantial contribution to the EU budget. The individuals that will actually make the compulsory contributions that end up in Brussels to cover public goods at the European level should be forgiven for considering these as EU taxes, and in addition, arguments that they technically do not qualify as such may be lost on them. In light of this it seems clear that we must take the issue of whether this is justified and justifiable seriously, including, for example, the question of whether these compulsory contributions rest on popular consent.

This overview provides a basis for making a simple but important point: you should take care to guard yourself against the ideas that the EU does not enjoy powers in the area of taxation or that tax sovereignty is something unique and exclusive to nation states, in this context the EU Member States. It appears that we find ourselves in a period of radical change when the EU exercises or seeks fiscal power in a way and to an extent that was unimaginable until quite recently,[93] and achieved by a creative reinterpretation of the Treaties. It is fair to say, as some have claimed, that NGEU in this regard is a 'game-changer'.[94] While it is true that there is currently a relatively limited number of EU measures in the area of taxation, recent developments highlight the EU's potentially significant fiscal powers. While the structure of the Treaties may act as an obstacle to the Union imposing and directly collecting some form of taxes from private entitles, the examples discussed demonstrate that these obstacles are not insurmountable.

NGEU has been characterised as an exceptional measure in response to an exceptional situation and many of its core elements are legally based on Treaty provisions providing exceptional powers in exceptional situations.[95] However, it is questionable whether NGEU really is a temporary, one-off event.[96] First, NGEU is not entirely a Covid-19 response but addresses problems that date back to the global financial crisis and the subsequent Euro crisis. Second, the EURI funds 'are mostly allocated on the basis of criteria that have little relevance for fighting COVID-19, such as climate neutrality, digital infrastructure, and social cohesion'.[97] Third, recent history has shown with perfect clarity that there is always an 'exceptional' crisis in Europe that justifies central fiscal arrangements. In fact, at the time of writing the EU is contemplating taking on additional joint debt for the reconstruction of Ukraine.[98]

[93] Fabbrini, 'The Legal Architecture of the Economic Responses to COVID-19' (n 28) 193.

[94] Fabbrini, 'The EU Economic Constitution after COVID-19' (n 74) 24.

[95] Especially Arts 122 and 175(3) TFEU.

[96] There are also many who see it as an opportunity for establishing permanent change. *cf* De Witte (n 12) 679 ('Time will tell whether it can be transformed into a permanent tool for common fiscal policy and macro-economic stabilization'). See also Sciancalepore, ch 7, section VI in this volume.

[97] Ruffert and Leino-Sandberg (n 2) 446.

[98] Jorge Valero, 'EU Weighs Joint Debt to Fund Ukraine's Long-Term Rebuilding' *Bloomberg* (10 May 2022), available at www.bloomberg.com/news/articles/2022-05-09/eu-weighs-joint-debt-to-fund-ukraine-s-long-term-reconstruction'; Dhara Ranasinghe, 'Analysis-Ukraine crisis another nudge for joint EU bonds' *Reuters* (21 March 2022) available at www.reuters.com/article/eurozone-bonds-issuance-analysis-idTRNIKCN2LI0UK.

3

Does the EU Have a Legitimate Power to Enact Direct Taxes?

RICARDO GARCÍA ANTÓN*

I. INTRODUCTION

IF SOMEONE HAD answered the question in this chapter's title in the affirmative 15 years ago, for example, such answer would have been the butt of everyone's jokes. The European Union (EU) does not provide direct services in areas such as education, health, security and transport. Since Member States have traditionally secured all these welfare benefits for their citizens, direct taxes at the national level ensure the right collection to support public spending in the areas mentioned above. Likewise, taxes traditionally convey a democratic ethos linked to the adagio 'no taxation without representation', and the EU has traditionally been accused of having a democratic deficit.[1] The attempts in the Treaty of Lisbon to enhance the role of the European Parliament in the EU legislative process have not resulted in a substantial democratic level comparable to the role of parliaments in the law-making process in the EU Member States.[2] Therein lies the strong disaffection of European citizens with

* Ricardo García Antón is Assistant Professor of International and European Taxation at Tilburg University (Fiscal Institute Tilburg, The Netherlands). The author would like to thank the organisers and participants of the Swedish Network for European Legal Studies (SNELS) conference, 'The Power to Tax in Europe' (Stockholm, 25–26 November 2021) for their insightful comments and remarks. I would also like to extend my gratitude to Hans Gribnau for his inspiring food for thought.

[1] On the democratic deficit of the EU, see the hallmark works from the late 1990s, M Newman, *Democracy, Sovereignty and the European Union* (St Martin's Press 1996); P Schmitter, *How to Democratize the European Union … And Why Bother?* (Lanham, Rowman and Littlefield Publishers 2000); JHH Weiler, *The Constitution of Europe: 'Do the New Clothes Have an Emperor?'* (Cambridge University Press 1999).

[2] On the limited role of the European Parliament and EU democracy, see D Grimm, *The Constitution of European Democracy* (Oxford University Press 2017); R Corbett, 'The Evolving Roles of the European Parliament and of National Parliaments' in A Biondi, P Eeckhout and S Ripley (eds), *EU Law after Lisbon* (Oxford University Press 2012) 249–61.

the EU as reflected, for example, in Brexit, the refugee crisis and the rise of Eurosceptic parties.[3] The EU is simply perceived as a '*Eurocrat* machinery'.

How is the EU perceived in tax forums? In the field of direct taxation, there is a strong prevailing narrative of the internal market of 27 countries.[4] The role of the EU in the field of direct taxation seems limited to removing obstacles that impede the exercise of EU fundamental freedoms in the internal market. Direct taxes belong to the domain of the Member States and the role of EU law is limited to the enforcement of the EU fundamental freedoms on a non-discrimination/restriction basis. Despite this serious limitation, there have been major achievements, for example, in the field of the cross-border mobility of workers. The *Schumacker*[5] successive series of cases (*Renneberg*,[6] *Commission v Estonia*,[7] *X*[8] and *Bj*)[9] challenges a classical principle of international taxation that the source state cannot take into consideration the personal and family circumstances of non-resident taxpayers.[10] It does not matter whether the amount of income at the Member State of source increases to 75 per cent, 60 per cent or 50 per cent, because what is really crucial is the fact that the country of residence cannot take into account the taxpayer's personal and family circumstances.[11] Such an extraordinary output contributes to reinforcing the idea of EU citizenship, as being something different from national citizenship.[12] Nevertheless, the internal market is far from being completed, and is still subject to many contradictions and inherent tensions between territoriality and neutrality.[13] The well-known metaphor of Professor Frans Vanistendael labelling the internal market as a room containing 27 small snooker tables, where access to these separate tables

[3] A Etzioni, 'Closing the Community Deficit in the EU' (9 September 2008) CEPS Policy Brief No 169, available at: ssrn.com/abstract=1333531 or dx.doi.org/10.2139/ssrn.1333531; E Hernandez and H Kriesi, 'Turning your back on the EU. The role of Eurosceptic parties in the 2014 European Parliament elections' (2016) 44 *Electoral Studies* 515.

[4] In the latest works published by scholars in the field of direct taxation, the recourse to the internal market is still quite dominant. See, eg, C Heber, *Enhanced Cooperation and European Tax Law* (Oxford University Press 2021) ch 5; JJAM Korving, *Internal Market Neutrality* (Sdu Uitgevers 2019).

[5] Case C-279/93 *Finanzamt Köln-Altstadt v Roland Schumacker* [1995] ECR I-00225.

[6] Case C-527/06 *Renneberg* [2008] ECR I-07735.

[7] Case C-39-10 *Commission v Estonia*, ECLI:EU:C:2012:282.

[8] Case C-283/15 X, ECLI:EU:C:2017:102.

[9] Case C-241/20 *Bj vs Belgium* (not yet published), ECLI:EU:C:2021:605.

[10] On the breach of the international taxation rule and the criticisms to the early rulings in this matter, see F Vanistendael, 'The consequences of Schumacker and Wielockx: two steps forward in the tax procession of Echternach' (1996) 33 *Common Market Law Review* 255.

[11] E Ros, 'EU Citizenship and Direct Taxation, The European Court of Justice in the Era of Public Decline for a Citizen's Europe' (2018) 27 *EC Tax Review* 147.

[12] On the links between EU citizenship and direct taxes, see my previous contribution, see R Garcia, 'Restoring the EU citizenship for tax purposes' (2019) 4 *Belgrade Law Review* 147.

[13] P Wattel, 'Anathema to the Internal Market' in P Pistone (ed), *European Tax Integration: Law, Policy and Politics* (IBFD 2018); W Schön, 'Neutrality and Territoriality – Competing or Converging Concepts in European Tax Law?' (2015) 69 *Bulletin for International Taxation* 271 (IBFD online).

is granted on a non-discriminatory basis, illustrates the traditional approach to EU direct taxation.[14]

Unlike the previous vision of national taxes as potential obstacles to achieving the internal market, this contribution aims to provide a rationale for the EU as a *polity* to levy its own direct resources. Answering this question requires the author to first shed light on the normative foundation of a tax (section II). Leaving aside the instrumental contribution of taxes to finance public expenditure, I will make the argument that taxes are compulsory exactions aiming to impose certain values on a particular territory. Such values endorse a sense of belonging to a community, meaning a reciprocal duty of the members to support each other on a reciprocity basis, and thus reflecting an ideal of solidarity. In section III of this chapter, the previous normative benchmark helps me to justify the legitimacy of direct EU taxes. Direct taxes require a connection between the individual and the territory, 'a sense of belonging' concerning the values that a community fosters. Beyond internal market logic, being a Member State of the EU implies the endorsement of the EU democratic and pluralist values under what is known as the 'European way of life'.[15] Finally, section IV is devoted to a presentation of how future EU taxes might promote and enhance solidarity and democracy within the Union.

II. A CONTINGENT CONCEPT OF TAX TO ACHIEVE CERTAIN VALUES IN A SOCIETY

Taxes are conceptualised as compulsory contributions paid in cash or in kind to the government to provide for public services without particular regard to the benefits received by the taxpayer.[16] Such a definition of taxes totally discards the postulates of a benefit or exchange theory of taxation, in which taxes are paid to gain access to public services, which was supported by eighteenth-century philosophers such as Hobbes, Smith and Hume.[17] The definition is linked to the

[14] F Vanistendael, 'The Compatibility of the Basic Economic Freedoms with the Sovereign National Tax Systems of the Member States' (2003) 12 *EC Tax Review* 136, 139.

[15] Among the priorities of the European Commission (2019–24), the protection of the European way of life has acquired an important role/a role of paramount importance. The European way of life is linked to the preservation of European values. See: ec.europa.eu/info/strategy/priorities-2019–2024/promoting-our-european-way-life_en.

[16] On a classical definition of tax, see WB Barker, 'The relevance of a concept of tax' in B Peeters et al (eds), *The Concept of Tax*, EATLP Congress, Naples (IBFD 2005); M Barassi, 'The Notion of Tax and the Different Types of Taxes' in B Peeters et al (eds), *The Concept of Tax* (IBFD 2005) 61; M Bowler Smith and H Ostik, 'Towards a Classification of the Central London Congestion Charge as a Tax' (2011) 4 *British Tax Review* 487.

[17] On the benefit theory, which was popular in the eighteenth century, see references to the writings of Thomas Hobbes and Adam Smith in Barker (n 16) 24. In the *Leviathan*, Hobbes considered only indirect levies based on consumption as fair taxes, insofar as they equally affect all citizens irrespective of their original income. For an insightful discussion of the benefit theory in the philosophers

instrumental justification of taxation to provide the necessary economic means of the state. Strikingly, the exchange theory has been the intellectual trigger to justify allocating taxing power to 'market jurisdiction' in the context of the digitalised economy.[18]

Discarding the exchange theory to justify taxes makes you wonder whether taxes go beyond the instrumental justification of financing public expenditure to achieve different goals. What is the rationale of levying taxes? Do taxes contribute to the democratic ethos of the state? When seeking a normative approach to taxes, the 2005 EATLP Congress provided relevant contributions. Vording explored the competing views of *libertarianism* and *utilitarianism* with regard to a philosophical perspective on the role of the state in levying taxes.[19] While the former approach advocates a minimal state that protects private property without engaging in redistribution and considers taxes as expropriation, the latter approach based on welfare theory justifies the state's intervention to correct market failures.[20] To the extent that there is a conceptual gap between the two positions (income redistribution versus private property), Vording defended a broad concept of tax to be employed when the state uses regulatory power to replace market mechanisms in order to restrain its taxation powers and to enforce constitutional guarantees.[21]

Assuming that taxes serve many goals, Barker addresses three different normative approaches. First, the normative prescription for tax is efficiency – 'an efficient tax is a neutral tax, thereby not influencing the prices of goods and services in the private sector'.[22] Second, the normative prescription of tax is justice based on the ability to pay principle, meaning that the burden of taxes should be allocated fairly among taxpayers.[23] Neither normative approach is entirely satisfactory. Not only can full neutrality not be achieved,[24] but in addition, the ability-to-pay principle does not yield uniform fair outcomes due to

of the Enlightenment, see H Gribnau and J Frecknall, 'The Enlightenment and Influence of Social Contract Theory on Taxation' (12 November 2021), available at: ssrn.com/abstract=3963285 or http://dx.doi.org/10.2139/ssrn.3963285.

[18] E Escribano, *Jurisdiction to Tax Corporate Income Pursuant to the Presumptive Benefit Principle* (Kluwer 2019). See my criticism of the benefit theory in R García Antón, 'Literature Review: Eva Escribano, Jurisdiction to Tax Corporate Income Pursuant to the Presumptive Benefit Principle, Kluwer, 2019' (2020) 48 *Intertax* 265.

[19] H Vording, 'The normative background for a broad concept of tax', in B Peeters et al (eds), *The Concept of Tax*, EATLP Congress, Naples (IBFD 2005).

[20] ibid 33–35.

[21] ibid 46.

[22] Barker (n 16) 23.

[23] On Stuart Mills's contribution to the strengthening of the ability to pay to achieve fairness, see Barker (n 16) 25.

[24] D Weisbach, he Use of Neutralities in International Tax Policy (2014) University of Chicago, Coase-Sandor Institute for Law & Economics Working Paper No 697; S-E Johansson, 'The Utopia of Neutral Taxation' in G Lindencrona, S-O Lodin and B Wiman (eds), *International Studies in Taxation: Law and Economics (Liber Amicorum Leif Muten)* (Kluwer 1999).

tensions between horizontal and vertical equity.[25] Third, the normative prescription of tax leads to a political question:

> Thus, a normative approach to the concept of tax is a study of politics … we cannot hope to derive a definition of tax law that will be good for all time and all places. As societies change, so too will their aims and purposes.[26]

In democratic societies, the goal is to achieve 'social equity' with the aim of relocating the wealth of the nation and reaffirming certain inherent values that a particular society endorses (ie, capitalist and democratic values). Barker supported the latter normative approach, thereby reaffirming a non-static concept of tax dependent on the particular values that a society wishes to reaffirm and its political system.

Although not entirely explicit in Barker's normative approach, I assume that the values of a particular society are clearly linked to the enhancement of the society itself, the sense of belonging to a group. Taxes are the cement that keep society united. In other words, taxes convey an idea of reciprocity and solidarity. Such a connection of values with the duty of reciprocity to sustain society has already been discussed in the literature. Based on the works of Rawls, Hans Gribnau refuted Peter Sloterdijk's proposal that citizens should be allowed to pay (part of) their taxes voluntarily and to decide the way this voluntary contribution should be spent.[27] In his essay, Gribnau argued that paying taxes goes beyond 'a minimalist rule-following, in the sense of strictly keeping to the letter of the law' to endorse a fair-pay duty of the members of a society. We pay our taxes trusting that everybody pays their fair share. Free-riders engaging in tax avoidance and tax evasion schemes damage that trust in society.[28] Additionally, the idea of taxes as an expression of reciprocity is also present in the inspiring work of Francisco Saffi based on Axel Honneth's theory of mutual recognition in order to liberate taxation from a purely instrumental rationale.[29] In his analysis, taxes secure the material conditions that make our living together possible under Honneth's third sphere of recognition (solidarity).[30]

[25] There is abundant literature on the different concepts of tax equity. Among others, see L Osberg, 'What's Fair? The Problem of Equity in Taxation' in A Maslove (ed), *Fairness in Taxation: Exploring the Principles* (Toronto University Press 1993); RA Musgrave, *The Theory of Public Finance* (McGraw-Hill 1959); L. Kaplow, 'Horizontal Equity: Measures in Search of a Principle' (1989) 42 *National Tax Journal* 139; J Repetti and D Ring, 'Horizontal Equity Revisited' (2012) 13 *Florida Tax Review* 135.

[26] Barker (n 16) 26–28.

[27] H Gribnau, 'Voluntary Compliance Beyond the Letter of the Law: Reciprocity and Fair Play' in B Peeters et al (eds), *Building Trust in Taxation* (Intersentia 2017).

[28] See also H Gribnau, 'Why Social Responsible Corporations Should Take Tax Seriously' in RK Feldthusen et al (eds), *Fair Taxation and Corporate Social Responsibility* (Ex Tuto Publishing 2019).

[29] F Saffie, 'Taxes as practices of mutual recognition: Towards a general theory of tax law' (PhD thesis, University of Edinburgh, 2013), available at: era.ed.ac.uk/bitstream/handle/1842/9589/Saffie2014.pdf?sequence=2&isAllowed=y.

[30] ibid 193. The three spheres of recognition that are identified by Honneth are love in intimate relations, law in legal relations and achievement in social hierarchies.

In this contribution, I depart from the last normative approach as a benchmark in order to build up my argument. This contingent vision of taxes is anchored in two arguments. First, in section II.A a historic view of taxes shows a strong link between political power and taxes, in which taxes contribute to affirm certain values of a particular society. Second, in section II.B, taxes are linked to the particular boundaries of territory.

A. Power, Values and Taxation

Such a contingent justification of taxes is reinforced under a historic vision of taxes. Throughout history, taxes have not adhered to a unique and uniform justification. While feudal levies were justified, not by a public purpose, but by personal rights and obligations that had a theological origin, in the absolutist state, the levies constituted an appropriation by the prince, reflected in Louis XIV's famous aphorism: '*l'état, c'est moi*'.[31] In a parliamentary state, the justification of taxes is derived from the consent of Parliament to increase public revenue:

> The levies of the parliamentary state were not tributary, nor were they appropriations. They were taxes properly so called. They had two ingredients that levies under the other systems so far discussed did not have: legislative authority, that is, the authority of the people's representatives, rather than divine or royal will; and legal compulsion.[32]

Finally, in the administrative state, the justification of taxes lies in enforcing fairness and repairing inefficiencies in the process of economic growth, without abandoning the role of parliament to impose them.[33]

The above justifications may lead to a dialectical relationship between taxes and a political balance of powers explored in the 2021 EATLP Congress in Antwerp.[34] At the risk of oversimplification, the main revolutions wherein taxes played an iconic role, scattered across the national reports – the Swedish revolts (1542–45), the Dutch Revolt against the Spanish '*alcabala*' (1568–1648), the Boston Tea Party (1773) and the French Revolution (1789)[35] – reflect the opposition of certain groups to the king or the political regime because they could not grant consent to be taxed. Rather than identifying democracy with

[31] See J Snape, 'The "Sinews of the State": Historical Justifications for Taxes and Tax Law' in M Bhandari, *Philosophical Foundations of Tax Law* (Oxford University Press 2017).

[32] ibid 27.

[33] ibid.

[34] See P Essers, 'General Report' in P Essers (ed), *The Dialectical Relationship between Taxation and the Political Balance of Power*, EATLP Congress 2021 (IBFD 2022). See the table of contents: www.ibfd.org/sites/default/files/2022-05/20_007_History_and_Taxation_The_Dialectical_Relationship_between_Taxation_final_web.pdf.

[35] See National Reports of Spain, the Netherlands, France, Sweden and the US in P Essers (ed), *The Dialectical Relationship between Taxation and the Political Balance of Power*, EATLP Congress 2021 (IBFD 2022).

taxation, at most, there is an ultimate claim for consent in order to be taxed. In fact, universal suffrage was not generalised and parliaments were segmented in states formed by privileged social classes.[36] The historical analysis of taxes matches the principle 'no taxation without consent' within a political dialectical balance of powers between those who pay taxes and those who decide what taxes should be levied.

What then is the role of the binomial democracy and taxation? Turning to Barker's normative theory, taxes are the device to accomplish certain inherent values that a particular society endorses. In our Western states, such values are undoubtedly linked to democracy and the redistribution of wealth. Conversely, in dictatorships, completely different values are associated with levying taxes.[37] Democracy is thus not in the *DNA* of taxes. A compelling argument to support the previous statement is provided by Professor Wolfgang Schön, who enumerates the numerous challenges associated with the link between democracy and taxation. Such a link does not always follow the principle of congruence: 'a tax should be identical with the people who pay the tax and with the people who benefit from the fiscal revenue, which is raised under the tax'.[38] Examples thereof are disagreement with the level of redistribution envisaged by the state (ie, the majority exploiting the minority), the conflicts between central government and regional governments in federal states, and the fact that tax residents, who are not citizens, are excluded from the right to vote.

In a nutshell, taxes are a manifestation of political power to impose certain values that sustain a particular society. In our Western societies, taxes foster first democratic values on the principle of 'no taxation without representation', which implies that the consent to be taxed must be derived from a parliament in which all a state's citizens are democratically represented,[39] and second solidarity. This contingent and axiological understanding of taxes deviates from reducing taxes to mere instruments to support public expenditure.

B. Territory and Taxation

Taxes are compulsory exactions which are levied within the boundaries of a particular territory. The territory functions as the physical space in which a state asserts its taxing right 'on the basis of both territorial link with the person of

[36] See W Schön, 'Fiscal Challenges to Democracy' in P Essers (ed), *The Dialectical Relationship between Taxation and the Political Balance of Power*, EATLP Congress 2021 (IBFD 2022) 101–26).

[37] See C Osterloh-Konrad, 'Tax Policy of Nazi Germany' in P Essers (ed), *The Dialectical Relationship between Taxation and the Political Balance of Power*, EATLP Congress 2021 (IBFD 2022) 59–68. The thematic report on the Tax Policy of Nazi Germany which stressed that the National Socialist tax policy searched for non-budgetary goals and imposed severe discrimination elements.

[38] See Schön, 'Fiscal Challenges to Democracy' (n 36); W Schön, 'Taxation and Democracy' (2019) 72 *Tax Law Review* 235.

[39] See Essers (n 34).

the taxpayer (ie on the basis of his or her fiscal residence) and territoriality link with the taxable object (ie on the basis of source of income)'.[40] In the literature, the second prong of territoriality has been profusely discussed in international taxation within the classical debate between source and residence.[41] The right of a state to tax the income generated in its territory has triggered literature on whether the principle of territoriality is becoming customary international law.[42] In the current discussions on the digitalised economy, the debate is still ongoing concerning whether it is fair to source taxing rights to market jurisdictions (the demand side) based on sales.[43]

Regardless of the eternal debate on the basis of source of income, it seems that there are no major concerns regarding the first prong of territoriality, which allocates taxing rights to the state on the basis of the tax residence of individuals and corporations. While the majority of countries in the world have a residence-based taxation system, only the United States and Eritrea still adhere to a citizenship-based system of taxation. In a world with increasing cross-border mobility, the latter approach becomes difficult to justify since it goes beyond the borders of the state to cover extraterritorial situations. It is wholly objectionable that US nationals living permanently outside the country without any real economic bonds with the United States, and no presence there (ie, 'the Accidental American') are still subject to the US tax system only because they happen to have an American passport. Hence, some authors convincingly argue that US regulations such as the Foreign Account Tax Compliance Act (FATCA) that aim to identify financial assets held abroad by US nationals in order to enforce citizenship-based taxation, violate international law.[44]

[40] See this definition in S Gadžo, 'The Principle of 'Nexus' or 'Genuine Link' as a Keystone of International Income Tax Law: A Reappraisal' (2018) 46 *Intertax* 194.

[41] In International taxation, there is abundant literature on the nexus and territoriality, which exceeds the scope of this contribution. See Gadžo, 'The Principle of 'Nexus'' or 'Genuine Link'' (n 40); LE Schoueri, 'Revisiting Territoriality as a Fundamental Principle of International Tax Law' in D Rosenbloom (ed), *Celebrating Twenty Years of the International Tax Program of the New York University School of Law 1996–2016* (New York University School of Law, 2016) 377.

[42] In favour of this thesis, see RS Avi-Yonah, *International Tax as International Law* (Cambridge University Press 2007); Gadžo, 'The Principle of 'Nexus' or 'Genuine Link'' (n 40); S Gadžo, *Nexus Requirements for Taxation of Non-residents' Business Income: A Normative Evaluation in the Context of the Global Economy* (IBFD 2018). Contrary to this view, see D Rosenbloom, 'International Tax Arbitrage and the 'International Tax System'' (2000) 53 *Tax Law Review* 137. In this line of thinking, Allison Christians argued that *opinio juris* is lacking in the fight against harmful tax practices in the pre-BEPS scenario. See A Christians, 'Hard Law & Soft Law in International Taxation' (2007) University of Wisconsin Law School Legal Studies Research Paper Series Paper No 1049.

[43] A Martín Jimenez, 'Value creation: a guiding light for the interpretation of tax treaties?' (2020) 74 *Bulletin for International Taxation* 197; W Schön, 'Ten Questions about Why and How to Tax the Digitalized Economy' (2018) 72 *Bulletin for International Taxation* 278; W Schön, 'Is There Finally an International Tax System?' (2021) 13 *World Tax Journal* (electronic version).

[44] Before FATCA was enacted, the US could not enforce worldwide taxation on grounds of citizenship on US nationals living permanently abroad. The design of the FATCA rules requires the cooperation and assistance of other states. Herein lies the potential violation of international law. See A Christians, 'A Global Perspective on Citizenship-Based Taxation' (2017) 38 *Michigan Journal of International Law* 193.

The extraterritorial dimension of citizenship-based taxation gives sufficient grounds for rejecting it and embracing residence-based taxation, as the majority of countries do. Such criticisms in the tax arena also echo parallel criticisms in legal and political literature. Citizenship is imbued with a nationalistic spirit, which reflects sentiments of attachment and common identity to a particular ethnic, political or historic group, but at the same time, it has unfortunately fed the politics of exclusion against non-citizens.[45]

Abandoning citizenship-based taxation leads by exclusion to the support of residence-based taxation. Yet in the residence-based systems, there are still 'citizenship footprints' that extend a state's taxing right over a citizen transferring his/her residence to a low tax jurisdiction or tax haven, in the nationality test in the tie-breaker rule in Article 4(2) of the OECD Model Tax Convention on Income and on Capital (OECD MC) (2017) to determine the tax residence under a treaty.[46] Residence-based taxation for individuals is also not exempt from criticism due to global cross-border mobility. In relation to the so-called digital nomads, those whose work can be easily exercised 'from any place that allows an internet connection' and no longer have a deep personal link with any certain country (ie permanent home, family), Kostic has demonstrated the inadequacy of the tie-breaker rules in Article 15 OECD UN MC to allocate taxing rights to any particular jurisdiction.[47]

Likewise, the tax residence of companies is beset with major concerns derived from the coexistence of several opposing legal criteria to determine the tax residence (place of effective management versus place of incorporation). The different legal cultures jeopardise a homogeneous definition of the tax residence of companies.[48] The 2017 revision of Article 4(3) OECD MC to remove dual-residence situations by the Mutual Agreement Procedure (MAP) presents serious breaches of the principle of legal certainty due to the excessive power granted to the tax authorities to determine the residence among several factors conducting a casuistic approach.[49]

To conclude, both citizenship-based taxation and residence-based taxation confirm the nexus of the individual/company with the territory, thereby justifying the state to levy taxes. However, regarding individuals, both systems also suffer from the effects of cross-border mobility. While with citizenship-based taxation, the state may tax on an extraterritorial basis (eg, 'accidental American'), in residence-based taxation it becomes extraordinarily difficult to

[45] For a critical account of citizenship, see D Kochenov, *Citizenship* (MIT Press 2019).

[46] In his article, Beretta argued in favour of disentangling citizenship from playing any role in tax matters, and therefore also of eliminating such 'footprints' in allocating taxing rights. See G Beretta, 'Citizenship and Tax' (2019) 11 *World Tax Journal* 227.

[47] S Kostić, 'In Search of the Digital Nomad – Rethinking the Taxation of Employment Income under Tax Treaties' (2019) 11 *World Tax Journal* 189.

[48] On the different domestic tests to determine tax residence between common law and civil law countries, either following a place of effective management considered as day-to-day management or strategic/key decisions, see G Maisto et al, 'Dual Residence of Companies under Tax Treaties' (2018) 1 *International Tax Studies* 3.

[49] ibid.

determine where digital nomads are tax residents. In the case of corporations, the interaction of different legal cultures and the internalisation of groups of companies may be extraordinarily difficult and uncertain in dealing with dual tax residence cases.

III. THE EU POWER TO TAX

In EU Council Decision (14 December 2020), the Union confirms the timid transition from Member States' contributions based on gross national income (GNI) to a proper sustainable system of new resources (2021–27).[50] However, the new basket of own resources is still far from producing a federal budget.[51] The Commission was empowered to borrow up to €750 billion on capital markets on behalf of the Union, of which €360 billion would be used for providing loans and up to €390 billion would be spent on non-reimbursable grants to the Member States.[52] The increase in the level of expenditure requires new taxes in the coming years such as a charge on plastic packaging waste, a carbon border adjustment levy, an EU digital tax, a business profit tax on businesses that mainly benefit from the operations of the EU internal market and a financial transaction tax.[53] The creation of new own resources are subject to the unanimity rule at the Council under Article 311 of the Treaty on the Functioning of the European Union (TFEU).[54]

In relation to the plastic packaging tax, Professor Vanistendael pointed out that 'for the first time we have a tax, that truly belongs to Europe and the scope, base, and rate are all determined exclusively by the EU Council and the European Parliament'.[55] However, a more cautious approach should be adopted

[50] Council Decision (EU, Euratom) 2020/2053 of 14 December 2020 on the system of own resources of the European Union and repealing Decision 2014/335/EU, Euratom [2020] OJ L424/1. See also, Council Regulation (EU, Euratom) 2021/768 of 30 April 2021 laying down implementing measures for the system of own resources of the European Union and repealing Regulation (EU, Euratom) No 608/2014 [2021] OJ L165/1.

[51] The in-depth analysis of the new basket of own resources exceeds the scope of this publication, which aims to provide normative grounds for the EU to levy its own resources. On a critical analysis of the new EU system of own resources, see A Martín Jimenez, 'The EU Own Resources and Budget after the Covid Pandemic: Still Far from a Closer European Union' in F Vanistendael and G Bizioli (eds), *The Roadmap to an EU Budget* (EU Law Live Press 2022) (forthcoming).

[52] On the COVID-19 Recovery Plan (Next Generation EU), see B De Witte, 'The European Union's COVID-19 Recovery Plan: The Legal Engineering of an Economic Policy Shift' (2021) 58 *Common Market Law Review* 635.

[53] See the enumeration of the new taxes in the 16 December Interinstitutional Agreement between the European Parliament, the Council of the European Union and the European Commission on budgetary discipline, on cooperation in budgetary matters and on sound financial management, as well as on new own resources, including a roadmap towards the introduction of new own resources [2020] OJ L433I/28.

[54] De Witte, 'The European Union's COVID-19 Recovery Plan' (n 52) 666.

[55] See F Vanistendael, 'Remembering 2020' (18 January 2021) 101 *Tax Notes International* 334.

in relation to the plastic waste own resource. It seems to be configured more as a contribution by the Member States than as a proper tax levied on the heads of EU citizens.[56] Despite defining the tax rate (€0.80 per kilogram), Member States retain important taxing powers to introduce lump sum reductions and to implement them.

The previous section deconstructed the normativity of taxes in three prongs: political power, territory and values. Following our broad and contingent benchmark, taxes are thus compulsory exactions imposed within a territory to achieve certain values to sustain a society, and as an extension, democracy and the redistribution of wealth in our Western states. Does the EU polity comply with the three prongs to justify levying direct taxes? The Covid-19 crisis has triggered a major step forward by giving an affirmative answer to the previous question, as this section will show.

The study of the first prong, the political power of the Union, involves an analysis of the theory of powers in international relations and legal philosophy, which would exceed the word-limit constraints of this contribution.[57] Taking for granted that the Union has political power, let me focus on the second and third prongs of the normative definition of taxes: whether EU law fosters certain values beyond access to the market (section III.A) and whether the territory of the EU differs from the sum of the territories of the Member States (section III.B). In both sections, I will demonstrate that the territory of the EU metaphorically connects with EU values, under the European way of life, meaning a sense of belonging beyond the frontiers of the Member States.

A. Beyond Access to the Internal Market: The Long March Towards Ensuring EU Values

Does the EU aim to achieve certain values beyond guaranteeing a proper functioning of the internal market? The tortuous path towards attaching values beyond the achievement of the correct functioning of the internal market is

[56] See Article 2(2) of EU Council Decision (14 December 2020) and Regulation 2021/770 of 30 April 2021 on the calculation of the own resource based on plastic packaging waste that is not recycled, on the methods and procedure for making available that own resource, on the measures to meet cash requirements, and on certain aspects of the own resource based on gross national income [2021] OJ L165/15; on this opinion, see Claudio Sciancalepore, 'The Reform of EU Own Resources under the Next Generation EU Programme: A Suitable Moment for the Introduction of a European Tax?, ch 7 in this volume; and Martín Jimenez, 'The EU Own Resources and Budget after the Covid Pandemic' (n 51).

[57] In the field of international relations, see the taxonomy of power in M Barnett and R Duvall, 'Power in International Politics' (2005) 59 *International Organization* 39. In the field of foreign policy and external relations, there is abundant literature on EU normative power: I Manners, 'Normative Power Europe: A Contradiction in Terms?' (2002) 40 *Journal of Common Market Studies* 235; R Whitman (ed), *Normative Power Europe: Empirical and Theoretical Perspectives* (Palgrave MacMillan 2011).

quite visible in the Court's slow-moving shift in the *Tobacco* saga in the 2000s.[58] In *Tobacco Advertising (I)*, Germany challenged Directive 98/43/EC, relating to the advertising and sponsorship of tobacco products, on the grounds that what is now Article 114 TFEU[59] was not the proper legal basis for harmonisation. As such, Article 114 TFEU should only be available as a legal basis for harmonisation in cases where obstacles to the exercising of fundamental freedoms and distortions of competition are considerable. In Germany's view, not only did Directive 98/43/EC not pursue the elimination of distortions of competition, it also created new obstacles to trade that did not previously exist (eg, a total prohibition of tobacco advertising).[60] The Court of Justice of the European Union (CJEU) accepted the arguments put forward by Germany and decided to restrict the meaning of 'establishment and functioning of the internal market'. Hence, the CJEU ruled that Article 114 TFEU did not confer on the European Union a 'general power to regulate the internal market':[61]

> If a mere finding of disparities between national rules and of the abstract risk of obstacles to the exercise of fundamental freedoms or of distortions of competition liable to result therefrom were sufficient to justify the choice of article 114 as a legal basis, judicial review of compliance with the proper legal basis must be rendered nugatory.[62]

Public health competence falls within the scope of the Member States, and thus the harmonisation proposed to prohibit tobacco advertising in the EU, in order to protect the public health of EU citizens, was rejected.

Despite the categorical outcome of this case, which, for the first time, annulled European law, not only the subsequent case law (eg, *Swedish Match* and *Tobacco Advertising II*), but also scholarly works have nuanced the meaning of *Tobacco Advertising I*.[63] In *Swedish Match*, the Court concluded that the prohibition of the marketing of tobacco for oral use in the EU in Council Directive 92/41/EEC was an equally effective way to combat nicotine addiction among young people. Thus, it was justified to use the legal harmonisation basis in what is now Article 114 TFEU. The growing importance of non-market

[58] Case C-376/98 *Germany v European Parliament and Council (Tobacco Advertising I)* [2000] ECR I-08419; Case C-210/03 *Swedish Match*; Case C-380/03 *Germany v European Parliament and Council (Tobacco Advertising II)* [2004] ECR I-11893.

[59] Then Art 100a of the EC Treaty.

[60] *Tobacco Advertising I* (n 58) paras 12–24.

[61] ibid para 83.

[62] ibid para 84.

[63] B De Witte, 'A competence to protect: The pursuit of non-market aims through internal market legislation' in P Syrpis (ed), *The Judiciary, the Legislator and the Internal Market* (Cambridge University Press 2012) 28: 'It seems therefore that the Court's statement in Tobacco Advertising that the European Community (read now: the European Union) does not have a general power to regulate the internal market was a rather isolated pronouncement whose significance should not be exaggerated'. See also D Wyatt, 'Community Competence to Regulate the Internal Market' (2007) Oxford University Faculty of Law Research Paper 9/2007, 23: 'The approach of the Court of Justice in subsequent cases has largely reversed the competence restricting effects of the *Tobacco Advertising* Case'.

goals, such as ensuring a high level of protection of EU individuals in health matters, weighs in on the reasoning of the CJEU in *Swedish Match*.[64] Yet, as De Witte correctly argues, such non-market values laid down in the Treaties (eg, the protection of health and safety, environment and cultural diversity) can only be achieved through internal market legislation as long as there is a specific competence elsewhere in the Treaty, the principle of subsidiary is respected and the measure must always contribute to the improvement of the conditions for the establishment and functioning of the internal market.[65]

In a nutshell, there must be a specific competence 'nexus' in the Treaty that allows the EU to pursue non-internal market values through internal market legislation. Since, for example, the area of public health is reserved to the Member States, the EU promotes the health protection of individuals by regulating the access to the market of medicines, food, human organs, alcohol, and biotech products.[66] The CJEU has adopted a similar circumventing approach in areas such as social security and reimbursement of medical expenses. Despite falling within the competence of the Member States, access to medical treatment in different Member States must not be jeopardised under the classical non-discrimination/restriction reasoning of the Court.[67]

In the field of the harmonisation of direct taxes, the competence nexus triggered a heated academic debate on whether the Anti-Tax Avoidance Directive (EU 2016/1164, ATAD) went beyond the framework provided in Article 115 TFEU. Accordingly, the Preamble to the ATAD justifies the legislative act through the need to strengthen the average level of protection against aggressive tax planning in the internal market, as well as to improve the resilience and effectiveness of the internal market as a whole against cross-border tax avoidance practices. Szudocky and Haslehner took the view that the mere existence of disparities between the tax rules of the Member States was not sufficient to justify the recourse to Article 115 TFEU.[68] As Haslehner conveyed,

> taxes by their very nature distort markets … Different taxes/rates therefore inevitably create distortions for the internal market. If that is sufficient to give the EU the

[64] In particular, see how the Court applies the proportionality principle in *Swedish Match* (n 58) para 56.

[65] De Witte, 'A competence to protect' (n 63) 35–37.

[66] See Directive 98/44/EC of the European Parliament and of the Council of 6 July 1998 on the legal protection of biotechnological inventions [1998] OJ L213/13; Directive 2010/45/EU of the European Parliament and of the Council of 7 July 2010 on standards of quality and safety of human organs intended for transplantation [2010] OJ L207/14.

[67] Case C-158/96 *Raymond Kohl* [1998] ECR I-01931; Case C-372/04 *Watts* [2006] ECR I-04325.

[68] R Szudoczky, *The Sources of EU Law and Their Relationships: Lessons for the Field of Taxation* (IBFD 2014) 361; Werner Haslehner, 'Anti-Hybrid Measures in the Parent Subsidiary Directive and the EU's Competence to Harmonise' (*Kluwer International Tax Blog*, 31 August 2015), available at: kluwertaxblog.com/2015/08/31/anti-hybrid-measures-in-the-parent-subsidiary-directive-and-the-eus-competence-to-harmonise/; and Werner Haslehner, 'The Commission Proposal for an Anti-BEPS Directive: Some Preliminary Comments' (*Kluwer International Tax Blog*, 5 February 2016), available at: kluwertaxblog.com/2016/02/05/the-commission-proposal-for-an-anti-beps-directive-some-preliminary-comments/.

> competence to mandate what to tax and what not, there are hardly any limits to that power and the Member State's 'sole competence' in direct tax matters is a mere illusion.[69]

Indeed, the measures envisaged by the ATAD aim to protect national tax bases against abusive practices and coordinate the responses of the Member States with the challenges undertaken in the OECD/G20 Base Erosion Profit Shifting BEPS project (BEPS). Neither the aim to eliminate obstacles to trade and competition, nor the aim to foster the exercise of the EU fundamental freedoms are very visible. This example shows the emerging frictions to foster non-internal market values (ie, the protection of Member States' revenue) under a strict internal access to market logic.

The recent Covid-19 crisis has revealed the EU's fragility in terms of public health. The narrative of 'access to market' to protect non-internal market values has shown dramatic results in terms of the loss of human lives due to the overwhelming weakness of our national health systems to tackle global pandemics. As such, the EU seems to have begun to free itself from the previous access to market narrative for goods, services and workers, embracing directly the human health concerns of EU citizens as a proper EU value to be achieved by transcending national borders.[70] As such, the Commission has put forward new legislative proposals under the legal basis of Article 168(5) TFEU 'on the adoption of incentive measures designed to protect and improve human health and in particular to combat major cross-border health scourges',[71] which has never previously been tested as a legal basis for harmonisation. While Article 168(1) TFEU narrows down the action of the Union to complementing national health policies, Article 168(5) increases the chances of having legislative actions of the Union under incentive measures, freed from the previous access-to-market narrative. However, will such new legislative actions in the EU ensure that the public health of EU citizens is protected regardless of the national health systems? Alemanno is entirely right when he argues that more actions at the EU level will not effectively protect the human health due to the structural inequalities in healthcare across the Member States.[72] That is where the value of solidarity to be attributed to the new EU taxes would lie (see section IV).

[69] Haslehner, ibid.

[70] A Alemanno, 'Towards a European Health Union: Time to Level Up' (2020) 11 *European Journal of Risk Regulation* 721.

[71] 'Proposal for a regulation of the European Parliament and of the Council on serious cross-border threats to health repealing Decision No 1082/2013/EU' COM/2020/727 final; 'Proposal for a Regulation of the European Parliament and of the Council amending Regulation (EC) No 851/2004 Establishing a European Centre for Disease Prevention and Control' COM/2020/726 final.

[72] Alemanno (n 70) 725.

B. Beyond the Member State Territory: The Territory of the EU

Since taxes are levied within the boundaries of a territory, the notion of territory acquires an important dimension to justify the EU's legitimacy to impose taxes on EU citizens. Can we speak about the territory of the EU as something different from the collection of territories of the Member States? Marzal has convincingly argued that the territory of the EU emerges as a distinct space of social relations, informed and delineated by the idiosyncratic values of the EU and thus something different from the mere sum of physical spaces under Member State sovereignty.[73] His claim is grounded in abundant case law wherein the CJEU applies EU law, not in order to ensure the effectiveness of the fundamental freedoms under the non-discrimination umbrella, but because the situation arises within the territory of the Union or retains close links with that territory.[74]

In its landmark decision in *Ruiz-Zambrano*,[75] the Court dealt with an expulsion order in the field of immigration. The Belgian authorities denied a third-country national from Colombia residence in Belgium as well as a work permit and ordered him to leave the country, despite the fact that his children had already received Belgian nationality and he made clear efforts to integrate into Belgian society. The Court stated that

> [a] refusal to grant a right of residence to a third country national with dependent minor children in the Member State where those children are nationals and reside, and also a refusal to grant such a person a work permit … would lead to a situation where those children, citizens of the Union, would have to leave the territory of the Union in order to accompany their parents. In those circumstances, those citizens of the Union would, in fact, be unable to exercise the substance of the rights conferred on them by virtue of their status as citizens of the Union.[76]

The territory of the Union as a place of ideals and values beyond the Member States' borders is reaffirmed in *Garcia Abello* in relation to the surnames.[77] Belgium denied Mr Garcia Avello and his spouse (Spanish nationals residing in Belgium) the change requested in the patronymic surname of their two children, who were born in Belgium. The justification for the rejection was based on the principle of the immutability of surnames as a founding principle of social order to prevent risks of confusion as to identity or parentage of persons.[78] The Court

[73] T Marzal, 'From World Actor to Local Community: Territoriality and the Scope of Application of EU Law' (2020), available at: papers.ssrn.com/sol3/papers.cfm?abstract_id=3549281.

[74] In this regard, see the applicability of EU freedoms to workers from Member States employed abroad, Case 237/83 *SARL Prodest* [1984] ECR 03153; Case 9/88 *Mário Lopes da Veiga* [1989] ECR 02989.

[75] Case C-34/09 *Ruiz Zambrano* [2011] ECR I-01177, para 44.

[76] ibid paras 43 and 44.

[77] Case C-148/02 *Garcia Abello*, ECLI:EU:C:2003:539.

[78] ibid para 40.

dismissed such a justification on the grounds that 'parentage cannot necessarily be assessed within the social life of a Member State solely on the basis of the criterion of the system applicable to nationals of that latter State'.[79]

What does the 'territory of the Union' mean? As Azoulai points out, rather than conceiving the territory of the Union as the sum of individual territories of the Member States, the Union territory should be conceived as

> a metaphor for a certain conception of the space referred to in Article 2 TEU as 'a [European] society in which pluralism, non-discrimination, tolerance, justice, solidarity and equality between women and men prevail. Following the Court of Justice's reasoning, leaving European territory means not only leaving Europe in the geographical sense; it means leaving a community of ideals and values; it means being deprived of a certain mode of existence corresponding to the standards of European society. As stated in *Ruiz Zambrano*, the territory of the Union 'transcends' the 'territorial framework of national communities'. It stands for the mix of material and immaterial things that determines the sustainability of individual existence; what we may call a 'European way of life'.[80]

The territory of the Union represents a metaphor of a sort of axiological nexus – 'the European way of life' – that unites European citizens beyond the geographical boundaries of the Member States. The recent rule of law crisis in Poland, together with the enactment of anti-LGBTQ law in Hungary, threaten the enforcement of EU common values and principles to which all the Member States have voluntarily committed themselves.[81] The joint statement of 18 EU Member States against the latter legislation reveals that the EU will react against serious breaches of the core values of the EU.[82]

Such metaphorical EU territory as a place for EU values becomes the normative basis on which to ground the EU's power of taxation. The territoriality principle within this metaphorical meaning urges us to replace the idea of the EU as an internal market with a federal narrative. In the long march towards a proper federal EU, which has been tentatively initiated in EU Council Decision (14 December 2020), there is much work to be done. Further research needs to be conducted on how the distribution of powers between the EU and the Member States would be made in order to prevent the overlapping of tax jurisdiction, and prevent EU citizens being taxed twice on the same taxable facts.

[79] ibid, para 42.

[80] L Azoulai, 'The (Mis)Construction of the European Individual' (2014) European University Institute, Florence EUI Working Paper Law 14, available at: cadmus.eui.eu/bitstream/handle/1814/33293/LAW_WP_%202014_14.pdf?sequence=1&isAllowed=y, 3.

[81] Case C-621/18 *Wightman et al v Secretary of State for Exiting the European Union*, ECLI:EU:C:2018:999, para 63: '[T]he European Union is composed of States which have freely and voluntarily committed themselves to those values, and EU law is thus based on the fundamental premiss that each Member State shares with all the other Member States, and recognises that those Member States share with it, those same values'.

[82] See Joint Statement 22 June 2021, available at: wilmes.belgium.be/en/thirteen-countries-unite-belgiums-initiative-defend-lgbtiq-rights-europe.

IV. EPILOGUE: EU TAXES TO ENFORCE THE SOLIDARITY AND DEMOCRACY AMONG EUROPEANS

Section II of this contribution rooted direct taxes in three normative prongs: 'compulsory exactions imposed by the political power (1) in order to enforce certain values to sustain society (2) over a specific territory (3). In section III, I advanced the argument that the EU has legitimacy to levy EU taxes inasmuch as it enforces certain values beyond guaranteeing the functioning of the internal market over an EU territory, irrespective of the Member States' territories. Although the new basket of own resources cannot properly be defined as EU taxes, I defend the position that EU taxes foster certain values, other than simply levering the increase of the level of EU expenditure. Such values represent a common sense of belonging, an idea of truly being united under a European way of life.

What are the values pursued by future EU taxes? In my view, future EU taxes will pursue the value of solidarity, first, and democracy, second. Yet, understanding the value solidarity in Articles 2 and 3(3) TEU does not lead to a univocal meaning. In supporting an integrated political community ('*a real political Union*'), Habermas relies on the value of solidarity as the trigger to achieve social justice and a just distribution of income and property among the EU citizens beyond the borders of the Member States.[83] Rather than a redistributive meaning of EU solidarity at the level of EU citizens living in the Member States, Eleftheriadis defends a corrective justice sense of solidarity at the level of the Member States, which requires that those who are unfairly burdened by an agreement (ie, Eurozone architecture) should be compensated by those who caused the unfairness.[84]

The Covid-19 crisis has initiated the transition towards a political Union, namely an ever-closer union among the peoples of Europe, pointing to Habermas's narrative. The recovery and resilience plans presented by the Member States and approved by the Commission to gain access to the €750 billion are a first step in that direction. The reforms and investments to be executed with EU funds by the Member States aim to make European States and societies more sustainable, the ensure their recovery, make them more resilient and better prepared for the challenges and opportunities of the green and digital transitions. The country-specific recommendations are linked so as to 'mitigate the socio-economic impact of the pandemic and on the measures to restart the economic activity in a safe way'.[85] Yet, as De Witte observes, while Member States do not need to incur new public debt to make the necessary economic

[83] J Habermas, 'Democracy, Solidarity, and the European Crisis' in L van Middelaar and P van Parijs (eds), *After the Storm: How to Save Democracy in Europe* (Lannoo 2015).

[84] P Eleftheriadis, *A Union of Peoples* (Oxford University Press 2020) 194–216.

[85] See COM(2020), Communication from the Commission on Country-specific recommendations.

reforms after the pandemic, this distribution of funds through the EU does not operate as a 'direct transfer from the richer to the poorer Member States, as the EUR 750 billion will neither be "German" nor "Greek" debt but truly common debt'.[86] The increased EU fiscal capacity to distribute loans and grants among the Member States is based on the issue of bonds, but not EU taxes. To put it in simple terms, as already stated in section III, there is no commitment to achieve fiscal federalism in the EU.[87] Until new EU taxes are approved, we will not have true EU solidarity represented in fiscal transfers from richer to poorer EU countries.[88] Materialising intra-EU solidarity by means of EU taxes could be limited to preventing uncontrolled spending by the EU and the Member States that leads to large budgetary deficits.[89]

Not only will solidarity be achieved through the approval of EU taxes, but EU democracy will also be substantially improved.[90] As such, while the revenue will come from the EU through its system of own resources, the expenditure will eventually be decided on by EU institutions, in particular the European Parliament. Such political transformation entails a clear assumption of the democratic principle of 'no taxation without representation' in a proper alignment between taxing and spending within a political Union.

[86] De Witte, 'The European Union's COVID-19 Recovery Plan' (n 52) 678.

[87] W Schelkle, 'Fiscal Integration in an Experimental Union: How Path-Breaking Was the EU's Response to the COVID-19 Pandemic?' (2021) 59 *Journal of Common Market Studies* 1; H Kriesi, M Ferrera and W Schelkle, 'The Theoretical Framework of SOLID – A Research Agenda' (2021) SOLID Working Paper, available at: solid-erc.eu/app/uploads/2020/12/theoretical-framework-paper.pdf.

[88] In this regard, see the Manifesto of EU tax professors, *European Solidarity Requires EU Taxes*, 21 April 2020, available at: eulawlive.com/op-ed-european-solidarity-requires-eu-taxes/.

[89] ibid.

[90] Fiscal autonomy must comply with democratic legitimacy. See AP Dourado and M Poiares Maduro, 'A Plead for the European Union Fiscal Autonomy' (2020) 48 *Intertax* 695; G Bizioli and E Traversa, 'Solidarity in the European Union in the Time of COVID-19: Paving the Way for a Genuine EU Tax?' (2020) 48 *Intertax* 743.

4

The Legitimacy of the EU's Tax-Based Own Resources

FRANÇOIS BARREAU*

I. INTRODUCTION

THE LISBON TREATY[1] introduced a new Article, Article 311, in the Treaty on the Functioning of the European Union (TFEU).[2] Article 311(3) TFEU is written as follows:

> The Council, acting in accordance with a special legislative procedure, shall unanimously and after consulting the European Parliament adopt a decision laying down the provisions relating to the system of own resources of the Union. In this context it may establish new categories of own resources or abolish an existing category. That decision shall not enter into force until it is approved by the Member States in accordance with their respective constitutional requirements.

The European Union (EU) can introduce new own resources with the approval of the Member States. Based on this Article, among others, the EU adopted Decision 2020/2053 on the system of own resources of the EU.[3] From 1 January 2021, the reorganisation of the resources of the EU is based on this decision. For instance, point (7) of the Preamble provides for a new category based on non-recycled plastic packaging waste.[4] Also, point (8) of the Preamble evokes 'proposals on a carbon border adjustment mechanism and on a digital levy with

* Doctoral Candidate, Research and Teaching Associate at the Institute for Austrian and International Tax Law, WU (Vienna University of Economics and Business).

[1] Treaty of Lisbon Amending the Treaty on European Union and the Treaty Establishing the European Community [2007] OJ 2007/C 306/01.

[2] Consolidated Version of the Treaty on the Functioning of the European Union [2012] OJ 2012/C 326/01 (TFEU).

[3] Council Decision (EU, Euratom) 2020/2053 of 14 December 2020 on the system of own resources of the European Union and repealing Decision 2014/335/EU, Euratom [2020] OJ L424/1 (Decision 2020/2053).

[4] Decision 2020/2053, point (7); Decision 2020/2053, Art 2 (for its implementation since 1 January 2021).

a view to their introduction at the latest by 1 January 2023'.[5] These examples can be added to other projects, such as the 'Business in Europe: Framework for Income Taxation' (BEFIT) Project,[6] and bring to light the tendency of the EU to put in place tax-based own resources.

European tax-based own resources raise some questions regarding the distinction between the competence to tax and the power to tax. Here, the competence to tax is the right to enact the tax law while the power to tax must be understood as the right to levy taxes.[7] An entity that finances its budget through its own taxes must have a right to levy these taxes. In modern European democracies, it generally means that the state has a consent to tax.[8] This contribution investigates whether the EU has this consent to tax in order to put in place tax-based own resources.

First, a certain distinction must be made between different possible designs of European taxes; the design that is chosen is relevant for the application of the consent to tax. There are three possibilities.[9] A first possibility is a revenue-sharing system.[10] In this system, a tax is fully harmonised in the EU (tax base and tax rate) and implemented at the national level. Then, the Member States transfer a partial share of the revenues to the EU. This system is also known as a *transfer system*.[11] Second, with a *surcharge system*, there is only a harmonisation of the tax base.[12] The EU 'levies a surcharge in addition to the national tax rate'.[13] This system is similar to the transfer system and is also based on a revenue-sharing arrangement. There is no direct tax claim from the EU. Third, the *separation system* is the introduction of a European tax completely distinct from the national systems.[14] These different systems do not have the same relation to the concept of consent to tax. The separation system implies a direct relation between the taxpayer and the EU, which levies its own taxes. In order to avoid any confusion, it must be highlighted that a harmonised tax is not a European tax. Under a transfer system, the EU has non-tax claims over the Member States, which have tax claims over the taxpayers.[15] What the EU receives is merely a contribution. The relationship between the taxpayer and the EU is

[5] Decision 2020/2053, point (8).

[6] Communication from the Commission to the European Parliament and the Council, 'Business Taxation for the 21st Century' COM(2021) 251 final.

[7] A Kallergis, *La Compétence Fiscale*, Nouvelle Bibliothèque de Thèses 175 (Dalloz 2018) 10.

[8] A Barilari, 'Le Consentement à l'Impôt' (2018) 49 *Bulletin de l'Académie des Sciences et Lettres de Montpellier* 1, 4.

[9] A Krenek and M Schratzenstaller, 'Tax-Based Own Resources to Finance the EU Budget – Potential Revenues, Summary Evaluation, from a Sustainability Perspective, and Implementation Aspects' (2019) WIFO Working Papers 581, 24.

[10] ibid.

[11] ibid.

[12] ibid.

[13] ibid.

[14] ibid 25.

[15] A Maitrot de la Motte, *Droit Fiscal de l'Union Européenne* (Bruylant 2016) 41.

indirect and the EU makes no direct tax claim. A European tax might exist only in a separation system. For the purpose of this chapter, harmonised taxes as well as future possibilities for European taxes are analysed in order to shed light on the relevance and possibility of a European consent to tax, which would involve a direct relation between the EU and the taxpayers. It means a direct consent from the European people for a fully independent European tax.

In order to do so, the central question, whether the EU has a consent to tax in order to put in place tax-based own resources, will be answered through the essential distinction between the *legal consent* to tax and the *political consent* to tax.[16] Even though this linguistic distinction might exist in other languages, it is a translation of the '*consentement à l'impôt*' (legal consent to tax) and '*consentement de l'impôt*' (political consent to tax) in the French language.[17] The legal consent to tax is the application of the principle of legality.[18] As long as the legal procedure is respected, there is a consent to tax. On the other hand, the political consent to tax is a social acceptance by citizens that they must pay the tax as being part of the society.[19] For instance, in the French Constitution, Article 14 of the Declaration of Human and Civic Rights expresses the political consent to tax: 'All citizens have the right to ascertain, by themselves, or through their representatives, the need for a public tax, to consent to it freely, to watch over its use, and to determine its proportion, basis, collection and duration'.[20] By comparison, article 34 of the French Constitution defines the legal consent to tax: 'Statutes shall determine the rules concerning: … Finance Act shall determine the revenue and expenditure of the State in the conditions and with the reservations provided for by an Institutional Act'.[21] Both articles are found in the Constitution but the second article is the legal basis and a clear explanation of the procedure to enact the tax rule (by the Parliament) while the first one contains the consent to be taxed by the citizens and cannot be invoked in a legal procedure.[22] This distinction highlights the difference between legal and political understandings of the consent to tax. This chapter will analyse the principle of the consent to tax in a European context. In a first step, through the notion of

[16] M Bouvier, *Introduction au Droit Fiscal Général et à la Théorie de l'Impôt* (LGDJ 2020) 34; A Maitrot de la Motte, 'Le Consentement à l'impôt et les Autorités Européennes' (2020) 150 *Revue française de finances publiques* 67.

[17] Bouvier (n 16) 34; Maitrot de la Motte, 'Le Consentement à l'impôt et les Autorités Européennes' (n 16) 67.

[18] Bouvier (n 16) 34; Maitrot de la Motte, 'Le Consentement à l'impôt et les Autorités Européennes' (n 16) 67.

[19] Bouvier (n 16) 34; Maitrot de la Motte, 'Le Consentement à l'impôt et les Autorités Européennes' (n 16) 67.

[20] Declaration of Human and Civic Rights of 26 August 1789 (FR) Art 14.

[21] Constitution of 4 October 1958 (FR) art 34.

[22] C const déc no 2010-5 QPC DC du 18 Juin 2010, *SNC Kimberly Clark*: the French Constitutional Council considers that Article 14 of the Declaration of Human and Civic Rights is put in application by Article 34 of the French Constitution and cannot be invoked by the taxpayer.

Exit and Voice,[23] applied to European integration by Weiler,[24] it will be observed to what extent the consent to tax is part of the European integration. In a second step, the legitimacy of the EU to exercise its power to tax is assessed.

In his article 'The Transformation of Europe', Weiler applied Hirschman's principles Exit, Voice and Loyalty to the process of European integration in order to demonstrate the equal importance of and the interactions between law and politics.[25]

Hirschman presented his principles in his book *Exit, Voice and Loyalty* in which he described three basic possible answers to the decline of firms or polities: quitting, speaking up, staying quiet.[26] Exit corresponds to the market force (quitting when you do not want the product any more).[27] Voice corresponds to non-market forces (manifestation in order to ask for change).[28] Loyalty is the renunciation of action (staying quiet).[29] Exit designates the more concrete world of economics while Voice designates the more abstract world of political science.[30] He demonstrates that to both worlds, the principle of the other world is useful and that reciprocity might be necessary.[31] Weiler applied the interactions between economics and political science to law and politics in the framework of European integration.[32] It is the distinction between hard law and 'hard law-making'.[33]

Exit is the legal field. There is, first, a formal or total Exit, which is a Member State taking the action of leaving the EU.[34] However, Weiler focused instead on the realistic alternative of a selective Exit, which means 'retaining membership'.[35] With selective Exit, the Member States can dampen the European integration, through their veto power for instance.[36] When there is a 'closure of selective Exit',[37] the EU takes away the possibility for the Member States to selectively apply EU law.[38] For instance, when the CJEU interprets EU law and enacts general principles such as the primacy of EU law, it definitively restricts the freedom of movement of the Member States. In this chapter, the use of the concept *Exit* is a reference to *selective exit*.

[23] A Hirschman, *Exit, Voice, and Loyalty: Responses to Decline in Firms, Organizations, and States* (Harvard University Press 1970).
[24] J Weiler, 'The Transformation of Europe' (1991) 100 *Yale Law Journal* 2403.
[25] ibid 2411.
[26] Hirschman (n 23).
[27] ibid 19.
[28] ibid.
[29] ibid 76.
[30] ibid 19.
[31] ibid.
[32] Weiler, 'The Transformation of Europe' (n 24) 2411.
[33] ibid 2426.
[34] ibid 2412.
[35] ibid.
[36] ibid.
[37] ibid.
[38] ibid 2413: application of different doctrines like the doctrine of direct effect.

Second, Voice is the field of politics. It is the decision-making process before hard law becomes imperative.[39] In Weiler's terms, it is divided between: '(1) the political impetus for a policy; (2) the technical elaboration of policies and norms; (3) the formulation of a formal proposal; (4) the adoption of the proposal; (5) the execution of the adopted proposal'.[40] When Exit (hard law) is put in place at the European level, it is almost impossible to avoid the Community obligations. This is why, when there is a 'closure of Exit',[41] the need for Voice (hard law-making) can increase in order to avoid too restrictive European obligations for the Member States.[42] This interplay has been applied to general EU law by Weiler. In the same vein, it will be applied here to the legal and political consent to tax while also making a distinction between indirect and direct taxes. The legal consent to tax is Exit and the political consent to tax is Voice. At the EU level, the legal implementation of indirect taxes is further advanced than it is for direct taxes. However, it does not mean there is a complete integration because the Member States are still using their Voice, which avoids a complete 'closure of selective Exit'.[43] Concerning direct taxes, the Voice of the Member States is still stronger than the capacity of the EU 'to close the Exit'.[44] It is a matter of national tax sovereignty (see section II.B.ii). The Member States can take advantage of their exclusive competence in this field. Finally, it is argued that Weiler's distinction is still pertinent,[45] especially for understanding European taxation. Thirty years and several European treaties later, European integration remains unfinished and the achievement of the Single Market is still an objective rather than a reality. This unachieved integration is especially perceptible in the field of European taxation, as will be demonstrated. The first section of the chapter will observe the interactions between European integration and the two aspects of the consent to tax.

The second section includes, beyond the factual situation, an assessment of whether the EU has the legitimacy to put in place tax-based own resources, or to put it in simple terms, whether a European consent to tax is democratically possible. In modern European states, the concept of legitimacy often involves the criterion of democracy. Here, it is not a question of making a conceptual distinction between democracy and legitimacy; legitimacy means that the EU has a sufficient democratic level.[46] Still, in Weiler's article, a distinction is

[39] ibid 2423.
[40] ibid.
[41] ibid 2412.
[42] ibid.
[43] ibid.
[44] ibid.
[45] G de Búrca, '*The Transformation of Europe Revisited*: Civilising Interstatal Relations' in MP Maduro and M Wind (eds), *The Transformation of Europe: Twenty-Five Years On* (Cambridge University Press 2017) 113; G Palombella, 'On the Past and the Future of *The Transformation of Europe*: Law, Governance, Rights, and Politics in the EU Evolution' in MP Maduro and M Wind (eds), *The Transformation of Europe: Twenty-Five Years On* (Cambridge University Press 2017) 184.
[46] Weiler, 'The Transformation of Europe' (n 24) 2468.

made between formal legitimacy and social legitimacy.[47] Formal legitimacy will apply to Exit and social legitimacy will apply to Voice. Formal legitimacy is the application of the principle of legality through a democratic process: the requirements of the law are respected and there is a formal validity *with a democratic foundation*.[48] Social legitimacy is a 'social acceptance of the system'.[49] There is social legitimacy when a government preserves and enhances values being part of the current political culture, such as justice, freedom and general welfare.[50] In modern European states, this culture is a democratic culture. That said, democracy seems to be essentially a question of representation in a state respecting the rule of law: the link between the citizen and the decisive bodies of the institution, and the preservation of the citizens' rights.[51] These two aspects will be assessed for indirect taxes and direct taxes together at the EU level. Certain distinctions could be made between the two types of taxes in terms of acceptance, especially as, from a market perspective in the process of the European integration, indirect taxes are directly linked to the objective of achieving the Single Market while direct taxes have a more general and indirect impact. This distinction is materialised at the EU level by the distinction between the EU competences in indirect and direct taxation. However, in the end democratic legitimacy must be the same for all kinds of taxes. The democratic side of the principle of consent to tax does not make a distinction.

Finally, the purpose of this chapter is to demonstrate the extent to which the principle of consent to tax affects European integration bearing in mind that law and politics are of equal importance and can lead to opposite solutions at the European level. Furthermore, if the EU wants to introduce European taxes in the future, these interactions will be of utmost importance in the process of democratic legitimisation of such taxes, as well as the principle in itself.

II. EXIT, VOICE AND THE CONSENT TO TAX

A. Exit, Voice and the Objective of Achieving the Single Market

i. The Ongoing Process of a 'Closure of Exit' for Indirect Taxes

Article 113 TFEU is written as follows:

> The Council shall, acting unanimously in accordance with a special legislative procedure and after consulting the European Parliament and the Economic and Social Committee, adopt provisions for the harmonisation of legislation concerning

[47] ibid.
[48] ibid.
[49] ibid 2469.
[50] ibid.
[51] ibid.

> turnover taxes, excise duties and other forms of indirect taxation to the extent that such harmonisation is necessary to ensure the establishment and the functioning of the internal market and to avoid distortion of competition.

This Article is the basis for the *harmonisation* of a limited number of indirect taxes and it cannot be seen as a legal consent to tax in the sense that it gives a power to tax to the EU. This harmonisation applies to existing indirect taxes. of the Member States for the objective of achieving the Single Market.[52] The harmonisation of current legislation refers to the competence to tax and not to the power to tax. However, a special legislative procedure applies according to which the Council has the initiative of the legislative procedure and unanimity voting is required.[53] The unanimity procedure provides all the Member States with a veto power when sitting in the Council. Also, if the EU wants to increase its resources, in accordance with Article 311(3) TFEU, the approval of each national parliament is required. Thus, each single Member State's national power to tax is preserved; the approval of both executive and legislative powers are constitutionally preserved in each Member State, and the principle of legality is respected.

Consequently, due to the *necessary application* of the objective of achieving the Single Market, as written in Article 113 TFEU, the Member States can use their national power to tax in order to create new European own resources. However, as Article 113 TFEU still only provides for harmonisation, these new European own resources would not be new tax-based own resources in the sense of European taxes. A separation system based on new taxes could not be established on the basis of Article 113 TFEU. Nevertheless, a transfer system and a surcharge system, such as the VAT system,[54] could be introduced.[55] The principle of legality, and so the legal consent to tax, would be respected. There is no European power to tax. However, there is a legal procedure in order to create new European tax-based own resources but these resources would be attributed to the EU by means of contributions.

Then, even if Article 113 TFEU is limited to already existing indirect taxes in the different Member States, other provisions of the TFEU can be used for different tax-based own resources: Articles 191, 192 and 194 TFEU. Article 191 TFEU provides the EU with a competence to adopt measures aiming at 'preserving, protecting, and improving the quality of the environment'.[56] Fiscal measures are possible according to Article 192(2) TFEU and Article 194(3) TFEU. The primary goal must not be revenue raising but the achievement of environmental objectives and objectives of energy policy.[57] Here, new taxes are possible as long

[52] TFEU Art 113.
[53] ibid.
[54] Decision 2020/2053, Art 2(1)(b).
[55] Krenek and Schratzenstaller (n 9) 24.
[56] TFEU Art 191.
[57] ibid Arts 192 and 194.

as they pursue an environmental objective.[58] There is the same special legislative procedure as for Article 113 TFEU and the EU could obtain new own resources based on indirect taxes because of these Articles.[59] However, they should not constitute a primary revenue source.[60] There is a legal procedure that gives legal consent to tax at the EU level. In terms of Exit, European taxes could be created for environmental reasons as a basis for new European tax-based own resources according to Article 311(3) TFEU and because the Union respects the shared competence of the Member States.

Concerning indirect taxes, a 'closure of Exit'[61] is possible in the EU. It already has a legal consent to tax in terms of environmental policy. If qualified majority voting were put in place for these taxes, closure could be realised. Article 311(3) TFEU applies for the creation of new categories of resources. New European taxes based on Articles 192(2) and 194(3) TFEU could be created in order to contribute to these categories. Also, through the objective of achieving the Single Market, legal consent could be extended to other kinds of indirect taxes. There is a legal basis for European indirect tax-based own resources, even if it is limited to environmental purposes for the time being. It increases the importance of Voice for the Member States.

ii. Voice and Loyalty: An Intriguing Relationship in the Field of Indirect Taxation

Concerning Voice, in the field of indirect taxation, the main example is the harmonisation of value-added taxation in the EU (VAT). Justified by a need to unify Europe after the Second World War and during the Cold War,[62] but also seen as a necessity for the construction and implementation of the Single Market,[63] the first VAT Directive was enacted in 1967.[64] Today, the VAT system is based on a directive from 2006.[65] This example of European integration in terms of taxation helps to remind us of the importance of politics, and thus of Voice, for the harmonisation of indirect taxes in the EU. Only the VAT basis is harmonised across Europe and the tax rates are still domestic rates. The VAT contribution to the EU budget is based on a surcharge system.[66] This

[58] Krenek and Schratzenstaller (n 9) 24.

[59] TFEU Arts 192 and 194.

[60] Krenek and Schratzenstaller (n 9) 24.

[61] Weiler, 'The Transformation of Europe' (n 24) 2412.

[62] A Konishi, 'Construire l'Europe par la Fiscalité: l'Harmonisation Fiscale Européenne (1950–1967)' [2018] *HAL* 19.

[63] ibid 20.

[64] First Council Directive 67/227/EEC on the Harmonisation of Legislation of Member States concerning Turnover Taxes [1967] OJ 71/1301.

[65] Council Directive 2006/112/EC of 28 November 2006 on the Common System of Value Added Tax [2006] OJ L347/1.

[66] Krenek and Schratzenstaller (n 9) 24.

still-restricted harmonisation can be seen as the consequence of the Voice of some Member States when the VAT system was implemented. These Member States refused to give up their decision-making power by moving from unanimity voting to qualified majority voting.[67] As a result of this unanimity voting, the Member States maintained their veto power and retained their political power during the process of 'hard law-making'.[68] In terms of the consent to tax, unanimity voting prevented further European integration, which could have led to a European power to tax in the field of indirect taxation. Two examples have been chosen to illustrate the importance of Voice in this matter.

First, in February 1957, while discussing the conditions of the VAT harmonisation, Germany proposed an article on the harmonisation of the indirect tax systems of the Member States, which became Article 99 of the Treaty of Rome at that time.[69] The Belgian Foreign Minister Paul-Henri Spaak, supported by Germany, wished that the Council would decide through qualified majority voting after a transitional period.[70] The French negotiators accepted the first draft of Article 99.[71] However, Paul Ramadier, the French Minister of Finance, reacted to the pressure of the French tax authorities and said that the unanimity rule was not negotiable.[72] In the end, the challenged disposition was withdrawn,[73] and the rule is still unanimity voting.

Second, the 'empty chair crisis' had an impact on the VAT construction.[74] In 1965, Charles de Gaulle refused two European reforms:

- The change from unanimity voting to qualified majority voting.
- The new rules for the financing of the Common Agricultural Policy (CAP).[75]

The new financing rules of the CAP would have involved increased power for the European institutions and an increase in EU own resources. They would not have been limited to the support of agricultural expenses.[76] During the debate on the CAP, Germany argued in favour of the suppression of tax frontiers within the European market. It would have involved mainly a common VAT system and the harmonisation of direct taxes.[77] In France, the government refused the elimination of the tax frontiers in order to avoid a loss of its tax sovereignty and

[67] Konishi (n 62) 70.
[68] Weiler, 'The Transformation of Europe' (n 24) 2412.
[69] F Tristram, *Une Fiscalité pour la Croissance – La Direction Générale des Impôts et la Politique Fiscale en France de 1948 à la Fin des Années 1960* (IGPDE 2005) 464–68.
[70] ibid.
[71] ibid.
[72] ibid.
[73] ibid.
[74] Konishi (n 62) 246.
[75] ibid.
[76] ibid 247.
[77] ibid 249.

an increase of VAT resources transferred to the European budget.[78] The French delegation left Brussels on 30 June 1965; its chair remained empty.[79] The crisis was resolved by the Luxembourg compromise in January 1966.[80] Among others, qualified majority voting was limited to certain subjects and the Member States retained their veto power in the field of taxation.[81] In addition, the EU accepted the idea of a common VAT system without suppressing the tax frontiers.[82]

This second example is maybe the most striking one of the use of Voice by a Member State. Nowadays, the rule for indirect taxes is still unanimity voting and the VAT contribution remains the same.[83] There is a European competence for tax harmonisation but no European power to tax, essentially because the rule is still unanimity voting as a consequence of political opposition.

Nevertheless, here, the notion of Loyalty according to Hirschman's principles might be important. There is Loyalty when the Member States, by staying quiet, let the EU extend its powers. The Voice of the Member States remains strong as a result of the unanimity rule. However, even if still limited, there is a political consent to tax in terms of indirect taxes, which is growing at the EU level. The objective of achieving the Single Market and contemporary concerns such as environmental issues demonstrate the impact of the Loyalty of the Member States, which would be willing to accept European dispositions that would give a political consent to tax to the EU. It is the example of the Carbon Border Adjustment Mechanism (CBAM).[84] The European Commission released a proposal on 14 July 2021 according to which a carbon price on imports of some products would be imposed in order to reduce carbon emissions in Europe, but the tax would directly contribute to the European budget as a tax-based own resource.[85] The initial concern is the protection of the environment but the impact on Voice is certain. Through such concerns, the EU would obtain the approval of the Member States for non-tax concerns but also a political consent to tax. A disproportionate number of such directives could become an issue in terms of legitimacy. Indeed, it would be a political consent to tax given by the governments of the Member States and not by the citizens themselves. This aspect will be considered in the next section.

[78] ibid 250.

[79] ibid.

[80] Final Communiqué of the Extraordinary Session of the Council [1966] *Bulletin of the European Communities* 3-66, 5-11.

[81] ibid 6.

[82] Konishi (n 62) 251.

[83] Decision 2020/205, Art 2(1)(b).

[84] Commission, 'Proposal for a Regulation of the European Parliament and of the Council Establishing a Carbon Border Adjustment Mechanism' COM(2021) 564 final.

[85] Decision 2020/2053, point (8).

B. Exit, Voice and National Tax Sovereignty

i. The Never-Ending Road Towards Exit

Article 115 TFEU is written as follows:

> Without prejudice to Article 114, the Council shall, acting unanimously in accordance with a special legislative procedure and after consulting the European Parliament and the Economic and Social Committee, issue directives for the approximation of such laws, regulations or administrative provisions of the Member States as directly affect the establishment or functioning of the internal market.[86]

Concerning direct taxes, there is no specific legal basis in the EU Treaties for their harmonisation. Article 115 TFEU has always been the indirect justification. Similar to the application of Article 113 TFEU, a special legislative procedure is required. A legal consent to tax is possible in the same context as for indirect taxes under Article 113 TFEU. The harmonisation is possible for already existing taxes if they excessively distort the Single Market.[87] A European tax could not be created and only a system based on a contribution is possible, meaning a transfer system or a surcharge system.

Furthermore, on the lack of basis for a direct legal consent to tax in the EU Treaties, the question could be raised whether Article 311 TFEU could be a direct legal basis for the creation of tax-based own resources. However, this possibility seems to have been easily discarded.[88] The German Federal Constitutional Court has asserted that Article 311(1) TFEU does not grant to the EU a *Kompetenz-Kompetenz*.[89] Article 311 TFEU provides no European legal consent to tax; it only enables the creation of new general categories of European resources and gives the EU no further competences with regard to taxation.

A 'closure of Exit'[90] is very unlikely to happen for direct taxes at the European level because the Member States still want to preserve their national tax sovereignty, keeping their competence to tax. Their Voice is predominant.

ii. Voice as a Veto in the Field of Direct Taxation

During the Foundational Period of the European Community (1958–70),[91] agreements for a common VAT system were found while a harmonisation

[86] TFEU Art 115.

[87] Krenek and Schratzenstaller (n 9) 23.

[88] C Waldhoof, 'Legal Restrictions and Possibilities for Greater Revenue Autonomy of the EU' in T Buettner and M Thöne (eds), *The Future of EU-Finances*, Beiträge zur Finanzwissenschaft 34 (Mohr Siebeck 2016) 152.

[89] Waldhoof (n 89) 152; BVerfG, Judgment of the Second Senate of 30 June 2009, 2 BvE 2/08.

[90] Weiler, 'The Transformation of Europe' (n 24) 2412.

[91] ibid 2403.

of corporate income tax was finally abandoned.[92] Since then, most of the Commission proposals have not succeeded. The most important attempt for harmonisation in direct taxation was the proposal for a common Consolidated Corporate Tax Base (CCCTB).[93] A proposal came out in 2011 but the Council could not agree on the adoption of a directive.[94] In 2015, the Commission took a different approach and transformed the proposal into one for a common company tax base.[95] There would have been no consolidation between the Member States in the first phase and the directive would have been applied only to large group of companies with an option for other groups of companies.[96] This new proposal is also still not adopted.

In 2021, the Commission proposed a new business tax agenda.[97] By 2023, a new proposal based on the OECD works[98] should be released: the BEFIT Project.[99] Nonetheless, until now, the Member States always refused to harmonise direct taxes within the Single Market. Achieving the Single Market has never been a sufficiently strong objective to overcome the Member States' will to preserve their national tax sovereignty and their national tax policy in terms of direct taxation. The political implications of direct taxation in terms of policymaking seems to be too important for the Member States' governments to give up their full independence in this matter. Direct taxes are closely linked to their social impact on the citizens in the political conscience.[100] Consequently, unanimity voting seems to be an insurmountable obstacle, even more because the EU does not have a competence to tax in this field. Finally, as it will be seen in the next section, legitimacy is of utmost importance for the taxpayer-citizen.

III. THE LEGITIMACY OF A EUROPEAN CONSENT TO TAX

A. The Formal Legitimacy of the EU

i. A Need for a Constitutional Consent to Tax

A further European integration for tax-based own resources necessitates enhanced legitimacy. In most European countries, a democratic legal consent

[92] Konishi (n 62).

[93] Proposal for a Council Directive on a Common Consolidated Corporate Tax Base (CCCTB) COM(2011) 121/4 final.

[94] H Kube, E Reimer and C Spengel, 'Tax Policy: Trends in the Allocation of Powers Between the Union and its Member States' (2016) 25 *EC Tax Review* 247, 253.

[95] Proposal for a Council Directive on a Common Corporate Tax Base (CCTB) COM(2016) 685.

[96] ibid art 2.

[97] Above (n 6).

[98] OECD, Statement on a Two-Pillar Solution to Address the Tax Challenges Arising from the Digitalization of the Economy [2021] OECD/G20 Base Erosion and Profit Shifting Project.

[99] Above (n 6) 11.

[100] See, eg, B de la Cuesta et al, 'Do Indirect Taxes Bite? How Hiding Taxes Erases Accountability Demands from Citizens' (2021) Princeton School of Public and International Affairs Working

to tax involves, at least, a constitutional basis.[101] This basis states that the Parliament has the power to enact the tax law and has the power to collect taxes – through their creation – by means of representation.[102] In terms of formal and so legal legitimacy, it involves two conditions, which are a consent to tax in the constitution and a respect of the popular sovereignty through representation.

At the European level, formal legitimacy is indirect.[103] The distinction between indirect and direct democratic legitimacy is especially important because of the possibility of a separation system. If the EU wants to put in place a separate tax system from those of the Member States and create a European tax, as there would be a direct link with the taxpayer-citizens, direct democratic requirements would be necessary. It must be remembered that the special legislative procedure (unanimity voting) and the necessity of the approval of national parliaments give only an indirect legitimacy to the EU. This formal legitimacy is not sufficient for a separation system, which would be possible under Articles 192(2) and 194(3) TFEU in terms of legal consent to tax.

Thus, representation and constitutional rights are of the utmost importance for producing direct democratic legitimacy. In this first subsection about the formal legitimacy of the EU, two aspects are addressed. The first is the respect for the rule of law in terms of consent to tax by the EU. The second is the principle of *no taxation without representation*.

The European Court of Justice (ECJ) ruled that the EU is a 'community based on the rule of law'.[104] It is enshrined in Article 6 of the Treaty on the European Union (TEU):[105]

> The Union recognises the rights, freedoms and principles set out in the Charter of Fundamental Rights of the European Union of 7 December 2000, as adapted at Strasbourg, on 12 December 2007, which shall have the same legal value as the Treaties.
>
> The provisions of the Charter shall not extend in any way the competences of the Union as defined in the Treaties.
>
> The rights, freedoms and principles in the Charter shall be interpreted in accordance with the general provisions in Title VII of the Charter governing its interpretation and application and with due regard to the explanations referred to in the Charter, that set out the sources of those provisions.

Paper: eg, the visibility of direct taxes impacts directly their perception by the citizens who will engage the accountability of their government.

[101] See, eg, art 34 of the French Constitution; art 43 of the Danish Constitution; art 60(1) of the Bulgarian Constitution; art 78(1) of the Greek Constitution; art 22.2.1–22.2.6 of the Irish Constitution, etc.

[102] See art 34 of the French Constitution for instance; the tax rules must be made through law and so by the legislative power.

[103] Weiler, 'The Transformation of Europe' (n 24) 2430.

[104] Case C-294/83 *Les Verts*, ECLI:EU:C:1986:166.

[105] Consolidated Version of the Treaty on the European Union [2012] OJ 2012/C 326/01 (TEU).

> The Union shall accede to the European Convention for the Protection of Human Rights and Fundamental Freedoms. Such accession shall not affect the Union's competences as defined in the Treaties.
>
> Fundamental rights, as guaranteed by the European Convention for the Protection of Human Rights and Fundamental Freedoms and as they result from the constitutional traditions common to the Member States, shall constitute general principles of the Union's law.[106]

The rule of law, as understood in the light of Article 6 TEU, involves different principles such as legal certainty. It is a general principle of EU law. This principle means that a law adopted by the EU and having effect in it must be certain, clear and precise; its legal implication must be foreseeable, especially concerning financial obligations and there must be a proper legal basis.[107]

In the EU, as an application of the principle of legal certainty, there is the misuse of powers test.[108] This test verifies whether a lawful power is not exercised for any other purpose than that for which it was conferred.[109] A tentative thesis is proposed here with the unique purpose of highlighting the lack of formal democratic legitimacy of the EU in terms of consent to tax. It must be remembered that there is a distinction between the competence to tax and the power to tax.[110] The latter is the right to levy taxes and requires a consent to tax. Furthermore, the Member States did not officially give to the EU a competence to tax in direct taxation and Article 115 TFEU merely covers 'approximation of laws'.[111]

The tentative thesis is that tax-based own resources of the EU are not in line with the rule of law and especially with the principle of legal certainty. First, it has been demonstrated in the first section that Article 311 TFEU cannot be used as a legal basis for new tax-based own resources as it does not give the '*Kompetenz-Kompetenz*'.[112] It means that the legal bases can only be Articles 113 and 115 TFEU, combined with the possibility of creating new categories of Article 311 TFEU. In this situation, the distinction between already existing taxes and new taxes is not necessary because the principle of the consent to tax is contained neither in Article 113 TFEU nor in Article 115 TFEU. Both Articles give a competence to tax that can be exercised at the EU level. In Article 113 TFEU, it is clearly detailed that harmonisation can be achieved subject to unanimity voting. In Article 115 TFEU, harmonisation in the field of taxation is implied and not clearly written, and still requires unanimity voting. There is an indirect democratic legitimacy concerning the competence to tax.

106 TEU Art 6.
107 Case T-115/94 *Opel Austria GmbH v Council of the European Union*, ECLI:EU:T:1997:3.
108 Case 105/75 *Giuffrida v Council of the European Communities*, ECLI:EU:C:1976:128.
109 ibid.
110 Kallergis (n 7) 10.
111 TFEU Art 115.
112 Waldhoof (n 89) 152.

The power to levy taxes is not considered and consent to tax is not expressed in the TFEU, nor can such consent be deduced from Article 311 TFEU. Thus, it is doubtful that a consent to tax for the EU itself follows from these Articles. If the EU puts in place tax-based own resources on the basis of these Articles, there is a risk of a misuse of powers if there is a creation of a European tax through a separation system. Indirect legitimacy is not sufficient because the constitutional provisions of a single Member State would not be able to protect the taxpayer-citizen any more. There would be a breach of the principle of legal certainty to the detriment of the European citizens in their direct relation with the EU, which would have been created by the separation system.

Democratically, and considering that the EU Treaties are a 'constitutional charter',[113] there is no constitutional right to levy taxes for the EU. In order to avoid uncertainty, a written consent to tax in the EU Treaties could help to draw its limits. However, there is already a legal consent to tax written in the EU Treaties at Articles 192 and 194 TFEU. The possibility to use fiscal measures is explicitly written in this specific case. The only limit to such environmental taxes is the unanimity voting and the main risk would be to use the environmental policy for tax purposes. The future will tell how the creation of new European tax-based own resources will be balanced with the protection of taxpayers' rights. Finally, these Articles do not allow the use of a separation system in terms of formal legitimacy when it comes to the principle of *no taxation without representation*: this system would be specific to the EU and should be approved at the EU level with a permanent representation and not with an indirect punctual approval of the national parliaments.

ii. No Taxation without Representation

The second important aspect in terms of formal legitimacy is the principle of *no taxation without representation*. Previously, the importance of writing the consent to tax in the Treaties has been discussed. This consent to tax implies that the people give the power to tax to their parliament by means of representation. Indeed, popular sovereignty implies that, in most European democracies, the people must govern even if they give their consent to be taxed to the power in place. This paradox is achieved through representation in a constitutional system. The importance of the role of the Parliament will be covered through a historical approach.

One of the first appearances of the consent to tax can be found in the Magna Carta of 1215.[114] At that time, the conception of the state was different from modern democracies. The monarch often had an absolute power of

[113] Above (n 105).
[114] Magna Carta Libertatum (1215).

vis et voluntas (force and will).[115] John Plantagenet, in old England, abused this power as he was levying high taxes in order to support war expenses even in times of peace.[116] Yet, in the late Middle Ages, when there was no need to unite in order to defend the kingdom, the king was living on his own like his vassals.[117] It means that, in times of peace, the king was not imposing taxes or heavy burdens on his vassals and was taking care of his own lands like them. King John Plantagenet abused of his right to levy taxes. This is why the Greater Charter of Liberties (Magna Carta) was signed after a short civil war between the king and his barons. Clauses 12 and 14 stated:

> No scutage nor aid shall be imposed on our kingdom, unless by common counsel of our kingdom, except for ransoming our person, for making our eldest son a knight, and for once marrying our eldest daughter; and for these there shall not be levied more than a reasonable aid. In like manner it shall be done concerning aids from the city of London.[118]
>
> And in order to have the common counsel of the kingdom for the levying of an aid, other than in the three instances aforesaid, or for the levying of scutage, we are to cause the archbishops, bishops, abbots, earls and greater barons to be summoned individually by our letters; and moreover we are to have a general summons made, through our sheriffs and bailiffs, of all who hold in chief of us; for a fixed day, at least forty days thence, and at a fixed place. And in all the letters of summons we are to set out its cause. And after the summons has thus been made the business is to go forward on the appointed day according to the counsel of those present, even if not all those summoned have come.[119]

The king was no longer able to put in place taxes without the approval of the 'common counsel'.[120] Different from the idea of representation, it was a first appearance of a consent to tax in a system different from modern democracies. Thus, it is in the American foundation that a consent through representation must be found.

After the Seven Years War, the British government faced a huge national debt.[121] New taxes were imposed on the American colonies.[122] In addition to already existing local taxes, they had to pay high import duties on the products coming from Great Britain among others.[123] Under the English Bill of Rights,[124] the imposition of taxes without the consent of Parliament was forbidden,

[115] MC Fregni, 'Legitimacy in Decision-Making in Tax Law: Some Remarks on Taxation, Representation and Consent to Imposition' in P Pistone (ed), *European Tax Integration: Law, Policy and Politics* (IBFD 2018) 129.
[116] ibid.
[117] ibid.
[118] Magna Carta Libertatum, clause 12.
[119] ibid clause 14.
[120] ibid.
[121] Fregni (n 115) 130.
[122] ibid.
[123] ibid.
[124] An Act Declaring the Rights and Liberties of the Subject and Settling the Succession of the Crown 1689.

and the American colonists did not have any representatives in the British Parliament.[125]

Two theses were in opposition. For James Otis, a Massachusetts lawyer and politician, 'taxation without representation is tyranny'.[126] The act of taxing unrepresented people in the Parliament is a direct attack on the most essential rights of freemen. It was the American position.[127] On the other side, the British position was that there was a virtual representation.[128] George Grenville and Thomas Whateley had previously theorised the idea that Members of Parliament could represent the people of a nation even if some of the people could not vote for them.[129] The American colonies were not the only ones to not be represented in the British Parliament. Samuel Johnson wrote a pamphlet, 'Taxation no tyranny', emphasising this aspect.[130]

The American colonists refused to agree to this position and many tax duties and tax disputes such as the controversial Stamp Act[131] and the Boston Tea Party[132] led to a secession and the American Declaration of Independence in 1776.[133]

Historically, the motto *no taxation without representation* became the pillar of modern democracies and the American democracy is one of the first democratic models. It seems to be preceded only by the Corsican Republic of 1755, whose Constitution already included the consent to tax and its vote by Parliament.[134] Consequently, the formal legitimacy of the modern democracies implies a constitutional consent to tax embodied by the representation through an elected parliament, which exemplifies the popular sovereignty. The European procedure for the adoption of European tax rules does not follow this process. Even if the European Parliament has a veto power,[135] it does not have the legislative power in tax matters and acts as a consultative body. Since 1979, the representatives of the European populations are directly elected by the people but they still do not have the tax powers that must involve the principle of *no taxation without representation*. Thus, there is a democratic flaw at the EU level.

Nevertheless, there is a democratic procedure but it is fulfilled at the national level of the Member States. For Vanistendael,[136] democratic legitimacy cannot

[125] Fregni (n 115) 130.
[126] J Otis Jr, *A Vindication of the Conduct of the House of Representatives* (1762).
[127] Fregni (n 115) 131.
[128] ibid.
[129] ibid 3.
[130] ibid 3.
[131] Duties in American Colonies Act 1765.
[132] Boston Tea Party of 16 December 1773 in reaction to the Tea Act 1773.
[133] US Declaration of Independence 1776.
[134] Corsican Constitution 1755.
[135] TFEU Art 352.
[136] F Vanistendael, 'On Democratic Legitimacy of European Tax Law and the Role of the European Parliament' in P Pistone (ed), *European Tax Integration: Law, Policy and Politics* (IBFD 2018).

be accomplished at both the European and national levels at the same time.[137] With the unanimity procedure and the approval of the parliaments, formal legitimacy is accomplished at the national level. In this sense, the EU does not have a formal legitimacy in itself. For a European separation system, the powers of the European Parliament in terms of taxation should be enhanced but the other two systems benefit from an indirect formal legitimacy.

B. The Social Legitimacy of the EU

i. The Absence of Demos of the European Community

The concept of virtual representation evoked in the previous subsection leads to the analysis of the social legitimacy of the EU in terms of tax-based own resources in order to assess whether a separation system could be put in place. There are two aspects. First, the taxpayer as a voter and so as a citizen questions the demos of the EU in terms of representation through the European Parliament. Second, the idea of a possible fiscal contract in order to put in place European taxes questions the possibility of a European ethos.

Before beginning the analysis, the distinction between indirect taxes and direct taxes must be mentioned. The relation between the taxpayer-citizen and the state as well as the fiscal contract concern both indirect taxation and direct taxation. However, this distinction exists at the European level as a consequence of the economic objectives of the EU. The relation between indirect taxes and the objective of achieving the Single Market could have given a social acceptance to such taxes. Like a kind of application of the benefit principle,[138] harmonisation of indirect taxes at the European level seems to be the price to pay in order to have a Single Market, which might be seen as an economic advantage for taxpayers. The same could be said about environmental taxes. They would be the fair price for a more effective protection of the environment. The future will determine to what extent this can be true and what will be the impact of the difference between contributions and European taxes on individuals. On the other side, this social acceptance is not true yet for direct taxes. More than a technical way of financing the state, they have an important social impact as can be seen in the history of political philosophy.[139]

Thus, the principle of *no taxation without representation* is a reference to the taxpayer-citizen. The members of a parliament, who represent the people, are elected by the citizens who are also taxpayers. The right to be represented in terms of taxation becomes an intrinsic element of belonging to a state as an

[137] ibid 104.
[138] M Stewart, 'The Tax State, Benefit and Legitimacy' (2015) TTPI Crawford School of Public Policy Australian National University Working Paper 1/2015, 22.
[139] JJ Rousseau, *Du Contrat Social* (1762); J Locke, *Two Treatises of Government* (1690).

individual. It implies the notion of nation state[140] where the sum of the individuals, as taxpayer-citizens, constitutes the nation of the state. There are two issues concerning the EU: the first is general and will only be mentioned, and the second is inherent to the EU.

First, the theory of the virtual representation has been developed because the link between the taxpayer and the citizen does not work in reality. Individuals are taxed as a result of residence and not as citizens. In a state, all the residents must contribute to taxes but they are not all citizens. Therefore, they do not all have a right to vote. Similarly, there are individuals who can vote but who are not taxed. This is why there is a theory of virtual representation. It is a general representation of a collectivity. In any nation state, this can be an issue in terms of social acceptance of a fiscal policy.[141] This issue is multiplied at the EU level.

Indeed, the notion of taxpayer-citizen implies the taxpayer belonging to a nation. This thesis is supposed to be an important part of the social acceptance of taxes.[142] The question is whether the EU can be understood as a nation or not, so whether it has a demos.[143] For instance, Weiler[144] considers this issue as being part of the 'new constitutional order'[145] that constitutes the EU. Due to the doctrine of direct effect, not only the Member States but also the individuals are subjects of the European order.[146] This is one of the justifications of the constitutionalisation of the EU.[147] However, it does not mean that the EU is de facto a nation.[148] European individuals can be subjects of the EU independently of national legislations but it must not reduce the notion of citizen to the application of a doctrine.[149]

'Citizens constitute the Demos of the polity'.[150] Demos is the collective side of citizenship, and an important side in terms of democracy.[151] Individuals must be members of the democracy. In Weiler's words, the authority and legitimacy of a majority is justified by the demos.[152] The nation as a sum of individuals being part of a same collectivity must be the place where the rules of the democracy can impose sacrifices. In the example of the political consent to tax of Article 14 of the French Declaration of Human and Civic Rights, it is the collective consent to tax that gives the right to the state to impose an individual burden.[153] Yet, the

[140] E de Crouy Chanel, 'La Citoyenneté Fiscale' (2002) 46 *Archives de Philosophie Du Droit* 39, 40.
[141] It was the case with the American Revolution.
[142] De Crouy Chanel (n 140) 40.
[143] J Weiler, 'European Neo-Constitutionalism: In Search of Foundations for the European Constitutional Order' (1996) XLIV *Political Studies* 521.
[144] ibid.
[145] ibid.
[146] ibid.
[147] ibid.
[148] ibid 522.
[149] ibid.
[150] ibid.
[151] ibid 523.
[152] ibid.
[153] Bouvier (n 16) 34.

thesis for now is that there is no demos at the European level.[154] It is a matter of empirical observation.[155] For instance, Swedish and Austrian people are part of two different nations. There are no Swedish representatives in the Austrian Parliament and vice versa. Now, with a majority rule at the European level and empowering the European Parliament (giving formal legitimacy), Swedish representatives could impose their tax views on the Austrian people. In other words, the nations represented by the minority would lose their democratic demos.

This leads to a simple observation. In terms of formal legitimacy of the European consent to tax, giving more powers to the European Parliament would substantiate the democratic legitimacy of the EU. However, in terms of social legitimacy, it would break the link between the taxpayer-citizens and their cultural backgrounds. It would be difficult to get social acceptance for a tax from the people of a Member State when the representatives of this State voted against it. In this situation, the democracy is separated from the nation state. However, a European ethos is still possible in order to create a European community and overcome this issue.

ii. A European Ethos for a European Fiscal Contract

Even if there is no European demos, a European ethos might exist. This ethos could be the foundation of a European fiscal contract. It expresses here the idea that a political and social acceptance of the individuals is necessary in order to put in place European taxes in terms of social legitimacy. From a democratic point of view, it is the expression of popular sovereignty – where individuals accept an intrusion into their right to property[156] – even if, afterwards, taxes are imposed.

The ethos can be understood as a general set of formal and informal values accepted by individuals who become part of a community founded on these values.[157] In the EU, a reference can be made to the already quoted Article 6 TEU, but also to Article 2 TEU:

> The Union is founded on the values of respect for human dignity, freedom, democracy, equality, the rule of law and respect for human rights, including the rights of persons belonging to minorities. These values are common to the Member States in a society in which pluralism, non-discrimination, tolerance, justice, solidarity and equality between women and men prevail.

These values can be the foundation of a common ethos in the EU. They are 'common to the Member States in a society'.[158] This reference to a society

[154] Weiler, 'European Neo-Constitutionalism' (n 143) 523.
[155] ibid.
[156] JJ Rousseau, *Discours sur l'Economie Politique* (1755): The real foundation of the civil society is the right to property.
[157] 'Ethos', *Oxford English Dictionary*, 2nd edn (Oxford University Press 1989).
[158] TEU Art 2.

requires a European integration, which is not legal but social. As there is no European demos, the only way to create this European community is through common values. If the different peoples of the EU recognise themselves in them, there is a possibility to create a community under EU law. In order to accomplish this integration in the specific field of taxation, and especially direct taxation, trust seems to be of utmost importance.

In the approach made here, trust is an important aspect of justice as it could be perceived by individuals. Even if, in a state, there is a theory of a collectively accepted fiscal contract, there is a duty for individuals to pay taxes.[159] In order to help them accept this duty, the administration must demonstrate to the taxpayers that they can trust it. This can be done through good management of public resources but also by the capacity of the state to deal with matters like tax evasion or tax fraud.[160] As an example, on this very last point, the EU has already begun to create the basis for a fiscal contract. The Union is more able than the Member States to deal with issues such as tax avoidance as it is not limited by the domestic frontiers. The ATAD directives,[161] which are applicable on the whole territory of the EU, are a good example of a step to an enhanced fairness between taxpayers. By enhancing social justice, the EU builds this contract of trust. It is as a supranational entity with its own fields of competence that the EU can get social approval on such aspects that cannot be resolved by the Member States alone. Even in the field of direct taxation, in corporate taxation, the progressive achievement of the Single Market, as the economic telos of the EU, could build an acceptance of a hypothetical fiscal contract.

A European ethos is possible and it is a part of European integration. A social legitimacy for European tax-based own resources, through a social and fiscal contract, is an aspect of this ethos and might exist in the future.

IV. CONCLUSION

In conclusion, the interactions between law and politics in the EU have been observed, especially in the process of putting in place European tax-based own resources. The analysis has been conducted through the prism of the consent to tax in the current European institutionalist context.

In the EU, the distinction between indirect and direct taxes is written into law. The integration process is different and Exit and Voice are different for both kinds of taxes. Concerning indirect taxes, through the objective of achieving the Single Market, a 'closure of Exit'[162] could be reached in the future. The Voice of the Member States might give room for a full Loyalty and a full consensus

[159] Fregni (n 115) 137.
[160] ibid.
[161] Council Directive (EU) 2016/1164 Laying Down Rules Against Tax Avoidance Practices that Directly Affect the Functioning of the Internal Market [2016] OJ L193/1.
[162] Weiler, 'The Transformation of Europe' (n 24) 2412.

in order to complete the EU objectives. On the other side, their Voice seems so important in the field of direct taxation that Exit barely seems to exist and is still a consequence of the application of national rules for the EU's benefit.

Hence, the technical possibilities offered by EU law in order to put in place European tax-based own resources can become problematic in terms of legitimacy. Yet, the consent to tax could be seen as a simple matter of procedure but it is also a founding element of the democracy. The EU must take it into account and there are two ways to do it: at the domestic level or at the European level.

Depending on the design of future tax-based own resources of the EU (kind of system), constitutional adaptations might be required in terms of formal legitimacy. These adaptations also relate to the respect of the rule of law as to the principle of *no taxation without representation*. However, as it has been seen, empowering the European Parliament could be an issue in terms of social legitimacy. This emphasises the distinction between indirect taxes and direct taxes for the EU. As Voice can be Loyalty concerning indirect taxes, it is conceivable that social legitimacy could be reached anyway for such taxes. The situation might be more difficult in the field of direct taxation.

At the moment, the EU as an institution seems to be in a democratic impasse or at least at a crossroads. Through a transfer system, for instance, it accepts its democratic deficit with the constant need to justify its actions. On the other side, a separation system would need some constitutional changes and a social acceptance that cannot be predicted. Nevertheless, in a globalised environment, the EU could develop its own legitimacy through a kind of market competence. Through situations that only the EU and not a Member State alone can resolve, it could attract a social legitimacy and give rise to some legal adaptations in order to reinforce its formal legitimacy. The European environmental policy is a possible glimpse of such a new transformation of Europe. Environmental taxes can be the first agents of this new and less institutional approach. The balance between law and politics will still be preponderant in order to find a democratic equilibrium between possibilities and limits for the EU in order to create its new tax-based own resources.

Back in history, the paradox of Montesquieu pointed out the correlation between democracy and taxes.[163] Increasing taxes would increase freedom. In democratic states, taxes are the price paid for freedom while in tyrannical states few taxes are levied. According to Barilari who tested this theory in modern states, the historical justification of this paradox is the intricate link between democracy and the consent to tax.[164] Whatever the evolution, the consent to tax must not be neglected.

[163] C Montesquieu, *De L'Esprit des Lois* (1748) Books XII and XIII.
[164] Barilari (n 8) 4.

5

From the Governance of National Tax Systems to Governing Through European Taxation: A Justification for the EU's Power to Levy Taxes

JUSSI JAAKKOLA*

I. INTRODUCTION

SINCE THE INCEPTION of the European Economic Community, European law has shaped Member States' tax systems. Throughout its existence, European law has addressed national tax systems' negative externalities on the functioning of the European market. From the mid-1990s onwards, an additional concern has been the adverse repercussions, such as tax policy competition and tax avoidance, of the European market on national tax systems. Since the Eurozone crisis, the measures of European macroeconomic governance have moulded national tax systems to be in line with the imperatives of financial stability and sound public finances. Gradually, the evolution of EU law has resulted in a bifurcated composition of the European Union's (EU) power to tax: while the Union significantly regulates how Member States exercise national taxing powers, it lacks the authority to levy taxes to the European public purse.[1] While endowed with regulatory faculties, the EU continues to lack the traditional 'core

* University of Turku, Faculty of Law. The original draft of the chapter was presented at the 'Power to Tax in Europe' Swedish Network for Legal Studies (SNELS) conference (Stockholm, 25–26 November 2021). For useful comments on improving the chapter, I thank the participants at the conference and Johan Lindholm in particular.

[1] AJ Menéndez, 'The Purse of the Polity' in EO Eriksen (ed), *Making the European Polity. Reflexive Integration in the EU* (Routledge 2005) 187–213; P Genschel and M Jachtenfuchs, 'How the European Union Constrains the State: Multilevel Governance of Taxation' (2011) 50 *European Journal of Political Research* 293; F Wasserfallen, 'Political and Economic Integration in the EU: The Case of Failed Tax Harmonization' (2014) 52 *Journal of Common Market Studies* 420.

state power' for the collection of tax revenues.[2] In the field of tax, the EU may be portrayed as a 'legislation-centred' polity,[3] as 'law remains the central instrument for both realising integration and for allowing the Union to govern'.[4] The EU thus shares the common feature of international organisations: rather than governing by taxes – ie, using taxes for ordering socio-economic conditions – international organisations engage in the governance of taxation – ie, shaping the national exercise of taxing powers through legislative standards.[5] Therefore, the contemporary EU lacks a genuine capacity to tax.

The power to collect taxes constitutes the lifeblood of government, as there is 'no public expenditure without taxation'.[6] The EU also needs resources to finance its functions. Certainly, since the EU is a second-order polity, it can and increasingly does extract resources from Member States' treasuries. Relying on national contributions, however, incites constant distributive struggles and divisions among Member States, and governments' *juste retour* behaviour erodes the EU's problem-solving capacities and output legitimacy.[7] The Eurozone and Covid-19 crises have only aggravated the situation. During both crises, massive political demand has put pressure on the EU to deal with the disruptions. However, the policy responses, such as macroeconomic stabilisation through financial rescue packages and recovery instruments, have involved enormous monetary resources, and reaching an agreement on these issues has proven to be a perplexing exercise in intergovernmental negotiations. It appears that in the absence of the power to levy taxes, the EU cannot engage in 'mutually beneficial mobilisation of resources on a scale that is commensurate to the many crises Europe is now facing'.[8] Therefore, conferring the power to collect taxes on the EU has been envisaged as a remedy to the EU's suboptimal problem-solving performance. In the Eurozone and Covid-19 crises, calls for the European power to levy taxes have accelerated tremendously. The former crisis marked

[2] P Genschel and M Jachtenfuchs, 'Conclusion: The European Integration of Core State Powers. Patterns and Causes' in P Genschel and M Jachtenfuchs (eds), *Beyond the Regulatory Polity? The European Integration of Core State Powers* (Oxford University Press 2013).

[3] N Walker, 'Freedom, Security and Justice' in B de Witte (ed), *Ten Reflections on the Constitutional Treaty for Europe* (European University Institute 2003) 159–81.

[4] D Chalmers, M Jachtenfuchs and C Joerges, 'The Retransformation of Europe' in D Chalmers, M Jachtenfuchs and C Joerges (eds), *The End of the Eurocrats' Dream: Adjusting to European Diversity* (Cambridge University Press 2016) 9.

[5] T Rixen and B Unger, 'Taxation: A Regulatory Multilevel Governance Perspective' (2022) 16 *Regulation and Governance* 621.

[6] AJ Menéndez, 'Taxing Europe: Two Cases for a European Power to Tax (with Some Comparative Observations)' (2004) 10 *Columbia Journal of European Law* 297, 337.

[7] J Le Cacheux, 'Funding the EU Budget with a Genuine Own Resource: The Case for a European Tax' (2007) 57 *Notre Europe Studies* 16; AR Leen, 'A European Tax: The Fiscal Sovereignty of the Member States versus the Autonomy of the European Union' in DA Frenkel and C Gerner-Beuerle (eds), *Financial Crisis, Globalisation and Regulatory Reform* (ATINER 2012); I Begg, 'Future Fiscal Arrangements of the European Union' (2004) 41 *Common Market Law Review* 775.

[8] PL Lindseth, 'The Perils of "As If" European Constitutionalism' (2016) 22 *European Law Journal* 696, 701.

the breakthrough of the political idea of a European 'fiscal capacity',[9] which soon became equated with the power to levy taxes,[10] especially in the context of the latter crisis.[11] The functional considerations indeed support using taxes as a means of governing at the EU level.

Notwithstanding the functional cause for establishing the European capacity to tax, the power to levy taxes has been considered as an exclusive prerogative of the nation state. Partly because of this normative presumption, the required consensus for conferring a genuine taxing power on the EU has not been reached among Member States. Therefore, extending taxing capacities beyond the nation state needs a proper justification. This chapter considers one possible pattern of justification. In so doing, it does not start from the principles of any *sui generis* approach to the EU. Rather, it reflects on the premise that has historically legitimised taxation in national political contexts and been authoritative in allocating taxing rights horizontally between nation states. In domestic settings, the core assumption has been a functional and reciprocal relationship between taxation and economy, in which both contribute to the other's conditions of possibility and which legitimises the collection of taxes. In the international environment, the idea thrived as an influential doctrine of economic allegiance. In the 2010s, the tenet re-emerged as a guiding idea for redesigning the international tax regime, as a host of policymakers and international organisations pleaded for the taxation of economic activities where economic value is created. This chapter proposes that the EU's power to levy taxes may be examined in the light of traditional principles that have preceded the existence of the EU and gained currency over a long historical process.

The chapter elaborates the mutually enabling relationship between taxation and economy and suggests it may be meaningfully applied to justify the vertical distribution of tax-collecting powers between the EU and its Member States. Relying on the idea of a systemic connection between the power to tax and economic value creation, the chapter concludes that the EU may make a legitimate claim to tax the economic activities that its legal system, together with national systems, enables. In this unconventional polity, there is a relevant reciprocal allegiance between the EU and economic activities taking place within the internal market, and this legitimises the EU power to levy taxes. Rather than a revolutionary and adventurous act, setting up the European capacity to tax is regarded here as a belated step in the integration process that even committed

[9] President of the European Council, 'Towards a Genuine Economic and Monetary Union'. Interim Report (Brussels, 12 October 2012). More extensively, see A Iara, 'Revenue for EMU: A Contribution to the Debate on Fiscal Union' (2016) 62 *CESifo Economic Studies* 301.

[10] F Fabbrini, 'Taxing and Spending in the Euro Zone: Legal and Political Challenges Related to the Adoption of the Financial Transaction Tax' (2014) 39 *European Law Review* 155.

[11] Communication from the Commission to the European Parliament, the Council, the European Economic and Social Committee and the Committee of the Regions, 'The Next Generation of Own Resources for the EU Budget' COM(2021) 566 final.

advocates of liberal Europe lack reason to resist. In developing this argument, the chapter proceeds essentially in three steps. Section II examines the reciprocally enabling relationship between taxation and economy in the domestic context, while section III spells out how this relationship has shaped the horizontal allocation of taxing powers between countries in the international context. Section IV reflects on the EU as a value-enabling community that has a legitimate cause to extract value from the European economy it makes possible. The concluding section V recapitulates and considers the implications of the chapter's arguments.

II. RECIPROCITY BETWEEN TAXATION AND ECONOMY IN THE LIBERAL SOCIAL ORDER

In the practice of modern government, the substantive legitimacy of taxation has rested on two properties. The first embraces the acceptable functions taxes serve vis-a-vis society, while the second involves the equitable distribution of the tax burden among individuals in society. Even though the latter permeated the twentieth-century quarrels over taxation, the rationale according to which taxes are imposed constitutes a primer that legitimises the collection of taxes in the first place.[12] This section traces such a raison d'être of taxation. In doing so, it relies on a moderate premise: rather than the pervasive role of taxes in the redistributive-interventionist and Keynesian policy regime, it considers the legitimacy of the revenue-raising function of taxes. This fiscal purpose was endorsed also in the liberal model of political rule, and long before espousing the social and interventionist orientation, 'the modern state was basically a state based on taxation, the bureaucracy of the treasury the true core of its administration'.[13] The functional and systemic legitimacy of taxation was formatively articulated in the liberal context of the limited government.

For the emergence of modern taxation, the functional separation between public and private spheres within the social order was key.[14] From the seventeenth century onwards, and reaching its climax in the nineteenth century, this differentiation developed as a separation between state and society, between government and economy.[15] In the liberal social model, the market system was

[12] S Huhnholz, 'Refeudalisierung des Steuerstaates? Vorüberlegungen zu einer politischen Theorie der Steuerdemokratie' in S Boysen, A-B Kaiser and F Meinel (eds), *Verfassung und Verteilung. Beiträge zu einer Grundfrage des Verfassungsverständnisses* (Mohr Siebeck 2015) 184–85.

[13] J Habermas, *The Structural Transformation of the Public Sphere: An Inquiry into a Category of Bourgeois Society* (trans Thomas Burger) (MIT Press 1991) 17.

[14] J Schumpeter, 'Die Krise des Steuerstaats' in R Hickel (ed), *Rudolf Goldscheid/Joseph Schumpeter. Die Finanzkrise des Steuerstaats. Beiträge zur politischen Ökonomie der Staatsfinanzen* (Suhrkamp 1976) 333–40.

[15] D Grimm, 'Die Bürgerlichkeit im Recht' in D Grimm, *Recht und Staat der bürgerlichen Gesellschaft* (Suhrkamp 1987); M Loughlin, *The Idea of Public Law* (Oxford University Press 2003) 72–98.

invented as a relatively autonomous institution, and it was seen as a primary site of promoting social and economic ends. The market was considered an action sphere of private actors, which entailed a confined role for the state. It was required that government does not dictate individuals' economic goals or reshape their commercial and contractual relations, and there was an expectation that these relations be shaped by the price mechanism and market considerations. The state was also supposed to abstain from directly engaging in market activities, therefore eschewing the role as an economic actor. The government surrendering its economic agency under the liberal premise was at the heart of the process that Rudolf Goldscheid portrayed as the 'expropriation of the state'.[16] Since expropriated from its traditional financial sources, the government was compelled to establish taxes as a permanent machinery of securing revenues. Yet, while their functional separation organised the life of a polity thoroughly, the state and the economy were not insulated from each other.[17] Rather, they were mutually embedded and served as conditions for each other's reproduction. This was most evident with respect to taxation, which functioned as a nexus between public and private involvement in the creation of value within the social order.

In the modern tax state, succeeding the collapse of the feudal order, taxes were collected as financing means, and they were essential for carrying out the general purposes that legitimised the existence and operation of the state.[18] According to political thought at the time, the government's task was seen as ensuring the life, liberty and estates of individuals. In establishing the political community, individuals were seen to aspire to preserve 'their lives, liberties, and estates, which I call by the general name, "property". The great and chief end, therefore, of men's uniting into commonwealths and putting themselves under government is the preservation of their property'.[19] Without a doubt, the government's political mandate was a limited one. However, taking care of the governing duties necessitated resources, and 'governments cannot be supported without great charge, and it is fit everyone who enjoys his share of the protection should pay out of his estate his proportion for the maintenance of it'.[20] Similarly, for Thomas Hobbes, the rationale of the state was to secure peace, liberty and proprietary rights, and taxes imposed 'on the people by the sovereign power, are nothing else but the wages, due to them that hold the public sword,

[16] R Goldscheid, 'Staat, öffentlicher Haushalt und Gesellschaft. Wesen und Aufgabe der Finanzwissenschaft vom Standpunkte der Soziologie' in R Hickel (ed), *Rudolf Goldscheid/Joseph Schumpeter: Die Finanzkrise des Steuerstaats. Beiträge zur politischen Ökonomie der Staatsfinanzen* (Suhrkamp 1976) 261–69.

[17] E-W Böckenförde, 'Die Bedeutung der Unterscheidung von Staat und Gesellschaft im demokratischen Sozialstaat der Gegenwart' in E-W Böckenförde, *Recht, Staat, Freiheit* (Suhrkamp 2013).

[18] J Snape, 'The "Sinews of the State": Historical Justifications for Taxes and Tax Law' in M Bhandari (ed), *Philosophical Foundations of Tax Law* (Oxford University Press 2017) 15–21.

[19] J Locke, *Two Treatises of Government* (Hafner Publishing 1947 [1690]) 184.

[20] ibid 193.

to defend private men in the exercise of their several trades, and callings'.[21] Enforcing property rights and contractual obligations was vital for the functioning of the economy, and this was possible only under the auspices of state authority, which in turn depended on taxes.[22] In the emerging liberal social order, taxation constituted a structural core among the systemic conditions enabling private production and exchange, and it was due to taxes that the creation and reproduction of value within the economic sphere could transpire.

While taxation enables the market economy, the collection of taxes itself is dependent on the private sphere. Since taxes are imposed on economic activities and private holdings, the private domain serves as a necessary underpinning that renders fiscal extraction feasible. This dependence is the fate of the expropriated state in the Goldscheidian sense, and it provoked Joseph A Schumpeter to characterise the tax state as an economic parasite.[23] In the liberal constitutional order, endorsing private ownership and entrusting economic efforts primarily to the private sphere, the state acts in the role of an external and non-contractual party, which takes part only in the market outcomes, which happens by means of imposing taxes.[24] Therefore, the market society is a socio-legal framework within which taxation achieves its mature design, and it functions as a systemic correlative of taxation.[25] The dependence of taxation on the market economy also entails that taxes may not frustrate the value-generating potential of the private economy, as this would eradicate the very conditions on which taxation rests.[26] Furthermore, given that taxation involves an extractive intrusion into the economy, the acceptable level of taxation became a heated issue in the liberal state. From the mid-eighteenth century onwards, political economy emerged as a pervasive disciplinary framework seeking to introduce economically rational boundaries for government powers, including taxation.[27] Still, even though the constraining principles on the power to tax were sought throughout the era of liberal state formation, and vehemently so among political economists, the role of taxation in enabling the private economy remained the premise that advised not to abolish taxes but to fix their proper position in the social and economic process of value formation.

[21] Thomas Hobbes, *The English Works of Thomas Hobbes of Malmesbury*, Vol III (John Bohn 1939 [1651]) 333–34.

[22] O Asbach, 'Thomas Hobbes und die Ambivalenzen des modernen Steuerstaates' in S Huhnholz (ed), *Fiskus – Verfassung – Freiheit: Politisches Denken der öffentlichen Finanzen von Hobbes bis heute* (Nomos 2018).

[23] Schumpeter (n 14) 346.

[24] P Kirchhof, 'Die verfassungsrechtliche Rechtfertigung der Steuern' in *Steuern im Verfassungsstaat. Symposion zu Ehren von Klaus Vogel* (CH Beck 1996) 32–33.

[25] S Huhnholz, 'Was soll das heißen: "Steuerstaat"?' in W Nienhüser and U Schmiel (eds), *Ökonomie und Gesellschaft: Jahrbuch 29. Steuern und Gesellschaft* (Metropolis Verlag 2017) 29–33.

[26] J Isensee, 'Steuerstaat als Staatsform' in R Stödter and W Thieme (eds), *Hamburg. Deutschland. Europa: Beiträge zum deutschen und europäischen Verfassungs-, Verwaltungs- und Wirtschaftsrecht. Festschrift für Hans Peter Ipsen zum siebzigsten Geburtstag* (Mohr 1977) 418.

[27] M Foucault, *The Birth of Biopolitics: Lectures at the Collège de France 1978–1979* (trans Graham Burchell) (Picador 2008) 10–73.

Since taxation enables private economy and vice versa, taxes and economy stand in a mutually reinforcing relationship, operating as each other's functional counterparts.[28] The relationship of mutual reinforcement between the public and private spheres, in which taxes contribute to the conditions of the economy and the economy provides for fiscal extraction, was essential in solidifying the conception that taxes and the economy constitute a more or less integrated socio-economic structure. By the end of the nineteenth century, this model of legitimising taxes had found a distinct form and become firmly settled in the theory of public finance, as demonstrated by Lorenz von Stein's ideas. Von Stein's justification for taxation was based on the social-theoretical assumption that it is

> beyond the possible that the community could provide for individuals, also economically, the conditions for their progress, unless individuals return [to the community] a portion of the economic rewards they derive under these conditions ... This is the economic principle of any human community.[29]

By means of law, this fundamental social-theoretical principle is translated into a tax system. A tax system serves as a legal framework within which the private sphere can flourish, and hence, the members of a society ought to contribute to the public purse in return. In this, von Stein sees 'the origin of the organic circuit in the innermost life of the state ...: tax potential [within the private economy] enables taxation, taxation provides for administration, and administration, in turn, engenders tax potential'.[30] Therefore, the production of economic value is a circular process, structured around public and private constituents, as prefigured by the exchange theories of taxation.[31]

On the face of it, conceptualising the relationship between taxation and society as one of mutual reproduction seems to follow the outright benefit theory of taxation. The most fully developed variant of the theory prescribes individuals to pay taxes in exchange for and in proportion to the benefits they receive from the government.[32] Thus, such a theory entails a specific criterion for distributing the fiscal burden between taxpayers. Because of its distributive premises, the benefit theory became fiercely contested at the turn of the

[28] UK Preuß, 'Rechtsstaat – Steuerstaat – Sozialstaat. Eine Problemskizze' in D Deiseroth, F Hase and K-H Ladeur (eds), *Ordnungsmacht? Über das Verhältnis von Legalität, Konsens und Herrschaft* (Europäische Verlagsanstalt 1981) 47–55.

[29] L von Stein, *Lehrbuch der Finanzwissenschaft: Zweiter Teil. Erste Abteilung* (FA Brockhaus 1885) 348. Quotations from von Stein have been translated by the author. For alternative translations, see L von Stein, 'On Taxation' in RA Musgrave and AT Peacock (eds), *Classics in the Theory of Public Finance* (Macmillan 1958).

[30] von Stein, *Lehrbuch der Finanzwissenschaft*, ibid 358.

[31] See FK Mann, *Steuerpolitische Ideale: Vergleichende Studien zur Geschichte der ökonomischen und politischen Ideen und ihres Wirkens in der öffentlichen Meinung 1600–1935* (Gustav Fischer 1937) 90.

[32] L Murphy and T Nagel, *The Myth of Ownership: Taxes and Justice* (Oxford University Press 2002) 16–19.

twentieth century, and the emerging political ideas of social justice transformed real-world tax systems.[33] To begin with, tax fairness required that the fiscal burden be distributed according to the principles of equal sacrifice or ability to pay. Furthermore, taxes were increasingly and deliberately harnessed to level socio-economic conditions and redistribute resources between individuals. Finally, the taxation of personal income forcefully asserted itself and complemented the traditionally prevalent consumption taxes. The three changes were intertwined. Tax fairness and redistribution necessitated that taxes be imposed in line with the individual taxpayer's socio-economic conditions, and the taxpayer's level of income was an important personal circumstance.[34] The abstract taxpayer of the liberal legal system was to be replaced with the more socially embedded individual, whose material and personal circumstances would be given due respect. As noted by Carl Schmitt, the concepts of the emerging tax law aimed at doing 'justice to the individual reality of living conditions, in order to conceive the economic circumstances in a fair manner with respect to taxation'.[35] Under this premise, the benefit theory was discredited for either endorsing inappropriate distributive criteria or neglecting a most vital issue of distribution altogether.

It should not be ignored that a number of liberal fiscal theories are indeed affiliated with the fully developed benefit theory of taxation. Yet, the doctrine of reciprocity between taxation and economy does not, as such, entail the fully developed form of the benefit theory. Since seeking to justify fiscal extraction from society at large, it leaves the issue of tax distribution as such unresolved. However, because this conception infers the legitimacy of taxation from the structural benefits provided by the state, it endorses what could be called the collective interpretation of the benefit theory.[36] Rather than a standard for individual tax shares, the mutual reproductivity serves as a principle for justifying the collection of taxes from a collective body of individuals. For this reason, the principle allows different interpretations of how the tax burden ought to be eventually allocated between taxpayers. In fact, from the early twentieth century onwards, governments increasingly incorporated both benefit and the ability-to-pay aspects of taxation, as they sought to strike a balance between impersonal (*ad rem*) and personal taxes. The core issue was 'to what *extent* these two contrasting principles – personal or impersonal taxation – shall be recognized in

[33] J Jaakkola, 'A Democratic Dilemma of European Power to Tax: Reconstructing the Symbiosis Between Taxation and Democracy Beyond the State?' (2019) 20 *German Law Journal* 660.

[34] AJ Menéndez, *Justifying Taxes: Some Elements for a General Theory of Democratic Tax Law* (Kluwer 2001) 101–05.

[35] C Schmitt, *Über die drei Arten des rechtswissenschaftlichen Denkens* (Duncker & Humblot 2006) 51.

[36] K Vogel, 'The Justification for Taxation: A Forgotten Question' (1988) 33 *American Journal of Jurisprudence* 19, 56–58. For a critical exposition of the principle, see JM Dodge, 'Does the "New Benefit Principle" (or the "Partnership Theory") of Income Taxation Mandate an Income Tax at both the Individual and Corporate Levels?' (2004) Public Law and Legal Theory Working Paper No 118.

our tax systems'.[37] While tax systems were rearranged under the interventionist welfare state premise, taxes continued to be legitimised also with reference to the benefits they rendered possible. Rather than endorsing an exclusive doctrinal background, the emerging tax systems implemented a dual composition and allowed two separate tax philosophies to intersect.

By the twentieth century, the systemic role of taxation in the socio-economic order was firmly entrenched, and this role legitimised the collection of taxes for fiscal purposes. Taxes enable the system of law and government, which in turn serves as an institutional precondition for creating and reproducing value within the private sphere. Taxation thus extracts value from the economy whose functioning it enables. While liberal political thought was a heterogenous tradition, its efforts to conceptualise the role of taxation in the overall economic process of value creation was one of its essential contributions to discourses on taxation. However, it undeniably lost its exclusivity as tax systems were thoroughly revamped in the political framework of the welfare state.

III. JURISDICTIONAL CONGRUENCE BETWEEN ECONOMIC VALUE FORMATION AND THE POWER TO TAX

Before the twentieth century, political thought on taxation did not significantly reflect on the territorial and international extension of the power to tax. The economy was chiefly assumed to operate within national borders, and the question regarding the activities that affiliate with a particular territory and allow a national exchequer to legitimately tax these activities was left unresolved. After the First World War, the problem of allocating taxing powers between national polities emerged rapidly. The adoption of income taxes, soaring tax rates and the quest for restoring the international economic order pushed the eradication of international double taxation onto the political agenda.[38] The double tax burden was an increasingly likely outcome, as the internationalisation of economy proceeded in parallel with states retaining their national tax sovereignty, resulting in the separation of fiscal and economic geographies.[39] With the purpose of alleviating double taxation, governments sought agreement on which state had a cause to tax and which ought to relinquish its fiscal claim. The task was to segregate taxing powers so that a proper territorial pairing between

[37] AA Young, 'Personal or Impersonal Taxation?' in *Proceedings of the Annual Conference on Taxation under the Auspices of the National Tax Association*, 10–13 August (National Tax Association 1915) 337 (emphasis original).

[38] P Genschel and T Rixen, 'Settling and Unsettling the Transnational Legal Order of International Taxation' in T Halliday and G Shaffer (eds), *Transnational Legal Orders* (Cambridge University Press 2015).

[39] On this background, see R Palan, *The Offshore World: Sovereign Markets, Virtual Places, and Nomad Millionaires* (Cornell University Press 2003).

economy and taxation would follow. This resulted in a search for suitable connecting factors that could be used to trigger the state's jurisdiction to tax.

In the nineteenth century, tax liability was generally based on national citizenship. By the time international efforts against double taxation commenced, nationality had already been largely displaced by other criteria.[40] In a famous report on double taxation, commissioned by the League of Nations and drafted by four prominent economists, the authors maintained that taxation based on nationality was predicated on the idea of political allegiance between state and individual. In their critical opinion, the economists insisted that political allegiance only had marginal relevance for tax liability. In 'the modern age of the international migration of persons as well as of capital, political allegiance no longer forms an adequate test of individual fiscal obligation'.[41] The economists suggested that political allegiance be replaced with economic allegiance, conveying material and economic factors that qualify, unlike a formal criterion of nationality, as genuinely pertinent for tax liability.[42] The concept of economic allegiance adhered in part to the notion of economic belonging (*wirtschaftliche Zugehörigkeit*) introduced by Georg Schanz[43] and developed further by Ernst Blumenstein.[44] For Schanz, the most essential aspect of economic belonging was the territorial origin of wealth and income, which referred to a territory in which wealth and income were generated. The four economists also deemed the territorial source of income a key element in economic allegiance, equating the economic origin with the community whose economic life 'makes possible the yield or the acquisition of the wealth'.[45] In addition, the economists perceived the taxpayer's country of residence as an important feature of economic allegiance. What emerged from the economists' reflections were two alternative proxies for tax jurisdiction: the residence of the taxpayer and the territorial source of income. Drawing on these, the right to tax is conferred either on the state of the taxpayer's residence or the state in which the taxpayer's income is generated.

From the 1920s to the mid-1960s, international cooperation against double taxation progressed significantly in the League of Nations and in the Organisation for European Economic Co-operation (later the Organisation for Economic Co-operation and Development (OECD)). The key goal was to opt for a proper connecting factor for tax jurisdiction and to safeguard the suitable congruence between economy and the power to tax. Framed by the four

[40] W Schön, 'Taxation and Democracy' (2019) 72 *Tax Law Review* 235, 282–87.

[41] League of Nations, *Report on Double Taxation Submitted to the Financial Committee*, document E.F.S.73. F.19; 5 April 1923 (Geneva, League of Nations, 1923) part II, section 1.

[42] ibid.

[43] G Schanz, 'Zur Frage der Steuerpflicht' (1892) 9 *Finanzarchiv* 1, 4–16.

[44] E Blumenstein, 'Die Steuer als Rechtsverhältnis' in H Teschemacher et al (eds), *Beiträge zur Finanzwissenschaft: Festgabe für Georg Schanz zum 75. Geburtstag, 12. März 1928. Band II* (JCB Mohr 1928) 3–15.

[45] League of Nations, *Report on Double Taxation* (n 41) part II, section 1.

economists' preparatory work, virtually the only proxies considered were the taxpayer's residence and the origin of income. Notwithstanding the agreement on these alternatives, the negotiations were afflicted with controversies over the actual choice between them. As recounted in the literature,[46] governments' stances oscillated between residence and source taxation. The overt background for this was countries' parochial fiscal interests. Capital-exporting countries sought to benefit from investments made abroad by their residents, which pushed them to advocate residence taxation. Capital-importing countries wished to extract from investments made by non-residents, which urged them to promote source taxation. In addition, practical concerns relating to the administration of taxes were raised, and these were prompted by the fear of tax evasion. However, there were profound tax-theoretical considerations in circulation, and these played a role in shaping the international settlement on the allocation of taxing rights, which was established by the mid-1960s.

A source country's entitlement to tax is associated with benefit taxation. In more precise terms, territorial taxation draws on the collective variant of benefit taxation, as interpreted in section II.[47] Thus, rather than only relying on an abstract international law argument about states being authorised to exercise sovereign authority within their territorial borders, source country taxation is associated with considerations characteristic to tax law and the ways of legitimising taxation in a domestic setting. In the double taxation context, the benefit doctrine expands its validity from a principle of legitimising taxation vis-a-vis the economy to an allocational rule of distributing tax bases between governments.[48] Since a source country's government provides enabling conditions also for non-residents' economic activities, 'foreigners, whose activities reach some minimum threshold, should contribute to the costs of services provided by the host government'.[49] Thomas Adams, who exerted major influence on the work against double taxation, asserted that national public bodies are constitutive in the economic process and should therefore be seen as 'silent partners in every business enterprise',[50] which legitimises taxation at the source of economic

[46] S Picciotto, *International Business Taxation: A Study in Internationalization of Business Regulation* (Cambridge University Press 2013) 1–63; T Rixen, *The Political Economy of International Tax Governance* (Palgrave Macmillan 2008) 86–116; S Jogarajan, *Double Taxation and the League of Nations* (Cambridge University Press 2018).

[47] See also K Vogel, 'Worldwide vs Source Taxation of Income: A Review and Re-evaluation of Arguments (Part I)' (1988) 16 *Intertax* 216; K Vogel, 'Worldwide vs Source Taxation of Income: A Review and Re-evaluation of Arguments (Part III)' (1988) 16 *Intertax* 393, 395; P Dietsch and T Rixen, 'Tax Competition and Global Background Justice' (2014) 22 *Journal of Political Philosophy* 150, 158.

[48] RA Musgrave and PB Musgrave, 'Inter-Nation Equity' in RM Bird and JG Head (eds), *Modern Fiscal Issues: Essays in Honour of Carl S Shoup* (University of Toronto Press 1972) 70–72.

[49] MJ Graetz, 'Taxing International Income: Inadequate Principles, Outdated Concepts, and Unsatisfactory Policies. The David R Tillinghast Lecture' (2001) 54 *Tax Law Review* 261, 298.

[50] Cited in MJ Graetz and MM O'Hear, 'The "Original Intent" of US International Taxation' (1997) 46 *Duke Law Journal* 1021, 1036.

activities. In benefit-based source taxation, a special importance was attributed to the country in which the economic value was generated as a result of entrepreneurial and productive activities.[51] The source country's privilege to impose taxes on various types of income, such as business income, was recognised in virtually all intergovernmental solutions to double taxation, and it solidified itself as a key element in the doctrine of economic allegiance.

In source country taxation, the primary proxy for aggregating income for tax purposes is the territorial origin of income. In an internationally scattered economy, this results in the geographical fragmentation of a person's tax liability. The architects of the international tax regime saw the dispersion of tax liability as a problem because they perceived it to compromise the ability-to-pay principle. Imposing taxes in line with a taxpayer's ability to pay and at a progressive scale required that the taxpayer's entire economic circumstances and total income were taken into consideration, which necessitated choosing the taxpayer as the primary unit for clustering income.[52] This was regarded inconsistent with the system of territorially fragmented tax liability, in which the category of taxpayer was less relevant for imposing taxes than the territorial source of income.[53] For this reason, a more intimately taxpayer-related proxy for tax jurisdiction was advocated. The connecting factor was found in the taxpayer's country of residence, which allowed taxation according to the taxpayer's worldwide income and at an appropriate progressive rate. This was pivotal already in the four economists' report, which relied expressly on the ability-to-pay principle and embraced residence taxation as the key method of implementing ability-to-pay taxation in an international context.[54] However, residence taxation did not figure as antithetical to economic allegiance nor to the normative tenet that taxes be paid in a country with an economy affiliated to the taxpayer.[55] Rather, also the place of residence indicated the location of the taxpayer's economic connections, and hence, it overlapped with the premise of source taxation. The economic ties of international taxpayers are many in number, not few. But since source country taxation was incapable of taking into account the taxpayer's worldwide income and accommodating inter-individual equity, as required by ability-to-pay taxation, the territorial origin of income as the exclusive connector for tax jurisdiction was not enough. Therefore, in eradicating double taxation, source and residence were both employed in the allocation of taxing rights.

[51] W Haslehner, 'Value Creation and Income Taxation: A Coherent Framework for Reform' in W Haslehner and M Lamensch (eds), *Taxation and Value Creation* (IBFD 2021) 47.

[52] W Schön, 'International Tax Coordination for a Second-Best World (Part I)' (2009) 1 *World Tax Journal* 67, 72.

[53] NH Kaufman, 'Fairness and the Taxation of International Income' (1998) 29 *Law and Policy in International Business* 145, 167–72.

[54] League of Nations, *Report on Double Taxation* (n 41) part II.

[55] J Li, J Bao and H Li, 'Value Creation: A Constant Principle in a Changing World of International Taxation' (2019) 67 *Canadian Tax Journal* 1107, 1112.

The tension between source and residence taxation reveals how the clash between the benefit and ability-to-pay principles, originally underlying the domestic discourse on taxation, shaped the international tax regime. In the formative phase of the regime, there was also tension in the separation between impersonal and personal income taxes, characteristic to national systems of taxation.[56] The former were imposed sporadically on the taxpayer's various types of income, with each tax having a separate tax rate. Because impersonal taxes were levied independently of each other, they were incapable of aggregating the taxpayer's total income for the purpose of graduated taxation. Personal taxes, in contrast, were general in a sense that they were charged on the taxpayer's combined income. In aggregating the taxpayer's entire income, personal taxes provided for taxation at a progressive rate.[57] Since impersonal taxes largely ignored the taxpayer's personal circumstances while personal taxes took them into consideration, the former were associated with benefit and the latter with ability-to-pay taxation.[58] Drawing on the connection to benefit and ability-to-pay taxation, the experts from the League of Nations maintained that regarding impersonal taxes,

> we have recognised the primary importance of the idea of origin, that is to say, the system of the assignment of income; in the case of the general or personal tax, on the contrary, we have recognised the primary importance of the idea of domicile [residence].[59]

Systemically scattered impersonal taxes could be matched with territorially fragmented source taxation, but integrated personal taxes entailed aggregate taxation by the country of residence. The demarcation between these basic categories exerted a major, even if not uninterrupted, influence on attributing different types of income to the jurisdictions of either the source country or country of residence. This stressed the nature of income tax as a 'dual thing' that must accommodate territorial as well as ability-to-pay considerations.[60] Thus, the classical tension between benefit and ability-to-pay taxation resurfaced and shaped the international tax regime.

Between the 1920s and the mid-1940s, several model conventions for alleviating double taxation were introduced by the League of Nations. In all of the

[56] See KC Wang, 'International Double Taxation of Income: Relief through International Agreement 1921–1945' (1945) 59 *Harvard Law Review* 73, 81–92; Jogarajan (n 46) 249–50.

[57] For a conceptual analysis of personal and impersonal taxes, see WH Coates, 'Double Taxation and Tax Evasion' (1925) 88 *Journal of the Royal Statistical Society* 403.

[58] JF Avery Jones, 'Sir Josiah Stamp and Double Income Tax' in J Tiley (ed), *Studies in the History of Tax Law: Volume 6* (Hart Publishing 2013) 9–10.

[59] League of Nations, *Double Taxation and Tax Evasion: Report and Resolutions Submitted by the Technical Experts to the Financial Committee*, document F.212 February 1925 (Geneva, League of Nations, 1925) part II, section 3; see also League of Nations, *Double Taxation and Tax Evasion: Report Presented by the Committee of Technical Experts on Double Taxation and Tax Evasion*, document C.216 M. 85. 1927 II (Geneva, League of Nations, 1927).

[60] Graetz and O'Hear (n 50) 1036.

models, the power to tax specifically enumerated types of income were allocated either with reference to the origin of income or the taxpayer's residence. In so doing, the models attempted to reconcile national fiscal interests and to strike a balance between benefit and ability-to-pay taxation. Importantly, the League of Nations embraced an either-or approach: a specific item of income, such as interest income, was attributed either to residence or source country. To some extent, this changed with the OECD's 1963 Model Convention.[61] Regarding some income types, the OECD also adopted an either-or approach. However, rather than granting either source country or country of residence an exclusive right to a particular income, the one and the same income could be taxed in part by the source country, in part by the country of residence. Technically, a maximum for a source country's tax rate would be agreed upon, while the country of residence would have a right to tax the same income without any upper limit, although it was expected to credit the tax imposed by the source country. For some items of income, this became a lasting element in the international tax regime. While this has been a relatively unnoticed policy shift, it is relevant for two reasons. First, it shows the intricacy of appreciating whether specific types of economic activities ought to be associated exclusively with the source country or country of residence. The same income could have an economic allegiance with multiple countries, with each country contributing to the production of the income. Thus, not only was it necessary to balance benefit and ability-to-pay taxation against each other but also the various economic and territorial connections of income. Second, the change of approach conceded that, in the case of more than one extracting treasuries, taxing the same income could be attributed to two exchequers. Economic activities could be taxed jointly across borders.

Since the turn of the millennium, the international tax regime has been fiercely criticised. It has frequently been asserted that the regime's basic principles have proven to be outdated under the conditions of globalised, financialised and digitalised economies.[62] Does this discontent suggest that the regime's underlying aspirations are becoming relics that ought to be abandoned? The answer is in the negative. Over the last 10-year period, a powerful political credo that 'profits are taxed where economic activities take place and value is created'[63] and that there ought to be a genuine 'link between taxation and where economic activity takes place'[64] has emerged. The plea has been fuelled by the jurisdictional

[61] AJ van den Tempel, *Relief from Double Taxation* (IBFD 1967) 31–34.

[62] For instance, see Graetz (n 49); ED Kleinbard, 'Stateless Income' (2011) 11 *Florida Tax Review* 700; R Mason, 'The Transformation of International Tax' (2020) 114 *American Journal of International Law* 353, 357 and references therein.

[63] Organization for Economic Co-operation and Development, Explanatory Statement, OECD/G20 Base Erosion and Profit Shifting Project (OECD 2015) 4.

[64] Communication from the Commission to the European Parliament and the Council, 'A Fair and Efficient Corporate Tax System in the European Union: 5 Key Areas for Action' COM(2015) 302 final, 6.

mismatch between taxation and economy. Even in a long-term perspective, this features as one of the most powerful articulations of economic allegiance, and one that has influenced the OECD's and the EU's efforts to address tax avoidance and the digitalisation of business. In academia, similar insights have been put forward, albeit under somewhat different conceptualisations.[65] These approaches to the international tax regime, and corporate tax in particular, have been informed by the aspirations of economic allegiance and the reciprocity between taxation and economy. The international tax regime's key flaw is found in its incapacity to implement, at the level of legal rules, the political and ideational aspirations that underlie the regime. It is advocated that rather than being deserted, these aspirations should be revitalised. However, many recent proposals for the overhaul of the international tax regime point beyond the elements that have traditionally governed the interpretation of economic allegiance.[66] For instance, emphasising the value-creating role of digital services' users may shift the economic allegiance from the production jurisdiction towards the market jurisdiction.[67] The exceptions aside, a host of recent reform proposals have pleaded that an essential link between taxation and economic value creation must be identified.

The international tax regime, as developed for the purpose of allocating taxing rights horizontally among countries, exhibits several important properties. First, it acknowledged the normative significance of the reciprocal relationship between taxation and economy. This was obvious in the doctrines of economic allegiance and territorial taxation, which enforced the benefit aspects of taxation. In this regard, it must be borne in mind that the international tax regime related merely to income taxation. Thus, in the overall system of taxation and besides income taxation, consumption taxes remained in operation and were imposed on a basis of economic allegiance, which once again emphasised the benefit aspects of taxation. Second, taxing rights were not distributed solely with reference to territorial connections. The ability-to-pay principle, having gained political and academic traction, insisted on accommodating income taxes to the taxpayers' overall and worldwide socio-economic circumstances, which reflected taxpayers' actual ability to pay taxes. The international tax regime was thus shaped by the ability-to pay as well as benefit aspects of taxation. Third, the coexistence of benefit and ability-to-pay premises resulted in a tiered or layered structure of the tax regime. Drawing on benefit taxation, the power to tax was allocated to the source country, while on the basis of

[65] For instance, see Dietsch and Rixen (n 47).

[66] See W Haslehner and M Lamensch, 'General Report on Value Creation and Taxation: Outlining the Debate' in W Haslehner and M Lamensch (eds), *Taxation and Value Creation* (IBFD 2021).

[67] J Hey, '"Taxation Where Value is Created" and the OECD/G20 Base Erosion and Profit Shifting Initiative' (2018) 72 *Bulletin for International Taxation* 203; J Becker and J Englisch, 'Taxing Where Value is Created: What's "User Involvement" Got to Do with It?' (2019) 47 *Intertax* 161; W Schön, 'One Answer to Why and How to Tax the Digitalized Economy' (2019) 47 *Intertax* 1003.

ability-to-pay taxation, it was assigned to the taxpayer's country of residence. Source country taxation respected territoriality and economic allegiance, and it was legitimised by ideas that had traditionally justified the exercise of the power to tax in a vertical relationship between state and individual. Country of residence taxation was also legitimised with respect to economic allegiance. Beyond that, however, taxation by the country of residence was founded on the capacity of the country of residence to enforce ability-to-pay taxation and generate tax fairness in a horizontal relationship between taxpayers. Thus, in the dual system of an international tax regime, separate political entities were allowed to assert their taxing rights under partly different premises. The source country makes a claim on the basis of the territorial connection between taxation and economy, while the country of residence also resorts to considerations pertaining to inter-individual tax fairness and social justice.

IV. THE EU AS A SECOND-ORDER SYSTEM OF ENABLING ECONOMIC VALUE FORMATION

In developing the international tax regime, the goal was the proper horizontal allocation of taxing powers among nation states. In the context of the EU, the issue transforms into the vertical allocation of taxing powers between the EU and its Member States. This vertical allocation of taxing powers differs from the interstate allocation in two related respects. First, in their horizontal relationship, states are politically autonomous governing units. In the multi-level European political structure, in contrast, there is a normative division of governing functions and competences between the EU and its Member States. The EU is thus legally and functionally intertwined with its Member States, and vice versa. Second, notwithstanding certain recent efforts regarding the determination of corporate tax bases[68] and even tax rates,[69] the horizontal allocation has not, so far, involved the positive construction of the power to collect taxes, as the key aspiration has been to avoid excessive tax burdens. The international tax regime prescribes the limits to the authority of states to tax but abstains from imposing on states any obligation to collect taxes.[70] In the EU, the problem is related to the positive construction of the EU's power to collect taxes. The power would be instrumental in enabling the functional allocation of governing

[68] Council Directive (EU) 1164/2016 of 12 July 2016 laying down rules against tax avoidance practices that directly affect the functioning of the internal market [2016] OJ L193/1.

[69] European Commission, 'Proposal for a Council Directive on Ensuring a Global minimum level of Taxation for Multinational Groups in the Union' COM(2021) 823 final.

[70] J Jaakkola and R Knuutinen, 'The International Order of Corporate Taxation: From Market-Building to Sustainable Fiscal Settlement?' in B Sjåfjell and CM Bruner (eds), *The Cambridge Handbook of Corporate Law, Corporate Governance and Sustainability* (Cambridge University Press 2020).

duties between the EU and its Member States. These two differences aside, this section reflects on whether the international tax regime's traditional principles and structures, legitimising tax collection in national polities, are meaningful for a review of the legitimacy of the EU's power to levy taxes.

The international tax regime's key lesson for the European power to tax is its dual structure. In this structure, taxation by the source country is legitimised through its value-enabling capacity, and taxation by the country of residence is legitimised through both its value-enabling capacity as well as its ability to execute socio-economic equity among individuals. In the relationship between the EU and its Member States, the dual structure of taxation has never been in operation: since the early phase of integration, Member States have retained their power to collect taxes, and the EEC and its successors have been financed by means mainly other than taxes, regardless of contrary political pursuits.[71] This is striking, as the dual structure of the international tax regime bears a relevant resemblance to the original two-tiered model of European integration, which was authoritative beyond tax-collecting powers. In this model, European market integration was assumed to generate economic growth and aggregate wealth across borders, while Member States had the mandate to redistribute resources between individuals and implement democratically established standards for social justice.[72] In this two-tiered system, the 'integration process was meant to expand the size of the (economic) cake, and the Member States were meant to redistribute that cake internally'.[73] The system was part of the broader post-war settlement of 'embedded liberalism',[74] in which national welfare regimes and international market order coexisted and reinforced each other.

To confer the power to collect taxes on the EU would not hinder Member States' prospects of using taxes for their democratically established ends. Member States, as the primary sites of the European taxpayer's social and economic ties, would retain their power to tax alongside the EU, and they would still be allowed to use taxes for various fiscal and redistributive purposes. In this sense, Member States would be reminiscent of countries of residence, whose right to tax was based on their contribution to the economic process, their capacity to enforce socio-economic fairness, and their ability to do justice to the

[71] AJ Menéndez, 'Neumark Vindicated: the Three Patterns of Europeanisation of National Tax Systems and the Future of the Social and Democratic *Rechtsstaat*' in D Chalmers, M Jachtenfuchs and C Joerges (eds), *The End of the Eurocrats' Dream: Adjusting to European Diversity* (Cambridge University Press 2016) 80–87.

[72] AS Milward, *The European Rescue of the Nation-State* (Routledge 1992); C Joerges, 'The Rechtsstaat and Social Europe: How a Classical Tension Resurfaces in the European Integration Process' in L Morlino and G Palombella (eds), *Rule of Law and Democracy: Inquiries into Internal and External Issues* (Brill 2010).

[73] F de Witte, 'The Architecture of a "Social Market Economy"' in P Koutrakos and J Snell (eds), *Research Handbook on the Law of the EU's Internal Market* (Edward Elgar Publishing 2017) 117.

[74] JG Ruggie, 'International Regimes, Transactions, and Change: Embedded Liberalism in the Postwar Economic Order' (1982) 36 *International Organization* 379.

taxpayer's personal circumstances. Therefore, dismantling national power to tax is not a part of the agenda. The question, rather, is whether there are legitimate grounds to grant the EU the power to collect taxes alongside Member States. Or, more precisely, can the EU be claimed to play a relevant similar role to the one that national polities, in their source country capacity, play in enabling value creation? Provided that the EU, as a second-order polity, makes a conceivable contribution, alongside Member States as first-order polities, to value creation, it could make a claim to tax the value it enables. In fact, over the last 10 years or so, this has emerged as perhaps the chief path of legitimising the EU's power to collect taxes.

Over the past decade, the EU's productive contribution to the accrual of economic value has been increasingly conceptualised as a 'European added value', which amounts to 'the value resulting from an EU intervention which is additional to the value that would have been otherwise created by Member States acting alone'.[75] I submit that there are two key mechanisms for the generation of a European added value or European public goods. The first is the legislative creation of the European internal market. Ever since the inception of the European communities in the 1950s, the European market has been the primary means of contributing to economic growth. Originally, this was intimately linked to the idea of 'dynamic growth', which characterised then-contemporary economic theories and which the architects of the European market equated with economies of scale, improved conditions of private competition, and increased productivity of investments.[76] For these rewards to emerge, competition law and the cross-border economic freedoms were established through European law. As a result, the regional system of Europeanised market economy, as a primary site of economic value creation, was no longer sustained solely through national legal systems, but a significant part of the legal substructure enabling private value creation was shifted to the European level. The second typical mechanism for generating European added value is budgetary expenditure and investment-type spending in particular. This spending has usually been implemented through various funds, from which pooled resources are distributed and whose significance has increased during the course of integration.[77] Recently, investment-type spending reached notable importance and topicality as the NextGenerationEU recovery instrument was adopted. The more these funds benefit the whole of the EU and the more they hold a genuinely European added value, the less they are bound to appear as an object of a *juste retour* zero-sum game in political bargaining.[78]

[75] European Commission, 'The Added Value of the EU budget' Commission Staff Working Paper SEC(2011) 867 final, 2.

[76] C Kaupa, *The Pluralist Character of the European Economic Constitution* (Hart Publishing 2016) 36–45.

[77] D Hodson, 'Regional and Structural Funds' in E Jones, A Menon and S Weatherill (eds), *The Oxford Handbook of the European Union* (Oxford University Press 2012).

[78] M Monti et al, 'Future financing of the EU: Final Report and Recommendations of the High Level Group on Own Resources' (December 2016) 30.

Drawing on the premise of benefit taxation, the European added value provides a basis for a European power to collect taxes. EU policies are contributory causes in the process of value creation, and the value not accrued in the absence of such policies may be taxed by the Union. This is most obvious with respect to the internal market, but the case can be made regarding public investments as well.[79] In line with the benefit theory, albeit routinely without reference thereto, it has been suggested that the focus of EU taxes 'should be on fresh receipts from activities immediately linked to the process of Europeanisation and globalisation', and that taxing this activity 'could quite reasonably and even profitably be mobilised to pay for the collective action that is its necessary concomitant and precondition'.[80] Without a doubt, the gains accruing in the internal market cannot be attributed entirely to the EU. Rather, the EU and Member States have a co-original effect in contributing to the existence of economic activity and the value it entails. This co-originality is familiar from the double tax context. In allocating taxing rights with deference to economic allegiance, it may be hard to determine the true and exclusive origin of specific activities. The right to tax dividend income, for instance, may be attributed to both source countries and countries of residence, as both may be seen to play a role in its formation. Likewise, in the European two-tiered system of economy, the public framework that enables market activities cannot be exclusively reduced either to its European or national pillar. This requires that the legal aspects of value creation are taken seriously. The EU does not come with its own population and it does entail a territorial extension, in a tangible and material sense. However, through its legal substructure and resource system, the EU contributes to value formation in an intangible way characteristic to the second-order and post-national systems of governance.

In allocating tax bases under the EU's taxing authority, the cross-border element of economic activities is a key, for two reasons. First, cross-border activities are a prototypical instance of the type of 'economic activity enabled by the internal market', and hence, they are linked to the European enabling policies and taxing authority.[81] From the benefit perspective, they are a legitimate target of taxation. Second, as a result of fiscal interdependence and tax competition, Member States' effective capacity to tax mobile tax bases within the internal market has diminished. Rather than being exogenous to the EU, this outcome can be traced back to the European market-making integration.[82] The internal

[79] G della Cananea, 'No Representation without Taxation in the European Union' in I Pernice and J Weiler (eds), *Legitimacy Issues of the European Union in the Face of Crisis* (Nomos 2017).

[80] D Tarschys, 'Entering a World of Footloose Tax Bases: Can the EU Generate Its Own Income?' in A de Feo and B Laffan (eds), *EU Own Resources: Momentum for a Reform?* (European University Institute 2016) 14.

[81] M Poiares Maduro, 'A New Governance for the European Union and the Euro: Democracy and Justice' (2012) RSCAS Policy Paper 11, 13.

[82] J Jaakkola, 'Enhancing Political Representation Through the European Economic Constitution? Regressive Politics of Democratic Inclusion' (2019) 15 *European Constitutional Law Review* 194.

market has thus facilitated an asymmetry between its benefits for private actors in their role as cross-border market citizens and disadvantages for governments in their role as tax collectors. However, the EU itself would be well positioned to tap mobile capital flows with a cross-border dimension, and it could 'aim for tax bases that are, more or less, beyond reach of individual states and accessible only by joint action'.[83] This would incorporate a corrective and balancing component into the European tax.[84] In essence, it would help Member States to adopt tax policies that are difficult to introduce and enforce under competitive pressures, prompted by transnational economic order. Addressing the negative fiscal externalities of integration would not interfere with the mandate of Member States to enforce their democratic conceptions of socio-economic fairness, but would rather compensate the losses incurred from the very process of integration. Therefore, in imposing taxes, the EU would act according to its perhaps primary functional role as an entity that solves collective action problems, and precisely in the field in which Member States have lost vital capacities to enforce their public policies.[85] In all this, the cross-border aspect and the taxpayer's degree of cross-border mobility would count as key factors in triggering the EU's legitimate power to collect taxes, and a European tax would relate to both positive and negative effects that the EU legal order entails.

Taxing cross-border activities by the EU would not merely generate revenues and limit fiscal externalities originating in the European market order. It could also alleviate Member States' struggles over the horizontal allocation of cross-border and mobile tax bases. In many cases, it appears notoriously hard to identify which Member State ought to be entitled to tax specific activities, as the territorial and value-enabling basis of taxation leaves much margin for interpretation. As stated in section III, the recent tax policy initiatives in the EU have widely endorsed the dogma of taxing where value is created. Implementing the principle in practice, however, has proven complicated, especially with respect to highly immaterial and mobile corporate activities. The EU's original common consolidated corporate tax base initiative of 2011, for instance, encountered fierce resistance because of the consolidation formula, according to which income was to be allocated between Member States.[86] Likewise, reinterpreting the concept of permanent establishment so that it would allow taxation of income (or revenue) from digital services in what is considered a proper site of economic activity has stalled.[87] Each time the reallocation of tax bases among

[83] Tarschys (n 80) 17. See also M Kumm, 'Democratic Challenges Arising from the Eurocrisis: What Kind of a Constitutional Crisis is Europe in and What Should Be Done about It?' in *Challenges of Multi-Tier Governance in the European Union: Effectiveness, Efficiency and Legitimacy* (European Parliament, 2013).

[84] Menéndez, 'Taxing Europe' (n 6) 324–25.

[85] Poiares Maduro (n 81) 11–16.

[86] For this, see European Commission, 'Proposal for a Council Directive on a Common Consolidated Corporate Tax Base (CCCTB)' COM(2016) 683 final.

[87] European Commission, 'Proposal for a Council Directive laying down rules relating to the corporate taxation of a significant digital presence' COM(2018) 147 final.

Member States is pursued by political means, obstacles emerge. In these cases, a European tax might be a part of the solution.[88] Rather than struggling to opt for one country or another, the proper site of taxation and also value creation might be the European level. This would not merely be a forced compromise in a situation where no other feasible solution appears in sight. On the contrary, in the complex value-enabling fabric of the European polity, the European level might well be the appropriate site of value creation, especially for cross-border activities.

Underlining the internal market benefits as a ground for instituting tax obligations often results in the conclusion that cross-border corporate entities and mobile financial capital ought to bear the tax burden, and correctly so. Yet, at the same time, European taxes are also portrayed as a conceivable means of fostering individuals' democratic citizenship and participation in the EU polity. Taxes could enhance European citizens' sense of political belonging in the EU, make the functioning of the EU system of governance more transparent to the citizens, raise their awareness of how the EU machinery functions, and increase their attentiveness to European politics.[89] To put it simply, European taxes would have a democratically productive role in reinforcing the link between individuals and the EU. This perception is affiliated with the broad strand of scholarship discussing the constructive role of taxation in building the modern state, nation and democratic institutions.[90] In the context of the EU, authors often stress that taxation would make the financial burden that the European polity imposes on individuals visible and transparent. However, on a more fundamental level, paying taxes is a key form of belonging to a political community and engendering a sense of authorship over the polity in which people's lives are essentially formed and through which individuals connect to each other's fate.

The two lines of reasoning above – the one considering mobile economic actors as an exclusive group of European taxpayers, the other stressing taxes as an essential means for a sense of political belonging – are difficult to accommodate simultaneously. If EU tax liabilities are merely allocated to cross-border corporate actors and financial capital, the European taxes are bound to remain distant to a great number of European citizens, and the broad-based financial

[88] See I Begg, 'The Challenges of Multi-Tier Governance in the EU: Budgetary Solidarity in a Multi-Tiered Union' in *Challenges of Multi-Tier Governance in the European Union: Effectiveness, Efficiency and Legitimacy* (European Parliament, 2013) 185.

[89] See Menéndez, 'Taxing Europe' (n 6); Le Cacheux (n 7); S Osterloh, F Heinemann and P Mohl, 'The EU Tax Revisited: Should There Be One? And Will There Be One?' (2008) 6 *Zeitschrift für Staats- und Europawissenschaften (ZSE) / Journal for Comparative Government and European Policy* 444, 449–51.

[90] For a discussion in different contexts, see RH Bates and D-HD Lien, 'A Note on Taxation, Development, and Representative Government' (1985) 14 *Politics & Society* 53; C Tilly, *Coercion, Capital and European States AD 990–1992* (Blackwell 1994); M Herb, 'Taxation and Representation' (2003) 38 *Studies in Comparative International Development* 3; ML Ross, 'Does Taxation Lead to Representation?' (2004) 34 *British Journal of Political Science* 229.

commitment to a polity, as a democracy-enhancing obligation, would still be missing. In fact, excluding European citizens from the body of taxpayers might facilitate the image of the EU as a community of capital and corporations, alienating citizens from the EU as a polity far from their own making. Therefore, if we consider fiscal obligations as essential components of democratic citizenship, associating the internal market benefits solely with corporations and financial capital might be counterproductive. Reducing the addressees of internal market benefits exclusively to corporate actors and finance might also disregard the fact that the internal market is not unconnected to European citizens, as citizens also have relevant economic ties to the European market. Furthermore, benefits from European investment-type expenditure are not confined to the corporate sector, of which the NextGenerationEU recovery package is a recent and in all likelihood not the last but rather an inaugural example. European citizens have relevant economic connections to the EU, and these are capable of justifying tax obligations beyond the business sector and providing for the political agency through citizen obligations. Therefore, an inclusive conception of European taxpayers would not entail that the link between the right to levy taxes and participation in the economy, as a basis for fiscal obligations, be abandoned. Indeed, the precise allocation of the tax burden between different groups of taxpayers is a topic that cannot be avoided in the EU context in the long run.

The fundamental question of who ought to be in the taxpayer position has been partly settled in the national context for quite some time, as national laws have embraced a broad taxpayer base. However, in the second-order polity of the EU, in which genuine tax obligations are still waiting to be introduced, the issue remains critical. I have proposed that the EU's contribution to the economic value formation provides a strong normative case for genuine EU taxes. The creation of these European taxes could involve pertinent reflections on various types of connections that exist between economy, taxation and individuals. Therefore, while the efforts of engineering EU taxes may rely on traditional tax policy principles, they may also entail a meaningful reinterpretation and rearticulation of those essentials. Future quarrels over the EU's revenue structure could thus make a significant contribution to tax-theoretical ideas, usually rather resistant to historical change.

V. CONCLUSION

In this chapter, the idea of systemic and functional reciprocity between taxation and economy has been treated as legitimising taxation in national, international and EU contexts. The chapter has put forward that in each setting, the power to collect taxes enables economic value creation, which justifies imposing taxes on the value being accrued. This pattern of thought has made an influential appearance through modern fiscal history and profoundly shaped the political rule. The chapter has also suggested that the EU's power to levy taxes, a capacity thus far non-existent in any significant sense, could be legitimised on such a basis. Although an admittedly unconventional polity, the EU's power to collect taxes may nonetheless be justified with reference to the powerful ideas developed in national and international contexts. In this view, the EU is considered a second-order value-enabling entity, whose power to collect taxes would match the already existing functions the EU plays in the European multi-level political structure. Rather than a revolutionary act, the conferral of tax-collecting power on the EU would signify a coherent step in the European integration process. In terms of institutional design, moving on from mere governance of national tax systems to governing through genuine European taxes would signify a considerable change. From a long-term historical and ideational perspective, however, even liberal political systems with limited government have allowed states to collect taxes to finance their governing functions. Therefore, rather than deeply ideational, the change would be real-political.

This chapter has asserted that the EU has a legitimate claim to tax the value it enables. In the nation-state context, the same argument has typically been employed to legitimise a very specific task of taxation, namely the fiscal function of raising revenues. This has also been the case in the present chapter, which has only reflected on the revenue-raising function of taxes at the EU level. In no way, however, has this approach been intended to constrain the use of taxation for various socio-economic purposes beyond collecting revenues. The starting point of the chapter has been the two-tiered structure of the European polity, in which the task of enforcing socio-economic fairness between individuals by means of taxation rests chiefly on the Member States. The EU, for its part, has its primary duty in providing genuinely European collective or public goods, which have an added value across borders and for the body of European citizens at large. The two-tiered division of labour, however, is not a fixed given. Should the EU adopt an orientation towards a more redistributive community, European taxes could well be designed according to these preferences and reviewed against further legitimising principles. In the contemporary Union, in which the almost total absence of European power to levy taxes prevails, legitimising such a power must start from a relatively moderate premise. In this sense, the value-enabling role of the EU is not a restrictive and exclusive premise for justifying European taxes. It rather shows how imperfectly the current revenue system of the Union corresponds even to the liberal conception of the polity and the confined role that taxes are expected to play therein.

The Eurozone and Covid-19 crises have provoked lively political debates on the finances and revenues of the EU. Since the European Commission has prepared to deliver proposals on the new sources of EU resources, and since these will include different forms of taxation too, 'the next phase of implementing the own resources roadmap will inevitably involve the discussion of new or harmonised forms of taxation'.[91] In this exchange of views, the proposals must be reviewed against the proper and sustainable grounds of justification.

[91] R Crowe, 'An EU Budget of States and Citizens' (2020) 26 *European Law Journal* 331, 342.

Furthermore, whatever the eventual response at the European level, it must naturally comply with the dictum of 'no taxation without representation', ie, it must come with democratic legitimacy. However, it has been pointed out that just as there cannot be taxation without representation, there cannot be representation without taxation.[92] The European Parliament that has some say over spending but lacks the power to decide on taxes covering that spending is a structurally bounded representative body. It is true that enhancing the power to tax is by no means a guarantee for a democratic organisation. Nonetheless, with this caveat in mind, European taxes could enhance the governing capacities at the European level and forge representative structures. In the end, a direct allegiance between the EU and the European individual in the role of a taxpayer could perhaps foster democratic agency in the polity that is in danger of remaining politically distant and opaque. The European connection between taxation and democracy might thus prove reciprocal and symbiotic.

[92] S Fabbrini, 'Representation Without Taxation: An Association or Union of States?' in A de Feo and B Laffan (eds), *EU Own Resources: Momentum for a Reform?* (European University Institute 2016); della Cananea (n 79).

6

Between Form and Substance: At the Root of the Limits of the EU Taxing Powers

FRANCESCO FARRI*

I. SOVEREIGNTY AT THE ROOT OF TAXING POWERS

TAXATION IS ONE of the most typical expressions of the 'sovereignty' of the legal entity that imposes taxes. Therefore, studying what limits the power to impose taxes by a legal entity (sovereign community, state, federation) is subject to, is tantamount to studying what the limits of its 'sovereignty' are.

This research requires facing a series of particularly complex and controversial questions. First, it is necessary to clarify the meaning of 'sovereignty'. Moreover, it is necessary to identify which legal entities may be the depositories of 'sovereignty'. Finally, it is necessary to verify whether or not the legal entity can be said to be a holder of taxing powers and if so, to what extent.

These questions must be answered in order to thoroughly examine the issue of the limits of the European Union's (EU) taxing powers, both from a current perspective (*de iure condito*) and from an evolutionary perspective (*de iure condendo*).

II. THE STRUCTURAL LINK BETWEEN SOVEREIGNTY AND PEOPLE

Over time, a veritable 'Babel of definitions',[1] each more or less 'historically placed',[2] has flourished around the concept of 'sovereignty'. Let us think, for

* Associate Professor of Tax Law, University of Genoa (Italy).

[1] To use the incisive words of A Morrone, 'Sovranità' (2017) 3 *Rivista AIC* 2. In the tax field see, in the same sense, Y Brauner, 'An Essay on BEPS, Sovereignty and Taxation' in SA Rocha and A Christians (eds), *Tax Sovereignty in the BEPS Era* (Wolters Kluwer 2017) 74.

[2] F Lanchester, 'L'erosione della sovranità nazionale' (1998) 2 *Rassegna parlamentare* 413; Brauner (n 1).

example, of how 'historically placed' the conception of sovereignty, elaborated by the controversial Carl Schmitt, can be considered as a power of decision on the 'state of exception'.[3] This conception is so 'historically placed' that it now appears outdated, at least until the pandemic has once again made the European peoples live in a painful 'state of exception'.

Beyond this, it is still possible to identify a basic definition of the concept of sovereignty in the power of self-determination, in the juridical sense, of an organised community, ie, with the power to choose the rules of its own civil life, power in which the possible choice to delegate the setting of the rules to external authorities is included. From this perspective, it is clear how taxation can be said to be intrinsically connected to sovereignty.

The power that organised communities exert in the choice of the expenditure to be made and in the regulation of the financing modalities, including the possibility of imposing taxes and of attributing powers to collective institutions to levy them, is a typical manifestation of the power of self-determination of a community and, as such, of sovereignty in the above-mentioned sense. The attribution of such powers of taxation pertains to one of the vital aspects of community life and, as such, pertains to the fundamental and supreme principles of the constitution of the community itself.

The sovereignty of a community can arise in diversified forms, because each of them is 'historically placed'. However, this does not change the conclusion drawn above. The acts of expression of sovereignty can be exercised directly by the local community (direct democracy), by its direct representatives (such as parliaments) or by a person who embodies it (such as a monarch). However, they always remain acts that are based on the exercise of a sovereign power. This is the case, in particular, for the acts through which taxes are imposed on a community.

We can ask ourselves whether it still makes legal and political sense to speak about 'sovereignty' in a globalised and digitised world, in a world of the web and multinationals, in a world in which the legal dimension often appears overwhelmed by the rapid evolution of facts and by their strength in a complex and 'pluralistic' world.

According to some influential thinkers, the very concept of 'State', to which sovereignty has historically been linked,[4] should now be considered as being in the process of being abandoned.[5] From another perspective, it is recognised that

> a political form in which the 'modern' returns to its original complexity … is far from requiring the radical removal of the principle of sovereignty … Indeed, it seems to

[3] C Schmitt, *Politische Theologie: Vier Kapitel zur Lehre von der Souveränität* (Duncker & Humblot 1922 and 1934).

[4] But that correspondence is not one-to-one: in fact, there may also be sovereignty outside the model of the state.

[5] *cf*, as an example, S Cassese, 'Fortuna e decadenza della nozione di Stato' in VvAA, *Studies in Honour of Massimo Severo Giannini* (Giuffrè 1988).

> require its restoration as a conservative principle of that plural order and that mutual obligation between rulers and ruled that we still wish to live in.[6]

In fact, 'sovereignty' is not a 'surmountable' concept and even less a concept about being abandoned. It is an element that a community that wishes to organise itself in that way cannot do without:

> Sovereignty is realism, conscious existence of a collective ego, not ego hypertrophy. The sovereignty of a political body is the ability to establish how to stay in the world and in history, how to relate to the external environment, how to recognise the permanent interests of a State.[7]

This is why sovereignty is an unfailing concept for an organised community. And it is for this reason that sovereignty does not emanate from the existence of a public organisation (state, federation, union), but from the community of persons, from the people, who give it life:

> Just as there is no soul without a body, nor a living body without a soul, so there is no sovereignty without the political body of which it is the vital impulse, nor a political body without sovereignty … This political body is not necessarily a tribal identity, a compact community: it is a complex society, crossed by tensions and conflicts, which is politically expressed in sovereignty.[8]

There is therefore no need to fear that a reference to the concepts of sovereignty and people will lead to dangerous nationalism or social exclusion. Sovereignty is by its nature 'popular', as properly recognised by the constitutions of democratic states.[9] Sovereignty 'belongs to the people', while it belongs to the State only indirectly, as the State is an expression of a population that poses itself as 'sovereign'.

If this dimension does not exist, as can happen for populations oppressed by a dictator, the act of expressing sovereignty is drained of substance and, sooner or later, is destined to create a fatal rift between the community and the tyrant who has taken the task of governing the community upon himself without having the necessary legitimacy, as a Leviathan.

This also applies in particular to tax sovereignty. Contrary to what we tend to believe, according to an authoritative conception rooted in pre-democratic contests,[10] tax sovereignty does not belong to the State as such, but is only an

[6] D Quaglioni, *La sovranità* (Laterza 2004) 120 (original in Italian, translated by the author).

[7] C Galli, 'Apologia della sovranità' (2019) 2 *Limes* 159; C Galli, *Sovranità* (Il Mulino 2019) (original in Italian, translated by the author).

[8] Galli, 'Apologia della sovranità', ibid (original in Italian, translated by the author).

[9] Think, eg, of Art 1 of the Italian Constitution; in the same sense also Art 1 of the Swedish Instrument of Government; Art 3 of the French Declaration of the Rights of Man and of the Citizen; Art 1 of the Spanish Constitution; the Preamble of the German Constitution; and Art 4 of the Polish Constitution.

[10] This theory has been considered particularly by traditional German doctrine (see, for instance, A Hensel, *Steuerrecht* (Springer 1933)); and it exerted a strong influence on the foreign doctrine (see, for instance, J Buisson, *Impôt et souveraineté* (2002) 46 *Archives de philosophie du droit* 25; M Ingrosso, 'Tributo e sovranità' in L Perrone and C Berliri (eds), *Diritto tributario e Corte costituzionale* (Edizioni Scientifiche Italiane 2006)).

expression of the existence of a sovereign population of which the State (whatever its form of government, monarchical or republican, may be) represents the public institutionalisation.

III. THE LACK OF SOVEREIGNTY IN THE CURRENT CONFIGURATION OF THE EU

In this light, an answer can be given to the question of whether the EU can, or cannot, claim to be the holder of sovereignty, in general, and of tax sovereignty, in particular. In fact, as it is currently configured, it is incontrovertible from a legal point of view that the EU is not an institution founded by a constituent moment expressed by a sovereign people. The EU has been founded and established by Member States, not by people.[11] Therefore, it is and remains exclusively an international organisation of Member States, although complex and evolved.

For this reason, it is easy to recognise that the EU cannot be considered to be endowed with its own sovereignty.[12] The inevitable consequence of this is that

[11] In this regard, it may be worth noting that the difference between the founding Treaties of the European Union and the federal or confederal constitutions is clear. In federal or confederal constitutions, it is the people who adopt the constitution, although possibly through federate or confederate states; in the European Treaties it is not. The US Constitution is established by 'We the people of the United States'; almost the same wording is used, *mutatis mutandis*, in the constitutions of India, Brazil and Argentina; the German Constitution is established by the '*Deustche Volk*' in its '*verfassungsgebenden Gewalt*', on the assumption that '*die Deutschen in den Ländern … haben in freier Selbstbestimmung die Einheit und Freieheit Deutschlands vollendet*'; a similar provision can be found in the Preamble of the Australian Constitution ('the people of New South Wales, Victoria, South Australia, Queensland, and Tasmania, humbly relying on the blessing of Almighty God, have agreed to unite in one indissoluble Federal Commonwealth under the Crown of the United Kingdom of Great Britain and Ireland, and under the Constitution hereby established'); the Swiss Constitution is established by the '*Swiss people and the cantons*'; similar are Arts 1 and 3 of the Belgian Constitution, with the reference to the '*trois communautés*' and the specification that '*tous les pouvoirs émanent de la Nation*' (Art 33); Art 3 of the Constitution of the Russian Federation states that 'the bearer of sovereignty and the only source of power in the Russian Federation shall be its multinational people. The people shall exercise their power directly, and also through the bodies of state power and local self-government'. Nothing similar is established by the European Treaties. The preambles of the Treaties themselves make it clear that the Heads of States that have signed them have acted in the ordinary prerogatives of international law, not as an expression of a people intending to form a confederate; indeed, the same Treaties specify that they propose to continue the process of creating an ever closer union among the peoples of Europe, but in this way, they take it for granted that it does not exist at the moment and mark the fact that under the juridical profile, it is not a matter of sovereign populations wishing to establish a federation of States, but rather States that wish to agree with each other in order to pursue common interests from which 'an ever closer union among the peoples of Europe' may be derived (as clearly expressed by Art 1 TEU). The exact opposite in fact of what happened regarding the Constitution of United States and other federal or confederal states. This is confirmed by the fact that when the Heads of State tried to adopt a Treaty establishing a Constitution for Europe (the Constitutional Treaty of 29 October 2004), the project was rejected by the sovereign peoples of some founding Member States and was therefore abandoned.

[12] I have analysed this issue in F Farri, *Tax Sovereignty and the Law in the Digital and Global Economy* (Routledge 2020) 96 ff; and in 'Tax Sovereignty Today' (2020) 2 *Revista técnica tributaria* 157, 166.

the competences of the EU must be circumscribed and limited to those specifically conferred to it by the Member States through the founding Treaties, as Article 5 of the Treaty on European Union (TEU) confirms.

A. The Intrinsic Limits to EU Taxing Powers

An initial but also definitive answer to the question initially posed is connected to this. There is, in fact, no reason to divert from what has been observed above regarding the competences of the EU in general when taxation is involved.

i. The Formal Level: The Absence of EU Sovereignty and the Consequent Lack of Power to Impose Taxes

Devoid of sovereignty, the EU – as it stands – also lacks in itself the power to impose taxes. Only through the 'filter' of the Member States, may the EU impose taxes on European taxpayers.

In this perspective, the fact that 'in the European Treaties there is no legal basis to claim an exclusive competence of the Member States to impose taxes', despite enjoying authoritative support[13] and now forming mainstream thinking,[14] seems to give rise to an inversion of levels. According to the Treaties, the competences of the EU are to be limited to those specifically attributed to it by the Member States through the Treaties, and not vice versa, where the competences that are left to the Member States suffer such a limitation. The powers reserved for the Member States are and continue to be of a residual nature, so everything that is not explicitly attributed to the EU remains the exclusive competence of the Member States.

With the possible exception of customs duties and perhaps also environmental taxes, there seems to be no doubt that there is no provision in the Treaties that confers the specific power of imposing taxes to the EU itself and the consequence of this is that the EU does not have any powers apart from the aforementioned, limited areas. And, as has already been said, this is not because of a lack of precision in the wording of the Treaties that can be overcome through a more expansive interpretation; it is instead due to a structural defect of sovereignty where sovereignty is the prerequisite for the imposition of taxes.

On the other hand, the fact that a tax can also take on additional functions above and beyond the fundamental one as a financing instrument for the

[13] See F Vanistendael, 'The European Union' in C Sacchetto and G Bizioli (eds), *Tax Aspects of Fiscal Federalism: A Comparative Analysis* (IBFD 2011) 589.

[14] See, for instance, E Traversa and A Pirlot, 'Tax Sovereignty and Territoriality under Siege: How Far Should the EU Freedoms of Movement Impact on the Territorial Allocation of Taxing Powers between Member States?' in C Brokelind (ed), *Principles of Law: Function, Status and Impact in EU Tax Law* (IBFD 2014) 129.

expenditure of a society, and in particular the fact that a tax can also take on the function of supporting the implementation of the values of the society that applies it, does not diminish the intrinsic nature of tax as an act of expression of the sovereignty of a society. The possible extra-fiscal functions of a tax, which may vary from context to context, are added, implemented and 'grafted' to the structural characteristics of a tax, and by their nature cannot be used to circumvent the lack of them.[15] It follows that, while political purposes can be expressed through various organisations and various legal entities, only those that are endowed with sovereign powers can translate these political purposes into the extra-fiscal purposes of a tax directly instituted by them. Otherwise, such entities and organisations may at most require entities with sovereign powers of taxation to take these extra-tax purposes into account in the application of the taxes imposed by the latter, but they will not be able to directly impose a tax attributing to it the extra-fiscal purposes that they advocate. Sovereignty is a logical and necessary antecedent for the application of a tax, a *condicio sine qua non*, which for the reasons expressed above cannot be done without, not even for the noblest extra-tax purposes.[16] To put it metaphorically, the body that thought of applying a tax to achieve certain extra-fiscal purposes without this being an expression of sovereignty is similar to the gourmet who, in order to enjoy the delicious berries that he has grown and harvested, pretends to use them as a topping on a cake without having any flour. An impossible recipe.

Nor, on the other hand, does it seem as if the implementation of extra-fiscal purposes, however noble, may justify overcoming the connection between sovereignty and people, as mentioned in the previous paragraph, which constitutes a direct result of democratic achievements. If entities without sovereign power, in a democratic sense, acted to collect sums in a society without them being the expression of the sovereign power of the society in question, their modus operandi would be comparable to that of 'conquerors' who exercise expressive acts of sovereignty over a society, without having legitimate representation from the society itself. To go back to the example above, it would be as if the gourmet fetched the flour from the neighbour's pantry without asking his permission. This time a possible recipe but with bitter consequences.

It fully corresponds to the Leviathan model of Hobbesian memory, according to which the imposition of taxes must be considered justified by the mere existence of the organisation that imposes them.[17] But this theory is hardly

[15] Neither is this kind of circumvention supported, as far as can be gleaned, by Baker's third tax 'normative' proposition (WB Barker, 'The relevance of a concept of tax' in B Peeters et al (eds), *The Concept of Tax*, EATLP Congress, Naples (IBFD 2005) 23).

[16] In this sense *cf* instead, Ricardo García Antón, 'Does the EU have a Legitimate Power to Enact Direct Taxes?', ch 3 in this volume, that actually seems to omit to deal with the concept of sovereignty.

[17] In this regard, see the complete demonstration by W Schön, 'Taxation and Democracy' (2018) 72 *Tax Law Review* 235 ff, section IV.

compatible with the stage of evolution of democratic Member States, and this is not exactly the model we have in mind for the progress of the EU.

Similarly, the fact that a governmental entity performs important functions and facilitates the creation of 'public goods' does not in itself constitute the prerequisite for attributing taxing powers to it to finance the functions it performs to create those 'public goods'.[18]

The 'public goods' created by this governmental entity can have an economic value, such as the 'added value' allowed for economic exchanges thanks to the existence of a common market whose functioning is facilitated by the aforementioned entity, or non-economic value, such as the guarantee of the exercise of some specific freedoms in a common space. It is not possible in either case that the role played by the entity in question for the production of such 'public goods' can give rise to the prerequisite for imposing taxes if the entity in question is devoid of sovereignty 'upstream'.

The creation of economic value can be a valid prerequisite for the distribution of taxing power between entities already endowed with taxing power, but it is not in itself valid for establishing taxing powers where it does not otherwise exist. The same is true, more generally, of the principle of benefit. Logically, the taxing power comes first, thereafter the identification of the criteria to be shared among those who possess it. Arguing that a criterion for sharing taxing power is sufficient in itself to establish a taxing power, is like confusing the *posterius* with the *prius*, the consequences of the assumptions, and therefore it gives rise to a conclusion that is not sustainable from a logical, let alone a juridical, point of view. For this reason, the assertion that if the EU contributes to creating value, it should consider itself endowed with a taxing power on that value on the basis of the international principles of sharing the taxing power between Member States (that are based in part on the principle of value creation and benefit), seems to give rise to an inversion of levels. These principles are valid for the distribution of the taxing power among entities (the Member States) that already have it (by derivation from the peoples who established them), but not for distributing it between governmental entities which in themselves lack sovereignty and therefore the power to impose taxes.

In a democratic system, sovereignty belongs to the people, not to the market, nor an economic value nor the economy in general. In addition, it is only if the entity that gives life to the economic value is endowed with sovereignty that it will be able to tax the values and benefits that it helps to generate. Otherwise, the taxing power on these (additional) values and (additional) benefits will

[18] According to Jussi Jaakkola, 'From the Governance of National Tax Systems to Governing Through European Taxation: A Justification for the EU's Power to Levy Taxes', ch 5 in this volume. Also G della Cananea, 'No Representation without Taxation in the European Union' in I Pernice and J Weiler (eds), *Legitimacy Issues of the European Union in the Face of Crisis* (Nomos 2017) 95 ff correlates the concept of 'public goods' with the tax imposition authority of the EU.

inevitably be referred to the sovereign communities that enjoy them, without prejudice to the possible powers of the former entity to possibly influence the regulation of this taxing power by the latter and request to participate in the revenue.

As for 'public goods' of a non-economic nature, in addition to the above, it must be taken into account that they cannot be considered prerequisites for the application of a tax to the extent that they do not meet the ability-to-pay principle.

ii. The Improper Concept of 'EU Taxes'

When we talk about EU taxes, we are therefore actually referring to an improper concept.[19] It is always the national or regional levels that (self)impose taxes on themselves, according to the specific procedures of each Member State.[20] The EU has the power to request the introduction of taxes in matters related to its functions, but not to impose them.

The only consolidated exception appears to be represented by customs duties where the Member States have specifically relinquished their own sovereignty (Articles 3, 28, 31 and 33 of Treaty on the Functioning of the European Union – TFEU)[21] and that are, consequently, subject to dynamics which are completely different from those applicable to all other taxes.[22] In fact, not only the delegation of powers to third parties, but also the decision to give up exercising certain types of sovereign acts constitutes an act of manifestation of sovereignty. This is what has happened in the matter of customs duties, for which the Member States have granted a full delegation to the Union, and which therefore escape the legal logic applicable to the generality of taxes.

Therefore, with the exception of customs duties, for which the Member States have decided to completely divest themselves of their sovereign prerogatives, the attribution of competences on the matter of taxation to the European Council and the requirement of the principle of unanimity provided for by the Treaties (Articles 113, 115, 192 and 194 TFEU) appear to be an unavoidable choice at the current stage of institutional evolution of the Union, to the extent that they represent the only possible connection mechanism between European institutions and Member States' sovereignty in tax matters.[23] As has been precisely

[19] '*Une fausse notion claire*', according to Isaac, 'La notion de ressources propres' in G Isaac (ed), *Les ressources financières de la Communauté Europeénne* (Paris 2004) 75.

[20] In particular, through the laws of Parliament.

[21] Treaty on the Functioning of the European Union (consolidated version) [2012] OJ C 326/01 (TFEU).

[22] On the contrary, it does not seem possible to include in the category of taxes the levies that the Council may introduce in the field of agriculture pursuant to Art 43 TFEU, making them strictly inherent to the function of regulating the prices of agricultural products.

[23] Likewise, the adoption of the majority principle in the matter of customs duties is consistent with the fact that the Member States have decided to completely divest themselves of their sovereignty on the matter.

observed, 'national democratic legitimacy is the only form of legitimacy that is currently recognized in the TFEU':[24] this is not a paradox but rather the normal consequence of the fact that each national community, even the smallest one, must consent to the imposition of taxes that concern it, as it is sovereign in the matter.

Beyond more or less legitimate political pressures, the fact that a national community, through its government representatives within the Council, vetoes a fiscal measure desired by other Member States and by the Commission,[25] cannot legally be overcome in other ways than by establishing a 'two-speed' Union. In fact, Article 116 TFEU (see the following paragraph IV.A.ii.c) does not prove to be usefully applicable to that goal, while enhanced cooperation is applicable pursuant to Article 20 TEU and Articles 326–34 TFEU.[26] Specifically, the enhanced cooperation could find a particularly fertile field of application among the Euro area countries.[27]

In particular, the instrument of enhanced cooperation would allow the Member States that feel more prepared for more in-depth integration (in particular, those belonging to the Euro area) to proceed in this direction without forcing the others to do the same and therefore respecting the sovereignties of the less dynamic Member States.

To be honest, you might object and say that the principle of unanimity is not even required within sovereign communities. The formation of the will of sovereign people is, in fact, almost by definition linked to the majority principle, and within the majority principle the aversion of the individual is taken into account and overcome. However, this derives from the fact that sovereignty is a manifestation of a unitary and indivisible character of the society that expresses it[28] and is not portioned out among its various members.[29] The question is instead radically different in the relations among different sovereign communities. In such relationships, each of them continues to bear their own unitary and indivisible

[24] F Vanistendael, 'On Democratic Legitimacy of European Tax Law and the Role of the European Parliament' in P Pistone (ed), *European Tax Integration: Law, Policy and Politics* (IBFD 2018) 111.

[25] For an insightful political and sociological reading of the consequences of the principle of unanimity in tax matters, *cf* C Brokelind, 'Smaller Countries versus Bigger Member States: How Can Their Voices and Goals Be Harmoniously Reconciled?' in P Pistone (ed), *European Tax Integration: Law, Policy and Politics* (IBFD 2018).

[26] See, on this issue, C Herber, *Enhanced Cooperation and European Tax Law* (Oxford University Press 2021).

[27] *cf* in that sense, F Gallo, 'L'Europa sociale e l'Europa fiscale dopo il Trattato di Lisbona' (2016) 5 *Diritto e pratica tributaria* 1789, 1799; F Gallo 'L'Europa in deficit di scelte e democrazia' (2017) 88 *Diritto e pratica tributaria* 639 640; F Gallo, 'Il diritto tributario italiano in Europa: coerenza o resilienza?' (2019) 6 *Giurisprudenza commerciale* 973, 983.

[28] *cf*, again, Galli, 'Apologia della sovranità' (n 7).

[29] A complete demonstration in this sense is made with reference to tax matters by Schön (n 17) section IV, para 5 where, also with reference to G Jellinek, *Allgemeine Staatslehre*, vol III (Springer 1929) ch 12, para 4, it is affirmed that: 'the (fiscal) decisions taken by the People acting as a homogeneous "organ" of the State in the sense of Rousseau, bear no conceptual relationship to the individual consent of a taxpayer or his peer group as required in the Lockean world'.

sovereignty. As such, the prerequisites for translating the principles that apply to the formation of the will within the single sovereign community do not apply. This substantial lack of prerequisites might not even be compensated by the introduction of additional checks and balances which are introduced to guarantee the rights of the minority against the majority within one same community.[30] This of course unless the various sovereign communities decide to dissolve their individual sovereignties by blending them with each other and creating a new sovereign community, unitary and distinct from the pre-existing ones. This, however, would mean the creation of a new constitutional phase, which at the moment does not concern the EU and which should meet the requirements that will be examined below.

In this context, another problem could also arise, namely that the bodies to which a Member State confers powers in the field of taxation (in particular, the parliament), intend to reject the position assumed in the European Council by the representatives of the Member States (in general members of the government).[31] In this – hypothetical – case, the will of the bodies which are competent in tax matters according to the internal law of any country should prevail. If the parliament not only delays but decides not to implement a European directive regarding the introduction of a given tax, that tax will not apply to the taxpayers of that Member State although requested by the EU. The European Commission, of course, would surely initiate an infringement procedure against the Member State which first, in the Council, allowed the introduction of a given tax, and then refused to implement it at the national level. But the infringement procedure would not produce any direct effect on taxpayers.

Furthermore, the exclusivity to manage tax issues that many constitutions grant to parliaments prevents such a decision by a parliament from being overruled by the administration and the courts through the direct application of European law: in fact, in the absence of a formal consent for imposition through an act of legislative power, internal systems do not recognise the existence of the prerequisite for the application of a tax on the citizens. At the administrative level, it is easy to imagine the earthquake that would occur, at an institutional and social level, if an administration demanded the payment of a tax not permitted by the parliament representing the sovereign people. Nor is it possible, for obvious reasons to imagine that national courts would initiate *ex officio* lawsuits to order taxpayers to pay taxes.

Nor will there be, for obvious reasons, the conditions for citizens to report a liability for their Member State for failure to transpose a directive according

[30] As requested by G Brennan and J Buchanan, *The Power to Tax: Analytical Foundations of a Fiscal Constitution* (Harvard University Press 1980) 187 ff, mentioned by Schön (n 17) section IV, para 5.

[31] The problem is raised also by Vanistendael, 'On Democratic Legitimacy of European Tax Law' (n 24) 114.

to the principles affirmed by the *Francovich* decision.[32] Not even residents of different countries will be able to complain to these national authorities about violations of competition or of European fundamental liberties, since they would remain free to operate in that territory and, in doing so, they would be treated in the same way as national operators; the fact that they would receive a different treatment abroad does not meet in itself, as mentioned earlier, the prerequisites for the application before the national authorities of the principles of the *Francovich* ruling.

Reserving the power to impose taxes for parliaments, therefore, must be considered a supreme principle of national constitutions and it can be similarly maintained that it should in any case prevail as a 'counter-limit' concerning European law and that it could not be made the object of constitutional reform at the national level, unless it is through a radical change of the entire constitution.[33]

[32] As is well known, the *Francovich* case was decided by the Court of Justice in the judgment on 19 November 1991, Cases C-6/90 and C-9/90. In the same perspective suggested above in the text see A Hultqvist, 'Legalitetsprincipen, skattedirektiv och tolkningen av mervärdesskattelagen' in J Bjuvberg and J Monsenego (eds), *Vänbok till Bertil Wiman* (Norstedts Juridik 2019) 126 and 130, where the author affirms that for an application to the detriment of the taxpayer the directive cannot be considered to have direct effect, since this direct effect can only be invoked by the individual, not by the State, nor by the financial administration. Therefore national legislation still remains the basis for taxation: private individuals can request that EU directives have direct effect in certain cases, but State authorities are not entitled to it against the taxpayer if the Parliament has not transposed them into national law.

[33] The concept of 'counter-limits', introduced by the Italian Constitutional Court with judgment no 183/1973, has been refined by judgments no 170/1984 and no 68/1991 and recently reaffirmed in the *MAS and MB* or *Taricco-2* case (Ordinance no 24/2017). In light of these developments, it seems possible to affirm that the reference made in decision no 183/1973 with regard to the fact that the parliamentary law exclusivity would not fall within these supreme of principle is worth reflecting on: just as the principle of the parliamentary law exclusivity was considered a supreme principle in criminal matters (Ordinance no 24/2017), there is no reason not to consider it in the same way as in other matters where it operates such as, in particular, tax matters. In fact, the difference between 'absolute' reserve and 'relative' reserve does not seem to have any relevance for this purpose. The concept of 'counter-limits' also emerges from French jurisprudence, which speaks of '*une règle ou d'un principe inhérent à l'identité constitutionnelle de la France*' (*cf* recently, Conseil Constitutionnel, decision of 15 October 2021, no 2021-940 QPC, *Air France*). In the doctrine, see M Cartabia, *Principi inviolabili e integrazione europea* (Giuffrè 1995). In tax law, Gallo, 'Il diritto tributario italiano in Europa' (n 27), highlights that, in tax matters, the conflict with the supreme principles could emerge not only in cases in which the fundamental internal principle, possibly colliding with EU law, is devoid of specific protection at the level of EU law (tax) – that is, when it is guaranteed only at the level of internal constitutional law – but also in the more frequent hypothesis in which the same principle possesses a multilevel protection both at the national as well as at the EU level. In the latter case, the contrast would be more evident when the European protection is, in its essential and irreducible core, different from that offered by the internal constitutional system. See also F Gallo, 'Ordinamento comunitario e principi costituzionali tributari' (2006) 2 *Rassegna tributaria* 407; F Gallo, 'La concorrenza fra il diritto nazionale e il diritto europeo (UE e CEDU) nella giurisprudenza costituzionale italiana' (2015) 42 *Giurisprudenza commerciale* 255, 260, which highlights that no constitutional provision excludes the qualification as 'counter-limits' of values of the State's legal culture which, despite being susceptible to constitutional revision, nevertheless perfectly characterise the State's political community and therefore marks its constitutional identity. For an extensive reading of the fundamental principles of the economic constitution, as such

In this sense, a system such as the Swedish one, in which the consultation of Parliament before the expression of the country's position at the European level is institutionalised and properly cared for, must be particularly commended.[34]

The approach considered above is not a problem of 'monist' or 'dualist' nature but the consequence of the awareness, to put it bluntly, that without the support of the national parliaments, the EU and its institutions, as currently configured, juridically would simply not exist.

a. The VAT Case

To make it simple through a paradox, if a Member State were to raise revenue in order to be able to meet its public expenditure without the application of a turnover tax, and if the parliament of the Member State in question consequently decided to abolish VAT, VAT would no longer apply in that Member State and the financial administration would lose each and every title to apply it.

The same wording of Article 117 TFEU seems to admit this. In fact, it considers the case of a Member State not complying with the Commission's recommendation not to adopt measures which may cause a distortion to the internal market, of which the above-mentioned situation undoubtedly is an example.

Naturally, the Commission would immediately try to start the procedure on the basis of Article 116 TFEU[35] and to initiate the infringement procedures it deems most appropriate, but it would be understood that until further notice the tax as such could not be applied to taxpayers of the Member State in question and a decision made by the parliament in that country.[36] Moreover, it would not even be taken for granted that the act, by the Commission, of imposing sanctions on the Member State would resist in the face of an appeal by the Member State submitted to the EU courts. Indeed, what the Treaty requires is that turnover taxes are harmonised where they are established, not that they

considered capable of prevailing over European norms, *cf* L Barra Caracciolo, *Euro e(o?) democrazia costituzionale. La convivenza impossibile tra Costituzione e Trattati europei* (Dike giuridica 2013) 237 ff; L Barra Caracciolo, *La costituzione nella palude* (Imprimatur 2015).

[34] B Wiman, 'Constitutional Issues in Developing International Tax Norms: A Swedish Perspective' in G Maisto (ed), *Current Tax Treaty Issues* (IBFD 2020) 157. In general, the importance of the involvement of national parliaments by governments in the matter of decisions on tax issues at the European level has been underlined by AP Dourado, 'No Taxation without Representation in the European Union: Democracy, Patriotism and Taxes' in C Brokelind (ed), *Principles of Law: Function, Status and Impact in EU Tax Law* (IBFD 2014).

[35] For a similar case relating to turnover tax, before the introduction of VAT, see the Commission 'Proposal for a special Council Directive on the 17th Law Amending the German Turnover Tax Act' COM (1967)277. Clearly, the will of the German Parliament prevailed and the procedure currently provided for by Art 116 TFEU was never implemented.

[36] In this regard, it may be interesting to note that, in some legal systems, the Constitutional Court has said that it possesses the authority to censor statutes with which a parliament has unjustifiably removed any of the limits of state sovereignty, determined through the law implementing the EU Treaties (see Italian Constitutional Court, no 170/1984).

are necessarily established.[37] And there is more. Previously, the rules on EU financing by the Member States required – Article 2, paragraph 2 B of Council Decision 2014/335/EU-Euratom – the devolution of a percentage of the VAT base, not of its revenue, with the consequence that this financing should have taken place even without the application of the tax to taxpayers. Currently, Article 2, paragraph 2 B of Council Decision 2020/2053/EU-Euratom determines the financing obligation of the Member States in relation to the VAT revenue, with the consequence that if the revenue is zero, nothing is due in relation to this item of financing obligation.

Article 1 of the First VAT Directive 67/227/EEC, moreover, was sufficiently clear in affirming that 'Member States shall replace their present system of turnover taxes by the common system of value added tax defined in Article 2' and that 'to effect this replacement' it is necessary that 'each Member State' enacts 'the legislation' due according to its national law. Consequently, the fact that all Member States envisaged a system of turnover tax (see the Recitals in the Prime Directive) and thus dutifully complied with the harmonisation required by the VAT Directives (see the Recitals in the Sixth VAT Directive), it is a fact that cannot be considered legally irreversible.

b. The Eco-Taxes Case

The considerations relating to possible taxes linked to environmental or energy purposes are perhaps more articulated in nature. On a terminological level, it is first of all necessary to do away with any possible misunderstandings. Although generally referred to as a *Plastic Tax*, the measure planned by Council Decision 2020/2053/EU-Euratom cannot be considered to be a tax per se. In fact, and this is well known, it is nothing more than a criterion for measuring additional financial transfers due from the Member States to the EU[38] and does not even require the Member States to introduce eco-taxes on non-recycled plastic, leaving them free to identify the means to cope with payment.[39] Beyond the name, therefore, it does not have the characteristics of a tax.

On the other hand, if the EU really decided to introduce a tax with an environmental or energy purpose, Article 192, paragraph 2 and Article 194, paragraph 3

[37] In this sense, François Barreau, 'The Legitimacy of the EU's Tax-Based Own Resources', ch 4 in this volume, also agrees by observing that 'Article 113 TFEU is limited to already existing indirect taxes in the different Member States' and 'it cannot be seen as a legal consent to tax in the sense that it gives a power to tax to the EU. This harmonisation applies to existing indirect taxes'.

[38] See Council Regulation (EU, Euratom) 2021/770 of 30 April 2021 on the calculation of the own resource based on plastic packaging waste that is not recycled, on the methods and procedure for making available that own resource, on the measures to meet cash requirements, and on certain aspects of the own resource based on gross national income [2021] OJ L165/15.

[39] *cf* Council Decision (EU, Euratom) 2020/2053 of 14 December 2020 on the system of own resources of the European Union and repealing Decision 2014/335/EU, Euratom [2020] OJ L424/1, Recital 7.

TFEU would seem to contain[40] an attribution of competence suitable to allow the Union to introduce such a direct and binding measure.[41] If this were the case, the role of national parliaments in this field could be circumvented as is already the case for customs duties.

Nonetheless, some clarifications need to be made in this regard. First, unlike customs duties, the Treaty does not confer exclusive competence on the Union in the matter of eco-taxes, so the Member States remain free to introduce their own tax measures in the field of environmental and energy taxation. Obviously, any such national measures should not be in conflict with European law, but that is enough to prove that we are not, in this matter, faced with an integral stripping of powers of the Member States as is the case with customs duties.

In the second place, the provisions of Articles 192 and 194 must be coordinated with the provisions of Article 311 TFEU. If it is true, in fact, that environmental or energy taxes may only be introduced by the Union in order to achieve a broader set of objectives attributed by the Treaties in those particular areas, they must have characteristics entailing that they are considered to be 'own resources' of the Union. If, however, they are configured as 'own resources', their introduction must be ratified by the national parliaments according to the procedure provided for precisely by Article 311 TFEU. Article 311 TFEU that expressly makes the application of own resources subject to approval 'by the Member States in accordance with their respective constitutional requirements'. In the absence of such approval, therefore, the EU decision to introduce a new own resource is ineffective.

[40] Indeed, from a terminological point of view, it does not seem reasonably possible to exclude measures with a tax-related nature from the concept of 'provisions primarily of a fiscal nature' used by the regulations in question, given that they by definition mainly assume a fiscal nature. This holds true, unless we refer to the clause 'without prejudice to Article 114', which is contained in para 2 of Art 192, to para 2 of the same Art 114, rather than, as seems more reasonable, to paras 4 et seq thereof.

[41] As regards the Carbon Border Adjustment Mechanism (CBAM), proposed as part of the 'Ready for 55%' plan, per Commission Communication COM(2021) 550 final, it is doubtful that it may be tracked back to the fiscal measures in question. It is proposed on a more formal level pursuant to para 1 of Art 192 TFEU (see COM(2021) 564 final) and related to the system of energy efficiency certificates provided for by Directive 2003/87/EC, but the relative mode of operation does not appear to be fully superimposable. The CBAM, in fact, directly imposes on the importer the obligation to purchase the 'certificates' issued by the European authorities against the payment of a given price and, in this, its taxation nature seems to prevail, while in the system under Directive 2003/87/EC, the more direct aspect is that about energy efficiency having a direct impact on the operators involved in the mechanism. Therefore, the use of the CBAM for the procedure in para 1 Art 192, instead of the one in para 2 or more simply the introduction of a compensatory duty on the import of products from polluting countries (in this perspective, see F Farri, 'Preliminary considerations on the usability of custom duties as environmental taxes' (2020) 1 *Rivista telematica di diritto tributario* 480), seems functional in order to avoid possible procedural aggravations or coordination problems with the WTO Treaties (which, moreover, need rethinking in many respects), but could pose problems concerning the correctness of identification of the regulatory basis of the measure (with all the possible consequences already highlighted by Case C-300/89 *Commission v Council, Titanium Dioxide*, ECLI:EU:C:1991:244).

The consequence is that behind the basis of the measure through which a possible new European eco-tax is introduced, there is still a sovereign decision of the Member States, guaranteed not only by the principle of unanimity to which Articles 192 and 194 subordinate the introduction of such a measure, but also by the specific intervention of national parliaments, ie, the depositary bodies of sovereign prerogatives in tax matters.

In the theoretical event in which the Union would introduce a new eco-tax[42] pursuant to Articles 192 and 194 without, however, considering it as its own resource pursuant to Article 311, there could really be a problem of divergence between the will of a national parliament not to introduce the tax and the position expressed in the European Council by the government of the same Member State allowing the binding introduction of the tax. A similar problem could arise in the event that the government of a Member State, after the introduction of a European eco-tax with the consent of the national parliament, would allow the matter to be regulated according to the ordinary European legislative procedure, thus giving up the prerogative of unanimity (as specifically permitted in this regard by the second line of Article 192, paragraph 2), without having received a mandate to that effect from its parliament.

Unlike what is indicated above for the other cases, it would be difficult in such events to conceive of a situation whereby an intervention by a national parliament blocks the application process of the European eco-tax: the parliament could not effectively repeal a provision that it did not issue but that produces direct effects based on the mechanisms of the Treaties. Except for the possible intervention at the European level by a new government, which, however, could only leverage the political dimension, the counter solutions from the perspective of domestic law could only be the most drastic ones, such as the partial repeal of the ratification law of the TFEU, in the part relating to the Articles under consideration, with consequences of utmost gravity at the international and European level, or the request for intervention by the Constitutional Court – by the operators legitimised by the law – to verify the compatibility of these provisions in the Treaties with supreme constitutional principles insofar as they would allow the introduction of eco-taxes devoid of the character of the Union's own resources without involving national parliaments.

c. The Role of the European Parliament

Leaving this last possibility aside, it is possible to affirm that what is reported above confirms that overcoming the democratic deficit of the institutions of the Union from a *de iure condendo* perspective, and in particular attributing greater

[42] Truthfully, it should be noted that most of the proposed measures, including the ones in the 'Ready for 55%' plan, give rise to regulatory interventions on existing taxes, such as excise duties in particular, and therefore not to the introduction of new types of taxes.

powers to the European Parliament which is directly elected by the European citizens, is not sufficient as grounds to attribute broader powers in tax matters to the Union. For that it is necessary that the European Parliament becomes the expression of a constituent sovereignty of the European peoples which, at the moment, simply does not exist.

A representative body is an expression of sovereignty, and as such suitable for exercising acts proper to sovereign power, if it represents a sovereign community, in the sense identified above; in the absence of this substantive substratum, representativeness is not in itself a guarantee of the respect for sovereignty, since the representative character of a body does not in itself make up for the lack of sovereignty on the part of the corporate body it represents. Representativeness of parliament, in fact, is the procedural expression of the sovereignty of a community, but if on a substantial level, this parliament is not the result of a population that poses itself as a constituent and sovereign one, representativeness is not sufficient to endow said parliament with the power to exercise sovereign powers in the name of a certain community.

If the parliament is not representative of a community that presents itself as being sovereign, it falls into a typical case in which the 'Rodrik trilemma'[43] is resolved by combining democracy with global economic integration, to the detriment of national sovereignty. But in the matter of taxation, it is not possible to overcome sovereignty, for the reasons given above.

Therefore, the correspondence between representation and taxation is not one-to-one, as is sometimes believed:[44] if there cannot, in a democratic system, be taxation without representation, there can still be representation without taxation powers.[45]

iii. Regulatory Competences Regarding Taxes Imposed by National Parliaments.

From another point of view, the Union has the power to specify what the regulation of taxes that it has requested to institute should be, and it has the power to intervene also in the regulation of other taxes if they interfere with its matters of competence. To the extent that European legislation of this kind is valid, which depends above all on whether it respects the Treaties and on the limits of

[43] 'Democracy, national sovereignty and global economic integration are mutually incompatible: we can combine any two of the three, but never have all three simultaneously and in full': *cf* D Rodrik, *The Globalization Paradox* (Oxford University Press 2011) ch 9.

[44] G della Cananea, 'No Representation Without Taxation in the European Union' in I Pernice and J Weiler (eds), *Legitimacy Issues of the European Union in the Face of Crisis* (Nomos 2017); S Fabbrini, 'Representation Without Taxation: An Association or Union of States?' in A de Feo and B Laffan (eds), *EU Own Resources: Momentum for a Reform?* (European University Institute 2016).

[45] An effective demonstration of this is provided by Schön (n 17) section V, para 2: 'in a modern democracy, parliamentary elections are not only about current taxing and spending but they affect many more long-term aspects of social, economic and political life'.

competence attributed to the Union, it is possible to maintain that the internal bodies of the Member States will have to apply the regulation itself even in the absence of a transposition by the national parliament,[46] since once the tax has been established, the principle of exclusivity of parliamentary statutory law in tax matters – which in this field is 'relative' and not 'absolute'[47] – is satisfied and the details of the regulation can also be established from different sources including, in particular, European ones.[48] But the first – and needed – choice should always be the transposition of the European law in tax matters into internal statutory acts, especially when the modification of the European law could be disadvantageous for taxpayers.[49]

The conclusions drawn above could be considered exclusively 'formal', just as the various decisions of national constitutional courts that have censored the overflow of competences by the European authorities,[50] which have often been considered 'formalistic'. In most cases, however, and except for extreme positions that may have occurred occasionally, they have done nothing but apply legal principles similar to those set out above.

[46] See, eg, what was stated in tax matters by the Italian Constitutional Court, sentence no 186/1991.

[47] For a comparative perspective on this point, *cf* Schön (n 17) section II.

[48] The same applies to the case in which, as allowed by the second line of para 2 of Art 192 TFEU, the Council unanimously decided that the regulation of the eco-tax introduced as its own resource pursuant to Art 311 TFEU can also be established with the ordinary European legislative procedure and, therefore, without the need to reach unanimity after the initial decision. Conversely, the principle of unanimity for the assumption of the initial decision to establish an own tax is mandatory not only according to the express formulation of Art 311, but also as a consequence of the applicability prohibition of the procedure referred to in Art 48, para 7 TEU set forth in this matter by Art 353 TFEU.

[49] Hultqvist, 'Legalitetsprincipen, skattedirektiv och tolkningen av mervärdesskattelagen' (n 32); in the same sense, see S von Bahr, 'Svensk anpassning till unionsrätten' in A Hultqvist, P Melz and R Påhlsson (eds), *Skattelagstiftning: Att lagstifta om skatt* (Norstedts Juridik 2015), as quoted by Hultqvist, 'Legalitetsprincipen, skattedirektiv och tolkningen av mervärdesskattelagen' (n 32) 131.

[50] Consider, in particular, the position taken by the German Constitutional Court regarding the ratification of the Lisbon Treaty (see BVerfG, 2 BvE 2/08 of 30 June 2009); but see also other decisions of the BundesVerfassungsGericht (as BVerfG, 2 BvR 2728/13 of 14 January 2014); of the Czech Constitutional Court, judgment of 31 January 2012, file no Pl ÚS 5/12, *Slovak Pensions XVII* (where the principles affirmed in the decision of the Court of Justice of the European Union (CJEU), judgment of 22 June 2011, Case C-399/09 *Landtová* (ECLI:EU:C:2011:415) have been defined as 'a failure to respect European history'); of the Danish Supreme Court, judgment of 12 June 2016, Case 15/2014 *Ajos*; of the French Conseil d'Etat, Assemblée of 21 April 2021, no 39309, Case *French Data Network*; and of the Italian Constitutional Court (Ordinance n 24 of 26 January 2017). In this latter case, the CJEU itself has substantially recognised the excess of competences to which its prior decision (CJEU, judgment of 8 September 2015, Case C-105/14 *Taricco*, ECLI:EU:C:2015:555) might have given rise to and has established that this decision should have been interpreted according to the constitutional principles of the Member States, following the preliminary deferment of the Italian Constitutional Court (CJEU, judgment of 5 December 2017, Case C-42/17 *MAS and MB* or *Taricco-2*, ECLI:EU:C:2017:936). The same constructive collaboration between courts did not take place in other cases, such as that of the German Constitutional Court which resulted in the decision on Quantitative Easing (BVerfG, 2 BvR 859/15, 2 BvR 980/16, 2 BvR 2006/15, 2 BvR 1651/15 of 5 May 2020) or the recent cases concerning the decisions of the Romanian Constitutional Court no 390/2021 of 6 June 2021 and of the Polish Constitutional Court no K 3/21 of 7 October 2021.

B. The Limits to the Competences in Tax Matters Deriving, on a Substantial Level, from the Permanent Central Taxation and Redistributive Function of the Member States

To be frank, the conclusions drawn above are not only based on the 'formal' data of the establishing foundation of the EU and the limitation of the competences attributed to it by the Member States, but they also rest on 'substantial' facts of central importance.

Typically, it is the administrations of the Member States that provide citizens with the services that taxes are meant to finance.[51] Furthermore, the collection of taxes is the responsibility of the national administrations. Thus, the fundamental aspect of the 'EU's own taxes' is essentially a regulatory one, while from an institutional point of view, from an administrative point of view, as well as from a functional and substantial point of view, taxes remain, to all intents and purposes, the remit of the Member States, without prejudice to their obligation to transfer the revenue in whole or in part to the Union in order for it to finance its operating expenditure.

The prospects provided by the Recovery Fund do not currently appear to significantly change this framework.[52] In fact, the function of the Union and the function it has in this context will essentially be one of redistribution among the Member States of the resources it will find,[53] while the use of resources geared towards certain communities will remain the responsibility of the nation states at least in a prevalent way.[54]

There will be a 'quantitative' change in the regulatory powers of the Union, which will undoubtedly increase, but this change will not necessarily be of a 'qualitative' character.

[51] See among many scholars, F Gallo, 'Giustizia sociale e giustizia fiscale nella prospettiva dell'unificazione europea' (2014) 85 *Diritto et pratica tributaria* 16; F Gallo, 'Giustizia sociale e giustizia fiscale tra decentramento e globalizzazione' (2004) 10 *Rivista di diretto tributario* 1069, 1074; Gallo, 'L'Europa sociale e l'Europa fiscale dopo il Trattato di Lisbona' (n 27) 1792; Gallo, 'Il diritto tributario italiano in Europa' (n 27).

[52] In this sense, F Vanistendael himself, 'Remembering 2020' in (2021) 101 *Tax Notes International* 334, where he hails the Plastic Tax as the first real European tax after customs duties, and recognises that the European dimension of the tax will continue to be essentially a regulatory one. This without prejudice to the fact that, for the reasons already explained in the previous section (III.A.ii.b), the Plastic Tax provided for by Council Decision (EU, Euratom) 2020/2053 cannot actually even be considered a tax.

[53] Both through transfers by the Member States themselves, also as a result of the application of new taxes requested by the Union itself, and through the use of public debt: Art 4 of the Council Decision (EU, Euratom) 2020/2053 establishes that 'The Union shall not use funds borrowed on capital markets for the financing of operational expenditure'.

[54] The collection of the Union's 'own' resources will also remain the responsibility of the Member States. See, even recently, Art 9 of Council Decision (EU, Euratom) 2020/2053: 'The own resources … shall be collected by the Member States in accordance with the national provisions imposed by law, regulation or administrative action. Member States shall, where appropriate, adapt those provisions to meet the requirements of Union rules'. The same applies to other taxes whose revenue Member States are fully or partially obliged to pay to the European Union.

In this regard, it is necessary to specify that the strengthening and institutionalisation of the controls performed by the Union on the national authorities of the Member States in charge of collecting the resources to be transferred to the Union itself, that follow from the approval of the Recovery Fund and is required by Regulation 2021/768/EU-Euratom, does not imply the attribution of direct powers to the European inspectors in the assessment and collection of taxes from taxpayers. It is more similar to the system of inspectors, from Roman governors and *procuratores* to Soviet *prokurory*, which the empires of every century sent with full powers to the vassal provinces to control, among other things, that treacherous *publicani* and corrupted local bureaucrats did not steal the revenue of taxes destined to the central power. The establishment of a European Public Prosecutor's Office for the protection of the financial interests of the Union (Article 86 TFEU, Regulation 2017/1939/EU) completes the 'police' framework, with a curious (or worrying?) analogy also in the terminology.

IV. CONSIDERATIONS ON THE FUTURE OF EU TAXATION

If the framework outlined above is to be considered the current one (*de iure condito*) in the present phase of evolution of the EU, it is possible to ask whether there is margin to go beyond it, ie, to concretely realise the 'United States of Europe' which we often hear about from parts of the political and cultural narrative. In addition, the inclusion of the EU in the matter of the distribution of taxation power between different levels of government clearly implies a context of federal evolution of the Union itself.

To answer this question, we must first ask ourselves what the conditions are for achieving a federal union. On this issue, which is of a general nature, there seem to be no in-depth considerations. It is necessary to go back to an essay from almost a century ago to find an overall study of the prerequisites of a federal state.[55]

In the case of the EU, two possible integration models are compared: a first model based on a 'functionalist' logic; and a second possible model based on an 'axiological' or 'value-based' logic.

A. The Unsuitability of the 'Functionalist' Logic to Support Greater Tax Integration

From the functionalist perspective, the fact that integration is the best option is a dogmatic assumption. A 'spillover' effect is sought by 'forcing' the competences attributed by the Treaties on the EU: this integration project is based on

[55] KC Wheare, *Federal Government* (Oxford University Press 1946).

the belief that a crisis or unexpected problems caused by the 'joining of forces' in an area of competence forces the Member States to take 'spillover steps' in integration.[56]

All the theories, which are now mainstream, and that see the health crisis as an opportunity to expand the Union's competences in fiscal and taxation matters mainly correspond to this functionalist logic.[57] In this regard, we have to observe that it is both undoubtedly the case and also understandable that the increase in the Union budget required to cope with the debt linked to the Recovery Fund also determines an increase in the volume of European regulation on the revenue side, starting with taxation. However, that does not imply the attribution of direct taxation powers to the European authorities. Nor is the argument that by attributing own resources to the EU, it would be possible to avoid burdening the exhausted finances of the Member States, very convincing. If new taxes have to be imposed to finance European action, the subjects that bear the burden are the taxpayers, not the Member States: this holds true irrespective of the fact that these taxes are collected by the administration of the Member States and then transferred to the Union, or, hypothetically, if they are to all intents and purposes real European taxes.

i. The Admissible Extensions of Competences in the Fiscal Field

Speaking about the functionalist perspective, a fundamental clarification is necessary. There may be a 'forcing' of the competences attributed by the Member States which, effectively, does not conflict with the sovereignty of the Member States themselves, since it is about maximising the expansive potential of matters already fully attributed to the competence of the Union.

Let us consider the case of monetary policy: it is already fully delegated to the competences of the Union, so its use in a more or less expansive sense does not conflict with the sovereignty of the Member States (as erroneously believed by the Constitutional Court of Germany in the well-known ruling of 5 May 2020, on the issue of Quantitative Easing), but it is a simple consequence of the delegation of powers that the Member States have decided (freely and 'sovereignly', at least from a legal point of view) to impose upon the Union.

[56] These words are borrowed from F Pepe, 'L'emergenza Covid-19 nell'Unione europea: verso una solidarietà tributaria "strategica"'? (2020) 1 *Rivista telematica di diritto tributario* 22.

[57] In the first place, see the influential declaration of European tax law professors P Pistone, F Vanistendael, G Bizioli, I Burgers, FA García Prats, D Gutmann, P Essers, W Haslehner, G Kofler, H Kube, AM Jiménez, E Reimer and E Traversa, 'European Solidarity Requires EU Taxes' in (2020) 98 *Tax Notes International* 577. See also, among many scholars: F Vanistendael, 'Will the Coronavirus Pandemic Cure the EU Budget?' (2020) 100 *Tax Notes International* 1417; and, before, in general terms, F Vanistendael, 'The Crisis: A Window of Necessity for EU Taxation' (2010) 50 *European Taxation* 394; E Traversa and G Bizioli, 'Solidarity in the European Union in the Time of COVID-19: Paving the Way for a Genuine EU Tax' (2020) 48 *Intertax* 743; A Cordewener, 'The COVID-19 Crisis: An Opportunity for EU Budget and Tax Reform' (2020) 29 *EC Tax Review* 258; AP Dourado and M Poiares Maduro, 'A Plead for the European Union Fiscal Autonomy' (2020) 48 *Intertax* 695.

ii. The Inadmissible Forcing of Competences in the Field of Taxation

There is, however, another form of 'forcing' of competences which is in direct contrast to the sovereignty of the Member States, because it seeks to attract new and different competences to the Union compared with those that the Member States have attributed to it through the Treaties and this is to the detriment of the competences that the Member States, by signing the founding Treaties, intended to keep for themselves.

a. The Financial Interests of the Union

The problem of ultra vires acts by the European authorities occurs in many areas and, for what is of most interest here, it occurs quite frequently also in tax matters, or in matters related to taxation.

At times, the Court of Justice appears to have been aware of the problem and it has paid attention, in some cases, to the constitutional context of the Member States, sometimes even establishing a dialogue with the national judges, to verify whether a tax subsidy, which according to European law could be regarded as State aid, corresponded in reality to a structural measure (and therefore not a selective one)[58] or, in any case, to a purpose that should be considered constitutionally necessary for the Member State that introduced the subsidy.[59]

In most cases, however, this does not seem to be the case. Despite a formal obsequiousness regarding Member States' tax sovereignty which is expressed in some decisions,[60] the CJEU has long since abandoned the self-restraint that was at the core of its behaviour during the golden age of its own jurisprudence.[61]

Consider, for example, the taking over of competences in the criminal field implemented by making use of the clause for the protection of the financial interests of the Union pursuant to Article 325 TFEU. It was only after the Italian Constitutional Court had proposed the use of the 'counter-limits' clause – or, in

[58] The issue of 'selectivity' is analysed in depth by J Monsénégo, *Selectivity in State Aid Law and the Methods for the Allocation of the Corporate Tax Base* (Kluwer Law International 2018). It should also be noted that the decision in the *Apple* case (judgment of 15 July 2020, Case T-778/16 and T-892/16 *Ireland v Commission – Apple*, ECLI:EU:T:2020:338) is essentially based on the failure to demonstrate the integration of the of the 'selectivity' requirement.

[59] C Brokelind, 'Competing Constitutional Concepts Relevant for International Taxation: Prohibition of Tax Subsidies' in J Englisch (ed), *International Tax Law: New Challenges to and from Constitutional and Legal Pluralism* (IBFD 2016) 147 ff, especially 154, 156 and 159, with reference to CJEU judgment of 8 September 2011 in Joined Cases C-78/08 to C-80/08 *Paint Graphos* et al, ECLI:EU:C:2011:550; CJEU, judgment of 11 September 2008 in Joined Cases C-428/06 to C-434/06 *UGT-Rioja*, ECLI:EU:C:2008:488; and CJEU, judgment of 22 November 2001 in Case C-53/00 *Ferring*, ECLI:EU:C:2001:627.

[60] See references in C Brokelind, 'The Anti-Tax Avoidance Directive under Scrutiny: A Matter of Competence?' in J Monsénégo and J Bjuvberg (eds), *International Taxation in a Changing Landscape: Liber Amicorum in Honour of Bertil Wiman* (Wolters Kluwer 2019) 46.

[61] A sort of break-up of this golden age can be said to have been symbolically constituted, in tax matters, by the *Hailfax* decision, CJEU, judgment of 21 February 2006 in Case C-255/02, ECLI:EU:C:2006:121.

other words, the partial voidness of the law implementing the European Treaties in the Italian internal system because it stands in contrast to the supreme principles of the Constitution – did the CJEU revise its position.[62]

Or let us take the matter of *res judicata*, again through the 'picklock' of the clause for the protection of the financial interests of the Union pursuant to Article 325 TFEU;[63] or to the ultra vires decisions in the field of direct taxes and local taxes through the clause prohibiting State aid (Article 107 TFEU).

It is important to recall, for example, the CJEU, Grand Chamber judgment of 6 November 2018 in Joined Cases C-622/16P and C-624/16P *Italy v Commission* (*Montessori*).[64] With such a decision, the European institutions have sanctioned the free determination of the Italian State on the subject of exemptions from local property tax of monastic guesthouses and private schools, although it is evident that they have never affected the European common market.

b. The Ban on State Aid

This case deserves to be examined more specifically, since it is emblematic of the trend that we intend to examine here with regard to the broader question of the interpretation of the ban on State aid.

In the case *Italy v Commission* (*Montessori*), the formulation prior to 2012 of the exemptions from property tax of monastic guesthouses and private schools was deemed to be unlawful State aid without the slightest consideration for the fact that, first, the charter school system is considered by the law to be a public service excluded from the application of the rule about competition and that, second, it is very difficult to imagine that the lower cost, represented by a lodging not having to pay the tax on the property,[65] would generate such barriers to entry or the exclusion of other operators to such an extent so as to threaten competition in the field of hotel tourism in Italy (as well as, and perhaps even more so, to threaten free trade between the Member States). Such a decision does not seem to be in compliance with Article 107 TFEU.

And yet, while Article 107 of the TFEU states that selective public subsidies for businesses are incompatible with the Treaty only in the face of the

[62] CJEU, judgment in Case C-105/14 *Taricco* (n 50); Italian Constitutional Court, ord n 24 of 26 January 2017; subsequent CJEU, Grand Chamber, judgment of 5 December 2017 in Case C-42/17 *MAS and MB* or *Taricco-2* (n 50) who has revised his prior positioning and agreed with the Italian Constitutional Court.

[63] CJEU, judgment of 3 September 2009 in Case C-2/08 *Olimpiclub*, ECLI:EU:C:2009:506.

[64] Joined Cases C-622/16P and C-624/16P *Scuola Elementare Maria Montessori v Commission*, ECLI:EU:C:2018:873.

[65] As rightly recalled by Brokelind, 'Competing Constitutional Concepts' (n 59) 137, in fact, tax subsidies do not translate into a direct subsidy (ie, a payment of a sum of money by a public body), but can be included in that concept only indirectly. However, there are doubts about the suitability of the concept of State aid pursuant to Art 107 TFEU to include tax benefits, because of the fact that in a competitive regime, the need to establish selective procedures to the positive payment of a sum of money is structurally correlated (except for possible exceptions having an exceptional character), while the same cannot be said for the measures constituting reductions of obligations and debts.

cumulative presence of two requirements (namely that these subsidies, on the one hand, '*distort or threaten to distort competition*' and, on the other, '*affect trade between Member States*'), the European institutions now[66] consider that even the mere 'threat' of an impact on inter-State exchanges is sufficient to consider the second requirement fulfilled.

Such an interpretation leads to a clear violation of the conventional rules. In fact, it is only in relation to the first requirement (distortion of competition) that these rules consider the mere risk of its occurrence to be enough to compromise the European interest; while in relation to the second requirement (impact on trade between Member States) it has been established that only the real and concrete occurrence of it is such so as to compromise the value protected by the European system.

The substantial elimination of this second requisite is not compliant with the Treaties, ie, with EU primary law.[67]

In fact, the Member States have signed treaties according to which selective advantage for a company falls within the prohibition of State aid and only if there is positive evidence that it causes damage to free trade between Member States. Therefore, eliminating this fundamental prerequisite during the application produces a flagrant violation of the competences that Member States have decided to entrust to the EU and, consequently, causes a real violation of the sovereignty of the Member States.[68]

The Court of Justice had initially taken this Treaty provision seriously, basing its decisions on State aid on an in-depth market analysis,[69] but it has subsequently simplified and distorted the sense of the rule and thought to 'summarise' the result of such analytical evaluations in a pseudo-principle by which the cost savings, which a legal entity would normally have had to make in its day-to-day management or normal activities, would distort in themselves

[66] See, among many decisions, the European Commission, Notice on the Notion of State Aid as Referred to in Article 107(1) of the Treaty on the Functioning of the European Union, 2016/C 262/01, para 6.3, point 190 ('it is not necessary to establish that the aid has an actual effect on trade between Member States but only whether the aid is liable to affect such trade'); CJEU, judgment of 14 January 2015 in Case C-518/13 *Eventech v The Parking Adjudicator*, ECLI:EU:C:2015:9; CJEU, judgment of 8 May 2013 in Joined Cases C-197/11 and C-203/11 *Libert et al*, ECLI:EU:C:2013:288.

[67] This substantial elimination is openly admitted by the European Commission, Notice 2016/C 262/01 (n 66) para 6.2, point 189: 'The definition of State aid does not require that the distortion of competition or effect on trade is significant or material'.

[68] According to G Luchena, 'I vincoli all'esercizio della sovranità economica statale per il tramite del controllo degli aiuti pubblici alle imprese: Prime osservazioni' [2018] *Amministrazione in Cammino* 11; and M Orlandi, *Le discriminazioni fiscali e gli aiuti di Stato nel diritto dell'Unione europea* (Aracne 2018) 15–17, the Commission's behaviour cannot even be recorded as the result of an accidental event, but it is part of a series of precise choices aimed at bypassing the competence limits established by the Treaties.

[69] See ECJ, judgment of 21 January 1976 in Case 40/75 *Bertrand*, ECLI:EU:C:1976:4; ECJ, judgment of 3 February 1977 in Case 52/76 *Benedetti v Munari*, ECLI:EU:C:1977:16; but see also ECJ, judgment of 14 February 1990 in Case C-301/87 *France v Commission* (*Boussac Saint Frères*) points 39–44, ECLI:EU:C:1990:67; ECJ, judgment of 6 November 1990 in Case C-86/89 *Italy v Commission*, point 15, ECLI:EU:C:1990:373.

the conditions of competition and trade between Member States, and would be limited to transcribing this routinely in a totally abstract, apodictic and assertive manner.[70]

On the contrary, it has been demonstrated for a long time now that the so-called 'absolute cost advantages', ie, the type of advantage that results from the selective reduction of the tax burden, do not generally lead to entry barriers that significantly influence competition rules.[71] In this context, for a tax advantage to be considered significant enough to create entry barriers that hinder competition or cause the expulsion of competitors from the market, it should be demonstrated that, thanks to this advantage, the operator can create economies of scale which, in turn, allow him to reduce the price to such an extent so as to exclude from the market those who cannot benefit from these economies of scale. This circumstance appears to be exceptional. It cannot be excluded in an absolute manner, but it is certainly worth having more in-depth demonstrations on individual concrete cases to verify if this exceptionality actually occurs.

In this way, the elaboration of a sort of *de minimis* aid concept has indeed taken place,[72] but it has served a highly discretionary and fluctuating application by the Commission and by the Court, which have ruled out the application of this specific clause in cases which, instead, should have been included, favouring a 'political' use of the instrument that contrasts with the lack of democratic legitimacy that characterises the institutions themselves.

To go back to the above-mentioned case, *Italy v Commission* (*Montessori*), what European entrepreneur in the hotel industry has ever been discouraged from carrying out his business in Italy due to the presence of monastic guesthouses? The European institutions have provided no reasonable response to this question. Instead, they should have asked themselves this question as a prerequisite before declaring an exemption like the one described above as being incompatible with European law.

c. Article 116 TFEU

Let us now imagine what would happen if this taking over of competences concerning Article 107 were transferred to Article 116 where it was also applied in tax matters, as the Commission and the European Parliament would like.[73] After all, the concept of 'provisions … distorting the conditions of competition

[70] See, eg, CJEU, judgment of 3 March 2005 in Case C-172/03 *Heiser*, point 55, ECLI:EU:C:2005:130; CJEU, judgment of 19 September 2000 in Case C-156/98 *Germany v Commission*, ECLI:EU:C:2000:467.

[71] S Bain, *Barriers to New Competition: Their Character and Consequences in Manufacturing Industries* (Harvard University Press 1956) ch 5.

[72] European Commission, Notice 2016/C 262/01 (n 66) para 6.3, points 196 and 197.

[73] See European Commission, 'Communication from the Commission to the European Parliament and the Council, An Action Plan for Fair Taxation Supporting the Recovery Strategy' COM(2020) 312 final. See also European Parliament, Resolution of 7 October on reforming the EU policy on harmful tax practices, P9_TA(2021)0416, para 16.

in the internal market' and such 'that the resultant distortion needs to be eliminated' has already been promptly assimilated to that of Article 107.[74]

However, the attempted extension of Article 116 TFEU to tax matters, and above all the attempts to exploit it to create deeper integration in tax matters, appears completely illegitimate.

On a preliminary basis, it should be noted that Article 116, like Article 311,[75] is not a rule on 'competences' that is suitable for establishing new Union competences, but it is only there to complement the competences already generally assigned to the Union by the Treaties and, as we have seen above, taxation is not one of them. To extend these competences without a formal amendment of the Treaties it would be necessary to use the procedure of Article 352 TFEU, which obviously requires unanimity and which, in any case, should not be applicable in tax matters. In fact, paragraph 3 of Article 352 expressly excludes the usability of this procedure to achieve harmonisation and approximation effects in matters that are excluded by the Treaties, as is the case for tax matters outside the attributions specifically assigned to the Union by Articles 113 and 115 TFEU. Whereas, in reference to the establishment of own taxes, the Treaties have a special provision – in fact that of Article 311 – which excludes the applicability of the residual rule of Article 352 by virtue of the ordinary hermeneutical principles for which *lex specialis derogat generali*.

Under a different profile, the use of Article 116 in matters for which the Treaty requires unanimity would, in this context, give rise to a real 'abuse of the law' by the European authorities if the principles of the *Halifax* doctrine were to apply.[76]

In any case, assuming that Article 116 TFEU were applied to taxation, it would also really be a 'nuclear weapon',[77] above all as regards the 'side effects'.

[74] As recalled by M Nouwen, 'The Market Distortion Provisions of Articles 116–117 TFEU: An Alternative Route to Qualified Majority Voting in Tax Matters' (2021) 49 *Intertax* 1, 16: 'the Commission's notes clarify this condition by referring to the Court's interpretation of the antitrust rules (Article 101 TFEU) and the State aid rules (Article 107(1) TFEU) that address any selectively advantageous measure that "distorts or threatens to distort competition"'.

[75] See, in this sense, the above-mentioned decision of the German Constitutional Court BVerfG, 2 BvE 2/08 (n 50). It may be helpful to observe that in all evidence, not even Art 48, para 7 TEU is an adequate rule for expanding the competences of the Union: in fact, it simply allows Member States to relinquish their sovereign prerogatives in matters which, according to the Treaties, would instead fully protect them by giving each of them the right of veto. It is no coincidence, in this regard, that for the effectiveness of this procedure a preliminary right of veto is foreseen and assigned to the bodies that directly represent popular sovereignty, ie, to each national parliament.

[76] From such a perspective, on the basis of the principles affirmed by the CJEU, the judgment in Case C-300/89 *Commission v Council* (*Titanium Dioxide*) (n 41), Nouwen (n 74) 24, observes that: 'it seems that any measure aiming at both tax harmonization and market distortion elimination, without one being incidental to the other, cannot simply be based on Article 116 TFEU. Allowing tax harmonization on the basis of the market distortion rules would undermine the unanimity rule laid down in Articles 113 and 115 TFEU'.

[77] J Englisch, 'Article 116 TFEU: The Nuclear Option for Qualified Majority Tax Harmonization?' (2020) 29 *EC Tax Review* 58, 61 states in this regard that 'as with any type of nuclear option, its use needs to be carefully pondered, both legally and politically'. Disagreement should be allowed in this regard: the use of nuclear weapons must not be 'carefully pondered' on, it must always be excluded: there can be no political or pseudo-legal reasons that hold.

A national community subject to this procedure, especially if interpreted extensively, would increase its distance from the Union, it would not decrease it. The foundations would in all probability be laid, not for greater aggregation, but for the disintegration of the Union. In addition, the procedure would be ineffective, since as seen in the previous section (III), as regards the taxpayers of the 'rebellious' Member State, in matter of taxation, its internal discipline would prevail anyway, over the hypothetical directive issued by the EU pursuant to Article 116 TFEU.

Therefore, the aforementioned perspective of enhanced cooperation appears to be surely preferable in the perspective of increasing integration in tax matters, allowing the willing ones to progress and the prudent ones to hold on, thus respecting the will of everyone, and leaving Article 116 with its coercive nature to its most appropriate purpose of exceptional safeguard clause.

B. The Counterproductive Effects of Forced Competences and Ultra Vires Acts

In this context, it is evident that this second type of 'forcing' of competences constitutes a violation of the sovereignty of the Member States that formed the Union and that the resistance of the single, delegating communities cannot be accused of 'sovereignism', but will constitute a legitimate manifestation to protect their fiscal sovereignty. As exactly observed,

> those popular requests for protection, for a return to the State, for defense from global dynamics and European rules, which are usually defined as 'sovereignism'… are not a manifestation of new barbarism, but of fearful creakings in the European construction.[78]

The major criticality of the functionalist logic is that it is characterised by an 'a priori' approach. It does not debate and does not adequately argue its assumption of whether or not integration in a specific field is the best option and under what conditions. This 'a priori' approach considers integration always good in itself. Even the legal thought, on the subject of the EU, is often soaked in this kind of dogmatism. But that sterilises a rational debate, instead of favouring it. As already reported,[79] it is no longer the era where emperors or auto-defined enlightened *elites* decide the fate of peoples around a table or on the battlefields without dealing with their will, their feelings, their traditions, their values, their culture.[80]

[78] Galli, 'Apologia della sovranità' (n 7) 163 (original in Italian, translated by the author).

[79] Farri, *Tax Sovereignty and the Law in the Digital and Global Economy* (n 12) 93 ff.

[80] The limits of the process of democratisation of supranational and international institutions are also highlighted by RA Dahl, *On Democracy* (Yale University Press 1998) 125, who notes that decisions will probably be taken through transactions between political and bureaucratic elites: administrators, delegates, ministers, diplomats, officials of governmental or non-governmental associations, managers, etc. Even if democratic processes can occasionally set external limits to this bargaining, to define as 'democratic' the political practice of international systems, it would be

And it is no longer the era of 'social engineering', although many writings on taxation and the EU budget examine this logic closely.[81]

Thus, on a juridical level it is useful to specify that any tolerance[82] of ultra vires acts stemming from European authorities does not create the conditions for overcoming the specific attributions of the Treaties, as outlined in the previous section. On the contrary, these abuses and the violations of the rule of law, in which they consist of preventing the formation of a trustworthy relationship[83] between the European authorities and the citizens of the Member States, hinder the formation of the social conditions for greater tax integration. It is difficult to report alleged erosions of the rule of law by national authorities if the first ones to erode the rule of law are the European institutions themselves when they go beyond their competences.

From another point of view, if it is stated that by virtue of this excess of competences of the European authorities, national sovereignty in tax matters is now undermined, the logical consequence cannot be that such a 'transfer' should be completed: the logic of the 'fait accomplit' should be considered incompatible with the rule of law. Thus, the logical consequence should be the prompt restoration of legality.[84]

Furthermore, once the method of forced competences has been 'established', there is a risk that it could be exploited by the Member States to the detriment of the interests of the supranational organisation.

Without dwelling on the details relating to the EU competences in the field of direct taxation[85] and the inveterate tendency of the Commission to

necessary to remove the term of any meaning. Classical are the works on the subject by C Lasch, *The Revolt of the Elite and the Betrayal of Democracy* (WW Norton & Company 1996) and, recently, by S Berman, 'The Pipe Dream of Undemocratic Liberalism' (2017) 28 *Journal of Democracy* 29, who clearly highlighted the problem that 'the more the people view democratically elected governments as being overruled by unelected bureaucrats, unaccountable regional or international institutions, and global economic forces, the more attractive populism's call to regain national sovereignty becomes'.

[81] Indeed, some papers explicitly refer to this logic: *cf*, eg, B De Witte, 'The European Union's Covid-19 Recovery Plan: The Legal Engineering of an Economic Policy Shift' (2021) 58 *Common Market Law Review* 635.

[82] A kind of 'Loyalty' in the perspective of J Weiler, 'The Transformation of Europe' (1991) 100 *Yale Law Journal* 2403, 2405 ff; and of A Hirschman, *Exit, Voice, and Loyalty: Responses to Decline in Firms, Organizations, and States* (Harvard University Press 1970), recalled by Barreau, ch 4 in this volume.

[83] On the importance of a trustworthy relationship as a base for a European Ethos for a European fiscal contract, see Barreau, ibid.

[84] Similarly, the fact that a supranational entity determines negative externalities in terms of revenue for the Member States that are part of it, by facilitating the mobility of capital and therefore the erosion of the tax base of the Member States, should logically give rise, not to a 'residual' taxing power on such 'nomadic' income by this entity (as maintained Jaakkola (n 18)) if – for the reasons explained – it is devoid of it, but instead to a form of economic compensation from it vis-a-vis the Member States.

[85] In this regard, it is necessary to observe that in Art 114 TFEU, the adjective 'direct' is not present, while it is instead present in Art 115 TFEU: thus, the approximation pursuant to Art 114 is possible in all cases in which the measure is necessary (even indirectly) for the establishment and functioning

force them,[86] the above-mentioned risk that the 'forcing' of competences by the EU authorities could be exploited by the Member States to the detriment of the interests of the EU itself has been acutely observed in fiscal matters with reference to the Anti Tax-Avoidance Directive (ATAD), insofar as the unanimity of the Member States in approving it lends itself to concealing more a desire to preserve national revenue than an effective step forward in removing direct obstacles to the functioning of the common market.[87]

In this way, the counterproductive effects (such as the violation of the rule of law by the European authorities and the feeding of 'sovereignism') generated by ultra vires acts and the violations of national sovereignties are not structurally counterbalanced by sufficient suitability of the increase in the powers of the Union to solve the problems of tax competition and tax avoidance.

V. THE NEED TO ADOPT A 'VALUE-BASED' LOGIC

On the contrary, a 'value-based' logic assumes that, in order to create a new sovereign reality, albeit a federal one, the existence of a population that perceives itself as a unitary, albeit plural, people is necessary. And to regard itself as such,

of the internal market, except in tax matters (expressly excluded by para 2 of the Art), whereas the approximation pursuant to Art 115, also applicable in tax matters, is only possible if the measures have a 'direct' impact on the establishment and functioning of the internal market. If words have a meaning, as they cannot fail to have, since the attribution of competences is sole and exclusive, the scope of application of Art 115 is therefore much more restricted than that of Art 114. Thus, considerations such as those by R Szudoczky, 'Is the CCCTB Proposal in line with the Principle of Subsidiarity? Negative Opinions Submitted by National Parliaments in the "Yellow Card Procedure"' in D Weber (ed), *CCCTB: Selected Issues* (Wolters Kluwer 2012) 112 and 114, where they are considered applicable to Art 115 TFEU the same principles affirmed by the Court of Justice (CJEU) in the judgment of 5 October 2000 C-376/98 *Tobacco Advertising*, ECLI:EU:C:2000:544, in relation to the provision now contained in Art 114 (at the time of the ruling, it had to do with Art 95 TEC, which, for what is of interest here, bears identical formulation to the current Art 114 TFEU), cannot be agreed. The same CJEU, judgment of 29 April 2004 in Case C-338/01 *Commission v Council*, ECLI:EU:C:2004:253 established that the current Art 114 cannot form the basis for the introduction of fiscal measures.

[86] Indicative in this regard, are the words used by Werner Haslehner, 'Anti-Hybrid Measures in the Parent Subsidiary Directive and the EU's Competence to Harmonise' (*Kluwer International Tax Blog*, 31 August 2015): 'The Commission starts to justify its proposal only indirectly with regard to that objective: rather than directly improving functioning of the internal market, it sees the change as necessary to protect the functioning of this directive … Uncoordinated tax regimes create market distortions; therefore coordination is necessary to remove distortions … Taxes by their very nature distort markets. Different taxes/rates therefore inevitably create distortions for the internal market. If that is sufficient to give the EU the competence to mandate what to tax and what not, there are hardly any limits to that power and the Member State's "sole competence" in direct tax matters is a mere illusion', available at: kluwertaxblog.com/2015/08/31/anti-hybrid-measures-in-the-parent-subsidiary-directive-and-the-eus-competence-to-harmonise.

[87] C Brokelind, 'EU Tax Law and the Return of the Nation-State' in A Bakardjieva Engelbrekt et al (eds), *The European Union and the Return of the Nation State:* Interdisciplinary European Studies (Palgrave Macmillan 2020). On the issue of the relationships between ATAD and competences of the Member States, see also A Hultqvist, 'Anti-Tax Avoidance Directive (ATAD) och subsidiaritetsprincipen: Svenska folkets urgamla rätt att sig beskatta eller EU:s rätt?' (2016) 12 *Skattenytt* 853.

a community must have common and shared values, which go beyond mere economic interest.

> Une des grandes erreurs de ce siècle est de croire que la constitution politique des peuples est une œuvre purement humaine; qu'on peut faire une constitution comme un horloger fait une montre.[88]

A. The Inadequacy of the Economic Logic of the Market to Give Substance to a Solid Integration of the Communities

Despite the statements of principle and wishes of Article 1, paragraph 2 TEU, 'simple Treaties do not create a new community by themselves'.[89] Nor would the democratisation of the institutions of the Union (eg, the attribution of greater centrality to a European parliament directly elected by the citizens), which is often spoken of as a panacea of evil, suffice. When we wish to talk about the foundation of a political community, the 'procedural justice' of Habermasian memory is not enough: contents are needed, and contents without a solid basis of values are fragile and transitory.

In today's context, a federal evolution can only take place between communities truly united through bonds that transcend the mere economic profile: money, however important, does not keep people together, in their lives, in their histories, in their traditions, in their values and, all the more so, they do not keep communities together. Furthermore, economic interests are by their nature too volatile to be able to represent an element of lasting cohesion among different communities and a basis on which they can found a self-perception as a unitary political body despite the pluralism of its composition. If there is no common planning of this kind, the delegation of functions will by its nature remain limited to certain interventions and will hardly be able to take on that properly political significance which constitutes the prerequisite for the exercise of an act of sovereignty.

The real question is, therefore, whether the axiological prerequisites exist for an evolution in the political sense of the EU, ie, if in the 27 Member States there is a European population which perceives itself as such on the basis of authentic values that are actually lived and shared. A Marxist scholar like Benedict Anderson wrote almost 40 years ago: 'market-zones, 'natural–geographic' or political–administrative, do not create attachments. Who will willingly die for

[88] ie, one of the greatest mistakes of this century is to believe that the political constitution of peoples is a purely human work; that a constitution can be built like a watchmaker builds a watch. J De Maistre, 'Etude sur la souveraineté', published posthumously in *Oeuvres complètes de J de Maistre Nouvelle édition contenant ses oeuvres posthumes et toute sa correspondance inédite* (1884) (but written in 1794) ch VII.

[89] A Sodano, *Per una nuova Europa* (Libreria Editrice Vaticana 2009) 23.

Comecon or the EEC?'.[90] Can this situation be said to have changed today? Influential doctrine, which for its academic, cultural and political past certainly cannot be 'accused' of 'sovereignism', maintains:

> Today it is really unlikely to think of a constituent power of the European peoples, which would imply their unification into a single people and a single political structure – however federal … A European sovereignty, even a federal one, would really be a super Leviathan.[91]

Conversely, the dramatic events of 2022 have revealed that a population ready 'to willingly die' in order to place itself in the European axiological and political space exists and has really shed its blood to resist the barbaric military action of those who, in order to oppose their own sovereign desire to place themselves in the space of Western civilisation, have perpetrated the most serious violations of international law: it is a people, the Ukrainians, of a state not yet a member of the EU, but undoubtedly, the receipt by the EU of its profound will to join Europe at the price of blood will constitute a fundamental verification and a turning point of the effective existence, within the Union, of a European demos that is beginning to present itself in the world as such and of institutions ready to adequately represent it.

Beyond this, finding 'values' in an EU that, apart from the formal affirmation of principles in Article 2 TEU, in Articles 8 ff TFEU and in the Charter of Fundamental Rights,[92] often makes of 'ethical nihilism' – and, consequently, of the substantial absence of 'values' – its 'value', is very complex. The programme of the Commission concerning the 'European Way of Life' can be considered as an example of this concept. It appears completely unsuitable to establish a set of true values on which to anchor a community: the very title of the project is testimony to this, which merely refers to a daily practice and, therefore, a fact of life, without any valuation claim of it in terms of justice. Its content, after all, says nothing about the concept of human life, the meaning of human dignity and the value of a human being and when it touches upon ethically sensitive issues, such as that of fundamental rights, it does so in a way that appears superficial, partial

[90] B Anderson, *Imagined Communities: Reflections on the Origin and Spread of Nationalism* (Verso 1983) 53.

[91] Galli, 'Apologia della sovranità' (n 7) 163 (original in Italian, translated by the author). In this sense, also L Conant, 'Contested Boundaries: Citizens, States, and Supranational Belonging in the European Union' in J Migdal (ed), *Boundaries and Belonging: States and Societies in the Struggle to Shape Identities and Local Practices* (Cambridge University Press 2004), while moving from a perspective that values the role of public powers in shaping the collective identity, observes that 'the dominant pattern of interaction' among individuals and civil society suggests that 'any new European foundation for belonging remains thin' (ibid 288).

[92] On the fact that the Nice Charter and Art 2 TEU have remained at the stage of enunciation of a general rule and that all these provisions should not be overestimated for tax purposes *cf* Gallo, 'L'Europa sociale e l'Europa fiscale dopo il Trattato di Lisbona' (n 27) 1792; Gallo, 'Il diritto tributario italiano in Europa' (n 27) para 2.1; Gallo, 'Ordinamento comunitario e principi costituzionali tributari' (n 33).

and sometimes anthropologically questionable and, in any case, contested by a significant part of the European population, which in some Member States represents a solid national majority. Besides, if this form of dispute occurs, it is a sign that beyond words there is no real common way of life, that what the Commission has planned does not correspond to truly shared values and that, ultimately, we are still far from the existence of a European people that can be said to be cohesive in their plurality, at least if we wish to concurrently embrace the entire community of 27 Member States. The spirit, for those who believe in the pro-European project, should be moved to working to modify this tendency. It is not enough to make the paradigm of the common market and competition an absolute whole, establishing on this totem a 'forcing' at all costs of the EU competences and a consequent 'divestiture' of national sovereignty:[93] if the container into which this sovereignty is transferred is structurally incapable of welcoming it, it generates results that in the long term prove to be sterile and counterproductive.[94] Acting on these aspects without acting substantially on the truly axiological aspect, ie, the one that pertains to a truthful vision of man and society, is like placing the cart before the horse: an initiative destined to fail and, indeed, counterproductive.[95]

[93] In this regard, Gallo, 'L'Europa sociale e l'Europa fiscale dopo il Trattato di Lisbona' (n 27) 1794 highlights a sort of 'schizophrenia' in European jurisprudence and debate, insofar as, on the one hand, it is argued that the logic of the market should not be the only one to guide the application of European law but, on the other hand, it 'ultimately tends to place itself in the visual angle of economic and property rights in preference to social ones. That is, it aims at asking itself within what limits the protection of social rights is compatible with market freedom and not to what extent the latter is compatible with social rights. The result is a de facto propensity to continue to privilege market and competition rules over other fundamental rights protected by the Union'. In the same sense Gallo, 'Ordinamento comunitario e principi costituzionali tributari' (n 33); Gallo, 'Il diritto tributario italiano in Europa' (n 27), where the 'economy-driven logic *of EU tax law*' is addressed and it is emphasised that 'even after the advent of the Nice Charter of Rights, in the tax field the scale of values is still the economic one, typical of free trade systems and of external and internal neutrality of the fiscal factor'.

[94] This is also acknowledged by the doctrine, which is generally critical towards national identity issues: see, for all, Y Mounk, *The People vs Democracy* (Harvard University Press 2018); G Nodia, 'The End of the Postnational Illusion' (2017) 28 *Journal of Democracy* 5, who claims that 'efforts to "liberate" democracy from the people will not end well. They will only generate more "populist" reactions by even more angry majorities'. With reference to the taxation in the European Union, F Vanistendal, 'Legal Pluralism and Higher Fiscal Coordination and Budgetary Supervision to Achieve Economic and Monetary Union' in J Englisch (ed), *International Tax Law: New Challenges to and from Constitutional and Legal Pluralism* (IBFD 2016) 209, 210, 212, 216, 217 comes to similar conclusions, pointing out that the current framework of the Treaties is not adequate for starting a fiscal union.

[95] In fiscal matters also Gallo, 'L'Europa in deficit di scelte e democrazia' (n 27) highlights that the 'excesses of economic-financial power' turn out to be 'obstacles to real European integration'. More specifically, such extremes, 'do not facilitate the achievement of the goal, to which every proponent of a more integrated European Union would aspire, of having a European own fiscal power as an essential step for the Union to take the place of the States as a producer of security for its citizens'. Gallo, 'Il diritto tributario italiano in Europa' (n 27).

B. The Need to Recover Non-negotiable Values and their Possible Relevance in Tax Matters

The true pro-European of today is therefore a person who seeks to give Europe (again) a soul based on 'non-negotiable' values.[96] A serious prospect of integration among Europeans to be based only on the sharing of truthful values.

That is the precondition for a more intense form of integration at the institutional level and, consequently, also at the fiscal level.[97]

Only from this perspective, therefore, will a possible strengthening of the role of the European Parliament in tax matters find a substantial foundation.[98] And only from this perspective can the increase in the democratic legitimacy of the system produce long-lasting positive effects.[99] The form needs to be given substance in order to obtain good results. Chances are that otherwise, everything will turn out to be an empty shell.

Moving from the institutional and formal to the substantive level, we have to realise that tax matters are not the primary field to be nurtured for the formation of a cohesive European people.

Contrary to what is often believed, paying common taxes does not in itself guarantee the creation of the foundations of a united people.[100] In fact, history teaches us that if common taxes do not correspond to common and shared values, then the conditions are laid for tax revolts, not for the strengthening of integration.[101] Only if the people are already united and cohesive, therefore

[96] To this extent, see the concept expressed by J Ratzinger, *Europe. Today and Tomorrow* (Ignatius Press 2007); J Ratzinger and M Pera, *Without Roots* (Basic Books 2007). The issue is anthropological and not linked to personal religious choices: see, in a comparable perspective, also influential non-Christian academics, such as JH Weiler, *Un'Europa Cristiana: Un saggio esplorativo* (Rizzoli 2003) translated into many languages.

[97] On the necessary coordination between these two aspects *cf* Gallo, 'L'Europa sociale e l'Europa fiscale dopo il Trattato di Lisbona' (n 27) 1797–98, that highlights how 'only a different institutional architecture of the EU in the direction of a federal state … could make it possible to overturn any different renunciative approach and the scale of values that is at its basis … and, consequently, … give the EU its own fiscal capacity'; Gallo, 'Il diritto tributario italiano in Europa' (n 27) 983.

[98] Similar to how for a mature evolution in a democratic sense of a state, it is not enough that it is endowed with formally democratic institutions, but it is necessary that it is enlivened by people educated in democracy (on this subject, see the considerations of C Galli, *Il disagio della democrazia* (Einaudi 2011) especially chs VI and VIII). For a mature evolution in the federal sense of the European integration project, it is not enough for the Union to endow itself with unitary democratic institutions: it is necessary that they represent a population that recognises itself as a unitary political body despite the plurality of its components.

[99] I have analysed this issue in *Tax Sovereignty and the Law in the Digital and Global Economy* (n 12) 65 ff and 87 ff; F Farri, 'El consenso a la imposición en la fiscalidad global' (2020) 76 *Themis* 13, 22 ff.

[100] Also the doctrine that dealt with the capability of political power to construct and conform identities through narrative and through the creation of credible stories from available cultural materials about the self-understanding of the collective subject and the answer to the questions 'who we are and who are they' (C Tilly, *Identities, Boundaries, and Social Ties*, 1st edn (Routledge 2005) 210 ff), points out that the directions to be followed for the construction and deployment of politically effective stories are different from the fiscal levy.

[101] C Adams, *For Good and Evil: The Impact Of Taxes On The Course Of Civilization* (Madison Books 2001).

only if there is a community that perceives itself as 'sovereign' already, is it possible to make a common front for strengthening financing public expenditure and the sense of belonging to the community itself, the solidarity within it and, ultimately, its solidity. As it has been demonstrated on a sociological level, in the more developed contexts, the relationship runs between representation and imposition, and it is not, on the contrary, the imposition to generate (and give meaning to) collective representativeness[102] and to transform into a 'community' groups of people that are not linked by other deep values in the above-mentioned sense.[103] Then again, it is not necessary to possess a particular sociological acumen to imagine that it will not be a digital service tax that will create a sense of belonging and community among European peoples, just as the introduction of common customs duties did not.

On the contrary, the perspectives opened by environmental taxes appear to be more significative, as mentioned in the previous section (III.A.ii.b). Indeed, there is no doubt that they are directly based on authentic values of care for creation. These values can be said to be, in their essential core, absolute and non-negotiable, without prejudice, of course, to the contingency and historical significance of their relative declinations and the need for them to always happen according to principles of rationality and functionality to the good of the human person.[104]

[102] On the subject see, ML Ross, 'Does Taxation Lead to Representation?' (2004) 34 *British Journal of Political Science* 229; M Herb, 'Taxation and Representation' (2003) 38 *Studies in Comparative International Development* 3; this even without reaching the conclusions for which the imposition would generate instability, to which it comes, KM Morrison, *Nontaxation and Representation* (Cambridge University Press 2014).

[103] After all, it is undeniable that paying taxes constitutes a form of evidence of the active belonging to a community: TR Davis, 'The tax-immigration nexus' (2017) 94 *Denver Law Review* 195, 210; IW Martin, AK Mehrotra and M Prasad, 'The Thunder of History: The Origins and Development of the New Fiscal Sociology' in IW Martin, A Mehrotra and M Prasad (eds), *The New Fiscal Sociology* (Cambridge University Press 2009) 3. In addition, it is easy to observe how the making of the perimeter of such a community constitutes a precondition for this form of active participation to grow. As clarified by ES Liberman, 'The Politics of Demanding Sacrifice: Applying Insights from Fiscal Sociology to the Study of AIDS Policy and State Capacity' in IW Martin, A Mehrotra and M Prasad (eds), *The New Fiscal Sociology* (Cambridge University Press 2009) 110 ff, the willingness to pay taxes requires a prior shared conception of the collectivity, a division of the world into 'us' and 'them', in-group and out-group: 'the stronger the identity … the more likely it is that citizens will sacrifice' by paying taxes. In this context, it is true that 'such feelings of collective identity are malleable and may be shaped … but preexisting boundary institutions are still likely' to be decisive. Therefore, it is not demonstrated, nor is it truthfully rationally evident, that the imposition of common taxes is adequate to strengthen groups of communities that are not otherwise deeply united. The effect of taxation on the creation of a sense of belonging to the community therefore seems only secondary and indirect.

[104] In this regard, some premises that are spreading on the subject are not good. First, the thesis that establishes improbable links between environmental protection and limitation of the human population on earth is clearly not acceptable, because it causes an inversion of the range of values to be safeguarded. From another point of view, the Decision of the EU Commission (COM(2022) 631 of 9 March 2022) to under certain conditions include nuclear energy among the forms of energy considered environmentally sustainable cannot be considered acceptable. Its harmfulness to the environment and human health has been witnessed by huge planetary disasters with a risk that does not seem likely to be eliminated with the use of new technologies.

Eco-taxes therefore represent a valuable tool, albeit not central from a systematic point of view, which can already be used in the context of the Treaties in force.

Without prejudice to what has been observed above about the role of taxation in the creation of a unified people, we can still identify at least two substantial aspects that the tax system itself can play to the advantage of the cohesion of a population or, at least, to hinder social disintegration. They add to the profile of environmental taxes, as mentioned above, and to general issues such as representativeness, rule of law and certainty of law,[105] as well as to the procedural issue of taxpayers' rights.[106]

These are the enhancement of the role that the peoples themselves have in the life of civil society, according to the principle of horizontal subsidiarity, and the reduction of inequalities between people.

These values must be implemented in European tax systems to make it an instrument of peoples' cohesion, rather than simply regulating the markets.

i. The Redistributive Function of Taxation

The aspect of reducing inequalities between people and the redistributive function of the tax levy is more specifically linked to the side of public spending and direct taxes.

In particular, it is certainly undisputed that personal taxes, such as income taxes levied on individuals and on corporations, are the most appropriate instrument for linking to taxation an opportunity to reduce economic inequalities between members of the community.[107] Although the redistributive finality also

[105] I have analysed these issues in *Tax Sovereignty and the Law in the Digital and Global Economy* (n 12) 77 f, where further references can be found.

[106] This issue has been studied in depth by the most influential doctrine: *cf*, among many, P Pistone, 'The EU Charter of Fundamental Rights, General Principles of EU Law and Taxation' in B Terra and P Wattel (eds), *European Tax Law* (Kluwer Law International 2018) 153 ff; P Pistone, 'The EU Law Dimension of Human Rights in Tax Matters' in C Brokelind (ed), *Principles of Law: Function, Status and Impact in EU Tax Law* (IBFD 2014); C Brokelind, 'The Role of EU in International Tax Policy and Human Rights: Does the EU Need a Policy on Taxation and Human Rights?' in P Pistone, G Kofler and M Poiares Maduro (eds), *Human Rights and Taxation in Europe and the World* (IBFD 2011). The EU Commission itself has launched an initiative in this field (see Communication on Taxpayers' Rights in the Single Market, Ares(2020)6140226).

[107] This aspect seems to be shared by the doctrine. See, for all, the following authors: E Vanoni, 'La finanza e la giustizia sociale' (1943) 11–12 *Studium* 358; F Gallo, *Le ragioni del fisco* (Il Mulino 2007) 59; M Luciani, 'Costituzione, tributi e mercato' [2012] *Rassegna tributaria* 831, para 3; RS Avi-Yonah, 'The Three Goals of Taxation' (2006) 60 *Tax Law Review* 1, especially at 12 ('a primary goal of the income tax historically was seen as redistributing wealth from the rich to everyone else'); RS Avi-Yonah, 'Os Três Objetivos da Tributação' [2008] *Direito tributário atual* 7. In general, on the subject of the redistributive function of taxes, *cf* F Gallo, 'Disuguaglianze, giustizia distributiva e principio di progressività' [2012] *Rassegna tributaria* 287; F Gallo, 'Potestà normativa di imposizione, mercato e giustizia sociale' [2018] *Giurisprudenza commerciale* 371; F Gallo, 'Il tributo quale indispensabile strumento di politiche ridistributive' [2021] *Rassegna tributaria* 273.

lends itself to be implemented on the side of the public revenue with the combination of other tax institutes, including a tax on personal general consumption,[108] the presence of a personal income tax is an indefectible element of the redistributive project in the public revenue side.[109]

Therefore, the redistributive function in the field of taxation can hardly be implemented in the current framework of the Treaties, which does not attribute to the Union direct competences in the matter of income tax and which outlines a different perimeter for consumption taxes from the one of the tax on personal general consumption. Only after an amendment to the Treaties, which in turn – for the reasons set out – can bring lasting positive effects only following a political and social maturation of the European people, can the redistributive function of the levy be fully realised at European level.

a. VAT Relevance Profiles

This does not mean that indirect taxes, as currently configured at the European level, do not have to comply with the principles of fiscal equity:[110] on the contrary, many interventions are necessary for this purpose.[111] This means, however, that the weapons made available by indirect taxes are structurally insufficient to achieve a redistributive effect of the levy that can be considered significant and of a general spectrum.

Among the necessary interventions in the field of indirect taxes and of European competences under current Treaties, an important sector that is suitable to generate redistributive effects is that of environmental taxes,[112] but some relevant aspects relating to the VAT Directive can also be underlined.

In particular, it needs to be improved to adequately take into account the need to exclude the *vital minimum* from taxation: the breadth of the transactions

[108] MJ Graetz, 'Implementing a Progressive Consumption Tax' (1979) 92 *Harvard Law Review* 1575.

[109] Gallo, *Le ragioni del fisco* (n 107) 112 and 119; Avi-Yonah, 'The Three Goals of Taxation' (n 107) 19 ff; RS Avi-Yonah, 'Why Tax the Rich? Efficiency, Equity, and Progressive Taxation' (2002) 111 *Yale Law Journal* 1391.

[110] For a possible constructive reading of the relevance in the European system of the 'ability to pay' principle, that may be considered an aspect of the broader redistributive function of taxation, see J Lang and J Englisch, 'A European Legal Tax Order Based on Ability to Pay' in A Amatucci (ed), *International Tax Law* (Wolters Kluwer); J Englisch, 'Ability to Pay' in C Brokelind (ed), *Principles of Law: Function, Status and Impact in EU Tax Law* (IBFD 2014).
F Vanistendael, 'The Ability to Pay Principle in the EU Legal Order' in L Salvini and G Melis (eds), *L'evoluzione del sistema fiscale e il principio di capacità contributiva* (Cedam 2014); F Vanistendael, 'Ability to Pay in European Community Law (2014) 23 *EC Tax Review* 121. On the wider issue of 'equality' in taxation see R Påhlsson, 'Equality in Taxation: Reflections on the Social Construction of Comparability in Tax Law' in C Brokelind (ed), *Principles of Law: Function, Status and Impact in EU Tax Law* (IBFD 2014).

[111] For an application of the principles of the Nice Charter to VAT matters *cf* KK Egholm Elgaard, 'The effect of the Charter of Fundamental Rights of the European Union on substantive VAT law' in M Lang et al (eds), *CJEU: Recent Developments in Value Added Tax* 2017 (Linde 2018).

[112] In this regard, see para 2.1. of the Commission's Communication 'Ready for 55%' COM (2021) 550 final.

excluded from the application of VAT should be extended to a more comprehensive basket of staple goods for families, children and the elderly. Let us not forget the need to exclude from taxation the supply of basic food products (bread, water, milk and such like) which, instead, Annex III to Directive 2006/112/EC only allows to be submitted to a reduced tax rate. Or let us not forget the need to extend the provision referred to in Article 132, paragraph 1(h), according to which 'the supply of services and of goods closely linked to the protection of children and young persons by bodies governed by public law or by other organizations recognised by the Member State concerned as being devoted to social wellbeing' are exempt. In addition to the services of orphanages, nurseries and youth hostels, large-scale exclusions should be provided for purchases of early childhood-related items (nappies, baby food, baby clothes).[113]

The same should be done for goods providing assistance to the elderly and disabled, which should be excluded from taxation well beyond the provision of Article 132, paragraph 1(g) of the Directive: in this regard, the reduction rate provided for in Annex III is not sufficient and the interpretation supplied by the Court of Justice is all the more 'frustrating'.[114]

Furthermore, these exclusions from taxation should also allow the deductibility of the VAT paid at the preceding stage, differently from what was also established in the previous regulations by Article 114 of the Directive.

b. The Equality Principle

The redistributive function of taxation at the European level may therefore have to be realised mainly downstream of a possible evolution in the political and sovereign sense of the EU. This is not only on a formal profile, it is also on a substantial one.

The principle of equality, to which the reduction of inequalities and the promotion of the redistributive function are connected, has elastic contents and can be applied with extremely different results.[115] The first consequence of the principle of equality is to require that equal situations be treated equally and different situations be treated differently: well, the identification of elements of similarity or dissimilarity between situations is a typical judgement influenced

[113] On this last subject *cf* H Kogels, 'The Application of the Zero VAT Rate on Children's Footwear' [2010] *British Tax Review* 688.

[114] Reference is made, in particular, to the cases in which the goods for the disabled were not even considered eligible to benefit from the reduction of the tax rate based on the fact that they could also be used by other subjects: *cf* CJEU, Case C-360/11 *Commission v Spain*, paras 84–89, ECLI:EU:C:2013:17; and CJEU, Case C-573/15 *Belgium v Oxycure Belgium SA*, para 34, ECLI:EU:C:2017:189.

[115] In particular, the difference between the content that the principle of equality assumes in the perspective of national constitutional rights and that it assumes in European law is clearly underlined by Gallo, 'Il diritto tributario italiano in Europa' (n 27). On the subject *cf* also A Perrone, *Tax competition e giustizia sociale nell'unione europea* (Cedam 2019) 180 ff.

by the values of the interpreter. Think of the issues relating to gender, which see extremely diversified and deeply rooted value judgements made by the various interpreters.

All the more so, the problem of the axiological substrate arises when passing from a logic of formal equality to a logic of substantial equality, such as that required by the redistributive function of taxation.[116] For this reason, a full implementation of the principle of equality in the EU in general, and in European taxation in particular, can only take place following the sharing of common values by a European population that has reached an appropriate level of social and axiological cohesion.

ii. Horizontal Subsidiarity

Conversely, the other aspect, namely that of horizontal subsidiarity, can from now on also be valued in the current Treaties' framework and it can really lend itself to favouring the rebirth among the European peoples of an attachment to values rooted in the depths of the human person and, therefore, to lay the foundations for the formation of a European people properly understood and that perceives itself as such.[117]

In each of the European societies, according to their own traditions, there are social groups which, despite being private, perform objectively public functions, ie, functions which, in the absence of the aforementioned social groups, should be carried out by the public administration. Think of the various charitable associations but also and, even earlier, of the family, which is central in taking care of fragile people (from children to the elderly). Here, the tax rules of the EU should immediately focus on the enhancement of these realities, much more so than they currently do. In fact, it is groups like these that naturally drive the formation of a people and give life to a common solidarity between persons.

a. VAT Relevance Profiles

From a fiscal point of view, these realities, while carrying out their services, are already contributing 'in kind' to public expenses: in fact, they provide

[116] It is matter debated by Cristina Trenta, 'Reconceptualising the Principle of Equality in EU Tax Law', ch 9 in this volume, and by U Spangenberg, A Mumford and S Daly, 'Navigating taxation towards sustainability: Contradictions between social, gender, environmental, and economic ambitions, obligations and governance capacities in the European tax law' (2018) FairTax Working Paper Series 16.

[117] On the relevance of the principle of horizontal subsidiarity in tax matters, *cf* L Antonini, 'Il principio di sussidiarietà orizzontale: da welfare State a welfare society' (2000) 1 *Rivista di diritto finanziario e scienze delle finanze* 999, 110 ff; L Antonini, *Sussidiarietà fiscale* (Guerini e Associati 2005); L Antonini and G Lombardi, 'Principio di sussidiarietà e democrazia sostanziale: profili costituzionali della libertà di scelta' [2003] *Diritto e società* 155; F Gallo, 'L'applicazione del principio di sussidiarietà tra crisi del disegno federalista e tutela del bene comune' (2014) 2 *Rassegna tributaria* 207, 221 ff.

a service that from an objective point of view is certainly of 'public' importance. Therefore, their contribution 'in kind' to public expenditure should be adequately taken into account when outlining their obligations to contribute 'in cash', ie, to pay taxes.

As an example, Articles 13 and 132 of the VAT Directive should be improved and, even more importantly, they should be given an appropriate application, both within the scope of the VAT system and in connection with the other sectors that the European jurisprudence includes in the field of taxation, such as in particular that of State aid.

In addition to what was specifically indicated in the previous section (IV.A.ii.b), it is hardly a reasonable approach whereby, for example, the services of private schools must rightly be exempted from VAT according to the Directive (Article 132, paragraph 1(i), but the choice of a Member State to exempt from property tax the real estate in which they are housed is regarded as undue State aid (see the above-mentioned *Montessori* case).

Going back to VAT, charity organisations should be excluded from the category of taxable persons, according to the same principles provided for public entities by Article 13. In any case, such entities should be allowed to provide services at a reasonable higher price than the mere direct cost, so as to also allow remuneration for the indirect costs of carrying out the activity, in the absence of which the activity of these subjects could not take place: the clauses of Article 132, paragraph 1(f) and (l), which make the exemption subject to the payment of a fee not exceeding the 'exact reimbursement of their share of the joint expenses' or a subscription fee, appear to be too strict. For this purpose, a clause that makes the exemption subject to the non-impact on market competition seems to be sufficient to guarantee compliance with the interests protected by European law: in this regard, once again the clause of the aforementioned rules appears to be too restrictive to the extent it considers a mere 'probability' of impact on competition to be sufficient to exclude the exemption.

If this is summed up to the exasperatingly restrictive interpretation provided by the CJEU to the exemption clauses of Article 132,[118] it is easy to observe how the limitations contained in the Directive for this purpose are unsuitable to adequately guarantee the social purpose taken into account here.

In addition, those goods and services which are indispensable to enable these social groups, in particular families, to perform their function of public importance, such as in particular the care of children, the sick and the elderly, should be exempted: in addition to the essential goods already indicated above, also babysitters'

[118] In this sense, the CJEU ruling in Case C-412/15 *TMD Gesellschaft für transfunsionsmedizinische Dienste*, ECLI:EU:C:2016:738, is indeed emblematic. In order to give a restrictive interpretation of the VAT exemption concerning the trade of human blood, milk and organs, linking them exclusively to their direct use for medical purposes, the Court ends up expressly legitimising (para 35) the trade and its taxability to purely industrial and economic purposes. The 'perfect' application of '*summum ius, summa inuiria*'.

and care-providers' services should be exempt (and not simply subject to a reduced tax rate, as it is currently established by Annex III to Directive 2006/112/EC); services which help families to care for fragile people without burdening public structures.

b. A New 'Social Accounting' System

Furthermore, while performing their services, these groups guarantee savings in the spending of public administrations: if there were no such groups, those services would have to be carried out by the public administrations and be paid for with public money. This saving in public spending should be taken into account when drafting public budgets: the budget balance, on which the Fiscal Compact is focused, should not only be measured on financial data, but also on substantial ones.

This step towards 'social accounting', rather than purely financial accounting,[119] appears to be the first step to take so that the European tax system can facilitate the formation of a European people who may perceive itself as such[120] and which, likewise, may open up to a change of the Treaties in the sense of a broader and also more substantial integration in terms of taxation.

[119] I have carried out an in-depth analysis of this matter in F Farri, *Un fisco sostenibile per la famiglia in Italia* (Cedam 2018) 37 ff.

[120] Instead of preventing this formation with a sterile forcing of competences which – as explained – violates national sovereignty and thus has no effect other than hiding behind them.

7

The Reform of EU Own Resources under the Next Generation EU Programme: A Suitable Moment for the Introduction of a European Tax?

CLAUDIO SCIANCALEPORE*

I. INTRODUCTION

THE HEALTH EMERGENCY caused by Covid-19 and the subsequent economic and social crisis posed a new challenge for all countries. The European Union (EU) decided to tackle this through extraordinary initiatives enhancing solidarity between Member States. The Next Generation EU (NGEU) relaunch programme represents an exceptional initiative that supports economic recovery in Europe through an expansion of public spending financed by bonds issued by the EU (so-called 'coronabonds').[1]

For the first time in its history, the EU has gained access to the financial markets through a massive use of debt under the NGEU programme by issuing bonds, including 'green bonds',[2] for a total of €750 billion until 2026,[3] which

* Tax Law researcher at University of Bari. Email: claudio.sciancalepore@uniba.it.

[1] Regulation (EU) 2021/241 of the European Parliament and of the Council of 12 February 2021 establishing the Recovery and Resilience Facility [2021] OJ L57/17. According to Francesco Costamagna and Matthias Goldmann, 'Constitutional Innovation, Democratic Stagnation? The EU Recovery Plan' (*VerfBlog*, 30 May 2020) 'Funding the ERI [European Union Recovery Instrument] through Own Resources allows on the one hand escaping the need to ask the Member States for financial guarantees and the actual or potential constitutional implications this may cause. On the other hand, it allows getting the European Parliament involved', available at: verfassungsblog.de/constitutional-innovation-democratic-stagnation/.

[2] By 2026, the European Commission will have issued about €250 billion of green bonds to finance the part of the NGEU dedicated to the environment. See also J Le Cacheux, 'Funding the EU Budget with a Genuine Own Resource: The Case for a European Tax' (2007) 57 *Notre Europe Studies* 16.

[3] Until now, the European Commission has registered four bond issues, each with a different maturity, raising a total of €54 billion. During the current financial year, it is expected to raise around €80 billion in bonds.

will be repaid directly through the European budget. Some commentators have defined this crucial historical phase as a 'Hamiltonian moment' for the EU since it is similar to what happened in the United States in the late 1700s when the first US Treasury Secretary, Alexander Hamilton, gave the impetus to mutualise war debts as they were transformed into public debt for the new federal government.[4]

In order not to be a burden on the public finances of the Member States through a request for greater transfers, the loans obtained will also be repaid through the revenues produced by the new European own resources,[5] some of which might have a juridical tax nature: a plastic tax that levies the weight of non-recycled plastic packaging waste, a carbon border adjustment mechanism,[6] a revenue-sharing scheme deriving from the Emissions Trading System,[7] a digital levy that will incorporate the evolution of the work of the Organisation for Economic Co-operation and Development on the taxation of the digital economy,[8] a financial contribution linked to the corporate sector or a new common corporate tax based on benefits gained from the European Single Market and, finally, a European Financial Transaction Tax.[9] The reimbursement of the coronabonds, therefore, is ensured, until 2058, through the resources of the EU, paving the way to an initial nucleus of tax levies belonging to the EU, ie, not deriving from the taxation of individual Member States.[10]

The possibility of creating a common fiscal capacity is necessary, not only to repay the debt deriving from the NGEU programme, but also to finance

[4] See L Lionello, 'Next Generation EU: has the Hamiltonian moment come for Europe?' (2020) 4 *Eurojus.it* 22.

[5] See A D'Alfonso, 'The own resources system: some questions on how to communicate a possible reform' in A de Feo and B Laffan (eds), *EU Own Resources: Momentum for a Reform?* (European University Institute 2016).

[6] See A Pirlot, 'Carbon Border Adjustment Measures: A Straightforward Multi-Purpose Climate Change Instrument?' (2022) 34 *Journal of Environmental Law* 25.

[7] See H Kogels, 'Energy Taxes and Emissions Trading on the Bumpy Road to a Climate Neutral EU' (2020) 29 *EC Tax Review* 208, 211 ff; L Del Federico and S Giorgi, 'The Coordination of Energy Taxes and ETS via Tax Exemptions: The Compatibility Test in the Context of Free and/or Auctioning Allowances and TFEU Rules' in M Villar Ezcurra and P Pistone (eds), *Energy Taxation, Environmental Protection and State Aid: Tracing the Path from Divergence to Convergence* (IBFD 2016); C Fuest and J Pisani-Ferry, 'Financing the European Union: new context, new responses' (2020) 16 Bruegel Policy Contribution 1, 7 ff, available at: www.bruegel.org/sites/default/files/wp_attachments/PC-16-2020-110920.pdf; R Ismer and M Haussner, 'Emissions Trading and Tax Treaties' (2015) 69 *Bulletin for International Taxation* 27.

[8] See also I Cugusi, 'Prospects for Taxation of the Digital Economy between "Tax Law and New Economy" and "Tax Law of the New Economy"' (2020) 12 *World Tax Journal* 763.

[9] See the Interinstitutional Agreement between the European Parliament, the Council of the European Union and the European Commission on budgetary discipline, on cooperation in budgetary matters and on sound financial management, as well as on new own resources, including a roadmap towards the introduction of new own resources [2020] OJ L433I/28. For the European Financial Transaction Tax, see L Denys, 'Why a Financial Transaction Tax? (2012) 21 *EC Tax Review* 2.

[10] See Carlos Closa, George Papakonstantinou and Miguel Poiares Maduro, 'EU and COVID-19: Time to think outside the box' (*EUIdeas*, Blogpost, 21 April 2020), available at: euideas.eui.eu/2020/04/21/eu-and-covid-19-time-to-think-outside-the-box.

European public goods, without increased national budgetary contributions, while at the same time promoting European objectives and policies. As a matter of fact, EU spending should be targeted at 'public goods'[11] of a European dimension which can provide the most benefit: the EU should focus only on those public goods that it can produce more efficiently/effectively than Member States alone (ie, European public goods such as research, infrastructure, border control, etc).[12] The attribution of fiscal sovereignty to the EU and the establishment of a European tax as a new fiscal own resource would, in fact, also allow an expansion of the size of the European budget, which is still too modest today to finance the number of functions that the Union is called upon to perform.[13]

In order to avoid worrying asymmetries between debt capacity and fiscal sovereignty, as well as to ensure that the EU is able to repay the loans by relying on future tax revenues deriving from the use of taxation power, it is necessary to investigate the possibility of establishing a supranational fiscal capacity as a necessary evolution of the European integration process.[14] Furthermore, the creation of an authentic fiscal union would make it possible to overcome the current rules of European economic governance which have formally respected the fiscal sovereignty of the Member States but have de facto ended up diluting similar national sovereignty and autonomy.[15] The strict rules of European

[11] For a definition of 'public good' see PA Samuelson, 'The Pure Theory of Public Expenditure' (1954) 36 *Review of Economics and Statistics* 387.

[12] The resources available to the EU amount to about 1.2% of European GDP, a negligible amount, especially when compared with the resources available to the Member States. According to C Fasone and N Lupo, 'The Union Budget and the Budgetary Procedure' in R Schütze and T Tridimas (eds), *Oxford Principles of European Union Law* (Oxford University Press 2018) 809: 'the Union budget ... is much smaller than the budgets of most Member States but, at the same time, it is three times bigger than that of the United Nations. Its size and, even more so, the EU procedures which set its expenditures – apart from its revenue – reveal that the EU aims to be something different from a mere international organization'. See also E Traversa and G Bizioli, 'Solidarity in the European Union in the Time of Covid-19: Paving the Way for a Genuine EU Tax?' (2020) 48 *Intertax* 743, 745; G Cipriani, '"Adding value", the raison d'être of the European Union' (2020) 3 *ECA Journal* 85; J Núñez Ferrer, 'Investing where it matters: An EU budget for long-term growth' in *CEPS Task Force Report* (Brussels 2012) 38; E Rubio, 'The "added value" in EU budgetary debates: one concept, four meanings' (2011) 28 *Notre Europe* 2.

[13] See J Haug, A Lamassoure and G Verhofstadt, *Europe for Growth: For a Radical Change in the Revenue of the European Union* (Bruxelles 2011) 30 ff; I Begg, 'An EU tax: Overdue reform or federalist fantasy?' (2011) FES Briefing Paper 11, 10 ff; I Begg, 'Mollifying Everyone, Pleasing No-one? An Assessment of the EU Budget Review' (2010) 14 *SIEPS European Policy Analysis* 1; I Begg, 'Rethinking How to Pay for Europe' (2010) 2 *SIEPS European Policy Analysis* 1.

[14] Since the Communication from the European Commission of 28 November 2012 – COM(2012) 777 final – entitled 'A Blueprint for a Deep and Genuine Economic and Monetary Union Launching a European Debate' it has been suggested that what is required is the creation of an autonomous 'proper fiscal capacity for the euro area to support structural reform on a large scale as well as for enabling forms of debt mutualisation' through the creation of 'a new taxation power at the EU level, or a power to raise revenue by indebting itself on the markets (presently barred by Articles 310 and 311 TFEU)'. See also M Buti and M Nava, 'Towards a European Budgetary System' (2003) 8 *EUI RSC* 3.

[15] See M Aulenta, 'The usefulness of the fiscal compact to supersede the domestic stability pact' (2016) 2 *Rivista di diritto finanziario e scienze delle finanze* 241.

public finance, in fact, have weakened national taxation, without creating supranational taxation, which ought to be remedied through the establishment of a fiscal union and the consequent distribution of taxation power between different levels of government.

II. 'NEGATIVE' AND 'POSITIVE' LEGAL INTEGRATION IN THE EU

Since the Treaties of Rome of 1957, the EU has never enjoyed taxing powers, despite the fact that it has always imposed the financing of the European budget through 'own resources'.[16] Although the Treaty of Paris of 1951 sanctioned that the European Coal and Steel Community be financed through tax levied on the production of coal and steel managed directly at the supranational level, the founding countries of the current EU decided to not re-propose such a provision and to remit Community funding to indefinite own resources.[17]

Due to the persistent lack of taxing powers, pressing spending needs and the growing number of common policies adopted, transfers from Member States, based on some macroeconomic variables, to the Union are still considered as 'own resources', despite the fact that they represent the majority share of the EU financing system. The paradoxical situation that has arisen, in which the Member States have decided not to provide the EU with its own taxing power but to impose that 'the budget shall be financed wholly from own resources',[18] indicates evidence of an *in itinere* integration process and is symptomatic of the uncertainty about the juridical definition of the Union, which oscillates between an international organisation and a federation of states.[19]

At the European level, therefore, there is no normative *corpus* that can be defined as a common tax system to be understood as an organic and systematic set of rules that are added to those of the Member States and regulate the exercise of supranational tax authority. European taxation, unlike that of Member States, does not aim to levy taxes to collect the resources necessary for the exercise of public functions; instead it only has the aim of coordinating the tax measures of Member States that could distort competition within the internal market. Even today, European measures in tax matters do not assume a 'fiscal' function intended as a contribution made by European taxpayers to common

[16] According to G Isaac, 'La notion de ressources propres' in G Isaac (ed), *Les ressources financières de la Communauté européenne* (Parigi 2004) 75 the definition of own resources is 'une fausse notion claire'. See also CD Ehlermann, 'The Financing of the Community: The distinction between financial contributions and own resources' (1982) 19 *Common Market Law Review* 571; M Bouvaert, 'Où est le droit fiscal européen?' [1966] *Cahiers de droit européen* 253.

[17] See G Benedetto, 'Institutions and the route to reform of the European Union's budget revenue, 1970–2017' (2017) 44 *Empirica* 615; R Ackrill and A Kay, 'Historical-institutionalist perspectives on the development of the EU budget system' (2006) 13 *Journal of European Public Policy* 113.

[18] Art 311 TFEU.

[19] See also G Melis and F Pitrone, 'Coordinating Tax Strategies at the EU Level as a Solution to the Economic and Financial Crisis' (2011) 39 *Intertax* 374.

public spending, but is aimed at achieving the coordination of Member State tax systems in order to ensure the functioning of the internal market.

The 'protectiveness' of Member States regarding their taxing powers has prevented a transfer, albeit partial, of tax sovereignty to the EU and the creation of a true European tax to finance the budget:[20] taxing power, as a fundamental index of the exercise of state sovereignty, is monopolistically and exclusively preserved by Member States. The European Treaties, in fact, do not qualify the EU as a tax entity and do not make legislative choices that determine and qualify the structure of a common tax system.

Nonetheless, the rules of European tax law appear rather pervasive and are heavily reflected in domestic tax systems, causing a compression of the sovereignty of Member States. These rules, in fact, end up limiting the autonomy of Member States in the tax field in order to prevent the tax instrument from posing obstacles to the exercise of fundamental freedoms or threatening competition in the Single Market. Taxation in the European context is not aimed at the establishment of a supranational tax order but assumes a mainly 'negative' value. This is also due to the 'creative' jurisprudence of the Court of Justice of the European Union (CJEU), aimed at controlling the legislative choices of Member States so that the proper functioning of the internal market is guaranteed by eliminating competition-distorting tax measures that prevent the creation of the level playing field as well as discriminatory ones which do not allow that equal conditions in trade exchanges are ensured. Therefore, European tax law assumes a 'negative' value, manifesting itself only in the coordination of national tax policies for the achievement of market interests.

Among the numerous limits and constraints sanctioned by European law, it is necessary to mention the principle of non-discrimination, the prohibition of adopting protectionist fiscal measures, the prohibition on the application between Member States of customs duties or taxes having equivalent effect as well as the prohibition of State aid.[21] European primary law imposes numerous prohibitions and limits on the national legislator in order to restrain the taxing powers of the Member States so that the tax aspect plays a neutral role in the autonomous dynamics of the market.

The objectives of freedom and competition in the Single Market are pursued not only through 'negative' integration, characterised by limits, prohibitions and constraints, but also through 'positive' integration based on the harmonisation and coordination of tax interventions of the Member States because, in some cases, the removal of tax obstacles requires the production of new common provisions. In this sense, there seems to be a European vision of taxation since

[20] See M Schratzenstaller, 'The EU Own Resources System: Reform Needs and Options' (2013) 48 *Intereconomics* 303; Le Cacheux (n 2).

[21] See A Fantozzi, 'The Applicability of State Aid Rules to Tax Competition Measures: A Process of "De Facto" Harmonisation in Tax Fields?' in W Schön (ed), *Tax Competition in Europe* (IBFD 2003) 127.

the Union not only has the role of stemming state taxing powers, but also has a propositional function.

The legal basis of positive integration can be found in Article 113 of the Treaty on the Functioning of the European Union (TFEU) regarding the harmonisation of legislation concerning turnover taxes, excise duties and other forms of indirect taxation and in Article 115 TFEU regarding the approximation of laws applied, in the tax field, to direct taxation.[22] In both cases, the Treaty requires compliance with a special legislative procedure that requires the unanimity of the Council and a merely consultative role for the European Parliament, demonstrating the unwillingness of the Member States to compromise their fiscal sovereignty. With a view to vertical subsidiarity, European intervention is allowed only to ensure the establishment and the proper functioning of the internal market and to avoid distortions of competition in order to support the interests of the free market.[23]

From the intertwining of such ‘negative’ and ‘positive’ integration, the so-called ‘anti-sovereign theory’ has been formulated. The theory is useful for describing the fiscal discipline developed at the European level where, from a multilevel legal system perspective, the fiscal sovereignty of Member States must respect fundamental freedoms and constraints for the proper functioning of the internal market.[24] In spite of the ‘negative’ European taxation that expresses a limitation to the taxing powers of the Member States, it is not substituted with ‘positive’ taxation meant as a fiscal sovereignty of the Union aimed at creating a new tax system based on common principles. The EU, therefore, is a kind of ‘anti-sovereign’ as it limits and eludes Member States’ sovereignty, without replacing it with a different sovereign order, and it leaves the choices concerning tax matters to market assessments and to the respect of fundamental freedoms. This phenomenon has been described as the ‘paradox of sovereignty’ in order to indicate the process by which the sovereignty of Member States, in relation to the EU, undergoes a metamorphosis:[25] they voluntarily give shares of their taxing powers to the Union, but only to allow it to control them at a supranational level.

It would seem as if the EU mainly regulates the cross-border aspects of taxation, especially regarding corporations,[26] and eludes the stringent unanimity rule

[22] See G Bizioli and C Sacchetto, ‘European Constitutional Integration: The Case of Direct Taxation’ in RS Avi-Yonah and M Lang (eds), *Comparative Fiscal Federalism* (Wolters Kluwer 2016). See also, extensively, L Cerioni, *The European Union and Direct Taxation: A Solution for a Difficult Relationship* (Routledge 2015); and M Isenbaert, *EC Law and the Sovereignty of the Member States in Direct Taxation* (IBFD 2010).

[23] See also MC Fregni, ‘EU Customs Union and Free Market. (Reflections on the Side-Lines of Brexit and the UK’s Withdrawal from the EU) (2019) 78 *Rivista di diritto finanziario e scienze delle finanze* 424.

[24] See P Boria, *Diritto tributario europeo* (Giuffrè 2015) 425 ff.

[25] See S Cipollina, *I confini giuridici nel tempo presente: Il caso del diritto fiscale* (Giuffrè 2003) 17 ff.

[26] See L Cerioni, ‘The European Commission Proposal for a 3% “Call Rate” as a New Suggestion for a EUCIT: An Assessment Against the Criteria for a Fair Taxation’ (2018) 27 *EC Tax Review* 237;

through the use of soft law instruments whose legal weakness does not compress the Member State tax sovereignty.[27] However, the results obtained from the approximation of direct taxation appear largely insufficient, making it necessary to fall back on initiatives of mere convergence in relation to transnational taxation, without losing sight of the objective of ensuring competition in the Single Market. Also, the recent significant progress in the coordination action in the fight against tax avoidance,[28] testify to the unanimous interest of Member States in fighting aggressive tax planning, with a view to the proper functioning of the Single Market (and the increase of national revenues), on specific aspects of the taxation, without any thought dedicated to a true European taxation. As a matter of fact, the timid positive signals coming from the coordination action undertaken by the European Commission regarding the fight against tax avoidance, where a consensus has been reached by the Member States, seem to be driven by the crisis in public finances.

III. THE FUNDAMENTAL TAX PRINCIPLES BETWEEN EUROPEAN PRIMARY LAW AND COMMON CONSTITUTIONAL TRADITIONS

A radical paradigm shift based on the attribution to the EU of its own taxing powers and on the establishment of a European tax system requires an amendment of the Treaties as well as a codification of the common fundamental principles. These principles are not stated in the provisions of the Treaties, which only enunciate the prohibition of discrimination, from which the principle of

B Peeters, 'EUCIT: For How Much Longer Will Political Objections Outweigh the Advantages?' (2015) 24 *EC Tax Review* 128; G Arachi and G Casalone, 'Trends in European Taxation' (2011) 3 *Rivista di diritto finanziario e scienze delle finanze* 332; V Ceriani, 'CCCTB and the Financial Sector' (2008) 17 *EC Tax Review* 159.

[27] See AP Dourado, 'The Commission proposal to replace unanimity with a qualified majority in the case of tax matters' (2020) 48 *Intertax* 341. See also MF Nouwen, 'The Market Distortion Provisions of Articles 116–117 TFEU: An Alternative Route to Qualified Majority Voting in Tax Matters? (2021) 1 *Intertax* 14 ff; J Englisch, 'Article 116 TFEU: The Nuclear Option for Qualified Majority Tax Harmonization? (2020) 29 *EC Tax Review* 58. See also S Hagemann, 'The EU Budget and Balance of Powers between the European Parliament and the EU Governments' (2014) 3 *European Policy Analysis* 1. According to P Pistone, 'A Plea for Qualified Majority Voting and the Ordinary Legislative Procedure in European Tax Law' in S Van Thiel, P Valente and S Raventós-Calvo (eds), *CFE Tax Advisers Europe – 60th Anniversary Liber Amicorum* (IBFD 2019) 23: 'This indirectly confirms the importance of qualified majority voting as a valid alternative to unanimity. From a qualitative perspective, it is therefore a better option than enhanced cooperation. Qualified majority voting steers the dynamics of consensus in a way that forces countries to pool their national interests without blocking the overall action in the interests of the European Union. Furthermore, unlike enhanced cooperation, it does not give rise to two-speed tax integration, thus not harming the exercise of the Member States that have decided not to join'.

[28] See Council Directive (EU) 2016/1164 of 12 July 2016 laying down rules against tax avoidance practices that directly affect the functioning of the internal market (Anti-Tax Avoidance Directive or ATAD I) [2016] OJ L193/1, amended by Council Directive (EU) 2017/952 of 29 May 2017 [2017] OJ L144/1 (ATAD II) in the wake of the work of the BEPS Project.

tax equality and, in this way, the principle of the ability to pay might somehow be derived. However, in European law, the principle of non-discrimination has a merely economic value, typical of free market systems, and it focuses on the neutrality of tax policies in order to avoid differentiations based on citizenship or residence or unjustified restrictions on economic freedoms, so that its meaning appears different from the equality principle applicable to tax matters. Indeed, the prohibition of discrimination, which is necessary for the proper functioning of the internal market, seems to contrast with the principles of redistribution and promotional taxation that are one of the functions of government according to Musgrave's Theory of Public Expenditures.[29]

In the absence of general principles in the field of taxation in the European Treaties, there is a need for the codification of some postulates of tax justice in European law. In particular, European primary law could express principles specifically relating to tax matters, and not just principles of European law reinterpreted from a fiscal point of view. In this regard, some scholars in Italy, coordinated by Professor Fantozzi, have identified a set of essential tax rules as an expression of constitutional traditions common to the Member States.[30] These principles should have been included in the Charter of Fundamental Rights of the European Union (Charter of Nice) through the introduction of a new chapter VI-*bis* – '*Taxation*' – and the addition of Article 50-*bis* regarding the '*Principles*'. Among these principles it is important to highlight the following: the consent to tax and the representative principle ('no taxation without representation'); the ability to pay principle; and the redistribution principle. The study group has also suggested giving the EU exclusive competence over its own resources which should be subject to the legislative procedure of co-decision in compliance with the democratic principle of consent to taxation.[31]

While awaiting the amendment of the Treaties, it is possible to start a study aimed at analysing the application in the European territory of principles on which any tax system should be based, including the rule of law, progressivity, redistribution, equality as well as reasonableness and proportionality. It is necessary to identify the fundamental rights of tax matters common to the Member States that can be raised to the European level either through an amendment of European primary law or through their mere existence since they already constitute general principles of the Union's law as 'they result from the constitutional traditions common to the Member States' ex Article 6(3) of the Treaty

[29] See also, extensively, RA Musgrave, *The Theory of Public Finance* (McGraw-Hill 1959).

[30] See Associazione per gli Studi e le ricerche sulla Riforma delle Istituzioni Democratiche e sull'innovazione nelle amministrazioni pubbliche – ASTRID, *Per la Costituzione dell'Unione europea. Convergenze, divergenze, percorsi possibili e qualche proposta* (February 2003), available at: www.astrid-online.it/static/upload/protected/Cost/CostituzioneUEperWeb.pdf.

[31] See also, MC Fregni, 'Legitimacy in decision-making in tax law: some remarks on taxation, representation and consent to imposition' (2017) 4 *Rivista di diritto finanziario e scienze delle finanze* 410.

on European Union (TEU).[32] In fact, these principles are able to guarantee a correct distribution of taxation among the affiliates and to limit the power of the Member States to impose taxes in order to protect the fundamental rights of taxpayers.[33]

Previous comparative studies have already made it possible to identify the presence of these principles in the legal systems of Member States and their compatible declination in European law regarding the ability to pay,[34] especially its corollary of maximum limit to taxation and prohibition of confiscatory taxation, the rule of law, the principle of equality, etc. These are principles of tax justice present in the legal systems of each Member State and widespread, almost through an osmotic process, in the European area as they implement fundamental values such as human dignity and the related rights and duties of solidarity.

Concerning the ability to pay, some scholars claim that it is not part of Union law as it represents a principle of domestic tax legislation only, while others are in support of its application in the EU.[35] From a comparative point of view, the ability to pay is expressly stated in the constitutional charters of some European countries; in the Member States where it is not expressly established, it emerges from a joint reading of the principles of reasonableness, fairness and equality relating to taxation. These principles, typical of a modern constitutional charter, regardless of their rigid or flexible nature, both written or unwritten, offer constitutional protection of the ability to pay, also thanks to the interpretations of the constitutional courts in various countries. Even in the absence of an explicit codification of the ability to pay in the Treaties, it appears unrealistic that it is not part of Union law since it is concretely and constantly applied in all Member States according to the logic of the circulation of constitutional principles and national legal models, albeit with contents and protections with 'variable geometries'. The ability to pay appears to be an example of a 'lowest common denominator' that unites the tax rules of Member States and which could be derived from an interpretation of the Treaties; in addition, its infringement would constitute an obstacle to the exercise of fundamental freedoms expressly protected by the Treaties.

Conversely, if a European tax were to infringe on the ability to pay, in addition to possible complaints that can be invoked before the European judges, the domestic system could react by raising the shields of 'counter-limits' as

[32] See F Vanistendael, 'The Role of (Legal) Principles in EU Tax Law' in C Brokelind (ed), *Principles of Law: Function, Status and Impact in EU Tax Law* (IBFD 2014) 41 ff.

[33] See also J Kokott and P Pistone, *Taxpayers in International Law: International Minimum Standards for the Protection of Taxpayers' Rights* (Bloomsbury 2022) 53 ff.

[34] See F Vanistendael, 'The ability to pay principle in the EU legal order' in L Salvini and G Melis (eds), *L'evoluzione del sistema fiscale e il principio di capacità contributiva* (Cedam 2014) 204 ff.

[35] See J Lang and J Englisch, 'A European Legal Tax Order Based on Ability to Pay' in A Amatucci (eds), *International Tax Law* (Wolters Kluwer 2012) 261 ff.

principles that could be opposed to the primacy of European law, albeit only in theory and hitherto never used in tax matters. The introduction of a European tax that does not respect the principle of the ability to pay because it is regarded as for example, unreasonable, arbitrary, etc, would be invoked before the constitutional court which would raise the shields of the 'counter-limits'.

In the jurisprudential field, the CJEU, also taking advantage of its 'creative' function, has developed some relevant principles for tax law starting from European primary law and national tax systems, although this contribution has often been limited to a statement of principles already developed by the Court with reference to other branches of EU law and applied to tax matters. Under the pressure of the Advocates General, the CJEU has often used the ability to pay principle in its judgments, not without some uncertainty, due to the constitutional traditions common to the Member States.[36]

The affirmation of the ability to pay as a European principle dates back to the well-known *Schumacker* case in which the Court underlined the relevance of the personal and family situation of the non-resident taxpayer for income tax purposes.[37] The CJEU offered protection to the global ability to pay expressed in the total income, with a particular emphasis on its personality characteristic.[38] Starting from the so-called '*Schumacker doctrine*', there has been a consolidated jurisprudential orientation in which the ability to pay and the related consideration of the personal and family situation of the taxpayer has gradually expanded to be applied in discrimination cases between residents and non-residents.[39]

Recently, in the *Vodafone Hungary* and *Tesco* cases, the CJEU treated the ability to pay as a general principle of Union law for the first time and, as such, applied it in its examination of the reasons for prosecuting an extraordinary Hungarian turnover tax which affects multinationals in order to assess

[36] See C Bardini, 'The Ability to Pay in the European Market: An Impossible Sudoku for the ECJ' (2010) 38 *Intertax* 2f.

[37] See Case C-279/93 *Schumacker*, ECLI:EU:C:1995:31; and Case C-9/14 *Kieback*, ECLI:EU:C:2015:406.

[38] According to G Bizioli and E Reimer, 'Equality, ability to pay and neutrality' in CHJI Panayi, W Haslehner and E Traversa (eds), *Research Handbook on European Union Taxation Law* (Edward Elgar Publishing 2020) 72: 'the CJEU seems nevertheless to have introduced a sort of minimum common standard applicable to all Member States: the overall individual and company ability to pay, seen as net income, should be taken into consideration by at least one Member State. In this interpretation, the ability to pay would acquire a definitive supranational dimension'.

[39] See Vanistendael, 'The ability to pay principle in the EU legal order' (n 34) 210 ff. In the jurisprudence see *ex multis* Case C-283/15 X, ECLI:EU:C:2017:102; Case C-632/13 *Hirvonen*, ECLI:EU:C:2015:765; Case C-527/06 Renneberg, ECLI:EU:C:2008:566; Case C-182/06 *Lakebrink* ECLI:EU:C:2007:452; and Case C-169/03 *Wallentin*, ECLI:EU:C:2004:403; Case C-385/00 *De Groot*, ECLI:EU:C:2002:750. See also PL Cardella, 'The cross-border use of losses incurred through foreign permanent establishments: wavering between the territoriality principle and the so-called 'Marks&Spencer exception'. The Bevola and Jens W Trock case' (2018) 3 *Rivista di diretto tributario internazionale* 175; I Richelle, 'Cross-Border Loss Compensation: State and Critique of the Judicature' in I Richelle, E Traversa and W Schön (eds), *Allocating Taxing Powers within the European Union* (Springer 2013) 103 ff.

its compatibility with EU law.[40] In these judgments, the European judges used the ability to pay in order to assess the compatibility of a national provision with Union law and, although they did not mention its European derivation, its use could be fundamental for the development of common tax law. The CJEU seems to raise the ability to pay to the rank of general principle of Union law, applicable to tax matters, in order to assess the rationality and reasonableness of the exercise of the taxing powers of the Hungarian legislator, especially with reference to the repercussions on the European legal system.[41] In the wake of this case law, the same parameter of the ability to pay was used by European judges to assess the legitimacy of a Polish progressive tax on the retail sector linked to turnover[42] as well as a Hungarian progressive tax on turnover related to advertising.[43]

Therefore, the jurisprudential evolution described above has seen a decisive strengthening and broad application of the ability to pay which could constitute a general principle of Union law as it results from the constitutional traditions common to the Member States *ex* Article 6(3) TEU. The ability to pay, as a principle shared at a constitutional level by Member States, represents a fundamental aspect for any form of European taxation aimed at delimiting the 'right tax' and guaranteeing the financing of public goods to meet the needs of the Community.[44]

IV. SOME THOUGHTS ON THE EUROPEAN PLASTIC TAX AS A MISUNDERSTOOD EXAMPLE OF A EUROPEAN TAX

Under current legislation, and in the absence of an express attribution of taxing powers to Europe, it is necessary to enhance and implement Article 311 TFEU which requires the financing of the European budget through own resources and, at the same time, the respect of the tax sovereignty of Member States.[45] Thus, it is necessary to conduct a legal study on the so-called 'European Plastic Tax' as a new own resource that levies the weight of non-recycled plastic packaging waste in order to verify its nature as a European tax and its compliance with the

[40] See Grand Chamber, Case C-75/18 *Vodafone Ungheria*, ECLI:EU:C:2020:139; and Case C-323/18 *Tesco-Global Áruházak*, ECLI:EU:C:2020:140. See D Stevanato, 'Are Turnover-Based Taxes a Suitable Way to Target Business Profits?' (2020) 59 *European Taxation* 538.

[41] According to F Vanistendael, 'Ability to pay in European Community Law' (2014) 23 *EC Tax Review* 121: 'The ability to pay principle itself has not been used by the ECJ as a principle on its own to establish infringements against EU law'.

[42] Case C-562/19 P *European Commission v Republic of Poland*, ECLI:EU:C:2021:201.

[43] Case C-596/19 P *European Commission v Republic of Hungary*, ECLI:EU:C:2021:202.

[44] See J Englisch, 'Ability to Pay' in C Brokelind (ed), *Principles of Law: Function, Status and Impact in EU Tax Law* (IBFD 2014) 453 ff.

[45] See A Cordewener, 'The COVID-19 Crisis: An Opportunity for EU Budget and Tax Reform' (2020) 29 *EC Tax Review* 258.

fundamental principles of taxation.[46] This levy was introduced with Council Decision 2020/2053 on the system of own resources of the EU and entered into force on 1 January 2021 as a result of the ratification of the aforementioned Decision by the national parliaments of all Member States.[47] Its establishment was agreed by the heads of state or government of the Member States a few months earlier, at the European Council of 17–21 July 2020 as the first new levy from a basket of new own resources of which the EU will equip itself in the near future in order to collect the revenues to be allocated to the repayment of the debts contracted under the NGEU programme.[48]

As regards the essential elements of the European Plastic Tax, it affects the non-recycled plastic packaging waste generated in each Member State through the application of a uniform levy rate, equal to €0.80/kg, on the weight of such waste.[49] This weight is calculated as the difference between the weight of plastic packaging produced in a Member State in a given year and the weight of plastic packaging waste recycled in the same year.[50]

The objective of such an own resource is mainly non-fiscal as it is intended to provide an incentive for Member States to reduce plastic packaging waste and pollution so as to promote recycling and discourage the consumption of single-use plastic products. In this way it is possible to give concrete implementation to

[46] According to M Allena, 'European Union Own Resources and Post-Covid Sustainability: The Italian Plastic Tax in the European Context' (2021) 61 *European Taxation* 417: 'The European plastic tax is part of a broader plan to define EU own resources to finance the post-COVID-19 recovery.'

[47] Council Decision (EU, Euratom) 2020/2053 of 14 December 2020 on the system of own resources of the European Union and repealing Decision 2014/335/EU, Euratom [2020] OJ L424/1

[48] According to G Cipriani, 'The case for a single and buoyant fiscal source to fund the EU budget' in A de Feo and B Laffan (eds), *EU Own Resources: Momentum for a Reform?* (European University Institute 2016) 43: 'Since the EU has no power to raise taxes, the introduction of new taxation to finance the EU budget would require convincing national governments to "promote" such taxes vis-à-vis their citizens. This would be a somewhat unpopular undertaking, as it would lead to an increase in overall taxation, or at any rate it would be perceived in that way. However, since the current volume of EU resources should remain unchanged, the proceeds from such taxes would only ultimately benefit national budgets. Governments may therefore be tempted to increase their own revenue and lay the blame on the EU'. See also J Haas and E Rubio, 'The future of the European budget' (2017) Notre Europe Policy Paper 199, 1, 3 ff; F Mesdag, 'Towards a new way to finance the EU budget? Reflections on the Monti Report' (2017) CEPOB Policy Brief 7, 1 ff; C Fuest, F Heinemann and M Ungerer, 'Reforming the Financing of the European Union: A proposal' (2015) ZEW Policy Brief 2, 1; AR Leen, 'Seigniorage: A True European Tax' (2012) 21 *EC Tax Review* 331; F Heinemann, P Mohl and S Osterloh, 'Who's afraid of an EU tax and why? Revenue system preferences in the European Parliament' (2009) 4 *Review of International Organizations* 73; S Plasschaert, 'Towards an Own Tax Resource for the European Union? Why? How? And When?' (2004) 11 *European Taxation* 470.

[49] See Council Regulation (EU, Euratom) 2021/770 of 30 April 2021on the calculation of the own resource based on plastic packaging waste that is not recycled, on the methods and procedure for making available that own resource, on the measures to meet cash requirements, and on certain aspects of the own resource based on gross national income [2021] OJ L165/15.

[50] In order to avoid excessively regressive effects on national contributions, annual flat-rate reductions have been envisaged and applied to the contributions of Member States with a per capita Gross National Income (GNI) lower than the European average.

the European strategy on plastics and to undertake a transition path towards a circular and sustainable economy.

For some time now, the EU has taken up the challenge of environmental protection by paying particular attention to the pollution caused by plastic waste: in the Communication entitled 'Towards a Circular Economy: A Zero Waste Programme for Europe',[51] the European Commission has adopted some proposals aimed at developing a more circular economy and promoting recycling in Member States, with a specific emphasis on plastic waste in order to eliminate landfill or incineration and to encourage the reuse of materials. The transition to a 'zero waste' economy was envisaged in the Communication 'Closing the Loop – An EU Action Plan for the Circular Economy'[52] where, with a specific reference to plastics, the Commission announced the study of specific provisions to encourage reuse and the cessation of their qualification as waste. In line with the European strategy for plastic waste,[53] the EU set out to increase the recycling of plastics, including packaging, to stimulate eco-design and to adopt provisions to facilitate cross-border trade in recyclable plastics. To this end, a Communication was adopted in 2018 containing a new 'European Strategy for Plastics in a Circular Economy'[54] aimed at protecting the environment from plastic pollution and, at the same time, promoting growth and innovation. The recent Directive 2019/904 of the European Parliament and of the Council on the reduction of the impact of certain plastic products on the environment, set new restrictions on certain single-use plastic products as well as ambitious collection and recycling targets for plastic bottles.[55] Finally, the European Green Deal[56] and the new Action Plan for the Circular Economy of the European Commission[57] contain a complex set of initiatives to tackle plastic pollution not only in Europe, but also globally.

In this regulatory context, the EU intends to pursue environmental targets through the application of the contribution on non-recycled plastic packaging. However, despite the aim of the own resource, the latter does not directly levy the behaviour of the taxpayer who does not differentiate plastic waste, but it

[51] Communication of 25 September 2014 COM(2014) 398 final 2.

[52] Communication of 2 December 2015 COM(2015) 614 final.

[53] Green Paper, 'On a European Strategy on Plastic Waste in the Environment' COM(2013) 123 final.

[54] Communication of 16 January 2018 COM(2018) 28 final.

[55] See also the Court of Auditors' review no 4/2020 entitled 'EU Action to Tackle the Issue of Plastic Waste'.

[56] Communication of 11 December 2019 COM(2019) 640 final. See E Traversa, 'The Tax Implications of Global Warming: Preparing for a Change of Climate' (2020) 48 *Intertax* 468; M Van Hulten, 'The Green Deal Consultations: Well-Being Aims and Tax Related Reforms' (2020) 29 *EC Tax Review* 263; T Rosembuj, 'Climate Change and the New Green Deal' (2019) 4 *Rivista giuridica AmbienteDiritto.it* 15. See also AP Dourado, A Pirlot and E Traversa, 'Editorial: Environmental Tax: International Tax Coordination & Global Environmental Challenges' (2021) 11 *Intertax* 866.

[57] Communication of 11 March 2020 COM(2020) 98 final entitled 'A New Circular Economy Action Plan. For a Cleaner and More Competitive Europe'.

'levies' exclusively the Member States, evidently in order to incentivise them into adopting domestic policies in favour of recycling, including the establishment of national plastic taxes.[58] However, such a 'strategy' risks generating fragmentation and heterogeneity in the taxation of plastic materials in the EU, with an inevitable impact on the proper functioning of the Single Market, given that each Member State sets domestic tax rules independently and without any coordination.[59] For example, there could be cases of double (or multiple) taxation since plastic packaging would be levied not only by the own resource, but also by the national Plastic Tax as well as landfill tax so that the entire industrial chain active in the plastics sector could be subjected to a heavy tax burden that would be passed on to the end consumer.

In spite of the *nomen juris* of the new own resource (European Plastic Tax), it does not appear to be a European tax, but a mere transfer from Member States to the EU in consideration of the continuing absence of taxing powers recognised at the supranational level of government. In addition, the European taxpayer is not aware of the existence of this new own resource and the deterrent effect seems to apply not to the citizen, but to the Member State: because, as indicated in the seventh clause of the Decision on Own Resources 2020/2053, the choice of the most appropriate measures to achieve the environmental objectives relating to plastics is referred to national policies in accordance with the principle of subsidiarity. Therefore, it would seem to be inconvenient to incorporate the EU own resource into a European Plastic Tax since it does not directly levy neither the producer nor the consumer of single-use plastic products but only the Member State: it is a national transfer to the European budget, invisible to the taxpayer.[60]

To prevent the new own resource from becoming a burden on the budgets of the Member States, a reorganisation of levies on polluting plastic packaging within Member States appears necessary, especially in order to effectively disincentivise failure to recycle plastic. In fact, the establishment of the European contribution on non-recycled plastic packaging waste generated in each Member State has not been followed by the simultaneous adoption of incentives aimed at developing waste collection services and improving recycling procedures.[61] In order to achieve the environmental objective, the new burden that discourages

[58] See E Scuderi, 'Towards a plastic-free economy: the Italian plastic tax' *Rivista di diritto tributario – Suppl online* (7 April 2021) 3, available at: www.rivistadirittotributario.it/2021/04/07/towards-a-plastic-free-economy-the-italian-plastic-tax/. See also A Cordewener, 'EU Budgetary Reform and Tax Harmonization: Becoming Brothers in Arms' (2022) 31 *EC Tax Review* 65. It is important to highlight that the UK Plastic Tax aims to encourage the use of recycled plastic, rather than new plastic, in plastic packaging.

[59] On similar risks of fragmentation in the taxation of the digital economy, see C Sciancalepore, 'Is the EU Heading Towards an ad interim Web Tax?' (2020) 2 *Diritto e pratica tributaria internazionale* 603.

[60] See also, G Cipriani, 'Reforming the EU's Budget Revenue: The case for a visible VAT-based resource' (2016) *CEPS Special Report 150*, 13; G Cipriani, *Rethinking the EU budget: Three unavoidable reforms* (CEPS 2007) 60 ff.

[61] See Allena (n 46) 9.

the production of waste ought to be applied together with specific tax expenditure aimed at offering economic support for the implementation of virtuous models of the circular economy. Moreover, the introduction of the own resource – with effect from 1 January 2021 – has prevented Member States from adopting timely and specific actions relating to the improvement of recycling procedures.

This own resource contributes to the pursuit of the ambitious European environmental protection objectives by levying a new index of ability to pay, different from the traditional ones, so as not to burden taxpayers already affected by the economic crisis resulting from the health emergency. However, from the point of view of public finance, the choice of allocating the revenue collected from the levy on non-recycled plastic to the repayment of the loans and related financial charges relating to the NGEU programme appears worthy of reflection. The direct legal basis used for the establishment of such a levy is Article 311 TFEU, and not Article 192, probably in order to avoid that the revenue collected may, wholly or in part, be used to finance European spending policies relating to the environment, as they will have to contribute to the repayment of the loans. Thus, the EU could not use precious resources to achieve the environmental objectives in the plastic waste sector through the financing of public expenditure or tax expenditure because these are earmarked to the payment of the common debt. Furthermore, there is a well-founded risk that where the new own resource determines a growing reduction in non-recycled plastic packaging in the coming years, the revenue trend could only be decreasing, causing inevitable difficulties for the EU to promptly fulfil its debts. Moreover, already with the transposition in all Member States of Directive 2019/904 of the European Parliament and of the Council on the reduction of the impact of certain plastic products on the environment, the production of single-use packaging is destined to decline drastically and, if the objective of the European strategy for plastics targeting all recycling of all plastic packaging placed on the market by 2030 is to be achieved, the own resource will not produce any revenue. The levy is, in fact, primarily aimed at changing the consumption habits of citizens, favouring the transition to an economy with a low environmental impact and, only secondly, at the production of public revenue. There is, in fact, an inverse function between the effectiveness of the environmental levy and the revenue since such a change in behaviour may, even in the short run, reduce the calculation base, generating inevitable financial coverage problems relating to the debt service, especially in relation to the NGEU programme, as loan repayments will last until 31 December 2058.

V. TOWARDS A NEW EUROPEAN TAX SYSTEM CHARACTERISED BY THE DUTY OF THE CONTRIBUTION AND A PROMOTIONAL FUNCTION

The establishment of the contribution on non-recycled plastic packaging waste seems to have strengthened the system of derivative contributions in the financing of the EU, disappointing the expectations of its conception as a new fiscal own resource, probably due to the fear of compressing the tax sovereignty of Member States.[62] It is true that without any Treaty amendments including a European fiscal capacity, the space available for the establishment of European taxes is narrow. However, a more courageous proposal would have had the merit of reopening the debate on supranational taxing powers that has now become unpostponable because of the global nature of certain phenomena such as climate change and the digital economy.

The need to adopt a common tax system intended as a tool to achieve the objectives of the Treaty that expand towards new horizons, no longer limited to the proper functioning of the Single Market, is increasingly pressing. The modern political challenges to which the EU is called to respond require the adoption of new and targeted spending actions that, in turn, require significant growth in the EU budget that can be pursued through the establishment of new fiscal own resources. Allowing the EU to levy taxes means allowing it to directly exercise a power of direction with reference to the financing choices for common expenditure and, more generally, to addresses political matters.

A European tax system can be designed to pursue not only the 'fiscal' purpose of acquiring the necessary public revenues that offer financial coverage to the expenses of the European budget for the pursuit of institutional purposes, but also the 'extra-fiscal' one since the common objectives can be reached both with public spending and by exploiting the incentive or disincentive function of the tax, especially if it is a Pigouvian one, on the behaviour of economic agents. Moreover, even today the European financing system is governed by an 'extra-fiscal' or functional purpose, albeit neutral as it is exclusively oriented towards avoiding distortions and alterations of competition in the Single Market. In this way, it is possible to implement Article 311 TFEU according to which 'the Union shall provide itself with the means necessary to attain its objectives and carry through its policies' so that, through its own resources, including fiscal ones, the Union is allowed to achieve its institutional objectives and common policies. For instance, the proposed 'green' own resources and the European taxation of the digital economy (as an own resource) could allow the EU to achieve its goals within the environmental policies and the creation of a digital Single Market.

Through the establishment of fiscal own resources, it is possible to achieve those common objectives of European significance that the Union's legal system acknowledges and which range from environmental and cultural heritage safeguards to the protection of social rights. The pursuit of these purposes cannot be of less importance than free competition given that, especially following the Lisbon Treaty, the EU should in addition to fundamental freedoms also pay

[62] See A Uricchio and F Giambrone, *European Finance at the Emergency Test* (Casa Editore 2020) 200 ff; extensively, M Schratzenstaller et al, 'EU Taxes as Genuine Own Resource to Finance the EU Budget: Pros, Cons and Sustainability-oriented Criteria to Evaluate Potential Tax Candidates (2016) Fair Tax Working Paper 3; I Begg, *Funding the European Union: A Federal Trust Report on the European Union's Budget* (2005) 26 ff.

increasing attention to social rights and environmental protection so that even taxation characterised by neutrality ought to be accompanied by one characterised by functionality and a promotional role for the achievement of European objectives. Even if we wish to give the EU a role that is attentive exclusively to the needs of the internal market and only, indirectly and subordinately, to the aforementioned 'social' objectives, it must be noted that the market forces, pushed by the 'invisible hand' of Adam Smith, are not able to ensure their achievement as a result of the so-called 'market failures'. For this reason, the common objectives can be achieved at a European level on a subsidiary basis, taking advantage of a supranational taxation characterised by 'extra-fiscal' purposes.[63] From this point of view, there seems to be a parity of objectives between those oriented towards the correct functioning of the Single Market and regarding social rights placed not in a relationship of contrast, but of integration, complementarity and even circularity since the relationship between the two spheres are not necessarily unilateral, but bilateral because it is clear that only sustainable development can ensure lasting economic growth in the free market. The wide variety of European objectives and policies, therefore, could operate within the Union legal system through the balancing of values. Therefore, a European system of taxation would adopt new tax models, different from those traditionally applied in the Member States, especially with regard to the purposes as European taxation is oriented towards the pursuit of extra-fiscal objectives. It seems that a new and innovative manifestation of the taxation phenomenon is taking shape at the European level where the redistributive and reallocation function of the tax is accompanied by the 'earmarking' function, always marked by solidarity effects, in which the levying of a European tax allows the pursuit of common purposes, with reference to environmental, social and employment issues. This evolution of the European tax system would allow easier integration with the systems of the Member States and represents a natural completion so that, in general, in the resulting tax system distributional purposes would coexist with fiscal justice, social equity and economic neutrality while respecting the principle of solidarity, which would justify the tax obligation in terms of duty, and within the limits of the ability to pay.

It is important to orientate the European legal order towards an autonomous and true system of fiscal own resources, especially through the adoption of a European system of taxation that requires the transfer of a share of the

[63] According to the Communication from the European Commission of 18 May 2021, COM(2021)251 final – entitled 'Business Taxation for the 21st Century' 'Behavioural taxes, such as environmental and health taxes, continue to be of growing importance for EU tax policies. Well-designed environmental taxes help to support the green transition by sending the right price signals, as well as implementing the polluter pays principle. They also generate revenue that could compensate some of the needed labour tax cuts. Similarly, health taxes, for example on tobacco or alcohol, can improve public health and save lives, while reducing the pressure on public health systems'.

taxing powers from the Member States to the EU, the enhancing of the decision-making by the European Parliament and the creation of a supranational and independent tax authority. The difficult evolution from an EU focused only on economic issues to a political Union inevitably requires the attribution at the European level of the power to establish taxes: the creation of a fiscal Union, in fact, represents only one piece of a true Union, economic and political.[64] *De jure condendo*, an amendment of the Treaties and a simultaneous transfer of fiscal sovereignty to the EU would allow the foundation of an authentic European system of taxation.

In the vision of a union conceived no longer as a union of states, but as a union of peoples which are granted specific rights – *in primis* those deriving from European citizenship, additional to and not a substitution for national citizenship – it appears necessary to shift the tax burden from the Member States to the citizens.[65] In fact, every day, European citizens and businesses make use of rights and freedoms, including the free circulation of goods, services, capital and people, thanks to the European legal order, without realising it and without contributing directly to its cost.[66]

It is necessary to introduce a proper European system of taxation that can legally and functionally be linked to the benefits ensured by the European legal order to create a link between taxation and common policies, as already exists today with reference to customs duties and the Customs Union. It is possible to levy the benefit achieved by the taxpayer, as a consequence of the activity of the EU, which allows the measurement of the ability to pay. Furthermore, a European system of taxation must be able to exploit the advantages of supranational taxation and levy international manifestations of wealth in order to produce added value: from the principle of a vertical subsidiarity perspective, the system should levy those incomes characterised by high mobility, which today escape from Member States, so as to attract new taxable income.

[64] See AP Dourado and M Poiares Maduro, 'A Plead for the European Union Fiscal Autonomy' (2020) 48 *Intertax* 695.

[65] According to M Bordignon and S Scabrosetti, 'The political economy of financing the EU budget' (2016) SIEP Working Paper 708, 10: 'Lack of citizen's accountability is also not an issue, as money belongs to Member State governments, not to citizens. Finally, "unfairness" across Member States is also not an issue; it is the potential result of a bargaining game across countries with side payments where some countries might have got more in some periods and less in others, to accommodate changing bargaining powers'.

[66] According to the reflection paper on the future of EU finances of the European Commission 'At around 1% of the combined gross national income (GNI) of its Member States, the EU budget is relatively small. For every €100 earned, European citizens pay an average of €50 each in taxes and social contributions, only €1 of which goes towards funding the EU budget. For less than the price of a cup of coffee a day, Europeans fund an EU budget that manages a wide range of issues that go beyond national borders and necessitate a European or international response. From climate and energy, to migration, consumer protection, globalisation, employment, the single market and the common currency, the budget contributes to the prosperity of EU citizens and the success of common policies. Experience has shown that even a modest budget at European level can have a major impact on the ground.' See also, A Alesina, I Angeloni and L Schuknecht, 'What does the European Union do?' (2005) 3 *Public Choice* 275.

Through their fiscal duty, European citizens will be made aware of their rights and the European added value they enjoy on a daily basis so as to make the Union an international organisation closer to the needs of the people.[67] The fiscal duty, in fact, would allow the development of a sense of belonging to a community characterised by a commonality of values, not only economic values, but mainly of solidarity. Therefore, it represents the other side of the coin of the production of common public goods directly by the EU in order to avoid the current misalignment between power and responsibility to respond to the needs of citizens that generates a democratic deficit and a disaffection of the latter. The institution of a European levy and the direct contribution of citizens could represent a catalyst for greater integration and social cohesion marked by the development of a European civic sense to make them participate in the management of *res publica*, albeit supranational, and allow them to evaluate the policies adopted by the EU according to the principle of accountability and disclosure.[68] Taxes are, in fact, imposed on taxpayers to finance public action that aims to meet the needs of the community with the application of the principles of redistribution and horizontal and vertical equity.[69]

The establishment of a European tax allows for a strengthening and enhancement of European citizenship, especially if used as a financing instrument for common public goods, including the creation of a European welfare system, as an expression of transnational solidarity that recognises and protects social rights more than those protected by each Member State.[70] Moreover, the principle of solidarity represents a general principle of the EU emerging from the combined provisions of Articles 2, 3 and 21 TEU, as well as a fundamental value traceable in the constitutional provisions of all Member States that must be applied not only among countries, but also among European citizens.[71]

[67] See C Lahusen and M Grasso, 'Solidarity in Europe: A Comparative Assessment and Discussion' (Palgrave Studies in European Political Sociology, 2018) 253 ff.

[68] See I Kalfin, 'The Importance of Own Resources in the EU Budget' in B Laffan and A de Feo (eds), *EU Financing for Next Decade Beyond the MFF 2021–2027 and the Next Generation EU* (European University Institute 2021).; G. Cipriani, 'Making Taxpayers' Contributions to the EU Budget Visible' in P Stephenson, ML Sánchez-Barrueco and H Aden (eds), *Financial Accountability in the European Union* (Routledge 2020); AR Leen, 'What an EU Tax Means (From Collective to Individual Net Positions)' (2011) 20 *EC Tax Review* 203.

[69] See F Vanistendael et al (eds), 'European Solidarity Requires EU Taxes' (4 May 2020) *Tax Notes International* 577–78.

[70] See Stefano Dorigo, 'The coronavirus emergency and solidarity in Europe: Is it time for a EU tax?' (*EU Law Live*, 26 June 2020) 23, 12 ff, available at: eulawlive.com/?s=Dorigo.

[71] According to M Poiares Maduro, 'A New Governance for the European Union and the Euro: Democracy and Justice' (2012) RSCAS Policy Paper 11, 13: 'If conceived in this way, the new EU own resources would not only provide the EU with the funds necessary to support the proposed budget increase but would also contribute to a clearer justification of the project of European integration. Furthermore, only in this way will we be able to legitimate solidarity within the Union on any meaningful and lasting basis. It is essential that the Union is seen as redistributing Union wealth and not merely the wealth of some Member States. It is equally important for this solidarity to be related to the different degree to which different social groups benefit from European integration and, particularly, the internal market'.

The tax represents an instrument of participation belonging to the European community and allows the overcoming of a 'restricted' concept of Union citizenship, often reduced to a mere appendix of the citizenship of a Member State, through the creation of a relationship of a contributory nature between the payment of the tax and the advantage given by the system of freedom and protections guaranteed by European law. This European system of taxation, governed by provisions of secondary law, ought to be to the advantage of the taxpayer and be derived from the action of the Union in the transnational dimension such as, for example, the internal market and the freedoms made available by the European system. Thus, the revenue should finance the European budget in order to feed the common expenditure aimed at the production of European public goods and the creation of added value, with a keen eye on solidarity and redistribution. A similar greater involvement of European citizens could be an opportunity for a push from below in order to reach ever-increasing levels of integration that could also lead to institutional changes aimed at building a federal union.

VI. CONCLUSIONS

The transfer of the share of national fiscal sovereignty should be achieved in favour of a new European political entity arising from the amendments of the Treaties and the abolition of the principle of unanimity. The European democratic deficit can, in fact, only be overcome through an evolution of integration so that the legislative process ought to be removed, at least in part, from the governments of Member States and attributed to democratically elected bodies – such as the European Parliament – which would also be responsible for controlling the work of the Commission. Only by decisively addressing the transition of the current European institutional model towards a federal union and, therefore, through a transfer of tax powers to the EU, is it possible to find a solution to the critical issues examined previously. The difficulties encountered in the process of reforming the financing system through the establishment of a European system of taxation can be overcome by following the path of fiscal integration that aims at abandoning the principle of unanimity and conferring new powers on the European Commission, but especially a fiscal law-making power to the European Parliament, with an inevitable downsizing of the political weight of the Council.

With the introduction of a federal institutional system, it would be possible to build a European tax order and establish a federal tax that finances EU public spending which is based on common principles of tax justice.[72] In this system, state and local taxes coexist with European ones within a federal tax system and

[72] See M Schratzenstaller, 'Tax-based Own Resource as a Core Element of a Future-Oriented Design of the EU System of Own Resources' (2018) 53 *Intereconomics* 301.

can be managed by the Member States and territorial divisions to pursue different purposes, fiscal or extra-fiscal, in compliance with common constraints. In this regard, the amendments of the Treaties necessary to introduce a federal institutional architecture should not be limited to positivising the financial autonomy of the EU as a federal state, but it will be necessary to attribute taxing powers and the power to coordinate national tax policies to the supranational level of government. It is thus conceivable to create a sort of European fiscal federalism, an alternative to harmonisation and approximation, within which to build a regulatory framework common to the Member States.

It is certainly true that such a reform could only be approved by Member States that would see their sovereignty eroded, especially in the current political context in which Europe does not yet seem ready for an acceleration of the integration process. The timing for a revision of the EU financing system is subject to the emergence of a favourable political framework, but the health emergency caused by Covid-19 could offer the propitious context in which to justify a reform of such importance.[73] In fact, it appears necessary to introduce a European tax system through the establishment of new own resources, destined to feed the European budget so as to finance, at least partially, the redistributive and anti-pandemic interventions, especially in the context of the NGEU programme which necessitated a strong exposure on the financial markets.[74]

The NGEU programme, albeit limited to the impacts of the health emergency, could be extended in the years to come where it would prove appropriate for the pursuit of European economic, social and environmental objectives, making it impossible to postpone the creation of supranational taxation, also through a transfer of taxing powers.[75] The coronabonds could act as a precursor for the creation of a fiscal union, characterised by a common fiscal capacity and financial autonomy.

[73] See F Vanistendael, 'Will the Coronavirus Pandemic Cure the EU Budget?' (20 June 2020) *Tax Notes International* 5; E Traversa and G Bizioli, 'Solidarity in the European Union in the Time of COVID-19: Paving the Way for a Genuine EU Tax?' (2020) 48 *Intertax* 743, 751 ff. See also K Pantazatou, 'Promoting solidarity in crisis times: Building on the EU Budget and the EU Funds' (2015) 7 *Perspectives on Federalism* 49.

[74] See G Cipriani, 'Improving the Accountability of the EU Budget's Multi-Level Implementation: Strengthening the Contribution of the European Court of Auditors' (2021) 22 *German Law Journal* 466. See also B Laffan, 'Own resources: the need for a reform' in A de Feo and B Laffan (eds), *EU Own Resources: Momentum for a Reform?* (European University Institute 2016).

[75] See F Vanistendael, 'The Crisis: A Window of Necessity for EU Taxation' (2010) 50 *European Taxation* 394.

8

A New System of EU Tax-Based Own Resources: How does it Affect the Fiscal Sovereignty of Member States?

MARIYA SENYK*

I. INTRODUCTION

PRIOR TO 1 January 2021, the system of EU own resources, established in 1970,[1] consisted of traditional own resources, such as customs duties, agricultural duties and sugar levies, the VAT-based own resource and the GNI-based own resource. Traditional own resources belong to the European Union (EU) but are collected by Member States in exchange for a collection fee.[2] The VAT-based own resource constitutes the application of a uniform call rate of 0.3 per cent to a complex statistical calculation of the harmonised VAT base paid by Member States from their tax income.[3] The GNI-based own resource serves as a balancing element calculated as the application of a uniform percentage levy on Member States' gross national income.[4]

A need to reform the system of EU financing has been in the air for decades.[5] In 2014, the high-level group on own resources (HLGOR) was created consisting of representatives from the European Commission, the European Parliament and the Council to find 'more transparent, simple, fair and democratically accountable ways to finance the EU'.[6] The HLGOR published its final report

* Senior lecturer, Faculty of Law, Lund University.

[1] 70/243/ECSC, EEC, Euratom: Council Decision of 21 April 1970 on the replacement of financial contributions from Member States by the Communities' own resources [1970] OJ L94 (no longer in force).

[2] European Parliament, Policy Department for Budgetary Affairs, Directorate-General for Internal Policies, *Reform of the EU own resources*, PE 690.963, March 2021, 6.

[3] ibid 6.

[4] ibid 7.

[5] See, eg, European Commission, 'Financing the EU Budget: Report on the Operation of the Own Resources System' Commission Staff Working Paper, SEC(2011) 876 final 2, Brussels 2011, Part 1 in section 5.

[6] HLGOR, Press release, 17 January 2017, available at: ec.europa.eu/info/strategy/eu-budget/long-term-eu-budget/2014-2020/revenue/high-level-group-own-resources_en.

in December 2016 with a number of recommendations about the reform of the EU budget. In particular, one recommendation concerned linking the EU budget to EU policies. In terms of impact on Member States, the EU budget should be measured by 'the collective benefit of the EU policies, economic synergies, cross-border effects and positive external outcomes'.[7] The reform of the EU own resources should be based on the principle of subsidiarity, whereby the powers of the national authorities to determine them should be respected and any expenditure should undergo a subsidiarity test to set a level at which it would be best done.[8] The final report of the HLGOR highlights the notion of a 'European added value' resulting from the EU's interventions.[9] When it comes to the composition of the EU budget, the HLGOR suggests a combination of new own resources options establishing a link with EU policies and reflecting the principle of a European added value, in particular:

- Resources linked to the Single Market and fiscal coordination – a reformed VAT-based resource, corporate income tax-based resource, financial transaction tax.
- Resources related to energy, climate, environmental, transport policies – a CO2 levy, proceeds from the EU emissions trading system, an electricity tax, and excise duties on fossil fuels.[10]

The necessity to introduce new own resources received a new impetus after the Covid-19 pandemic, which led to the adoption of an economic recovery plan – Next Generation EU (NGEU) – a temporary instrument channelled through the EU long-term budget aimed at boosting the recovery of economic and social damages after the pandemic.[11] Inasmuch as the NGEU is to be financed through external borrowings on capital markets, new own resources are necessary to repay the debts. A political agreement on the introduction of new own resources (Own Resources Decision)[12] was reached during the negotiations on the Multiannual Financial Framework (MFF) for 2021–2027[13] with a new own resource based on non-recycled plastic packaging waste in place since 1 January 2021 (the so-called, 'EU Plastic Tax').[14] The roadmap for the introduction of new own resources was

[7] HLGOR, *Future Financing of the EU – Final report and recommendations of the High Level Group on Own Resources* (December 2016) 7.

[8] For a complete list of recommendations, see HLGOR (December 2016) (n 7) 10–14.

[9] ibid 11.

[10] ibid 12.

[11] Council Regulation (EU) 2020/2094 of 14 December 2020 establishing a European Union Recovery Instrument to support the recovery in the aftermath of the COVID-19 crisis [2020] OJ L433 I/23 (EURI Regulation).

[12] Council Decision (EU, Euratom) 2020/2053 of 14 December 2020 on the system of own resources of the European Union and repealing Decision 2014/335/EU, Euratom [2020] OJ L 424/1 (Own Resources Decision).

[13] *Reform of the EU own resources* (n 2) 6.

[14] Own Resources Decision (n 12).

laid down in Annex II of the Interinstitutional Agreement concluded between the European Parliament, the Council and the Commission on budgetary discipline, cooperation on budgetary matters and sound financial management (Interinstitutional Agreement).[15] Among other things, the Interinstitutional Agreement is aimed at establishing cooperation regarding the introduction of new own resources over the period of the MFF between 2021 and 2027 for the repayment of the European Union Recovery Instrument (EURI) established under the EURI Regulation:[16]

> [I]n order to enhance the credibility and sustainability of the European Union Recovery Instrument repayment plan, the Institutions will work towards introducing sufficient new own resources with a view to covering an amount corresponding to the expected expenditure related to the repayment.[17]

The introduction of new own resources should also reduce the national GNI-based contribution to the EU budget and attain better expenditure at the EU level on common public goods, which would be more efficient in comparison to national spending. According to the Interinstitutional Agreement, the new own resources of the EU should meet the following criteria (not exhaustive list):

- Be aligned with EU policy objectives and should support Union priorities, such as the European Green Deal and fit for the Digital Age.
- Contribute to fair taxation and the strengthening of the fight against tax fraud and evasion.
- Aim at reducing red tape and burden for companies.
- Fulfil the criteria of simplicity, transparency, predictability and fairness.[18]

The first step in the introduction of the new own resources under the Interinstitutional Agreement encompasses an 'EU plastic tax', revenues from the Carbon Border Adjustment Mechanism (CBAM), a digital levy and a reviewed EU Emissions Trading System (ETS) with a possible extension to include aviation and maritime transport. Additional own resources will be proposed by the Commission to be introduced by 1 January 2026 with a possible inclusion of a Financial Transaction Tax (FTT) and a financial contribution linked to corporate taxation.[19]

In December 2021, the Commission proposed three new own resources to be included in the first basket with an implementation date on 1 January 2023,

[15] Interinstitutional Agreement between the European Parliament, the Council of the European Union and the European Commission on budgetary discipline, on cooperation in budgetary matters and on sound financial management, as well as on new own resources, including a roadmap towards the introduction of new own resources [2020] OJ L433I/28.

[16] See n (11) above.

[17] Preamble to Annex II of the Interinstitutional Agreement (n 15) point F.

[18] Annex II Part A of the Interinstitutional Agreement (n 15).

[19] Annex II Part B of the Interinstitutional Agreement (n 15).

namely, a part of the revenues generated by the ETS, an own resource based on the CBAM and the share of the residual profits of the largest and the most profitable multinational enterprises reallocated to the EU based on an international agreement on Pillar One.[20] Undoubtedly, the NGEU will have an impact on the budgetary powers of the Member States for a long period of time by creating considerable financial liabilities for the EU, which would have to be repaid through the own resources of the EU.[21] Furthermore, the EU may have recourse to the Member States in case of a lack of own resources.[22] The introduction of new own resources also gives rise to a question of their interplay with the fiscal sovereignty of Member States, and the more general question of whether the EU is moving towards obtaining its own fiscal sovereignty.[23] The aim of this chapter is, therefore, to analyse how the new system of own resources of the EU, which is currently on the agenda of the EU legislature, will affect the fiscal sovereignty of Member States. This links to a broader question about what limitations concerning the fiscal sovereignty of Member States are the result of membership of the EU and, in particular, the extent to which the Member States have given up their fiscal sovereignty in favour of the EU. The chapter ends with a conclusion regarding the impact of the new own resources of the EU on the fiscal sovereignty of Member States including their power to decide over their national tax systems.

For the purposes of the discussion, it is necessary to first define what the fiscal sovereignty of a state actually means and how it is challenged by the necessity to address global issues which cannot be resolved by individual states. This will be done in section II. Section III briefly outlines the competence of the EU in tax matters and more specifically lists the legal mechanisms that may be employed by the EU to affect the sovereignty of Member States in this area. Section IV concerns the definition of the term 'EU tax' along with the criteria that have to be met to fall within the scope of this definition. This is required to assess which of the proposed new own resources resemble the features of an 'EU tax', which is done in section V. A classification of a tax-based own resource as an 'EU tax' may serve as an argument for claiming that the EU is obtaining its own fiscal sovereignty. Finally, the conclusions are presented in section VI.

[20] Communication from the Commission to the European Parliament, the Council, the European Economic and Social Committee and the Committee of the Regions, 'The next generation of own resources for the EU budget' COM(2021) 566 final. See also Proposal for a Council Decision amending Decision (EU, Euratom) 2020/2053 on the system of own resources of the European Union COM(2021) 570 final.

[21] *Budgetary power* is inherent in a state's sovereignty; it refers to a state's ability to determine its own budget on a revenue and expenditure sides in accordance with its constitutional commitments.

[22] Art 9(4) Own Resources Decision (n 12).

[23] Another issue recognised by scholars concerns the creation of constitutional issues in the Member States. This, however, lies outside the scope of this chapter. For more information, see, eg, L-S Päivi, *Between European Commitment and 'Taking the Law Seriously': The EU Own Resources Decision in Finland, VerfBlog*, 2021/4/29, available at: verfassungsblog.de/between-european-commitment-and-taking-the-law-seriously/, DOI: 10.17176/20210429-181619-0.

This chapter focuses on the legal aspects of the introduction of new tax-based own resources of the EU as a consequence of the NGEU recovery plan. An overview of the proposed own resources is limited to those resources that the Commission has suggested should be introduced in the first basket on 1 January 2023.[24] The effectiveness of the introduction of certain tax measures at the EU level is left outside the scope of this chapter. Likewise, it is not within the scope of this contribution to analyse whether a possibility to attract borrowed funds under the NGEU is compliant with the provisions of the EU Treaties governing the budgeting powers of the EU, in particular when it comes to the interpretation of Articles 310 and 311 of the Treaty on the Functioning of the European Union (TFEU).[25]

II. THE PRINCIPLE OF FISCAL SOVEREIGNTY

A. Defining the Concept

The concept of 'sovereignty' may be viewed from different angles, in particular, as an attribute of people who constitute a source of power or a state as a supreme authority.[26] Different theories about how to understand the notion of 'sovereignty' may be found in the literature.[27] Some conceive it as a means of protection from external threats while others see it as a means to attract external assets even if it requires a transfer of certain competences to the supranational level.[28] Notwithstanding the existence of different perceptions of the notion of 'sovereignty', a common feature of most of the definitions is that it is a supreme authority within a certain territory.[29] When it comes to the scope of matters over which an authority holder is sovereign, the distinction may be made between absolute and non-absolute.[30] An example of non-absolute sovereignty in certain matters is EU Member States that have conferred a part of their sovereignty in a number of areas on the EU. Some scholars make a distinction between domestic, Westphalian and international legal sovereignty.[31] Domestic sovereignty denotes the legitimacy and effectiveness of the authority within a state; Westphalian

[24] COM(2021) 570 final (n 20).

[25] Consolidated version of the Treaty on the Functioning of the European Union [2016] OJ C 202.

[26] F Farri, *Tax Sovereignty and the Law in the Digital and Global Economy* (Routledge 2020) 9.

[27] See, eg, P Nagan Winston and M Haddad Aitza, 'Sovereignty in Theory and Practice' (2012) 13 *San Diego International Law Journal* 429, available at: scholarship.law.ufl.edu/facultypub/293/.

[28] *Europe and sovereignty: Reality, limits and outlook*, Conference report by F Frigot and E Bonadonna (Robert Schuman Foundation 2016), available at: www.robert-schuman.eu/en/european-issues/0410-europe-and-sovereignty-reality-limits-and-outlook.

[29] See the definition of 'sovereignty' in the Stanford Encyclopedia of Philosophy, available at: plato.stanford.edu/entries/sovereignty/.

[30] ibid.

[31] P Dietsch, 'Rethinking sovereignty in international fiscal policy' (2011) 32 *Review of International Studies* 2109.

sovereignty is based on the principle of non-intervention in the internal affairs of other states, whereas international legal sovereignty outlines the status of the states in the international community.[32]

A central attribute of sovereignty is the jurisdiction of a state, which is a corollary of the former, and may be defined as the lawful power to make and enforce rules and to control the conduct of natural and juridical persons in a narrow sense, and in a broader sense, as a lawful power to act and to decide whether and how to act.[33] Fiscal jurisdiction, ie, the power to impose taxes, may be defined as 'the power to determine the territorial application of tax laws in accordance with the principles recognised by international law'.[34] In the context of tax law, the terms 'fiscal sovereignty' and 'fiscal jurisdiction' are often used interchangeably, although this might not be correct from the perspective of international law.[35] For the purposes of this contribution, the term 'fiscal sovereignty' will be used to denote both terms.

Traversa and Pirlot identify different aspects of tax sovereignty,[36] namely:

- So-called 'technical autonomy' – the ability to define all aspects of a tax system, such as a tax base, tax rates etc.
- 'Exclusive territorial application' – the power to determine the territorial application of tax laws in accordance with the principles of international law.[37]

Fiscal sovereignty should be delineated from fiscal policy. The latter encompasses measures employed by governments to stabilise the economy, specifically by manipulating the levels and allocations of taxes and government expenditure.[38] Thus, the exercise of fiscal policy includes several aspects, whereby an ability to decide on taxes is one side of the coin and deciding the volume and the direction of expenditures is the other.[39] By comparing fiscal sovereignty, on the one hand, with fiscal policy, on the other, one may speak about the distinction between the legitimate authority and available tools to conduct such an authority.

[32] ibid 2109.

[33] R Bernhardt, *Encyclopedia of Public International Law*, vol 3 (1997) 55. Brownlie also defines 'the principle of jurisdiction' as a corollary to sovereignty distinguishing between three aspects thereof, namely, judicial, legislative and administrative aspects. See I Brownlie, *Principles of Public International Law*, 6th edn (Oxford University Press 2003) 297.

[34] E Traversa and A Pirlot, 'Tax Sovereignty and Territoriality under Siege: How Far Should the EU Freedoms of Movement Impact on the Territorial Allocation of Taxing Powers Between Member States?' in C Brokelind (ed), *Principles of Law: Function, Status and Impact in EU Tax Law* (IBFD 2014) 128.

[35] RSJ Martha, *The Jurisdiction to Tax in International Law: Theory and Practice of Legislative Fiscal Jurisdiction* (Kluwer Law and Taxation Publishers 1989) 13.

[36] The terms 'fiscal' and 'tax' are used interchangeably in this chapter. 'Fiscal' – ie, pertaining to public revenue. See the definition given in the *Oxford English Dictionary*: www.oed.com.

[37] Traversa and Pirlot (n 34) 128.

[38] The definition is taken from *Encyclopedia Britannica*, available at: www.britannica.com.

[39] F Vanistendael, 'Federalism and the Euro Crisis' (2011) 3 *World Tax Journal*, para 3.4.1.

The 'power of the purse' was a primary prerogative of the legislature, whereby the allocation of resources among competing claims 'was critical to establishing the legitimacy and authority of the legislature as an institution competing with the monarchy'.[40] In many constitutions of the Member States the source of the power to tax is vested on parliaments as representatives of the people. In Sweden, for example, the people are the source of the public power, which is realised through a representative and parliamentary polity and through municipal self-governance.[41] The Swedish Parliament has the competence to adopt decisions on taxes and how the state funds shall be used.[42]

Taking into account the existence of different definitions of the notion of sovereignty, for the purposes of this chapter, 'fiscal sovereignty' refers to the supreme power of a state to decide its own tax system, namely, by defining all constituent elements of a particular tax, as well as, the territorial reach of a tax.

B. Fiscal Sovereignty in the Twenty-First Century

The concept of sovereignty is not static, and it has therefore been developing for a long time with a national state as a starting point, which, however, changed with the formation of supranational institutions and organisations and an increased interdependence between states. Dietsch proposes a new meaning of sovereignty as assigning not only rights but also duties, which corresponds to the notion of sovereignty as a 'responsibility'.[43] In fiscal terms, this implies the obligation of a state to respect the fiscal choices of other states and to ensure a certain redistributive justice in favour of poorer states.[44] Nowadays, the notion of Westphalian sovereignty is challenged when policies of one state may affect other states even though it is without a direct exercise of authority over their policies.[45]

New challenges to national sovereignty were brought about by technological and economic development and a rising need for collective efforts. Some issues may be resolved within a small community, while others are beyond the reach of single states. Over time, communities are required to sustain a large number of joint endeavours, which Tarschys calls 'upward pushing of collective efforts'.[46]

[40] P Posner and C-K Park, 'Role of the legislature in the budget process: Recent trends and innovations' (2007) 7 *OECD Journal on Budgeting* 3, 3.

[41] Regeringsformen, 1 kap 1 §: 'All offentlig makt i Sverige utgår från folket. Den förverkligas genom ett representativt och parlamentariskt statsskick och genom kommunal självstyrelse.'

[42] Regeringsformen, 1 kap 4 §.

[43] Dietsch (n 31) 2108.

[44] ibid 2117–20.

[45] ibid 2111.

[46] D Tarschys, *New funds for the EU: the case for a market access fee* SIEPS (2022), 8, available at: www.sieps.se/en/publications/2022/new-funds-for-the-eu-the-case-for-a-market-access-fee/.

This eventually has an impact on the sovereignty of states, whereby the latter have to give up a part of their sovereign rights in pursuit of global endeavours.

One of the challenges in the tax world relates to tax competition between states resulting in a weakening of the tax base. Tax competition is detrimental to domestic sovereignty in fiscal matters and requires international cooperation in order to be tackled. Different models of international tax cooperation depending on the impact on fiscal sovereignty of a state are possible. Dietsch distinguishes between 'sovereignty – preserving', ie, a form of cooperation which does not require a transfer of sovereign rights, 'sovereignty – compromising', which implies a partial giving up of sovereignty but without establishing a supranational institution, and a world tax authority with substantial powers, where the most realistic scenario lies somewhere in between.[47] International cooperation has the objective of creating an institutional framework to protect the interests of citizens so that they are not undermined by other states. The constraints such an institutional framework imposes should not be viewed as constraints on sovereignty but as constraints of sovereignty.[48] If one views sovereignty as a responsibility, tax cooperation will not be detrimental but rather beneficial to preserving national sovereignty.

It is difficult to disagree with the statement that in the twenty-first century there can be no total national sovereignty due to the existence of global problems like terrorism or global warming.[49] International cooperation underlies a new dimension of fiscal sovereignty, which may be perceived as a multi-tiered concept:

> In a context of interdependence in which cooperation is vital, in areas such as the economy, defence and the climate, we have to consider a type of multi-tiered sovereignty as the embodiment of modern sovereignty, a premise in which the States are sovereign to varying degrees and in different areas.[50]

One can go even further and claim that the people of the world should be regarded as an attribute of international sovereignty. Without going into extremes, the author of this chapter shares a view that fiscal sovereignty in the twenty-first century may only be achieved through international cooperation.

III. COMPETENCE OF THE EU IN TAX MATTERS

The EU has an attributed competence, ie, competence conferred on it by the Treaties.[51] Consequently, the EU cannot decide on its own competence but may

[47] Dietsch (n 31) 2108.
[48] ibid 2116.
[49] Frigot and Bonadonna (n 28).
[50] ibid.
[51] P Craig and G de Búrca, *EU Law: Text, Cases and Materials*, 7th edn (Oxford University Press 2020) 106.

only exercise those powers that are laid down in the Treaties.[52] According to Article 4 of the TEU, 'competences not conferred on the Union in the Treaties remain with the Member States'. Since the power to tax, ie, the power to introduce and levy new taxes, has not been conferred on the EU, it remains within the scope of the fiscal sovereignty of Member States. In other words, the current versions of the EU Treaties do not provide for a legal basis for the imposition of taxes at the EU level and, accordingly, appropriate changes to the EU Treaties would be required for this purpose. Even if a legal mechanism to levy 'EU taxes'[53] had existed, the EU would not have had the power to enforce their collection on the territories of the Member States and, therefore, would have to rely on the latter in this regard. At the same time, the EU is empowered to finance itself through the system of own resources.[54] Any decisions of the Council on the introduction and/or abolition of the existing own resources is subject to the unanimity requirement.

In the area of taxation, the EU has a few exclusive competences but many shared competences with the Member States. Article 3 TFEU establishes the areas of exclusive competence of the EU, which include, inter alia, the Customs Union, wherein the EU may legislate and adopt legally binding acts, whereas the Member States may only do so if empowered by the EU or for the implementation of the EU acts.[55] Import and export duties and other levies established in respect of trade with third countries, as indicated earlier, constitute traditional resources of the EU.[56]

The EU's tax competence serves as an instrument to prevent distortions of competition and the establishment and functioning of the internal market.[57] It differs when it comes to direct and indirect taxes. The harmonisation of the latter was historically considered vital for the establishment of the common market.[58] As such, Article 113 TFEU provides for a full and direct legislative power of the EU for harmonisation[59] in the area of indirect taxation. The EU has exercised its competence regarding the harmonisation of indirect taxes in respect of Value

[52] In the context of the competence in tax matters, the relevant EU Treaties are the Treaty on European Union (consolidated version 2016) (TEU) and TFEU.

[53] The definition of 'EU tax' is given in section IV.

[54] Art 311 TFEU.

[55] Art 2(1) TFEU read in conjunction with Art 3 TFEU.

[56] Art 2(1)(a) Own Resources Decision (n 12).

[57] U Spangenberg, A Mumford and S Daly, 'Navigating taxation towards sustainability: Contradictions between social, gender, environmental, and economic ambitions, obligations and governance capacities in the European tax law' (2018) FairTax Working Paper Series 16, 6.

[58] See, eg, Neumark Report (unofficial translation by Dr H Thurston), in the EEC Reports on Tax Harmonization: the fiscal report of the Fiscal and Financial Committee and the reports of the Sub-groups A, B and C (IBFD 1963).

[59] The concept of 'harmonisation' refers to the process of removal of fiscal barriers and discrepancies between the EU Members. See Organisation for Economic Co-operation and Development (OECD), Glossary of Tax Terms, available at: www.oecd.org/ctp/glossaryoftaxterms.htm.

Added Tax (VAT),[60] excise duties,[61] taxes on the raising of capital[62] and taxes on heavy goods vehicles.[63] In particular, Member States may not impose national taxes that may be regarded as turnover taxes.[64] This prohibition has been introduced to prevent the functioning of the common system of VAT from being jeopardised by the introduction of taxes, duties or charges levied on the movement of goods and services in a way comparable to VAT.[65] Furthermore, the exercise by the Member States of extraterritorial fiscal jurisdiction in the field of VAT is limited due to highly harmonised VAT rules and their interpretation by the European Court of Justice (ECJ).[66] Although belonging to a harmonised area, the VAT Directive provides Member States with a certain degree of discretion, for example, the ability to determine the national VAT rates subject to the conditions of the VAT Directive.

In contrast to indirect taxes, in the area of direct taxation the competence of the EU is rather limited. However, the EU may still affect the exercise of tax competence by the Member States through the adoption of tax coordination measures under Article 115 TFEU and the process of so-called 'negative integration', which is done through legally enforceable prohibitions on certain tax measures of Member States if they violate the internal market requirements, such as, for example, the free movement of goods, persons, capital and services.[67] According to the principle of sincere cooperation, Member States shall take appropriate action to ensure the fulfilment of their obligations under the Treaties and shall refrain from any measure which could jeopardise the attainment of the Union's objectives.[68] Therefore, even though Member States

[60] Council Directive 2006/112/EC of 28 November 2006 on the common system of value added tax [2006] OJ L347 (the VAT Directive).

[61] Council Directive 2008/118/EC of 16 December 2008 concerning the general arrangements for excise duty and repealing Directive 92/12/EEC [2009] OJ L009. In addition to that, other directives govern the application of excise duties to specific types of products, such as alcohol, tobacco and energy.

[62] Council Directive 2008/7/EC of 12 February 2008 concerning indirect taxes on the raising of capital [2008] OJ L46.

[63] Directive 1999/62/EC of the European Parliament and of the Council of 17 June 1999 on the charging of heavy goods vehicles for the use of certain infrastructures [1999] OJ L187.

[64] According to Art 401 of the VAT Directive, Member States may introduce taxes on insurance contracts, taxes on betting and gambling, excise duties, stamp duties or any taxes, duties or charges on the condition that they are not characterised as turnover taxes and provided that their collection does not give rise to cross-border formalities within the EU. For the clarification of the meaning of 'turnover tax' see, eg, case C-200/90 *Dansk Denkavit ApS and P Poulsen Trading ApS, supported by Monsanto-Searle A/S v Skatteministeriet*, EU:C:1992:152.

[65] Case C-200/90 *Dansk Denkavit*, para 11.

[66] The ECJ has particularly stated that the exercise of extraterritorial jurisdiction in respect of VAT should not encroach the jurisdiction of other Member States. See Case 283/84, *Trans Tirreno Express SpA v Ufficio provinciale IVA*, EU:C:1986:31, para 20.

[67] ECCM Kemmeren, 'Sources of EU Law for European Tax Integration: Well-Known and Alternative Legal Instruments' in *Traditional and Alternative Routes to European Tax Integration* (GREIT Series, IBFD 2010) section 2.4.

[68] Art 4(3) TEU.

possess fiscal sovereignty, they may not exercise their taxing powers without taking into account powers conferred upon the EU, in particular in relation to the establishment and functioning of the internal market.[69]

Yet another legal mechanism providing the EU with the possibility to influence the tax policies of Member States is a State aid prohibition laid down in Article 107(1) TFEU. The objective of this prohibition is to prevent distortions of competition resulting from assistance received by companies from their governments.[70] The existence of a wide scope of what may constitute aid, and a limited compatibility regime, result in the limitation in Member States' ability to pursue different policy objectives through fiscal measures.[71] Therefore, State aid provisions in the TFEU may be used by the EU to affect the fiscal sovereignty of Member States.

In the context of the exercise by the EU of its legislative powers in the tax area, the principles of subsidiarity and proportionality should be mentioned in addition to the principle of conferral.[72] The principle of subsidiarity entails that political decisions should be taken at the lowest efficient level.[73]

Under the principle of proportionality, a Union action shall not exceed what is necessary for the achievement of the objectives of the EU Treaties. It also serves as an instrument that limits public authorities in exercising their competence determining the rights and obligations of private parties so that no disproportionate restrictions are imposed on the exercise of the rights by the latter.[74] When it comes to the exercise of fiscal jurisdiction, it is believed that political decisions should be made at the lowest possible level in order to take local conditions into account.[75] This, however, does not exclude that certain actions are best achieved at a more global level.

IV. 'EU TAX'

In order to determine which of the new tax-based own resources may be characterised as an 'EU tax', it is first necessary to define what contributions may be

[69] See in this regard, Case C-279/93 *Finanzamt Köln-Altstadt v Roland Schumacker*, EU:C:1995:31, para 21.

[70] Craig and de Búrca (n 51) 575.

[71] D Pelekis, 'Taxation and state aid: the notion of fiscal state aid and the Commission's new approach' (University of Edinburgh Law thesis and dissertation collection, 2021) 29, available at: era.ed.ac.uk/handle/1842/38109.

[72] The peculiarities of the application of the principles of subsidiarity and proportionality in the process of the adoption of new legislative EU acts are laid down in Protocol No 2 annexed to the TEU and TFEU.

[73] Art 5(3) TFEU.

[74] A Zalasiński, 'The Principle of Proportionality and (European) Tax Law' in C Brokelind (ed), *Principles of Law: Function, Status and Impact in EU Tax Law* (IBFD 2014) section 13.4.1.

[75] Dietsch (n 31) 2114.

classified as a 'tax'. The OECD's working definition of a tax is a 'compulsory unrequited payment to the government'.[76] The following elements are usually recognised in the definition of a tax: (1) a compulsory levy; which (2) is imposed by a governmental body; (3) for public purposes; (4) without a regard to particular benefits received by a taxpayer.[77] The definition of a 'tax' is not definite and may vary from state to state. According to the principle of legality, a tax has to be based on the law. Another feature of a tax is its enforceability,[78] ie, the existence of a legal mechanism for the obedience of taxpayers. Taxes perform a fiscal function by imposing a compulsory contribution on entities and individuals, therefore, on private parties. No tax may be imposed on sovereign states by governmental bodies or organisations. A state may undertake to make compulsory contributions on the basis of a particular agreement, such as in the case of the own resources of the EU. Such contributions, however, may not be considered 'taxes' inasmuch as only sovereign entities may impose taxes. Moreover, contributions based on a particular agreement are not enforceable in contrast to taxes imposed by states on individuals. In particular, in the former case, no property may be seized from a state by another state or organisation in order to ensure that the latter complies with its undertakings to pay a contribution, while other legal instruments may be employed in this regard.

It follows from the above that the imposition of an EU tax would presuppose the possession by the EU of sovereign powers. As stated in section III above, the EU's competence is of an attributed character and is based on those competences which are granted to it by the EU Treaties. The introduction of an EU tax would imply the existence of legislative and revenue EU competences,[79] which is not the case at the current state of the development of the Union. The following criteria may particularly indicate that a particular tax measure resembles features of an EU tax:

- No national legislative actions are required for the implementation of the tax measure.
- The EU has the authority to decide all constituent elements of the tax measure.
- A tax is imposed by the EU legislature and flows directly to the EU budget.
- The EU authorities possess enforcement powers as to the collection of tax revenues.[80]

[76] OECD, Glossary of Tax Terms, available at: www.oecd.org/ctp/glossaryoftaxterms.htm#T.

[77] M Helminen, *General Report* (IFA Cahiers 2016).

[78] ibid.

[79] C Waldhoff, 'Legal Restrictions and Possibilities for Greater Revenue Autonomy of the EU' in T Büttner and M Thöne (eds), *The Future of EU Finances* (Mohr Siebeck 2016).

[80] This function may be delegated by the EU to the Member States.

Different ways of designing a tax-based own resource are possible, and not all of them may be characterised as so-called 'EU taxes'. The following design options could be possible:

- **A revenue-sharing system.** Under this system, a tax is introduced by Member States but constitutes a harmonised area. A part of the revenues collected by the Member States is transferred to the EU budget. This system is also called a 'transfer system'. Currently, a revenue-sharing system is applied in respect of the VAT-based own resource.
- **A surcharge system.** This system presupposes the levying of an EU surcharge in addition to the existing national tax rates, whereby the revenues from the surcharge go to the EU budget. A surcharge system requires the harmonisation of the tax base. A surcharge system has not been implemented by the EU yet.
- **A separation system.** According to this system, the EU introduces a specific tax at the EU level and collects the revenues therefrom. It requires the existence of legislative and revenue competences of the EU.[81]

A separation system would seem to be the only system where one can speak about resembling the features of a genuine EU tax. Currently, such a system applies in respect of customs duties, although the enforcement thereof is still exercised by the Member States. In the customs area, the EU carries out its legislative powers primarily in the form of regulations, which are directly applicable in the Member States. However, this 'exclusive power' to regulate the Customs Union does not flow directly from the Union as a supranational organisation, but has been granted by the Member States that have given up a part of their sovereign competences in favour of the Union.

V. NEW TAX-BASED OWN RESOURCES OF THE EU

A. The Legal Basis for the Introduction

The EU's own resources can be defined as 'revenue allocated irrevocably to the Union to finance its budget and accruing to it automatically without the need for any subsequent decision by the national authorities'.[82] This is a very similar decision to the one a central government would take in order to attribute some fiscal revenue to decentralised regions or smaller geographical entities. Upon

[81] These design options are outlined by M Schratzenstaller and A Krenek, 'Tax-based Own Resources to Finance the EU Budget: Potential Revenues, Summary Evaluation from a Sustainability Perspective, and Implementation Aspects' (2019) FairTax Working Papers Series No 25, 27–28.

[82] HLGOR (December 2016) (n 7) 20.

the approval by the Member States of a new own resource of the EU, the identified source of revenue legally belongs to the EU. However, the Member States have different perceptions concerning the EU's own resources. Some of them consider the GNI-based own resource in particular, as well as the VAT-based own resource, as a transfer from their own budgets.[83]

Several Articles of the TFEU are used by the EU legislature as the legal basis for the introduction of new tax-based own resources. One of them is Article 113 TFEU laying down the Council's competence on the harmonisation of indirect taxes. The author believes that Article 113 TFEU does not constitute a proper basis for the introduction of new taxes at the EU level since the main purpose of the mentioned provision is to harmonise existing taxes and not to impose new ones in those Member States where the latter have not been adopted. The same is true in respect of Article 115 TFEU which is the legal basis for the positive approximation of the legislation of Member States concerning direct taxes. As mentioned in section II.A. above, the power to introduce taxes is traditionally considered to be a prerogative of the national parliaments as representatives of the people.

Another possibility for the introduction of new tax-based own resources follows from Articles 192 and 194 TFEU. The first paragraph of Article 192 TFEU authorises the European Parliament and the Council acting in the ordinary legislative procedure and after consulting the Economic and Social Committee and the Committee of the Regions to take actions in order to achieve environmental objectives listed in Article 191 TFEU. The second paragraph of Article 192 provides for a special legislative procedure to adopt measures of a fiscal nature. Therefore, the Council acting unanimously may adopt fiscal measures required for the achievement of environmental objectives. Similarly, Article 194(3) TFEU constitutes a legal basis for the adoption of fiscal measures, by a special legislative procedure requiring the unanimity of the Council, to attain energy objectives listed in Article 194(1) TFEU. The Articles mentioned may serve as a legal basis for the introduction of new environmental EU levies flowing directly to the EU budget (this, for instance, could be a duty adopted in the form of a regulation, which would be directly applicable in the Member States) subject to unanimity voting in the Council. This, however, may raise constitutional issues in the Member States with constitutions where the source of the power to tax is vested in parliaments representing the people. Notably, the environment and energy form an area of shared competence between the EU and the Member States.[84] This implies that the Member States may exercise their competence in these areas to the extent the EU has not exercised/decided to relinquish its competence.[85]

[83] ibid 21.
[84] Art 4 TFEU.
[85] Art 2 TFEU.

Articles 192 and 194 TFEU do not seem to be a proper legal basis for the introduction of revenue sources to comply with the external borrowing obligations of the EU under the NGEU and, as such, with the main purpose of fiscal nature. Still, such revenue sources may serve as an additional source on the premise that the primary purpose of a tax is the achievement of environmental/energy goals[86] and not the generation of revenue.[87] In other words, environmental taxes should have environmental effects and promote environmentally friendly behaviour. There should be an explicit link between the revenues received from the introduction of environmental fiscal measures and the achievement of environmental and/or energy objectives.

Yet another possibility for the introduction of tax-based own resources could be an enhanced cooperation procedure based on Article 329 TFEU. In its final report, the HLGOR suggested the use of differentiation in justified cases, particularly, by virtue of the enhanced cooperation procedure.[88] According to Article 20 TEU, Member States may establish enhanced cooperation in areas which do not belong to the exclusive competence of the EU, ie, in areas that constitute shared cooperation under Article 4 TFEU. Enhanced cooperation should aim at attaining the objectives of the EU, protect its interests and reinforce integration. The Council adopts the decision authorising enhanced cooperation if the objectives of such cooperation cannot be attained within a reasonable period of time by the Union as a whole, and provided that at least nine Member States participate in it.[89] An example of the use of enhanced cooperation procedure is the introduction of the financial transaction tax. Generally, expenditure for the implementation of an enhanced cooperation procedure is made by the participating Member States except for administrative costs for the institutions. New revenues may arise as a result of the enhanced cooperation by respective Member States. The latter may assign the proceeds for the EU budget and, accordingly, benefit from such proceeds. The participating Member States may also agree through the Own Resources Decision to use the revenues from such enhanced cooperation as own resources for such Member States thus reducing their GNI-based contributions.[90]

[86] Regulation (EU) No 691/2011 of the European Parliament and of the Council of 6 July 2011 on European environmental economic accounts Text with EEA relevance defines 'environmentally related tax' as a 'tax whose tax base is a physical unit (or a proxy of a physical unit) of something that has a proven, specific negative impact on the environment, and which is identified in ESA 95 [The European System of Accounts] as a tax'.

[87] Schratzenstaller and Krenek (n 81) 27.

[88] Two types of differentiation are mentioned in the final report of HLGOR, namely, 'multi-speed' integration, whereby a core group of Member States are willing and able to go further in the integration process on the assumption that other Member States will follow suit, and 'variable geometry' referring to a permanent differentiated integration. See HLGOR (December 2016) (n 7) 62.

[89] Art 20(2) TEU.

[90] HLGOR (December 2016) (n 7) 66.

In view of the fact that enhanced cooperation is established between participating Member States, it cannot authorise the introduction of a new tax-based measure by the EU.

B. An Overview of New Tax-Based Own Resources of the EU

As mentioned in section I above, in the roadmap laid down in the Interinstitutional Agreement, four new own resources are listed for the introduction in the first step, namely, the plastic-based contribution, an own resource based on the CBAM and the ETS, as well as a digital levy. A digital levy, however, has been abandoned for the moment, and the Commission has instead proposed a new own resource amounting to a share of the residual profits of the largest multinational enterprises reallocated to the Member States.[91] Therefore, currently, the four following new resources are to be introduced by 1 January 2023:

1. The EU Plastic Tax

The first tax-based own resource, which has already been introduced and which entered into force on 1 June 2021, constitutes a statistical aggregate calculated as the weight of plastic packaging waste generated in each Member State that is not recycled multiplied with a uniform call rate of €0.80 per kilogram.[92] An annual lump sum of reductions is available to some of the Member States listed in paragraph 3 of Article 2(2) of the Own Resources Decision. The introduction of the plastic-based own resource is linked to the EU policy on a circular economy[93] and, particularly, the objective to promote the recycling of plastic waste.[94] Notably, the management of packaging and packaging waste is harmonised at the EU level.[95] The introduction of the plastic-based own resource will urge Member States to adopt appropriate fiscal measures to achieve the goals of reducing single-use plastic, fostering recycling and boosting the circular economy.[96] Concrete national measures will be decided by the Member States in view of the principle of subsidiarity.[97] The procedure for calculation and making

[91] COM(2021) 566 final (n 20).

[92] Art 2(1)(c) Own Resources Decision (n 12).

[93] Communication from the Commission to the European Parliament, the Council, the European Economic and Social Committee and the Committee of the Regions, 'Closing the loop – An EU action plan for the Circular Economy' COM(2015) 614 final.

[94] Communication from the Commission to the European Parliament, the Council, the European Economic and Social Committee and the Committee of the Regions, 'A European Strategy for Plastics in a Circular Economy' COM(2018) 28 final.

[95] European Parliament and Council Directive 94/62/EC of 20 December 1994 on packaging and packaging waste [1994] OJ L365.

[96] *Reform of the EU own resources* (n 2) 12.

[97] See, eg, about Italian Plastic Tax in M Allena, 'European Union Own Resources and Post-Covid Sustainability: The Italian Plastic Tax in the European Context' (2021) 61 *European Taxation* 417.

the plastic-based own resource available is laid down in Council Regulation (EU, Euratom) 2021/770.[98] Although it is referred to as an 'EU tax', the plastic-based own resource constitutes a compulsory contribution by the Member States to the EU budget directly linked to the EU policy aimed at the reduction of unrecyclable single-use plastic.

2. ETS-Based Own Resource

The EU Emissions Trading System (ETS) launched in 2005[99] constitutes a cap and trading system with the objective of gradually reducing the cap on the total amount of greenhouse gas (GHG) emissions.[100] The cap is set at the EU level and the default method of allocating allowances is an auction.[101] Currently, revenues from the auctioning of allowances go to the Member States respectively but at least 50 per cent of the auctioning revenues must be spent on climate and environmentally related purposes. The Commission has proposed to direct 25 per cent of the revenues from selling ETS allowances to the EU budget.[102] The ETS system is an EU tool aiming at the reduction of GHG emissions with the current purpose of achieving a climate-neutral EU by 2050 and a reduction in GHG emissions of at least 55 per cent compared with 1990 by 2030.[103] The reduction in GHG emissions is also a part of the European Green Deal.[104] Thus, the introduction of the ETS-based own resource is linked to the EU policy in the field of the climate and the functioning of the internal market.

3. An Own Resource Based on CBAM

The purpose of a carbon border adjustment mechanism (CBAM) is to prevent carbon leakage where carbon-intense production is moved abroad due to increased carbon prices in the EU. This policy measure corresponds to the EU's

[98] Council Regulation (EU, Euratom) 2021/770 of 30 April 2021 on the calculation of the own resource based on plastic packaging waste that is not recycled, on the methods and procedure for making available that own resource, on the measures to meet cash requirements, and on certain aspects of the own resource based on gross national income [2021] OJ L165/15. It should be read in conjunction with Council Regulation (EU, Euratom) 609/2014 of 26 May 2014 on the methods and procedure for making available the traditional, VAT and GNI-based own resources and on the measures to meet cash requirements [2014] OJ L 168/39.

[99] Directive 2003/87/EC of the European Parliament and of the Council of 13 October 2003 establishing a scheme for greenhouse gas emission allowance trading within the Community and amending Council Directive 96/61/EC (Text with EEA relevance) [2003] OJ L275.

[100] *Reform of the EU own resources* (n 2) 12.

[101] ibid.

[102] COM(2021) 570 final (n 20).

[103] *Reform of the EU own resources* (n 2) 13.

[104] Communication from the Commission, the European Parliament, the European Council, the Council, the European Economic and Social Committee and the Committee of the Regions, 'The European Green Deal' COM(2019) 640 final.

undertakings in the decarbonisation of the economy,[105] and is linked to the ETS system. The legal basis for the CBAM is Article 192(1) TFEU. The CBAM is supposed to be introduced in the form of a regulation which would be directly applicable in Member States and will not require any implementing measures. The sale of CBAM certificates constitutes a new levy to be introduced in the exercise of the EU of its competence in the field of environment policy. The proceeds corresponding to the price of CBAM certificates at the price calculated by the Commission will be collected by the competent authorities of the Member States.[106] The intention is to reallocate 75 per cent of revenues from the sale of the CBAM certificates to the EU budget as the EU own resource in the form of a national contribution.[107] The Commission will act as a central administrator to maintain an independent transaction log recording the purchase of CBAM certificates, their holding, surrender, re-purchase and cancellation and ensure the coordination of national registers.

4. The Share of a Residual Profit of Multinational Enterprises Reallocated to Member States

Another new own resource which was proposed by the Commission in its amended proposal in December 2021 is the 15 per cent of the share of a residual profit of multinational enterprises reallocated to Member States which are end-market jurisdictions. Reallocation is to be based on a directive on the implementation of the global agreement on the reallocation of taxing rights under Pillar One.[108] A directive is to be proposed by the Commission in 2022.[109] The EU actively supports the work of the OECD/G20 Inclusive Framework on BEPS aimed at reaching a global consensus on fair taxation of multinational enterprises. The legal basis for the introduction of a directive should be Article 115 TFEU, which serves as a basis for the approximation of direct tax legislation of Member States to achieve the proper functioning of the common market. This new tax-based own resource is within the EU's framework for the establishment of fair business taxation within the EU, and is linked to a number of EU policies, such as the European Green Deal, the Digital Agenda for Europe, the New Industrial Strategy, etc.[110]

[105] See Explanatory Memorandum to Proposal for a Regulation of the European Parliament and of the Council establishing a carbon border adjustment mechanism COM(2021) 564.

[106] Proposal for a Regulation of the European Parliament and of the Council establishing a carbon border adjustment mechanism COM(2021) 564.

[107] COM(2021) 570 final (n 20).

[108] In October 2021 more than 135 members of the OECD/G20 Inclusive Framework on BEPS (Base Erosion and Profit Shifting) reached a political agreement on a two-pillar solution addressing tax challenges arising from the digitalisation and globalisation of the economy. Pillar One (Amount A) concerns the reallocation of residual profits of in-scope multinational enterprises to market jurisdictions provided nexus criteria are met.

[109] COM(2021) 570 final (n 20).

[110] Commission, Communication from the Commission to the European Parliament and the Council 'Business Taxation for the 21st Century' COM(2021) 251 final.

C. The Impact on the Fiscal Sovereignty of Member States

As indicated in section II.A above, fiscal sovereignty presupposes a supreme power to decide on a tax system, as well as the territorial reach of a tax. In the context of the EU, the Member States have already transferred a part of their competences in fiscal matters to the EU resulting in the latter having a direct impact on the exercise of the fiscal policies of Member States.[111] Therefore, one could speak of shared competences and cooperation between the Union and its members. This, however, does not change the fact that the sovereign power to tax originates in the Member States, and may subsequently be delegated to the Union.

As has been illustrated in section V.B above, all four new own resources are directly linked to various policies of the EU. In other words, they relate to those objectives which may not be attained within a single state but rather by collective efforts within a larger community, which is the Union. As such, in all those areas, the EU already has some of the competences. When it comes to the 'Plastic Tax', which is not a genuine tax but rather a contribution based on specific indicators, it may be concluded that this new own resource does not directly affect the fiscal sovereignty of Member States. The introduction of the plastic-based contribution by the Own Resources Decision does not explicitly require the introduction by Member States of corresponding domestic taxes. However, it may indirectly influence the legislative choices of Member States which are implicitly urged to cover the expense that has to be transferred to the EU budget.[112] At the same time, Member States are free to define all substantial elements of a specific tax on a non-recycled plastic and its territorial application as long as this kind of tax does not constitute a harmonised EU area.[113] Therefore, the Plastic Tax does not induce the transfer of fiscal sovereignty in terms of the power to tax to the EU.

Another new own resource based on the ETS consists of a part of revenues which will flow from the auctioning of ETS allowances by the Member States. The proceeds from the sale of ETS allowances are linked with particular benefits which taxpayers receive, ie, acquiring the ability to release greenhouse gases into the atmosphere and, accordingly, they do not possess the features of a tax.[114] Furthermore, the ETS system is already a harmonised EU area and, therefore, the Member States have already transferred a part of their competences to the EU. It looks like the introduction of the ETS-based own resource will not bring about any additional constraints on the fiscal sovereignty of Member States.

[111] See section III above.

[112] eg, such a plastic tax has been already introduced in Italy. See Allena (n 97).

[113] Subject to the existing restrictions on the sovereignty of Member States in the form of the prohibition of State aid and the compliance of tax legislation with the conditions of the internal market (negative integration).

[114] See the definition of 'tax' in section IV above.

In contrast to the plastic-based and ETS-based own resources, the introduction of the CBAM and the sale of CBAM certificates seem to affect the fiscal sovereignty of Member States. This fiscal mechanism is directly linked to the environment, which constitutes a shared competence between the EU and the Member States. As soon as the EU introduces this environmental measure with a fiscal character, Member States will lose the possibility to legislate in this particular area to the extent the EU has exercised its competence.[115] In this sense, it may be asserted that the CBAM will have an impact on the fiscal sovereignty of Member States and, in particular, on their power to tax. Similar to the proceeds from the sale of ETS allowances, an own resource based on the sale of CBAM certificates may not be regarded as a 'tax' inasmuch as it relates to specific benefits received by the holders of such certificates. At the same time, this own resource reveals the features of an explicitly EU levy.

The adoption of an EU directive on the implementation of the global agreement on the reallocation of taxing rights under Pillar One would be another step in the approximation of the national legislation of Member States to ensure the proper functioning of the internal market. Although an own resource based on the residual profits of multinational enterprises reallocated to the Member States should not be classified as an 'EU tax', the introduction of such a measure would have an impact on the fiscal sovereignty of Member States. The reallocation of taxing rights under Pillar One will be based on a directive, which will have to be implemented by the Member States through the adoption of the respective national legislation. Although it is difficult to comment to what extent the provisions of this directive would be a constraint on Member States' ability to define the reallocation mechanism before the relevant directive is proposed by the Commission, the author assumes that this tax measure will not leave much discretion for the Member States inasmuch as it would jeopardise the interests of the internal market.

VI. CONCLUSION

As members of the EU, Member States have already transferred certain of their competences in fiscal matters to the EU for the achievement of common goals. The EU has in particular a substantial impact on the fiscal sovereignty of Member States through the various legal instruments made available by the EU Treaties and developed by the ECJ in its jurisprudence. Even in the field of direct taxes, which has been traditionally considered to belong to the exclusive competence of the Member States, the EU may constrain the exercise of fiscal policies by Member States.[116] Therefore, the fiscal competences of Member

[115] According to Protocol (No 25) of the TFEU, this concerns specific elements governed by the EU act and not the entire area belonging to the shared competence.

[116] See section III above.

States have been diluted in favour of cooperation and the achievement of the common EU goals.

The introduction of some of the new tax-based own resources of the EU may affect the fiscal sovereignty of Member States, either directly or indirectly. In particular, the launching of the CBAM or the adoption of a new resource based on the implementation of the global agreement under Pillar One will directly affect the fiscal sovereignty of Member States as these measures require the further approximation of the national tax legislation of the latter and, therefore, will limit their technical autonomy.[117] In the case of the Plastic Tax, one could speak about an indirect effect on the national legislative choices of Member States inasmuch as the Member States preserve their technical autonomy but will eventually be forced to adopt respective national legislative measures. The ETS-based own resource relates to an already harmonised area and accordingly will not cause any additional limitations on the technical autonomy of Member States.

None of the new tax-based own resources may be characterised as an 'EU tax'. An own resource based on CBAM has, at the same time, the characteristic of a levy in respect of trade with third countries which may fall within the category of traditional own resources.[118] The competences of Member States concerning the sale of CBAM certificates would be rather limited. Furthermore, the CBAM will be based on a regulation directly applicable in the Member States, and would not require the adoption of the respective national legislation. Besides that, according to the current vision of the EU proposal, most of the revenues from the sale of CBAM certificates, namely 75 per cent, will flow to the EU budget. The residual part of revenues which is left for the Member States may be perceived as a fee for the collection carried out by the competent authorities of Member States. The sale of CBAM certificates will be under the direct management of the Commission, which will determine the price. It would appear that an own resource based on CBAM will be a genuine EU levy.

Although the introduction of some of the new own resources of the EU will have repercussions on the exercise of the fiscal authority by Member States, it is too early to draw the conclusion that they may be viewed as a step towards more fiscal sovereignty for the EU. Notwithstanding that the EU is apparently obtaining more fiscal competences (this, in particular, would be the case if an own resource based on the CBAM were adopted), these competences originate from the Member States and are not acquired by the Union automatically but rather shared by the Member States for the attainment of common goals. Neither the Plastic Tax, nor the ETS-based own resource reveal features of an 'EU tax' but rather a transfer of a part of the revenues of the Member States to the EU budget under a 'revenue-sharing system'.[119] The same is true in relation to the share of

[117] See section II.A above.
[118] Art 2(1)a Own Resources Decision (n 12).
[119] See section IV above.

residual profits of multinational enterprises. For the application of the proposed tax-based resources in the Member States, for example, the collection of residual profits of multinational enterprises in market jurisdictions, Member States have to adopt appropriate national legislation. Accordingly, the competence to collect such revenues would have its source in national, not EU legislation. The only own resource that has the features of an EU levy is the one based on the sale of CBAM certificates.

What is common for all new tax-based resources, listed in section V.B above, is that they are all connected with EU policies, such as the environment and the proper functioning of the internal market. As such, it may be asserted that they possess an 'intrinsically pan-European character'. None of the policy objectives underlying the tax measures which serve as a basis for the new own resources of the EU may be achieved by a single Member State but rather through collective efforts at the EU level. Moreover, since the goals of such EU policies would be beneficial for all the people of the EU, this would substantiate the transfer of the revenues collected in respect of such policies to the EU budget.

As claimed in section II.B above, international cooperation, which presupposes giving up a part of sovereign rights, may be viewed as a measure aimed at preserving national interests in tax matters and, therefore, as having a positive impact on the fiscal sovereignty of Member States. One example relates to measures, which could be adopted by the EU for the taxation of multinational enterprises. It may be assumed that EU measures in this regard would have a positive effect on the fiscal policies of Member States which will be able to tax a part of the profits generated by such enterprises within their national territories. This would not be possible by exercising the fiscal sovereignty of an individual Member State but exclusively by the means of international cooperation at the EU level.

9

Reconceptualising the Principle of Equality in EU Tax Law

CRISTINA TRENTA*

I. INTRODUCTION

THE CHAPTER EXAMINES the principle of equality as it is traditionally interpreted and applied in European Union (EU) tax law, with the aim to understand the extent to which it is necessary to reconceptualise it after the Lisbon Treaty[1] and the introduction of the EU Charter,[2] which have rendered fundamental and human rights and sustainable development binding principles for the Union.

EU law is built on the principle of equality[3] and on an interpretation of it that has economic origins relating it to the concept of formal equality, firmly tied to the creation of the Common Market in 1957 and to the European Economic Community (EEC) as a community of trade based on the four fundamental freedoms.[4] EU governance in matters of taxation as originally framed in the Treaty of Rome[5] was informed by this view, and led to an EU tax law framework aimed at ensuring equality in terms of competition on the one hand, and

* Associate Professor of Tax Law at Örebro University, Örebro, Sweden. The author is grateful to the Torsten Söderbergs Stiftelse foundation for the financial assistance that made writing this chapter possible.

[1] European Union, Treaty of Lisbon Amending the Treaty on European Union and the Treaty Establishing the European Community [2007] OJ C 306 (Treaty of Lisbon).

[2] European Union, Charter of Fundamental Rights of the European Union [2012] OJ C 326.

[3] Joined Cases 117-76 and 16-77 *Albert Ruckdeschel & Co and Hansa-Lagerhaus Ströh & Co v Hauptzollamt Hamburg-St Annen*; *Diamalt AG v Hauptzollamt Itzehoe*, ECLI:EU:C:1977:160, para 7. See also J Croon-Gestefeld, *Reconceptualising European Equality Law: A Comparative Institutional Analysis* (Hart Publishing 2017) 4.

[4] See European Union, Consolidated version of the Treaty on the Functioning of the European Union [2012] OJ C 326 (TFEU) Art 26(2): 'The internal market shall comprise an area without internal frontiers in which the free movement of goods, persons, services and capital is ensured in accordance with the provisions of the Treaties'. C Bernard, *The Substantive Law of the EU: The Four Freedoms* (Oxford University Press 2016).

[5] European Union, Treaty Establishing the European Community (Consolidated Version), Rome Treaty, 25 March 1957 (Rome Treaty).

economic freedoms on the other.[6] This prevailing aim has led to a 'systematic imbalance between economic and non-economic interests'.[7]

In EU tax law, this modus operandi has resulted in regulations that only implement the concept of formal equality, and which casts taxpayers solely as '*homines oeconomici*', 'agents of the production system'.[8] This is ascertainable, for example, in the line of reasoning followed by the Court of Justice of the European Union (CJEU) in its judicial review of whether the tax systems and the tax regulations of Member States were to be considered a restriction to the exercise of the European economic freedoms, and whether national regimes discriminate against cross-border activities when compared with domestic ones.[9] As a consequence of this approach, overcoming tax discrimination within the EU has been and still is largely dependent on the functioning of the mechanisms of the internal market.[10]

The introduction of a system of protections for fundamental and human rights and for sustainability as part of the EU legal framework implies the addition of a second, substantive dimension to the conceptualisation of the right of equality.[11] This necessarily poses the issue of reassessing the meaning and bearing of the concept itself, and the impact it would have on the power of taxation of the EU.[12]

This chapter investigates whether a substantive model of equality should be adopted in EU tax law in response to the renewed attention given to fundamental and human rights following the Lisbon Treaty, especially considering the impact that the application of these rights is bound to have on taxation and on the power to tax of the Union, with the goal of outlining a more rounded and cohesive approach centred on 'policy integration, linkage and coordination'[13] that considers European taxpayers as human beings and not merely as economic agents.[14]

[6] U Spangenberg, A Mumford and S Daly, 'Navigating taxation towards sustainability: contradictions between social, gender, environmental, and economic ambitions, obligations and governance capacities in European tax law' (Umeå universitet 2018).

[7] G Davies, 'Democracy and Legitimacy in the Shadow of Purposive Competence' (2015) 21 *European Law Journal* 2.

[8] P Boria, *Taxation in the European Union* (Springer 2017) 197.

[9] J Jaakkola, 'Democratic Dilemma of European Power to Tax: Reconstructing the Symbiosis Between Taxation and Democracy Beyond the State?' (2019) 20 *German Law Journal* 660.

[10] F Gallo, 'Principi di diritto tributario: problemi attuali' (2008) 51 *Rassegna tributaria* 919 ff.

[11] C Nikolaidis, *The Right to Equality in European Human Rights Law: The Quest for Substance in the Jurisprudence of the European Courts* (Routledge 2014) 148.

[12] Gallo, 'Principi di diritto tributario: problemi attuali' (n 10).

[13] Davies (n 7).

[14] G de Búrca, 'New Modes of Governance and the Protection of Human Rights' in P Alston and O De Schutter (eds), *Monitoring Fundamental Rights in the EU: The Contribution of the Fundamental Rights Agency* (Hart Publishing 2005) 30.

II. METHODOLOGY

Equality is a central principle for liberal democracies, and one that is frequently employed to monitor, evaluate and balance the relationship between the public authority and individuals.[15] Consequently, the chapter investigates two of the fundamental questions for a reassessment: how the principle of equality should be reconceptualised to account for its substantive dimension as required by the Lisbon Treaty; and how the said reconceptualisation would affect the very foundations of the power to tax in the Union.

To answer these research questions, the chapter applies a methodological approach based on a dynamic interpretation of EU law. This is an approach which has been upheld by the CJEU[16] and is connected with the need for interpreting provisions of EU law in the light of the EU legislative system as a whole:[17]

> [E]very provision of community law must be placed in its context and interpreted in the light of the provisions of community law as a whole, regard being had to the objectives thereof and to its state of evolution at the date on which the provision in question is to be applied.[18]

Such an interpretative approach is particularly important in the area of the EU internal market and of the fundamental freedoms, since these are principles which are 'drafted in general terms'.[19] One of the goals of dynamic interpretation is that of 'promot(ing) a transformation, an evolution of Community law'[20] and thus contributing to draft and develop EU policy.

Therefore, consistently with what was set out in the *CILFIT* case, this chapter investigates the possible need to reconceptualise the principle of equality as interpreted and applied in EU tax law in the context of the European legal system as a whole, while taking into account the evolving case law of the CJEU. An immediate consequence of this approach is that the sources used for the

[15] EM Belser, 'Concluding Remarks' in EM Belser, T Bächler, S Egli and L Zünd (eds), *The Principle of Equality in Diverse States Reconciling Autonomy with Equal Rights and Opportunities*, Series: Studies in Territorial and Cultural Diversity Governance, Vol 13 (Brill Nijhoff 2021).

[16] K Lenaerts and JA Gutierrez-Fons; 'To Say What the Law of the EU Is: Methods of Interpretation and the European Court of Justice' (2014) 20 *Columbia Journal of European Law* 3. See also, Y Arai-Takahashi, *The Margin of Appreciation Doctrine and the Principle of Proportionality in the Jurisprudence of the ECHR* (Intersentia 2002) 199.

[17] I McLeod, *Legal Method* (Macmillan International Higher Education 2013) 316.

[18] Case 283/81 *Srl CILFIT and Lanificio di Gavardo SpA v Ministry of Health*, ECLI:EU:C:1982:335, para 20.

[19] J Monsenego, *Taxation of Foreign Business Income within the European Internal Market: an analysis of the conflict between the objective of achievement of the European internal market and the principles of territoriality and worldwide taxation*, vol 22 (IBFD 2012) 22.

[20] G Itzcovich, 'The Interpretation of Community Law by the European Court of Justice' (2009) 10 *German Law Journal* 537; M Derlén, 'Multilingualism and the Dynamic Interpretation of European Union Law' in G Abi-Saab, K Keith, G Marceau and C Marquet (eds), *Evolutionary Interpretation and International Law* (Hart Publishing 2019).

analysis span the entirety of EU law, considered as a single autonomous legal system,[21] and are not limited to the field of EU tax law. Additional sources of international law are used to complement and improve the definition of EU concepts and precepts where necessary, and the investigation does not extend to a discussion of how the reconceptualised model of equality could be implemented in EU tax law.

III. THE FORMAL MODEL OF EQUALITY

The most basic conceptualisation of equality is that of formal equality, based on consistency and usually interpreted to mean that 'likes must be treated alike'.[22] Formal equality finds its root in the Aristotelian notion of treating equals equally:[23] its symmetrical nature implies the application of an equal treatment to comparable situations and of a differential treatment to different situations.[24]

Equality is intimately linked to the principle of non-discrimination, to the extent that it could be said that equality and non-discrimination are positive and negative statements of the same underlying values: a person is treated equally when she or he is not discriminated against, and is discriminated against if he or she is not treated equally.[25] This emerges quite clearly from the definition of discrimination provided by the UN Human Rights Committee established under the UN Covenant on Civil and Political Rights.[26] The Committee stated that discrimination is a basic and general principle relating to the protection of human rights, which rejects

> any distinction, exclusion, restriction or preference which is based on any ground such as race, colour, sex, language, religion, political or other opinion, national or social origin, property, birth or other status and which has the purpose or effect of nullifying or impairing the recognition, enjoyment or exercise by all persons, on an equal footing, of all rights and freedoms.[27]

[21] Case 26-62 *NV Algemene Transport- en Expeditie Onderneming van Gend & Loos v Netherlands Inland Revenue Administration*, ECLI:EU:C:1963:1. See also, A von Bogdandy, 'The Legal Case for Unity: The European Union as a Single Organization with a Single Legal System' (1999) 36 *Common Market Law Review* 887.

[22] C Barnard and B Hepple, 'Substantive Equality' (November 2000) 59 *Cambridge Law Journal* 562.

[23] Aristotle, *Nicomachean Ethics*, V.3. 1131a10–b15; Nikolaidis (n 11) 15.

[24] M De Vos, 'The European Court of Justice and the march towards substantive equality in European Union anti-discrimination law' (2020) 20 *International Journal of Discrimination and the Law* 62.

[25] S Besson, 'Gender Discrimination under EU and ECHR Law: Never Shall the Twain Meet?' (2008) 8 *Human Rights Law Review* 647.

[26] ibid.

[27] UN Human Rights Committee (HRC), CCPR General Comment No 18: Non-discrimination [1989].

Both equality and non-discrimination require not only abstention from discrimination, but also the positive absence of discrimination.[28]

A. The Formal Model of Equality in EU Law

EU law is built around the principle of equality.[29] This principle has economic roots, close to the concept of formal equality, that tie it to the EEC and the creation of a common market based on freedom of movement (of persons, goods, services, capital) and freedom of competition. Article 2 of the Treaty of Rome states that:

> The Community shall have as its task, by establishing a common market and progressively approximating the economic policies of Member States, to promote throughout the Community a harmonious development of economic activities, a continuous and balanced expansion, an increase in stability, an accelerated raising of the standard of living and closer relations between the States belonging to it.

The Treaty of Rome was based on market principles essentially introducing regulations aimed at abolishing barriers to trade and at ensuring the fundamental freedoms.[30] These four fundamental freedoms are now part of the Treaty on the Functioning of the European Union (TFEU),[31] Article 26(2) of which states that '(t)he internal market shall comprise an area without internal frontiers in which the free movement of goods, persons, services and capital is ensured in accordance with the provisions of the Treaties'.[32] The creation of the internal market itself is still one of the main goals of the EU, as stated in Article 3(3) of the Treaty on European Union (TEU).[33]

The concept of the common market has been further defined by the CJEU in the *Gaston Schul* case,[34] as that of an economic market for the benefit of commerce and of private persons conducting economic transactions:

> The concept of a common market as defined by the court in a consistent line of decisions involves the elimination of all obstacles to intra-community trade in order to merge the national markets into a single market bringing about conditions as close as possible to those of a genuine internal market. It is important that not only commerce

[28] S Besson, 'The Principle of Non-Discrimination in the Convention on the Rights of the Child' (2005) 13 *International Journal of Children's Rights* 433.

[29] Joined Cases 117-76 and 16-77 (n 3) para 7. Croon-Gestefeld (n 3) 4.

[30] Spangenberg, Mumford and Daly (n 6).

[31] TFEU (n 4).

[32] Before the Lisbon Treaty the Treaties were referring to the common market, and now after Lisbon the reference is to the internal market.

[33] M Costa and S Peers *Steiner and Woods EU Law* (Oxford University Press 2020) 327.

[34] Case 15/81 *Gaston Schul Douane Expediteur BV v Inspecteur der Invoerrechten en Accijnzen, Roosendaal*, ECLI:EU:C:1982:135.

as such but also private persons who happen to be conducting an economic transaction across national frontiers should be able to enjoy the benefits of that market.[35]

The principle of equality is also a superset of the principle of non-discrimination in EU law.[36] The relationship between the two can be quite clearly discerned in the CJEU *Albert Ruckdeschel* case: '[t]he prohibition of discrimination laid down in the aforesaid provision is merely a specific enunciation of the general principle of equality which is one of the fundamental principles of Community law'[37] and, more recently, in Advocate General Kokott's Opinion in *Association Belge des Consommateurs Test-Achats*: 'as there is no fundamental difference for the purposes of the present case between the concepts "principle of equal treatment", "principle of non-discrimination" and "prohibition of discrimination", I will use them as synonyms'.[38]

In these cases, both the CJEU and the Advocate General interpreted the prohibition of discrimination as a specific elaboration of the general principle of formal equality, stating that likes must be treated alike, because discrimination 'involves the application of different rules to comparable situations or the application of the same rule to different situations'. This approach has been confirmed in numerous other cases.[39] The CJEU has further elaborated it in respect of the general principle of equal treatment, which requires that comparable situations are not treated differently and that different situations are not treated alike unless such treatment is objectively justified,[40] and which is factually an implementation and elaboration of the principle of formal equality.

B. The Formal Model of Equality in EU Tax Law

EU governance in the area of taxation has been strongly influenced by the economic concept of the common market as outlined in the Treaty of Rome,[41] leading EU tax law to support equality in competition on the one hand, and economic freedoms on the other.[42] The EEC also included a Customs Union[43]

[35] ibid para 33.

[36] Besson, 'Gender Discrimination under EU and ECHR Law' (n 25).

[37] Joined Cases 117-76 and 16-77 (n 3) para 7.

[38] Case C-236/09 *Association Belge des Consommateurs Test-Achats ASBL and Others v Conseil des ministres*, Opinion of Advocate General Kokott delivered on 30 September 2010, ECLI:EU:C:2010:564, para 29. For an analysis of the role of the Advocate General in the development of EU law, see N Burrows and R Greaves, *The Advocate General and EC law* (Oxford University Press 2007); T Tridimas, 'The role of the Advocate General in the development of Community law: Some reflections' (1997) 34 *Common Market Law Review* 1349.

[39] Case C-394/96 *Mary Brown v Rentokil Ltd*, ECLI:EU:C:1998:331, para 30; Case C-342/93 *Joan Gillespie and others v Northern Health and Social Services Boards*, ECLI:EU:C:1996:46, para 16; Case C-279/9 *Finanzamt Köln-Altstadt v Roland Schumacker*, ECLI:EU:C:1995:31, para 30.

[40] Case C-313/04 *Franz Egenberger GmbH Molkerei und Trockenwerk v Bundesanstalt für Landwirtschaft und Ernährung*, ECLI:EU:C:2006:454, para 33.

[41] Nikolaidis (n 11).

[42] Spangenberg, Mumford and Daly (n 6).

[43] Rome Treaty (n 5) Art 8 (1)(2): 'The common market shall be progressively established during a transitional period of twelve years. This transitional period shall be divided into three stages of four

which Article 9 of the Treaty of Rome described as covering 'all trade in goods' and 'involv[ing] the prohibition between Member States of customs duties on imports and exports and of all charges having equivalent effect'. The Customs Union also required ensuring the four fundamental freedoms.

The free movement of workers between Member States was also considered in economic terms: 'from the outset' it was to be understood 'as the guarantee of the free movement of an economic production factor and not as recognition of a fundamental human right'.[44] Such a set-up only required a working model of formal equality to function.

The same European model of formal equality described here has been widely used by the CJEU through the years and until the present day in the field of EU tax law. The judicial reviews of the CJEU routinely rule on issues relating to whether the Member States' tax systems and norms pose restrictions on the exercise of the European economic freedoms, or whether national regimes discriminate against cross-border activities when compared with domestic ones.[45]

It is following this line of reasoning that the CJEU has decided that, in the field of direct taxation, the situations of residents and of non-residents are not, as a rule, comparable.[46] Resident and non-resident taxpayers differ in terms of their source of income, ability to pay and family circumstances.[47] Therefore, formal discrimination between the two is unjustified only if it is demonstrable that the underlying factual conditions are similar.

In EU tax law, the principle of formal equality has resulted in taxpayers being essentially cast as '*homines oeconomici*' and 'agents of the production system'.[48] There is an evident parallelism between this idea of taxpayers as agents of the production system and the early EEC conceptualisation of workers as an 'economic production factor' in which work does not receive 'recognition of a fundamental human right'.[49] In the words of the Spaak Report,[50]

> the common market will go beyond the pooling of existing resources; it will call for the creation of new resources by the development of backward areas and the

years each; the length of each stage may be altered in accordance with the provisions set out below. To each stage there shall be assigned a set of actions to be initiated and carried through concurrently'. See also, H von der Groeben, 'The EEC is now a Customs Union' (1968) 3 *Intereconomics* 226; R Ranieri, 'The Origins and Achievements of the EEC Customs Union (1958–1968)' in A Varsori (ed), *Inside the European Community: Actors and Policies in the European Integration* (Nomos 2006).

[44] P Vielle, 'How the Horizontal Social Clause Can Be Made to Work: The Lessons of Gender Mainstreaming' in N Bruun, K Lörcher and I Schömann (eds), *The Lisbon Treaty and Social Europe* (Hart Publishing 2012) 120–21.

[45] Jaakkola (n 9).

[46] Case C-279/93 *Finanzamt Köln-Altstadt* (n 39) paras 30–31; Case C-80/94 *GHEJ Wielockx v Inspecteur der Directe Belastingen*, ECLI:EU:C:1995:271, para 17. See also N Bammens, *The Principle of Non-discrimination in International and European Tax Law*, vol 24 (IBFD 2012) 949; G Porcaro, 'Interessi "in uscita" al vaglio della Corte di Giustizia tra (non) discriminazione e libertà di circolazione dei capitali' (2010) 2 *Rassegna tributaria* 545 ff.

[47] Case C-279/93 *Finanzamt Köln-Altstadt* (n 39) para 32.

[48] Boria (n 8).

[49] Vielle (n 44).

[50] F de Cecco, 'Fundamental Freedoms, Fundamental Rights, and the Scope of Free Movement Law' (May 2014) 15 *German Law Journal* 383.

> employment of labour forces hitherto unused; assistance, where needed, in the conversion of industry and retraining of workers; and finally, to facilitate these measures, free circulation of the factors of production, capital and manpower.[51]

We can safely conclude that the area of free movement of workers was not the only area affected by 'the logic of pure market instrumentalism',[52] since the same logic has been applied to taxpayers in the context of EU tax law.

In the area of free movement of workers, the principle of the primacy of the person over that of the worker as a mere factor of production or 'manpower' has developed over time in such a way that substantial equality can be ensured when it comes to access to and opportunities for employment. In an early Opinion of Advocate General Jacobs in the *Bettray* case we read that

> labour is not, in Community law, to be regarded as a commodity and notably gives precedence to the fundamental rights of workers … the concern of the Treaty and of the legislation on the free movement of workers is to ensure equality of access, for all Community citizens regardless of their nationality, to employment opportunities.[53]

Traditionally, the specific function of taxes in EU tax law is not social in nature, but rather economic, and directed at protecting the four freedoms. As such, it requires formal equality only. The goal of the internal market is to ensure the free movement provisions: it therefore prevents Member States from introducing legal and fiscal barriers to cross-border trade, and from adopting measures that are likely to deter, discourage or dissuade economic operators from moving freely within the borders of the EU.[54] The actual extent of said barriers or measures has no weight in the matter.[55]

This led the CJEU to rule that discrimination deriving from domestic law is illegitimate, from a Community perspective, if it leads to restrictions of the fundamental freedoms, and is not justifiable on any other grounds.[56]

[51] P-H Spaak, *Report of the Heads of Delegation to the Ministers of Foreign Affairs, Intergovernmental Committee on European Integration* (Spaak Report 1956) 12, para II: 'On 21 April 1956, the Intergovernmental Committee established by the Messina Conference held on 1 and 2 June 1955 submits its report to the governments of the ECSC [the European Coal and Steel Community] Member States. This document, known as the "Spaak Report", includes proposals regarding the aim, resources and organization of an investment fund which would seek to establish conditions for the balanced, smooth development of the Common Market'. The original document and additional information in the English version are available at the University of Luxembourg's CVCE.eu research infrastructure: www.cvce.eu/obj/report_of_the_heads_of_delegation_to_the_foreign_ministers_brussels_21_april_1956-en-4dd69921-433b-4bc0-acec-808f72fec9ae.html. See also, D Kramer 'From worker to Self-Entrepreneur: The transformation of Homo Economicus and the Freedom of Movement in the European Union' (2017) 23 *European Law Journal* 172.

[52] de Cecco (n 50).

[53] Case C-344/87 *I Bettray v Staatssecretaris van Justitie*, Opinion of Advocate General Jacobs, ECLI:EU:C:1989:113, paras 29–30.

[54] Case C-35/98 *Staatssecretaris van Financiën v BGM Verkooijen*, ECLI:EU:C:2000:294, para 34.

[55] W Schön, 'Neutrality and Territoriality – Competing or Converging Concepts in European Tax Law?' (2015) 69 *Bulletin for International Taxation* 271.
Case C-9/02 *Hughes de Lasteyrie du Saillant v Ministère de l'Économie, des Finances et de l'Industrie*, ECLI:EU:C:2004:138, para 43.

[56] Porcaro (n 46).

Tax law measures should thus not hinder companies and taxpayers from entering the internal market: tax rules have to ensure that homogeneous categories of taxpayers carry the same tax burdens.[57] In his Opinion on the *Cadbury Schweppes* case,[58] Advocate General Léger states that in EU law the principle of equality applies to comparisons between internal and cross-border situations, as well as to comparisons between two cross-border situations.[59] This same approach has also been consistently adopted by the CJEU in its rulings.[60]

Consequently, the model of equality of EU tax law may compare taxpayers, and this comparison may of course include variables: for instance, profits are generally considered as an acceptable criterion by which to compare taxpayers' ability to pay. Comparing profits from two companies and expressing these in different currencies will require some form of conversion from one currency to another in order to understand which company earned more.[61]

Commentators have consistently argued that fundamental rights and freedoms in the internal market have the primary aim to protect and guarantee the economic freedom of individuals in cross-border situations.[62] In EU tax law, this has led to individuals and organisations being appraised only 'in relation to the formal aspect of the production of a single event economically significant (act or activity) and not further discriminated with reference to the subjective position overall'.[63]

Part of the doctrine sees the prohibition of tax discrimination in EU tax law as a specific expression of the general principle of equality emanating from EU law.[64] Other authors interpret this prohibition in relation to the principle of fiscal neutrality.[65] The principle of fiscal neutrality is not directly regulated in

[57] Boria (n 8).

[58] Case C-196/04 *Cadbury Schweppes plc and Cadbury Schweppes Overseas Ltd v Commissioners of Inland Revenue*, Opinion of Mr Advocate General Léger, ECLI:EU:C:2006:278, para 77: 'Even if the legislation at issue were tax-neutral compared to a purely domestic situation, however, that would not call into question the existence of unequal treatment and the disadvantage to Cadbury in comparison with the position of a resident company which has established a subsidiary in another Member State which has a less favourable tax regime than that in effect in the International Financial Services Centre'.

[59] S Douma, 'The Three Ds of Direct Tax Jurisdiction: Disparity, Discrimination and Double Taxation' (2006) 46 *European Taxation* 522.

[60] See, for instance, Case C-512/13 *CG Sopora v Staatssecretaris van Financiën*, ECLI:EU:C:2015:108, para 25: 'Secondly, having regard to the wording of Article 45(2) TFEU, which seeks to abolish all discrimination based on nationality "between workers of the Member States", read in the light of Article 26 TFEU, the view must be taken that that freedom also prohibits discrimination between non-resident workers if such discrimination leads to nationals of certain Member States being unduly favoured in comparison with others'.

[61] LE Schoueri, 'Arm's Length: Beyond the Guidelines of the OECD' (2015) 69 *Bulletin for International Taxation* 690.

[62] S Douma, 'Optimization of Tax Sovereignty and Free Movement' (2011) IBFD Doctoral Series no 21, 108, available at: ssrn.com/abstract=2997412.

[63] Boria (n 8).

[64] Case C-354/9 *The Queen v Minister for Agriculture, Fisheries and Food, ex parte, National Farmers' Union and Others*, ECLI:EU:C:1997:379, para 61. S Capolupo, 'Recupero dell'IVA addebitata su operazioni non imponibili' (2021) 2 *il fisco* 131.

[65] F Gallo, 'Ordinamento comunitario, ordinamenti nazionali e principi fondamentali tributari' (2006) 77 *Diritto e pratica tributaria* 1137; G Bizioli and E Reimer, 'Equality, ability to pay and

primary EU law, but it is widely acknowledged in tax doctrine where it specifically supports economic efficiency on the one hand, and the development of the internal market on the other.[66] That is to say, that the principle of fiscal neutrality has as its final goal the protection of the four fundamental freedoms, and therefore to counteract market imbalances, including economic discriminations. The Member States' legislative systems and the various EU-level harmonisation processes are supposed to collaborate to prevent or eliminate distortions within the internal market.[67]

The CJEU has routinely used the neutrality principle as a manifestation of the principle of formal equality.[68] The principle is also applied by the CJEU in the field of indirect taxation as a final test to assess whether national VAT regulations are harmonised with EU VAT law.[69]

Furthermore, in the area of EU VAT law,[70] the principle of equal treatment is linked to the principle of neutrality,[71] with particular attention being paid to the principle of neutrality in competition.[72] These concepts only rely on formal equality and offer a procedural approach to equality consistent with the Union's traditional core economic values and principles, but that presents three different weaknesses: it is passive and static; it does not consider outcomes; and, most importantly, it neglects any substantive perspective on inequality.[73]

neutrality' in CHJI Panayi, W Haslehner and E Traversa (eds), *Research Handbook on European Union Taxation Law* (Edward Elgar Publishing 2020) 59.

[66] J Chen Shu-Chien, 'Neutrality as Tax Justice: The Case of Common Consolidated Corporate Tax Base under the EU law' (2018) 5 *European Studies: The Review of European Law, Economics and Politics* 33. See also, Schön, 'Neutrality and Territoriality' (n 55).

[67] Chen Shu-Chien (n 66).

[68] Case C-498/03 *Kingscrest Associates Ltd and Montecello Ltd v Commissioners of Customs & Excise*, ECLI:EU:C:2005:322, para 54: 'it must be recalled that the principle of fiscal neutrality precludes, in particular, treating similar supplies of services, which are thus in competition with each other, differently for VAT purposes'.

[69] J Englisch, 'Ability to Pay' European Tax Law' in C Brokelind (ed), *Principles of Law: Function, Status and Impact in EU Tax Law* (IBFD 2014).

[70] See, for instance, Council Directive 2006/112/EC of 28 November 2006 on the common system of value added tax [2006] OJ L347.

[71] Case C-309/06 *Marks & Spencer plc v Commissioners of Customs & Excise*, ECLI:EU:C:2008:211, para 49: 'it is important to bear in mind that the principle of fiscal neutrality is the reflection, in matters relating to value added tax, of the principle of equal treatment'.

[72] KK Egholm Elgaard, 'The Effects of the Charter of Fundamental Rights of the European Union on Substantive VAT law' in M Lang et al (eds), *CJEU – Recent Developments in Value Added Tax 2017*, vol 109 (Schriftenreihe IStR Band 2018) 26–27, mentioning Recital no 4 of the EU VAT Directive 2006/112: 'The attainment of the objective of establishing an internal market presupposes the application in Member States of legislation on turnover taxes that does not distort conditions of competition or hinder the free movement of goods and services. It is therefore necessary to achieve such harmonisation of legislation on turnover taxes by means of a system of value added tax (VAT), such as will eliminate, as far as possible, factors which may distort conditions of competition, whether at national or Community level'. See also, Case C-240/05 *Administration de l'enregistrement et des domaines v Eurodental Sàrl*, ECLI:EU:C:2006:763, para 55: 'even for the purpose of remedying a possible distortion of competition undermining the Community principle of equal treatment, which is reflected in the area of VAT by the principle of fiscal neutrality'.

[73] M de Vos, 'Beyond Formal Equality: Positive Action under Directives 2000/43/EC and 2000/78/EC' (Office for Official Publications of the European Communities 2007) 10.

The formal model of equality requires a comparison between two entities, but it does not clarify which indicators have to be considered, or according to which criteria two individuals are to be treated equally. It then fails to answer the most important questions: 'equal to whom?',[74] 'equality of what?'.[75]

When two entities have equal status in at least one normatively relevant aspect, they must be treated equally in respect to that aspect. The most sensitive question which arises with formal equality is that of identifying which aspects are normatively significant and which are not. If we pose that same question in the field of EU tax law, it should be reformulated/reworded as 'are taxpayers equal among them in the same economic category, or are there other profiles that should also be considered?' This question presumes answers that will change with the changing social understanding of the meaning of equality and inequality.[76]

IV. TOWARDS A SUBSTANTIVE MODEL OF EQUALITY

The formal model of equality focuses on equal treatment and on symmetry of treatment. The substantive model of equality focuses on results rather than on treatment; attention is shifted to whether there is fair distribution of benefits. It could be said that it targets disadvantage rather than aiming at neutrality.[77]

The same rationale also applies to EU tax law: the application of the substantive model of equality to taxpayers aims to achieve equality in outcomes, targeting fiscal disadvantage rather than fiscal neutrality.

While the EU began as a free trade zone, with economic freedom taking precedence over social rights,[78] the Treaty of Rome[79] had already introduced a number of non-economic regulations on matters of social policy in its Title III.[80] In EU law, the process has continued through the years, with the principle of equality acquiring facets going beyond the mere formulation of economic or formal equality, mirroring the transition from the economically centred ECC to an EU community of values and rights.[81]

The respect of fundamental rights as a general principle of EU law was first codified in the text of the Treaties in 1986, with the Single European Act.[82]

[74] de Vos, 'The European Court of Justice and the march towards substantive equality' (n 24).

[75] A Sen, 'Equality of What?' (1980) The Tanner Lecture on Human Values 1, 197–220. Croon-Gestefeld (n 3).

[76] F Vanistendael, 'Is Fiscal Justice Progressing?' (2010) 64 *Bulletin for International Taxation* 526.

[77] S Fredman, 'Substantive Equality Revisited' (2016) 14 *International Journal of Constitutional Law* 712.

[78] S Fredman, 'Transformation or Dilution: Fundamental Rights in the EU Social Space'(2006) 12 *European Law Journal* 41.

[79] Rome Treaty (n 5).

[80] J Zglinski, *Europe's Passive Virtues: Deference to National Authorities in EU Free Movement Law* (Oxford University Press 2020) 166.

[81] Croon-Gestefeld (n 3) 5.

[82] Single European Act [1987] OJ L169/1.

Its Preamble, the first major revision of the 1957 Treaty of Rome, states that the Union is

> [d]etermined to work together to promote democracy on the basis of the fundamental rights recognized in the constitutions and laws of the Member States, in the Convention for the Protection of Human Rights and Fundamental Freedoms and the European Social Charter, notably freedom, equality and social justice.

In the years since the Maastricht Treaty of 1992,[83] the weight of fundamental rights in the interpretation of EU law has increased greatly, and the Union has embraced social and political values which have taken it radically beyond its initial, almost exclusively economic focus.[84]

A. The Substantial Equality Model as for the CJEU

Understanding the constitutional structure of what is the EU today requires not only a reading of the Treaties, but also of the interpretations of those texts offered by the CJEU, in the light of the role of a 'constitutional court' framing the constitutional status of the EU played by the CJEU according to doctrine.[85] In respect to the shift documented in this chapter, this means reaching back all the way to 1969, when the CJEU used the general principle of respect of fundamental rights for the first time in *Stauder*:[86] '[i]nterpreted in this way the provision at issue contains nothing capable of prejudicing the fundamental human rights enshrined in the general principles of Community law and protected by the Court'.[87] One year later, in 1970, the Court linked the fundamental rights of the EU to the constitutional tradition of the Member States in the *Internationale Handelsgesellschaf* case:[88]

> In fact, respect for fundamental rights forms an integral part of the general principles of law protected by the court of justice. The protection of such rights, whilst inspired by the constitutional traditions common to the Member States, must be ensured within the framework of the structure and objectives of the community.[89]

This pattern was confirmed in subsequent years.[90] In *Nold*,[91] the Court ruled that it was not possible to accept measures which are incompatible with fundamental

[83] European Union, Treaty on European Union [1992] OJ C 191.

[84] Zglinski (n 80) 166.

[85] Nikolaidis (n 11) 107–08.

[86] Case 29-69 *Erich Stauder v City of Ulm – Sozialamt. Reference for a preliminary ruling: Verwaltungsgericht Stuttgart – Germany*, ECLI:EU:C:1969:57.

[87] ibid para 7.

[88] Case 11-70 *Internationale Handelsgesellschaft mbH v Einfuhr- und Vorratsstelle für Getreide und Futtermittel*, ECLI:EU:C:1970:114.

[89] ibid para 4.

[90] O De Schutter, 'The European Pillar of Social Rights and the Role of the European Social Charter in the EU Legal Order' (2018) Council of Europe 14.

[91] Case 4-73 *J Nold, Kohlen- und Baustoffgroßhandlung v Commission of the European Communities*, ECLI:EU:C:1974:51.

rights recognised and protected by the constitutions of the Member States involved:

> As the court has already stated, fundamental rights form an integral part of the general principles of law, the observance of which it ensures. In safeguarding these rights, the court is bound to draw inspiration from constitutional traditions common to the Member States, and it cannot therefore uphold measures which are incompatible with fundamental rights recognized and protected by the constitutions of those states. Similarly, international treaties for the protection of human rights on which the Member States have collaborated or of which they are signatories, can supply guidelines which should be followed within the framework of community law.[92]

More recently, in the 2000 *Deutsche Telekom AG v Lilli Schröder* case,[93] the CJEU explicitly reversed any previous hierarchy between the economic aim and the social aim of the Union:

> [T]he economic aim pursued by Article 119 of the Treaty, namely the elimination of distortions of competition between undertakings established in different Member States, is secondary to the social aim pursued by the same provision, which constitutes the expression of a fundamental human right.[94]

B. After the Lisbon Treaty

The transition of the Union from a free trade zone to a place where fundamental and human rights are not only proclaimed, but also upheld, continued with the Lisbon Treaty and with the adoption of the Charter of Fundamental Rights (EU Charter) as a legally binding instrument.[95] Equality is now a fundamental value in both primary and secondary EU law: the TEU[96] has it at its centre, and the EU Charter[97] devotes an entire title to it: Title III.

Article 8 TFEU requires the Union to eliminate inequalities in all of its activities:[98] the way current EU policymaking interprets and implements this request, via a redefinition of equality as a complex, multifaceted concept, is rendering obsolete the simpler principle of formal equality among taxpayers

[92] ibid para 13.

[93] Case C-50/96 *Deutsche Telekom AG v Lilli Schröder*, ECLI:EU:C:2000:72.

[94] LFM Besselink, 'Case C-50/96, Deutsche Telekom AG v Lilli Schroder, Joined Cases C-234/96 and C-235/96, Deutsche Telekom AG v Agnes Vick and Ute Conze, Joined Cases C-270/97 and C-271/97, Deutsche Post AG v E' (2001) 38 *Common Market Law Review* 437.

[95] Treaty of Lisbon (n 1).

[96] Consolidated version of the Treaty on European Union [2012] OJ C 326 (TEU).

[97] European Union, Charter of Fundamental Rights of the European Union [2012] OJ C 326, Art 23.

[98] TFEU (n 4).

used in EU tax law.[99] This conclusion finds support in several EU provisions: Article 6(3) TEU states that the

> [f]undamental rights, as guaranteed by the European Convention for the Protection of Human Rights and Fundamental Freedoms and as they result from the constitutional traditions common to the Member States, shall constitute general principles of the Union's law.

Article 2 TEU further maintains that

> [t]he Union is founded on the values of respect for human dignity, freedom, democracy, equality, the rule of law and respect for human rights, including the rights of persons belonging to minorities. These values are common to the Member States in a society in which pluralism, non-discrimination, tolerance, justice, solidarity and equality between women and men prevail.

Doctrine affirms that Article 2 TEU is one of the more remarkable and distinguishable demonstrations of this evolutive process of the EU towards the proclamation and guarantee of human and fundamental rights, and an important contribution to the redefinition of equality.[100]

Among the 13n values listed in Article 2 we find freedom, equality and minority protection, together with constitutional principles such as dignity, pluralism and solidarity. Articles 8–10 TFEU require the EU to promote other important fundamental rights, such as gender equality, employment, adequate social protection and to fight social exclusion, combating any type of discrimination based on sex, racial or ethnic origin, religion or belief, disability, age or sexual orientation.[101]

C. Sustainable Development

The fundamental values listed in Article 2 TEU must not be interpreted in 'clinical isolation',[102] separated from all other provisions of the EU Treaties: they must be read in accordance with the core objectives of the EU as stated in Article 3(3) TEU, which also outlines a concept of sustainable development for Europe:

> The Union shall establish an internal market. It shall work for the sustainable development of Europe based on balanced economic growth and price stability, a highly competitive social market economy, aiming at full employment and social progress,

[99] E Muir, *EU Equality Law: The First Fundamental Rights Policy of the EU* (Oxford University Press 2018) 5.

[100] Zglinski (n 80) 166.

[101] ibid.

[102] M Cremona, 'Shaping EU Trade Policy post-Lisbon: Opinion 2/15 of 16 May 2017: ECJ, 16 May 2017, Opinion 2/15 Free Trade Agreement with Singapore' (2018) 14 *European Constitutional Law Review* 231.

> and a high level of protection and improvement of the quality of the environment … It shall combat social exclusion and discrimination, and shall promote social justice and protection, equality between women and men, solidarity between generations and protection of the rights of the child.

The Lisbon Treaty introduced relevant changes in the field of sustainable development with the concepts of a 'sustainable development of Europe' and a 'sustainable development of the Earth' as goals of the EU in Article 3(3) and (5) TEU respectively.[103]

Sustainable development is deeply embedded in EU primary legislation: it is part of the TEU, the TFEU[104] and the EU Charter.[105] For the purpose of our discussion, it is interesting to note that the Preamble of the TEU links the principle of sustainable development to 'the accomplishment of the internal market and of reinforced cohesion and environmental protection'. The EU Charter similarly includes the principle of sustainable development in its Preamble and links it not only with the protection of indivisible, universal values, but also with ensuring the free movement of persons, services, goods and capital, and the freedom of establishment:

> Conscious of its spiritual and moral heritage, the Union is founded on the indivisible, universal values of human dignity, freedom, equality and solidarity; it is based on the principles of democracy and the rule of law. It places the individual at the heart of its activities … The Union contributes to the preservation and to the development of these common values … it seeks to promote balanced and sustainable development and ensures free movement of persons, services, goods and capital, and the freedom of establishment.

The European Commission has constantly reiterated that sustainable development is one of the basic values of the TEU, and its achievement one of the top priorities of the Union.[106] In a recent Communication concerning the EU Action Plan on Human Rights and Democracy,[107] the link between sustainable development and the human rights frameworks deriving from the UN's 2030 Agenda and Sustainable Development goals[108] have been reinforced, with the Agenda and the Goals being called 'an extraordinary opportunity to ensure that the

[103] MM Kenig-Witkowska, 'The Concept of Sustainable Development in the European Union Policy and Law' (2017) 1 *Journal of Comparative Urban Law and Policy* 64.

[104] See TFEU, Art 11.

[105] J Verschuuren, 'The growing significance of the principle of sustainable development as a legal norm' in D Fisher (ed), *Research Handbook on Fundamental Concepts of Environmental Law* (Edward Elgar Publishing 2016).

[106] European Commission, Sustainable Development Goals, available at: ec.europa.eu/info/strategy/international-strategies/sustainable-development-goals_en.

[107] JOIN(2020) 5 final, Joint Communication to the European Parliament and the Council EU Action Plan on Human Rights and Democracy 2020–2024. Brussels [2020].

[108] UN General Assembly, Transforming our World: The 2030 Agenda for Sustainable Development A/RES/70/1 (2015).

commitment to inclusion feeds into the promotion of human rights and democracy worldwide'.[109]

The Universal Declaration of Human Rights (UDHR),[110] the international human rights treaties[111] and the UN Convention on the Rights of the Child,[112] all have a specific role in the framework laid out by Agenda 2030,[113] as does the UN Declaration on the Right to Development (UNDRTD).[114] Article 1 of the UNDRTD defines the right to development as 'an inalienable human right (b)y virtue of which every human person and all peoples are entitled to participate in, contribute to, and enjoy economic, social, cultural and political development, in which all human rights and fundamental freedoms can be fully realized'.[115]

D. Human and Fundamental Rights

The introduction of the human rights framework in the EU legislative framework has added a second substantive dimension to the Union's model of equality,[116] with symmetry of treatment becoming one of several criteria to consider.[117] Such a change has repercussions on the principle of formal equality and the way in which it has been traditionally applied in EU tax law.

The adoption of the EU Charter plays a central role in this discourse. Its Preamble states that 'the Union is founded on the indivisible, universal values of human dignity, freedom, equality and solidarity'. 'Indivisible' is a key word here: it can be interpreted to mean that the fundamental rights are a single corpus and that any artificial categorisation and separation should be rejected. The adoption of the EU Charter also emphasises the institutional duties of states and of international bodies to respect and protect rights and values in their essence and substance as an obligation descending from the EU Charter, while refusing formality and rigidity in classifications and definitions.[118] This also applies to the principle of equality.

[109] JOIN(2020) 5 final, Joint Communication (n 107) 3, para 2. JP Yimbesalu and D Zakus, 'The Sustainable Development Goals as Human Rights' in M Raymond Izarali, O Masakure and I Bonny (eds), *Expanding Perspectives on Human Rights in Africa* (Routledge 2019).

[110] UN General Assembly, Universal Declaration of Human Rights, 10 December 1948, 217 A (III).

[111] RE Kaufman, 'Localizing Human Rights in the United States through the 2030 Sustainable Development Agenda' (2017) 49 *Columbia Human Rights Law Review* 99.

[112] UN General Assembly, Convention on the Rights of the Child, 20 November 1989, United Nations, Treaty Series, vol 1577, 3.

[113] UN General Assembly, Transforming our World (n 108) para 67.

[114] ibid para 67. UN General Assembly, Declaration on the Right to Development [1986] A/RES/41/128. See also N Schrijver, 'A new Convention on the human right to development: Putting the cart before the horse?' (2020) 38(2) *Netherlands Quarterly of Human Rights* 84.

[115] UN General Assembly, Transforming our World (n 108) para 67. UN General Assembly, Declaration on the Right to Development (n 114). See also, K Arts, 'Inclusive sustainable development: a human rights perspective' (2017) 24 *Current Opinion in Environmental Sustainability* 58.

[116] Nikolaidis (n 11) 148.

[117] ibid 193.

[118] J Kenner, 'Economic and Social Rights in the EU Legal Order: The Mirage of Indivisibility' in T Hervey and J Kenner (eds), *Economic and Social Rights under the EU Charter of Fundamental Rights: A Legal Perspective* (Hart Publishing 2003) 1–4.

Contemporary doctrine interprets human rights not only as universal and indivisible, but also as interdependent and interrelated.[119] This interpretation derives from the UDHR and its non-hierarchical assertion of inalienable rights that encompasses shared societal values. Once again, the Preamble of the EU Charter expresses a factual obligation to uphold the fundamental rights as they are expressed in the constitutional traditions and international obligations common to Member States:[120]

> This Charter reaffirms, with due regard for the powers and tasks of the Union and for the principle of subsidiarity, the rights as they result, in particular, from the constitutional traditions and international obligations common to the Member States, the European Convention for the Protection of Human Rights and Fundamental Freedoms, the Social Charters adopted by the Union and by the Council of Europe and the case-law of the Court of Justice of the European Union and of the European Court of Human Rights.

V. DISCUSSION

In EU tax law, the CJEU has used the residence criterion to assess whether two taxpayers could be said to be in a comparable situation. Consequently, the tax-related situations of all EU citizens are in principle comparable unless the residence criterion comes into play. It could also be said, flipping this perspective, that if their residence is the same 'all EU citizens are as a matter of principle in equal positions'.[121] Current law doctrine considers this a simplistic and problematic approach, maintaining that 'the people of Europe are too heterogeneous [and] taxation is not only a revenue raiser, it is also a nuanced tool to steer taxpayers' behaviour, achieve justice and equal opportunities through redistribution, and address economic needs'.[122] Economic doctrine supports this view, considering the concept of '*homo oeconomicus*' to be relatively unproblematic in market settings but presenting 'potentially seriously misleading implications when applied outside this sphere'.[123]

After the Lisbon Treaty, the economic functions of the internal market must be in balance with other, non-market, values[124] deriving from the attention given by the EU to human and fundamental rights and to sustainable development.

[119] UN General Assembly, Vienna Declaration and Programme of Action [1993] A/CONF.157/23, para I.

[120] Spangenberg, Mumford and Daly (n 6).

[121] R Påhlsson, 'Equality in Taxation: Reflections on the Social Construction of Comparability in Tax Law' in C Brokelind (ed), *Principles of Law: Function, Status and Impact in EU Tax Law* (IBFD 2014).

[122] C Heber, *Enhanced Cooperation and European Tax Law* (Oxford University Press 2021). See abstract, 12.

[123] H Gintis, 'Beyond Homo economicus: evidence from experimental economics' (2000) 35(3) *Ecological Economics* 311.

[124] N de Sadeleer, 'Trade v Environmental Law' (2015) 45 *Environmental Policy and Law* 23.

To consider EU taxpayers simply in their role as '*homines economici*' would today be in direct conflict with EU primary legislation, and specifically with the TEU, the TFEU and the EU Charter, whose principles and obligations rank high in the hierarchy of EU law. Articles 3(5)[125] and 21(1)[126] TEU require the EU to support the advancement of human rights:[127] tax law doctrine has proposed that fiscal neutrality based on the formal model of equality could be considered to be 'discriminatory by nature',[128] since it does not ensure the *fair differentiation* among different groups of taxpayers that logically follows from the evolution of EU law.[129] Formal equality prohibits any form of discrimination, which paradoxically results in not considering the differences that may exist between taxpayers belonging to specific social groups.

It is quite evident that the model of equality currently used in EU tax law, anchored to the primacy of the economic factors, and the model of equality adopted by EU law after the Lisbon treaty, based on the upholding of human rights, are in conflict. Table 1 below illustrates the difference between the way the principle of equality is interpreted in EU law, considering a person's 'inherent self-worth' (left), and in EU tax law, considering instead just a person's economic worth (right).

Table 1 Models of equality in EU law and EU tax law after the Lisbon Treaty

EU law	EU tax law
'People are to be valued not just because they are economically or otherwise useful but because of their inherent self-worth'.[130]	Taxpayers as *homines oeconomici* and agents of the production system.[131]
Model of Substantive Equality	Model of Formal Equality

[125] TEU, Art 3(5): 'In its relations with the wider world, the Union shall uphold and promote its values and interests and contribute to the protection of its citizens. It shall contribute to peace, security, the sustainable development of the Earth, solidarity and mutual respect among peoples, free and fair trade, eradication of poverty and the protection of human rights, in particular the rights of the child, as well as to the strict observance and the development of international law, including respect for the principles of the United Nations Charter'.

[126] TEU, Art 21(1): 'The Union's action on the international scene shall be guided by the principles which have inspired its own creation, development and enlargement, and which it seeks to advance in the wider world: democracy, the rule of law, the universality and indivisibility of human rights and fundamental freedoms, respect for human dignity, the principles of equality and solidarity, and respect for the principles of the United Nations Charter and international law'.

[127] C Pavel, and S Besson, 'The Bearers of Human Rights' Duties and Responsibilities for Human Rights: A Quiet (R)evolution?' (2015) 32 *Social Philosophy and Policy* 244.

[128] TM Porcano, 'Distributive Justice and Tax Policy' (1984) *Accounting Review* 619.

[129] Case C-450/93 *Eckhard Kalanke v Freie Hansestadt Bremen*, ECLI:EU:C:1995:105, Opinion of Mr Advocate General Tesauro delivered on 6 April 1995, para 16. See also R Nielsen, 'Is EU Equality Law Capable of Addressing Multiple and Intersectional Discrimination Yet?' in D Schiek, and V Chege (eds), *European Union Non-Discrimination Law: Comparative Perspectives on Multidimensional Equality Law* (Routledge 2009).

[130] A Bruce et al, 'Human rights and disability: The current use and future potential of United Nations human rights instruments in the context of disability' (United Nations Press 2002).

[131] Boria (n 8).

Since it only addresses equal treatment and does not consider any form of fair differentiation among groups of taxpayers, the formal model of equality applied in EU tax law is inadequate to address any substantive disadvantage. In this sense, the formal model of equality has become inadequate in the light of the principles that came into play after the entry into force of the Lisbon Treaty: European taxpayers not only have the right to receive equal treatment, they also have a right to the fair differentiation bestowed upon them by EU law.

In EU tax law, the principle of equality has been, and still is, primarily applied in its formal model, in strict respect of the priority of economic values. This has led the EU and the CJEU to compare and differentiate situations and taxpayers with the sole aim of correcting market imbalances.[132]

EU tax law is itself primarily considered a tool to protect property rights, the internal market and the four fundamental freedoms: in this perspective, taxation is a possible factor for the evaluation of distortion of competition, and henceforth taxes have to be harmonised, coordinated and controlled. What EU tax law is not under this view is a tool for the collection of tax revenue in support of societal goals and principles of equal, fair distribution.[133] EU tax law does not contribute to guarantee distributive justice, and tax law is not concerned with evaluating the personal and social conditions of taxpayers.[134] Erroneously ensuring substantive equality is not seen as an EU tax law goal: at this stage we can only conclude that any preoccupation with substantive equality is still missing from the discourse in EU tax law.

The shift to a substantive equality model is necessary to support human and fundamental rights and to force EU tax law to refocus on the underlying conditions that cause inequality rather than on treatment criteria.[135] This implies an acknowledgment that European taxpayers may no longer be identified as simple '*homines oeconomici*': they must be considered in their fullness as complex political, social and moral individuals who also have an economic side. In the words of Advocate General Tesauro of the CJEU:

> [T]he principle of substantive equality necessitates taking account of the existing inequalities which arise because a person belongs to a particular class of persons or to a particular social group; it enables and requires the unequal, detrimental effects which those inequalities have on the members of the group in question to be eliminated or, in any event, neutralized by means of specific measures.
>
> Unlike the principle of formal equality, which precludes basing unequal treatment of individuals on certain differentiating factors, such as sex, the principle of substantive equality refers to a positive concept by basing itself precisely on the relevance of those different factors themselves in order to legitimize an unequal right, which is to be

[132] Gallo, 'Principi di diritto tributario: problemi attuali' (n 10).
[133] Gallo, 'Ordinamento comunitario' (n 65).
[134] ibid.
[135] A Broderick, *The Long and Winding Road to Equality and Inclusion for Persons with Disabilities: The United Nations Convention on the Rights of Persons with Disabilities* (Intersentia 2015).

> used in order to achieve equality as between persons who are regarded not as neutral but having regard to their differences. In the final analysis, the principle of substantive equality complements the principle of formal equality and authorizes only such deviations from that principle as are justified by the end which they seek to achieve, that of securing actual equality. The ultimate objective is therefore the same: securing equality as between persons.[136]

Substantive equality has also been framed as a 'group justice' approach because of its focus on group characteristics and of the specific attention it pays to 'redress(ing) existing or historical disadvantages … to enhance voice and participation, or to accommodate differences and achieve structural societal change'.[137] The limitations of the principle of formal equality in EU tax law clearly stand out if we consider vulnerable groups such as women, children, youths and the future generations: by refocusing on outcomes, substantive equality offers a way to rebalance this imbalance. Substantive equality concerns itself with the effects of standing regulations and processes, and evaluates group dimensions[138] to address structural or social inequality that situates formally equal individuals, or '*homines oeconomici*', in different positions in society preventing them from competing on an equal footing. As a consequence, it calls for group-sensitive and asymmetrical methodologies[139] that lie far from the 'mathematical equality'[140] of methods centring on a symmetry of treatment between taxpayers.

EU tax law requires changes in line with current European economic and social developments as outlined and supported by the principles contained in the EU Treaties and the EU Charter.[141] This 'social function of equality'[142] is implied in the changes to the EU framework set in motion with the Lisbon Treaty.

Acknowledging its substantive dimension in European law in full is a necessary step, and one that requires EU tax law to move away from a simplistic application of the principle of formal equality to a more holistic view, in which the economic dimension of taxpayers is one of many elements at play and not an end in and by itself.[143]

[136] Case C-450/93 *Eckhard Kalanke* Opinion of Mr Advocate General Tesauro (n 129) para 16.

[137] M De Vos, 'Substantive Formal Equality in EU Non-Discrimination Law' in T Giegerich (ed), *The European Union as Protector and Promoter of Equality* (Springer 2020) 246–47.

[138] de Vos, 'Beyond Formal Equality' (n 73) 10.

[139] European Commission, 'European Equality Law Review' Directorate-General for Justice and Consumers (2018) 40.

[140] S Denys, 'SABENA is dead, Gabrielle Defrenne's case is still alive: the old lady's testament' in M Poiares Maduro and L Azoulai (eds), *The Past and Future of EU Law: The Classics of EU Law Revisited on the 50th Anniversary of the Rome Treaty* (Hart Publishing 2010) 267.

[141] O Fontana, 'Un sistema fiscale europeo per il XXI secolo, Commento 222' (2021) Centro Studi sul Federalismo, available at: www.csfederalismo.it/it/pubblicazioni/commenti/1604-un-sistema-fiscale-europeo-per-il-xxi-secolo.

[142] Muir (n 99) 4–5.

[143] A Veldman and S de Vries, 'Regulation and Enforcement of Economic Freedoms and Social Rights: A Thorny Distribution of Sovereignty' in T van den Brink, M Luchtman and M Scholten (eds), *Sovereignty in the Shared Legal Order: On the Core Values of Regulation and Enforcement in the EU* (Intersentia 2015).

The possibility of rebalancing the relationship between the free market economy and the fundamental principles of solidarity is, at least for now, absent from EU tax law because of the way tax discrimination is solely handled as an economic problem part of a market based on the observance of competition rules.[144] The adoption of a substantive model of equality would then profoundly alter de facto[145] the taxing power of the EU: consistently with human and fundamental rights, the Union could introduce rebalancing measures that derogate from the principles of the free market economy.[146] The outcomes of such a shift would be similar to what is achieved via the protection of 'distinct identities, needs or priorities' in federal systems, where the 'quest for autonomy is often also one for equality'.[147]

In this respect, it is worth noting that the CJEU has repeatedly stated that 'as Community law stands at present, direct taxation does not as such fall within the purview of the Community'.[148] This could be interpreted as a push towards considering a federal structure a somewhat necessary prerequisite for the application of the substantive model of equality in EU tax law: that is not the case. The enforcement of the fundamental freedoms as per the EU Treaties has already created 'new taxing rights'[149] that did not exist previously, and the process of normative integration between the EU and its Member States has produced a regulatory landscape that shares traits with federal models:[150] all of this without a compelling need, tactically speaking, to change the political structure of the EU. Therefore, a similar line of reasoning can surely be applied to the implementation of the principle of substantive equality even if it would lead to the creation of new, additional EU taxing rights.

VI. CONCLUSIONS

This chapter investigates whether and how the principle of equality in EU tax law should be reconceptualised after the Lisbon Treaty, and how this reconceptualisation would affect the very foundations of the power to tax in the Union. A dynamic, and 'evolutionary'[151] approach to the interpretation of EU

[144] Gallo, 'Ordinamento comunitario' (n 65).

[145] ibid. For a similar discussion in the field of State aid Rules, see A Fantozzi, 'The Applicability of State Aid Rules to Tax Competition Measures: A Process of "De Facto" Harmonization in Tax Fields?' in W Schön (ed), *Tax Competition in Europe* (IBFD 2003). See also F Nanetti and G Mameli, 'The Creeping Normative Role of the EC Commission in the Twin-Track Struggle Against State Aids and Harmful Tax Competition' (2002) 11 *EC Tax Review* 185.

[146] Gallo, 'Ordinamento comunitario' (n 65).

[147] Belser (n 15).

[148] Case C-279/93 *Finanzamt Köln-Altstadt* (n 39) para 21.

[149] F Vanistendael, 'Does the ECJ have the power of interpretation to build a tax system compatible with the fundamental freedoms?' (2008) 17 *EC Tax Review* 52.

[150] G Bizioli and C Sacchetto, 'European Constitutional Integration: The Case of Direct Taxation' in RS Avi- Yonah and M Lang (eds), *Comparative Fiscal Federalism* (Wolters Kluwer 2016).

[151] Derlén (n 20).

law, holistically addressed as one single system, has been applied to the investigation with the final goal of 'promot[ing] a transformation, an evolution of Community law'.[152]

An analysis of the principle of equality in EU law reveals that the values it embodies have been dynamically adjusting to changes occurring in society and to the redefinition of the Union from an economic pact to a political entity: discussing the possibility or necessity of its reconceptualisation requires taking into account these contemporary values and objectives the EU wants to pursue. It also requires that the principle be examined in the light of the EU legal system as a whole, rather than in isolation.

As documented here, such an approach clearly demonstrates that a dynamic interpretation of EU law shows that the principle of equality in the field of EU tax law is still seriously affected by the early conceptualisation of the Union as an economic free trade area. Doctrine calls this the 'economic DNA' that 'arose under the auspices of the then European Economic Community'[153] and that still permeates the concept of equality, stating that the 'hegemony enjoyed by the economic freedoms … since 1957, become tantamount to a constitutionally valid tenet within Europe'.[154]

The EEC was established back in 1957: its goal was to facilitate and support the free movement of persons, services, goods and capital. The protection of human rights was not a concern at the time.[155] On the other hand, EU citizens in the 2020s enjoy fundamental and human rights that extend beyond the four fundamental freedoms and that impact their taxpayer status. In EU tax law, the rigid application of formal equality does not acknowledge this new substantive dimension which has instead been addressed, for example, by the Supreme Court of Canada in *Andrews v Law Society of British Columbia*.[156] The Canadian Court abandoned its formalistic approach, recognising that the 'similarly situated should be similarly treated' approach does not lead to equal results and stating a need for a new approach to equality as a tool to build a more equal society. Similarly situated tests, says the Court,

> cannot be accepted as a fixed rule or formula for the resolution of equality questions … Consideration must be given to the content of the law, to its purpose, and its impact upon those to whom it applies.[157]

The TEU, TFEU and the EU Charter have placed human and fundamental rights at the centre of the European legislative framework. Equality and

[152] Itzcovich (n 20).

[153] de Vos, 'Substantive Formal Equality in EU Non-Discrimination Law' (n 137).

[154] Vielle (n 44) 120–21.

[155] C Kollonay-Lehoczky, K Lörcher and I Schömann, 'The Lisbon Treaty and the Charter of Fundamental Rights of the European Union' in N Bruun, K Lörcher and I Schömann (eds), *The Lisbon Treaty and Social Europe* (Hart Publishing 2012) 89.

[156] *Andrews v Law Society of British Columbia* [1989] 1 SCR 143.

[157] ibid.

non-discrimination are principles that belong to the constitutional identity of the EU. They are governing precepts for the EU legal system and the rule of law of the EU and its Member States.[158] As a consequence, in EU law, the principle of equality went through a transformation from a fairly rigid mechanism for economic integration to one for the substantive and multifaceted protection of human dignity and rights.[159]

A similar transformation has not been seen in the field of EU tax law, where formal equality is still the rule.

Such a paradigmatic change would have vast repercussions and at least partially redefine the very foundation of the power to tax in the Union: but without a reconceptualisation of its own principle of equality, EU tax law will increasingly find itself in friction, if not open conflict, with the substantive and non-discriminatory values of the Union, preventing not only the upholding of fundamental and human rights, but also the realisation of a more substantive economic freedom 'before public authorities ... in the single market and in daily life'.[160]

[158] S Kadelbach, 'Are Equality and Non-Discrimination Part of the EU's Constitutional Identity?' in T Giegerich (ed), *The European Union as Protector and Promoter of Equality* (Springer 2020) 23.

[159] S Prechal, 'Non-discrimination Does Not Fall Down from Heaven': The Context and Evolution of Non-discrimination in EU Law' (2009) Eric Stein Working Paper No 4/2009.

[160] Kadelbach (n 158).

10

The Power to Tax in International and EU Tax Law: Who is Sitting Behind the Wheel?

CÉCILE BROKELIND*

I. BACKGROUND

THIS PUBLICATION IS dedicated to addressing a burning problem of international tax law based on a cross-disciplinary approach, involving constitutional law, tax law and international law. The present contribution deals with the question of where the power to tax originates from. The answer to this question generates follow-up questions, such as how to share the tax pie, in other words, which jurisdiction is entitled to tax income or value creation. The most important question remains, however, and concerns understanding the legal grounds and reasoning behind the power of states to tax in a world in constant evolution facing an obsolete legal framework. The traditional tax base division based on a territorial limitation of the power to tax seems to be challenged in current business models which create tensions in the present legal environment and have led to proposals for change.

In the aftermath of the trade tax war between the United States (US) and the European Union (EU),[1] and the initiative of the Organisation for Economic

* Professor of Business Law, Department of Business Law, School of Economics and Management, Lund University. This chapter summarises the author's keynote speech held at a conference in Stockholm on 25 November 2021, trying to answer the question raised by the organisers: 'Who is sitting behind the wheel in international tax law?' It builds on the author's previous publications such as 'EU Harmonization of Tax Nexus: Lessons from Past Experiences' in E Traversa (ed), *The New Tax Nexus in International and EU Tax Law*, GREIT Series 15 (IBFD 2022); C Brokelind, 'EU Tax Law and the Return of the Nation-State' in A Bakardjieva Engelbrekt et al (eds), *The European Union and the Return of the Nation State: Interdisciplinary European Studies* (Palgrave Macmillan 2020).

[1] As a follow-up of the implementation by some states of a Digital Services Tax (DST) targeting mainly US MNEs, the US Trade Representative implementing s 301 US Trade Act (1974) initiated the application of 25% tariffs *ad valorem* on a series of products imported from Austria, India, Italy, Spain, Turkey and the UK. Notice of actions 7 June 2021. See G Kofler, 'The Future of Digital Services Taxes' (2021) 30 *EC Tax Review* 50.

Co-operation and Development (OECD) on the introduction of a new regime for corporate income taxation encompassing the untaxed profits of Multinational Enterprises (MNEs) in its 'Inclusive Framework' project of a multilateral convention, the present contribution addresses selected EU tax law issues arising from the reform in question. The taxation of the digital economy (Pillar one) is particurly suitable to investigate these questions, since it homes in on the main issue of this chapter: the lack of clear territorial connection with tax sovereignty.

The most important question is whether states can do whatever they wish in the field of taxation, and adopt any kind of new tax system meant to limit tax base erosion caused by new business models. As witnessed during and after the Covid-19 crisis, the EU has taken steps to organise a rescue package to the benefit of the EU Member States issuing bonds on the international financial markets in the name of the Member States,[2] and at some point, the loans will have to be repaid. Hence, finding larger tax bases has become even more critical for states. How does the law as it stands uphold these needs? How far can states' tax sovereignty be exercised to fulfil that goal?

Member States are bound by EU primary and secondary law in matters where the EU has either exclusive competence (competition law, external relations, custom duties) or exercised its shared competence in matters relating to the internal market among others. In other words, when implementing Pillar 1 (income from digital business or activities) and Pillar 2 (minimum effective taxation around the globe) rules in their domestic legislation, Member States will have to consider certain risks of incompatibility with other superior norms, such as the freedom of establishment, the free movement of capital and services provision (Articles 49, 56 and 63 of the TFEU), as well as the prohibition of State Aid (Article 107(.1) TFEU).[3] Needless to say, even if the EU adopts the proposed directives on the minimum level of taxation for MNEs,[4] on shell companies, or on Business in Europe: the Framework for Income Taxation (BEFIT), the implementation of such directives will not carry out a full harmonisation, and will compel Member States to take primary law into consideration in their implementing laws.[5]

But what is the problem exactly? Corporate Income Tax (CIT) bases disappear into the blue somewhere between the shores of well-defined state territories, a phenomenon which may remind us of Atlantis the lost world to quote

[2] On the plans for business taxation in the aftermath of sanitary crisis recovery, see European Commission, available at: ec.europa.eu/taxation_customs/communication-business-taxation-21st-century_en.

[3] For more details, see C Brokelind, 'An Overview of Legal Issues Arising from the Implementation in the European Union of the OECD's Pillar One and Pillar Two Blueprint' (2021) 75 *Bulletin for International Taxation* 212.

[4] EU Commission, 'Proposal for a Council Directive on ensuring a global minimum level of taxation for multinational groups in the Union' COM(2021) 823 final.

[5] See, for instance, CJEU, Case C-6/16 *Eqiom SAS*, EU:C:2017:641, para 15.

Peter Wattel.[6] This is the case for many reasons, one of which being the adoption of new business models challenging the outdated rules on the allocation of tax bases. Another is the inadequacy of transfer pricing rules to allocate residual profits in an efficient way that accommodates market jurisdictions, linked to the fact that risk assumption generating higher returns can be freely reallocated through contracts between associated companies.[7] Another reason is the ill-functioning US taxation of MNEs, which despite the recent rule changes leave unrepatriated income untaxed.[8] Tax havens and tax competition lie at the heart of the vanishing tax bases. However, the question is: on what legal grounds may a state tax income in Atlantis? Is this tax jurisdiction legally justified to tax for the simple reason that a few reluctant taxpayers exploit regulatory competition, or use their knowledge of different legislation and end up paying a global tax close to zero, despite an ability to pay more? Will the problem disappear if an effective CIT rate of 15 per cent is applied worldwide as suggested in the OECD's Pillar 2?

II. A SIMPLE METAPHOR: WHO IS SITTING BEHIND THE WHEEL?

As suggested by the drafters of the call for chapters for this book, it is possible to address the present trends on international taxation in many ways, and in addition, in the exact same way we speak about driving a car. Car drivers can do whatever they wish and go anywhere they feel like going provided they have a driving licence and insurance. These are the fundamental legal prerequisites of the right to drive. Transposed to the area of taxation, just as drivers need a driving licence to sit at the wheel of a car and drive, states need a legitimate taxing power in order to be able to levy taxes. This is a matter of constitutional, internal affairs, for which international tax law and EU tax law have little or even no bearing at all at the time of drafting this chapter.

However, at the very moment when drivers press the ignition button and start driving, they start interacting with other drivers and this may lead to a collision or an accident. States in search of additional tax bases also cause a risk of collision. International tax law and EU tax law establish rules for the traffic indicating the lanes the drivers should stay in to avoid an accident.

In which direction should they subsequently go? Drivers can go wherever they want to, that is an expression of their free will, as long as they stop at a red light and stick to the right lane. What about states? Can they go wherever

[6] PJ Wattel, 'Stateless Income, State Aid and the (Which?) Arm's Length Principle' (2016) 44 *Intertax* 791.

[7] W Schön, 'One Answer to Why and How to Tax the Digitalized Economy' (2019) 47 *Intertax* 1003.

[8] T Fensby, 'The FDII Regime – OECD Headache or Opportunity?' (3 December 2018) 98 *Tax Notes International* 989.

they feel like going? May they attract foreign investors, encourage exports, only support domestic production in the name of sustainability? Who writes the traffic laws for international taxation as they stand today, and how do we make sure that the passengers will reach their destination safely?

To start driving, a driver needs to trigger the ignition of the engine, which exported to the field of international taxation corresponds to the right to tax allocated between states as regulated in Double Tax Treaties (DTT). Some would say that these rules are so old and have reached such a level of acceptance that they would fit into the framework of customary international public law. Others would say that there is no such thing as customary tax law, at least not yet.[9]

The starting point of the problem raised in the literature is that the right to tax income at source is regarded as ill-functioning as it is based on a purely territorial approach.[10] Territoriality and globalisation do not go hand-in-hand. However, it is quite logical to define the power to tax with a reference to a territory in a world where tax sovereignty is defined by the right of a state to legislate solely on its own territory. Accordingly, the question arises regarding the meaning of sovereignty in an international context and in a changing world where all economic transactions are dematerialised. In the context of the current reform carried out by the OECD within the Inclusive Framework project, with the aim of targeting profits arising from digital commerce that are untaxed as yet, it does make you wonder whether the mere fact that a tax is not levied in another tax jurisdiction suffices to justify another state's jurisdiction over income lost in Atlantis. Is this reason a sufficient nexus?

Many authors seek solutions to this problem in international law, which provides for a legal framework concerning the concept of sovereignty, as noted by Kingston quoting parts of the ruling in the *Lotus* case of 7 September 1927:

> [T]he first and foremost restriction imposed by international law upon a State is that – failing the existence of a permissive rule to the contrary – it may not exercise its power in any form in the territory of another State.[11]

[9] See, for instance, P Hongler, *Justice in International Tax Law: A Normative Review of the International Tax Regime* (IBFD 2019) 64 ff, who gives an account of both sides.

[10] For a problem description see, for instance, M de Wilde, 'On the Future of Business Taxation' (2020) 12 *World Tax Journal* 1; I Cugusi, 'Prospects for Taxation of the Digital Economy between "Tax Law and New Economy" and "Tax Law of the New Economy" (2020) 12 *World Tax Journal* 763; J Kokott, 'The "Genuine Link" Requirement for Source Taxation in Public International Law' in W Haslehner et al (eds), *Tax and the Digital Economy: Challenges and Proposals for Reform* (Kluwer Law International 2019); S Gadžo, 'The Principle of Nexus or Genuine Link as a Keystone of International Income Tax Law, a Reappraisal' (2018) 46 *Intertax* 194; M Greggi, 'Rise and Decline of the Westphalian Principle in Taxation: The Web Tax Case' (2020) 29 *EC Tax Review* 6.

[11] Judgment of the Permanent Court of International Justice, *Lotus*, Judgment 9, 1927, PCIJ, Ser A, No 10, 18–19, quoted by S Kingston S (2016) 'Territoriality in EU (Tax) Law: A Sacred Principle, or Dépassé?' in J Englisch (ed), *International Tax Law: New Challenges to and from Constitutional and Legal Pluralism* (IBFD 2016).

In other words, a state may exercise its jurisdiction within its territory, in any matter, even if there is no specific rule of international law permitting it to do so. In these instances, states have a wide measure of discretion, which is only limited by the prohibitive rules of international law. However, this also means that a state cannot exercise its jurisdiction outside its territory unless an international treaty or customary law permits it to do so.

In the current state of international tax law research, the limitations on states' taxing powers is expressed as 'the nexus requirement'. Seen as a principle of customary tax law, the nexus requirement aims to ascertain tax jurisdiction by finding a qualifying connection between the taxpayer or the tax activity and the taxing state. For some, the nexus requirement expresses the principle of international customary law, which prohibits income taxation in lack of sufficient personal or territorial nexus.[12]

The concept of 'tax nexus' originally applies in the context of transaction taxes, more specifically, the US state laws on sales tax, under which retailers must have some kind of presence in a state before the state in question may require a retailer to collect sales tax from buyers in that state. For a long period of time, sales tax was easy to avoid in the United States when consumers did not remit sales tax at the point of sale. In this case, they passed on to the seller the duty to collect sales taxes. As most US state laws required a physical presence in the state in question, when the seller had no presence in the destination state, no tax was due, and that of course provided decisive advantages for online sellers.[13] However, as from 21 July 2018, the US Supreme Court acknowledged a more economic nexus to justify a state's right to tax on its territory of the kind adopted in South Dakota (200 sales or US $100,000 per year). Physical presence should therefore not be a prerequisite in the collection of sales tax, as this nexus has the 'consequent potential for internet retailers to maintain a pervasive presence within a State despite their lack of employees or tangible property there' in the terms of the US Office of the Solicitor General.[14]

Under EU tax law, the issue has already been summarised by Advocates General (AG) in their Opinions on cases dealing with extraterritoriality or with too-loose nexus rules. For instance, in the case of *United Kingdom v Parliament and Council*,[15] the United Kingdom contested the validity of Directive 2013/36/EU on the Bankers' Bonus provision (Article 94(1)(g)) introducing reporting obligations in the EU of all offshore-related bank offices for computing the maximum individual bonus. The United Kingdom found that the Directive

[12] J Kokott, 'Nexus within the New Tax World Order' in E Traversa *Nexus and Jurisdiction in International and EU Tax Law* GREIT Series 15 (IBFD 2022).

[13] For an explanation, see R Mason, 'Implications of Wayfair' (2018) 46 *Intertax* 810 and section 5.3 for the consequences of the 2018 EU-Digital service tax proposal, since withdrawn.

[14] US Supreme Court, No 17-494, *South Dakota v Wayfair, Inc et al* (21 June 2018).

[15] Case C-507/13 *United Kingdom v Parliament and Council*, Opinion of AG Jääskinen delivered on 20 November 2014, EU:C:2014:2394, para 39. Case withdrawn.

had an extraterritorial range in breach of international law. However, the AG suggested that the United Kingdom could not blame the EU for this large range, as 'the Lotus judgment establishes a kind of burden of proof entailing that the link invoked by a state to justify its legislative jurisdiction is sufficient, absent of a rule of international law to the contrary',[16] and that there was no such rule to the contrary. The Court of Justice of the European Union (CJEU) was not in a position to address the issue as the case was withdrawn.

Likewise, the extraterritorial reach of the Financial Transaction Tax (FTT) proposed in a Directive proposal COM (2013)71 also raised the issue of the potential breach of international law. Indeed, the FTT proposal included authorising Member States participating in the enhanced cooperation proposal to levy a transaction tax in several situations, ie, when a financial instrument was traded by one party established in the territory of a Member State, either the seller or the buyer, or when the financial instrument was issued in the territory of a Member State but traded outside these states, such as the United Kingdom, which did not participate in the enhanced cooperation around the FTT Directive. Arguing that this situation raised concerns of sovereignty for the EU to legislate on that point, the United Kingdom challenged the proposed Directive in a case before the CJEU and claimed that the FTT draft Directive would infringe international public law requiring a reasonable nexus for legislation, inasmuch as the extraterritorial effects of the future FTT stemming from the counterparty principle (ie, a buyer or a seller established outside the EU) and the issuance principle (ie, any instrument generated in the EU but traded outside the EU) were not justified in the light of any accepted rule of tax jurisdiction under international law.[17] However, the CJEU dismissed the claim in its ruling dated 30 April 2013 on procedural grounds and never took a position on the claim of a 'too weak nexus'.

Interestingly, many transaction taxes such as digital service taxes, taxes on advertisements/advertising, taxes on gambling, and taxes on telecommunications have a similar universal nature, or even offer a weaker link. Despite the numerous occasions offered when contesting the sufficient link to a legislative power to tax, the CJEU has never taken the opportunity to rule on the difficult problem that is caused by too weak a nexus. For instance, in the case of *Google Ireland*[18] decided by the Grand Chamber on the same day as the *Vodaphone* and *Tesco* cases,[19] the AG acknowledged the right for the Member States to levy a tax on advertising because of the language used, irrespective of where the

[16] Judgment of the Permanent Court of International Justice, *Lotus*, Judgment 9 (n 11).

[17] CJEU, Case C-209/1330 *UK v Council*, EU:C:2014:283, paras 20–21.

[18] CJEU, Case C-482/183 *Google Ireland*, EU:C:2020:141.

[19] CJEU, Case C-323/18 *Tesco Global*, EU:C:2020:139; and Case C-75/18 *Vodaphone*, EU:C:2020:140.

service provider (*Google Inc* was incorporated in Ireland) or the target of the advertisement were located.[20] The CJEU did not confirm the statement but did not challenge it either.

III. THE CJEU AND THE LOOSE NEXUS OF DOMESTIC FINANCIAL TRADE TAXES

The contemplated reform by the OECD to provide a new allocation key for the taxable profits of major MNEs is based solely on the access to market through consumers, or what is referred to as 'value creation'. A physical link between the income to be taxed and the state's sovereignty is no longer required, since the requirement for local source taxation through a permanent establishment and tangible presence on that territory does not apply any longer. In other words, and in the language of international law, the taxing state will be able to exercise its taxing power on extraterritorial bases. The mere access to a foreign market will be sufficient to trigger the power to tax an MNE in scope. Furthermore, the usual permission of allocating taxing rights organised in DTT forming part of customary law will not apply either.

The lack of a clear allocation of taxing rights may very well result in double economic taxation without the benefit of the usual tie-breakers organised in DTT. The CJEU has had a recent occasion to deal with this situation in the Italian case of *Société Générale SA*.[21] Both France and Italy had implemented domestic legislation as a copycat of the FTT proposal discussed in the previous section. According to Italian law, any financial transactions of shares or securities were liable to a transaction tax of 0.2 per cent of the value of the transaction, regardless of the state of residence of the issuing entity, the state of residence of any contracting party, or the place of conclusion of the transaction. In addition, the law covered transactions involving derivative financial instruments; the purpose of the tax was to ensure a contribution to public expenditure from any entity carrying out transactions relating to financial instruments linked to the territory of the Italian state. The latter were subject to a fixed tax assessed with reference to the number of transactions involved.

The French bank Société Générale had a branch in Italy, through which a number of transactions involving underlying Italian financial instruments were liable to the fixed tax in question as well as the French Financial Tax on equivalent terms, causing a double exposure to FTT. It therefore challenged the Italian Financial Tax as both residents and non-residents were liable to the same tax,

[20] Case C-482/18 *Google Ireland*, Opinion of AG Kokott delivered on 12 September 2019, EU:C:2019:728, paras 48–55.

[21] CJEU, Case C-565/1830 *Société Générale SA*, EU:C:2020:318.

despite the different situations in which they were causing a discriminatory treatment in breach of Article 63 TFEU. The French bank also claimed that the double administrative charge of filing for the FTT in both Member States was also an obstacle to market access and that it discouraged cross-border transactions. Most interestingly, the claimant also objected that the Italian FTT lacked an effective and objective territorial link between the tax and the Italian legal order. The Italian Constitutional Court had indicated that there is an effective and objective link of an economic nature between the taxable event and the Italian state, namely the negotiation leading to the conclusion of a derivative financial instrument expressing an ability to pay, as well as an indissoluble link between the value of such an instrument and that of the underlying security.

In his Opinion of 21 November 2019, AG Hogan did not find the last claim relevant for the determination of an infringement of Article 63 TFEU. He nevertheless suggested that it is questionable whether Italy is entitled to levy a tax irrespective of where the operation was carried out in an international public law meaning. He also mentions that the lack of adherence to common principles of international law remains out of the scope of the CJEU's field of competence, and several previous cases where the CJEU has obviously avoided to rule on the matter of the competence of states to tax.[22]

In a nutshell, the CJEU's approach to the FTT can be seen as a forerunner of the potential cases triggered by the digital service taxes adopted domestically and unilaterally by Member States. The CJEU traditionally finds no breach to the Fundamental Freedoms (Articles 49–63 TFEU) where the double taxation problem arises from the parallel exercise of tax jurisdiction. The Court has also avoided taking a position in its case law when the problem arose from the lack of a genuine link in the transaction tax cases. However, will the OECD's contemplated reforms on taxing the *profits* of the largest MNEs in the world be compared to a case law on taxing transactions?

IV. THE OECD INCLUSIVE FRAMEWORK: POSSIBLE OBSTACLES FOR TAXING RESIDUAL PROFITS OF DIGITAL COMMERCE UNDER PILLAR 1

The OECD's contemplated reform, which is followed closely by the EU,[23] means to change the rules of allocating profits between states, with more weight on the access to market as the 'value creation' (Pillar 1), and more weight on the fight against low tax jurisdictions (Pillar 2, 15 per cent). The ambition is to move away from physical presence indicators to other proxies that reflect more accurately

[22] CJEU, Case C-48/15 *NN (L) International*, EU:C:2016:356; and Case C-725/19 *Anton van Zantbeek VOF*, EU:C:2020:54.

[23] European Commission, press release on 'historic shift in the world of taxation', available at: ec.europa.eu/taxation_customs/system/files/2021-12/Factsheet Pillar 2.pdf.

the market penetration of companies and their socio-economic engagement with a particular country (revenue threshold, user-based factors, digital factors, etc).

The underlying assumption is that some MNEs[24] do not pay 'their share' of CIT and this fact only legitimises reforms. If the EU follows up on this reform, the legal question is whether the EU is competent to tax income that is not taxed in third states, just because they are not taxed there by choice, or by accident. You may wonder whether this is not in breach of the customary international public law requirement of a reasonable genuine link.

As said earlier, and in the words of AG Kokott herself,

> income taxation presupposes a genuine link to the taxing state. Just providing or selling services via the Internet has not generally been considered sufficient. However, States' practice is becoming more lenient. The notion of user- or consumption-based value creation is gaining round. Insofar as some link to the taxing state can be established through at least an intangible presence, apportionment can contribute to a fairer distribution of tax revenues between the EU Member States. However, it presupposes a common consolidated tax base and at least similar apportionment formulas.[25]

The OECD's Inclusive Framework contemplates the adoption through a multilateral convention of an instrument for allocating taxing rights of the digital economy. This new rule will lead to a steeply progressive tax system targeting major MNEs only. It intends to leave aside certain businesses with tangible activities, such as the extraction of natural resources, or banking activities. The 'digital tax' remains, however, a direct tax levied on a specific part of taxpayers' income, defined by a formulaic key of the allocation of gross profits within a market jurisdiction. Tax sovereignty is therefore exercised by the mere access to the domestic (large) market but not on a net income basis that best reflects the ability-to-pay principle. This shift in the underlying tax principle has been commented on at length in several doctrinal authoritative publications,[26] highlighting the problem of the lack of a common agreement in international tax policy priorities between the major and the minor market states. The most burning issue about steeply progressive taxes is their intentional effect of only targeting major MNEs which are usually (but not systematically) non-residents of the jurisdiction in question.

The CJEU case law on steeply progressive taxes may be an indication of whether tax sovereignty expressed in an EU-compliant rule implementing the changes recommended for 140 tax jurisdictions by the OECD would pass the test of compatibility with EU primary law. As commented at length,[27] the CJEU

[24] Commonly addressed in the press as the GAFA (Google, Amazon, Facebook and Apple).

[25] J Kokott, 'Nexus within the New Tax World Order', GREIT Series 15 (IBFD 2022).

[26] See above (n 10) for references.

[27] R Szudoczky and B Károlyi, 'Case Law Trends: The CJEU's Approach to the Objectives of Progressive Turnover-Based Taxes: Respect for the Member States' Fiscal Sovereignty or Authorization

in its most recent case law found a steeply progressive trade tax actually paid mostly by non-resident taxpayers with a greater ability to pay than domestic business operators to be in line with both the fundamental freedoms.[28] Targeting major retail distribution undertakings rather than minor ones also does not fall under the prohibition of State aid as the advantage provided to minor operators who do not pay the trade tax is not a deviation from the general benchmark set by the ability-to-pay principle.[29] In contrast, the Court previously ruled in the 2014 *Hervis* case that the Hungarian tax on trade was not in line with the freedom of establishment. In this case, the tax entailed a combined application of highly progressive rates of turnover tax and a turnover consolidation rule for related companies, resulting in taxpayers belonging to a group being taxed on the basis of a 'notional' turnover. The tax had a clear extraterritorial scope, but the Court did not mention this reason for finding a breach. It left it open to the referring court to check whether

> on the store retail market in the Member State concerned, the taxable persons belonging to a group of companies and covered by the highest band of the special tax are, in the majority of cases, 'linked', within the meaning of the national legislation, to companies which have their registered offices in other Member States, in which case, the application of the steeply progressive scale of the special tax to a consolidated tax base consisting of turnover is liable to disadvantage, in particular, taxable persons 'linked' to companies which have their registered office in another Member State.[30]

Since the tax in question was subject to further litigation in the 2020 and 2021 cases, it can be assumed that the referring court did not find any such disadvantage, and that the tax was still levied and disputed before the domestic courts once again.

In a nutshell, this means that the CJEU does not interfere with the exercise by Member States of their taxing powers when they design a tax meant to cover non-resident companies only, based on their greater ability to pay tax

for Circumventing EU Law?' (2022) 50 *Intertax* 82; R Mason and L Parada, 'Company Size Matters' (2019) 64 *British Tax Review* 610; R Szudoczky and B Károlyi, 'The Troubled Story of the Hungarian Advertisement Tax: How (Not) to Design a Progressive Turnover Tax' (2020) 48 *Intertax* 46; R Szudoczky and B Károlyi, 'Progressive Turnover Taxes under the Prism of the State Aid Rules' (2020) 19 *European State Aid Law Quarterly* 251; P Nicolaides, 'Multi-rate Turnover Taxes and State Aid, A Prelude to Taxes on Company Size?' (2019) 18 *European State Aid Law Quarterly* 226; Phedon Nicolaides, 'The Problem with Turnover Taxes' in 'The Problem with Turnover Taxes – Free State Aid' blog article (*lexxion.eu*, 30 July 2019); D Deák, 'Cloaking Member State Objectives Through Legislative Instruments' (2021) 30 *EC Tax Review* 111; L Parada, 'How the Vodafone Magyarország Opinion Affects EU Debate on Turnover-Based Digital Taxes' (14 August 2019) 95 *Tax Notes International*; JFP Nogueira, 'The Compatibility of the EU Digital Services Tax with EU and WTO law: Requiem Aeternam Donate Nascenti Tributo' (2019) 2 *International Tax Studies* 3.

[28] CJEU, Case Case C-75/18 *Vodafone Magyarország*, EU:C:2020:139; CJEU, Case C-323/18 *Tesco-Global Áruházak*, EU:C:2020:140.

[29] CJEU Case C-596/19 P *Commission v Hungary*, EU:C:2021:202; Case C-579/19 P *Commission v Poland*, EU:C:2021:201.

[30] CJEU, Case C-385/12 *Hervis Sport- és Divatkereskedelmi Kft v Nemzeti Adó- és Vámhivatal Közép-dunántúli Regionális Adó Főigazgatósága*, EU:2014:47, para 39.

than domestic operators. This results from both the FTT and the trade tax case law, in which the possible extraterritorial effect of the taxes as an obstacle to the fundamental freedoms was left out of the rulings. Exported to the case of Digital Services Tax (DST), or even the Pillar 1 reform, it is expected that the CJEU will not jeopardise a project such as the Inclusive Framework or the EU directives (minimum taxation and fight against shell companies) just because the domestic law implementing these common rules lacks a *genuine link* to the domestic territory.

However, a number of unfortunate situations involving extraterritorial taxation will inevitably lead to multiple taxation and litigation when the rules on Pillar 1 take effect. First, taxing a residual profit in excess of what transfer pricing rules provide for may lead to economic double taxation, which only a dispute resolution mechanism will be able to resolve, especially if two or more jurisdictions do not agree on the order of priority of these rules. Even if the rules in Pillar 1 are adopted in the EU by way of a minimum tax directive, which coordinates the allocation of taxing rights in the EU, it is highly likely that the digital business income will be taxed once again outside the EU. Indeed, you can understand that states may not be able to agree on how to share the tax pie, just because some tax jurisdictions (including the EU itself through a directive) will exercise an extraterritorial taxing power. When acknowledging the right to tax where the consumers of a digital service are located, despite the lack of physical or stable presence in the same place, the EU will tax business income which is taxable in the state of residence only, by definition outside the EU. It is unlikely that the state of residence of this MNE will let this business income be taxed in the destination state, ie, where the consumer is located, and provide for the credit of foreign taxes on business income. In addition, this presupposes that the DTT between the Member States and the third state allows for the credit method of the foreign taxes on business income. This is not uncontroversial, as the nature of the levy in question will have to be categorised as qualifying CIT in the words of the DTT.

Second, part of 'Amount A' (automated digital services, ADS) of Pillar 1 contemplated in the OECD proposal is based on the assumption that the profits of digital commerce arise from the lack of taxation on an MNE in the tax jurisdiction where services are purchased. The October 2021 statement introduces a special-purpose nexus rule permitting the allocation of Amount A to a market jurisdiction when the in-scope MNE derives at least €1 million in *revenue* from that jurisdiction. For smaller jurisdictions with a GDP lower than €40 billion, the nexus will be set at €250,000.[31] In other words, the link with the territorial taxing power is expressed in terms of access to market and sales figures, not

[31] OECD, 'Statement on two-pillar solution to address the tax challenges arising from digital economy', available at: www.oecd.org/tax/beps/brochure-two-pillar-solution-to-address-the-tax-challenges-arising-from-the-digitalisation-of-the-economy-october-2021.pdf.

in terms of a permanent establishment's ability to pay as in a traditional CIT system. Whereas the CJEU acknowledged the *turnover* as an expression of the ability to pay in the trade tax cases rendered in 2020 and 2021,[32] it remains to be seen whether the *revenue* (ie, the sales cashed in by the seller) matches the same features. Indeed, in the digital economy, the number of sales is not dependent on the location of the service provider, but on the size of the state's population in question. This provides for a mere presumption that a large number of people with internet access legitimises taxation at source. Is this a genuine nexus? How can a minor state agree to a new allocation factor for CIT based on the number of sales in its territory? Who is this tax system helping? Who is sitting behind the wheel?

V. CONCLUSIONS

The pressure on the OECD members to accept a new allocation model for business profits generates certain questions in terms of international law. Taxing corporate profits arising from the digital economy requires a genuine nexus for a legitimate power to tax to be born. International law forbids a state to exercise its jurisdiction outside its territory unless an international treaty or customary law permits it to do so. The OECD is organising a new model of taxation under the umbrella of the Inclusive Framework which, if accepted by all members through a multilateral treaty on digital profits, will legitimise taxing rights far beyond the mere requirement of a genuine nexus to a particular tax jurisdiction.

To round off this chapter and finish with the metaphor of driving cars, this new international legal framework will lead to accidents, just like when cars change lanes without indicating or do not stop when a traffic light turns red. Despite a licence to drive (multilateral convention) or an insurance policy (dispute resolution mechanisms in DTT or in EU tax law involving transfer pricing), there will be collisions and accidents, and the CJEU will not be able to overrule the commitment of Member States to such a new model of taxation. After all, if the Member States agree on a Directive on the allocation of taxing powers in the EU, implementing the OECD's Inclusive Framework, there will be no possibility for the judges to protect small tax jurisdictions against tax base erosion to the benefit of larger states, even within the EU. At least not on the basis of the required genuine nexus of international law.

It remains to be seen whether the contemplated reform will reach its goal of making the wealthiest MNEs pay more CIT than they do today. The OECD claims for Pillar 1 an 'additional USD 125 billion of profit to be reallocated to market jurisdiction each year'.[33] Alternative research claims, however, that

[32] See above, nn 28, 29 and 30.
[33] OECD, 'Statement on two-pillar solution' (n 31) 16.

only US $200 million are to be expected, and for a majority of residual profit to be earned by MNEs with headquarters in just 10 countries (United States receives 30 per cent).[34]

Finally, it is worth mentioning that the EU's draft Directive on Pillar 2 contemplating the adoption of a minimum effective tax of 15 per cent in the EU will not include any economic impact assessment, as the work was already carried out at the OECD level.[35] The same will probably be repeated for the next draft on Pillar 1 on taxation of digital business income. In that respect, the economic impact assessment released by the OECD states:

> The effect of Amount A of Pillar One on the global tax base equals zero. This is because Amount A reallocates tax base across jurisdictions without changing the global tax base. The jurisdiction groups benefitting most from this tax base reallocation (as a share of their GDP) are middle and low income jurisdictions, while tax base gains tend to be more modest among high income jurisdictions … In contrast, investment hubs would lose tax base in the reallocation, reflecting that a significant share of residual profit is currently located in investment hubs. Results by statutory CIT rate groups offer a consistent picture. Tax base gains are largest among jurisdictions with higher rates (20–30%, and even more above 30%), while jurisdictions with lower rates (10–20%, and even more 0–10%) tend to lose tax base.[36]

Based on this quote, it is time to answer the question raised by the conference organisers regarding who is sitting behind the wheel. Probably the G7 Members and their fairly high CIT rate will push forward the reform of the century. Unfortunately, this will undeniably generate more tension and obstacles to the mobility of free capital, as anticipated in the literature, for instance by Rodrik and his 'trilemma' in 2011, who exposed that it is impossible to attain economic hyper-globalisation, national sovereignty and democracy simultaneously, because only two of these can be achieved at any one time.[37] Within the EU, the rise of 'European sovereignty' seems to lie behind the adherence to the proposed OECD Inclusive Frameworks, which will request more scrutiny on the other side of the triangle, ie, democracy, as globalisation is not decreasing.

[34] S Beer, RA de Mooj, S Hebous, M Keen and L Liu, 'Exploring Residual Profit Allocation' (February 2020) IMF WP 20/49, available at: www.imf.org/en/Publications/WP/Issues/2020/02/28/Exploring-Residual-Profit-Allocation-48998.

[35] European Commission, 'Proposal for a Council Directive on ensuring a global minimum level of taxation for multinational groups in the Union' SWD (2021)580 final, COM(2021) 823 final, 4.

[36] OECD, Economic Impact Assessment, para 2.9.1, available at: www.oecd-ilibrary.org/sites/0e3cc2d4-en/1/3/2/index.html?itemId=/content/publication/0e3cc2d4-en&_csp_=60cbdb3f912de71310706737fc50a27f&itemIGO=oecd&itemContentType=book - section-d1e7174.

[37] See: drodrik.scholar.harvard.edu/links/trilemma.

11

Interpretation of EU (Direct) Tax Directives: The Judges Will Decide

JASPER KORVING*

I. INTRODUCTION

FOR A LONG time, in the absence of harmonisation in the field of direct tax law, national provisions in the field of direct taxation were especially affected by EU law through case law from the Court of Justice of the European Union (CJEU). The CJEU negatively integrated direct tax laws by determining whether provisions in domestic tax laws treated cross-border situations less favourably than domestic situations. Most of the time, the CJEU used its mantra that although direct taxation falls within the competence of the Member States, they must nonetheless exercise that competence consistently with EU law and, in particular, the fundamental freedoms guaranteed in the Treaty on the Functioning of the European Union (TFEU).[1] The EU itself had no power to tax of its own, at least not in the field of direct taxation, but Member States were held to take into account fundamental freedoms when applying their domestic power to tax.

Along the way, Member States started to agree on harmonisation of parts of direct taxation. This harmonisation, or positive integration, in the field of direct taxation started with the entry into force of the Parent-Subsidiary Directive[2] and the Tax Merger Directive.[3] Later, other directives followed, such as the

* Dr Jasper Korving is assistant professor in tax law at Maastricht University and employed at the Netherlands Knowledge Management of Deloitte Belastingadviseurs BV.

[1] See, for instance, CJEU, Case C-98/14 *Berlington Hungary and Others*, ECLI:EU:C:2015:386, point 34.

[2] Council Directive 2011/96/EU of 30 November 2011 on the common system of taxation applicable in the case of parent companies and subsidiaries of different Member States [2011] OJ L345/8).

[3] Council Directive 2009/133/EC of 19 October 2009 on the common system of taxation applicable to mergers, divisions, partial divisions, transfers of assets and exchanges of shares concerning companies of different Member States and to the transfer of the registered office of an SE or SCE between Member States [2009] OJ L310/34.

Interest & Royalties Directive[4] and the Anti-Tax Avoidance Directives 1[5] and 2,[6] with number 3[7] in the making. Other directives, which do not directly relate to substantive direct tax law, have also had an impact on how direct taxation but from the side; an example being the Directive on Administrative Cooperation[8] and, especially, its fifth amendment requiring intermediaries to provide information on cross-border reportable transactions.[9]

Such positive harmonisation in the field of direct taxation takes the form of a directive. Consequently, EU Member States are obligated to implement the directive into domestic law. The directive determines the objective of the result that is to be reached, whereas the individual EU Member States can freely choose the form and wording of the actual implementation, as long as the directive's objective is achieved.

The implementation of directives into national law may lead to interpretational issues. Not every term, phrase or word is clearly defined in the directive itself. Also, due to the freedom EU Member States have in the implementation process, individual Member States can simply choose to not copy the text of the directive and instead opt for using other words. Where harmonisation of a result is the objective of a directive, the effect of the harmonisation is not necessarily the same in each Member State. That is not solely due to the different wording of implementation legislation, it is also the result of interpretational differences.

In this contribution, the author researches when national provisions are within the scope of directive-consistent interpretation (section II). Subsequently, the allocation of competences and the relevance of EU and national sources respectively in the interpretation of provisions originating from directives in the field of direct taxation will be examined (section III). The core of this contribution consists of research on interpretation methods that are relevant and accepted for interpreting terms that are used in directives (section IV), followed by some practical examples relating to the two more recent EU directives with relevance to direct taxation, ie, ATAD2 and DAC6 (section V). This contribution ends with some concluding remarks (section VI).

[4] Council Directive 2003/49/EC of 3 June 2003 on a common system of taxation applicable to interest and royalty payments made between associated companies of different Member States [2003] OJ L157/49.

[5] Council Directive 2016/1164 of 12 July 2016 laying down rules against tax avoidance practices that directly affect the functioning of the internal market [2016] OJ L193/1.

[6] Council Directive 2017/952 of 29 May 2017 amending Directive (EU) 2016/1164 as regards hybrid mismatches with third countries [2017] OJ L144/1.

[7] Commission, 'Proposal for a Council Directive laying down rules to prevent the misuse of shell entities for tax purposes and amending Directive 2011/16/EU' COM(2021) 565 final.

[8] Council Directive 2011/16 of 15 February 2011 on administrative cooperation in the field of taxation and repealing Directive 77/799/EEC [2011] OJ L64/1.

[9] Council Directive 2018/822 of 25 May 2018 of 25 May 2018 amending Directive 2011/16/EU as regards mandatory automatic exchange of information in the field of taxation in relation to reportable cross-border arrangements [2018] OJ L139/1.

II. INTERPRETATION IN CONFORMITY WITH A DIRECTIVE

Older directives in the field of direct taxation effectively benefited taxpayers, for instance by requiring EU Member States to apply a withholding tax exemption on profit distributions by qualifying resident companies.[10] As the withholding tax exemption was clear and unconditional, the provision had direct effect.[11] Consequently, if an EU Member State would not – or was late, or incorrect – in transposing the withholding tax exemption into domestic law, taxpayers could start litigation proceedings in order to exercise the right to which they were entitled under the directive.

A directive may, however, also have an indirect effect, meaning that national law should be interpreted in conformity with the directive.[12] This obligation to interpret a domestic legal provision applies not solely to courts, but also to competent authorities.[13] They are at least held to apply the indirect effect when the time limit for implementation has expired.[14] The *Adeneler* judgment, in which this was decided, however, concerned a belated implemented provision, meaning that there was still no legal provision that could have been interpreted before the implementation deadline had expired. In the author's opinion, a national provision should be interpreted in conformity with the directive as of the moment the domestic provision implementing the directive provision – or a pre-existing provision already achieving the required effect – effectively applies, even if that is before the expiration of the implementation deadline.

From a content perspective, the interpretation in accordance with a directive means that domestic legislation implementing a directive must be interpreted in light of the wording and purpose of that directive.[15] Whether an interpretation in conformity with a directive is possible also depends on the flexibility of the provision of national law to be interpreted.[16] Courts must even consider the entire body of national law in order to assess the extent to which it can be applied in such a way so as not to produce a result which is contrary to that sought by the directive.[17] However, an interpretation in accordance with the directive has its limits, as the interpretation of a provision of national law may not be stretched to bring it into line with the directive provision to such an extent that it results in

[10] Art 5 of Directive 2011/96 (n 2); and Art 1, para 1 of Directive 2003/49 (n 4).

[11] For the withholding tax exemption in the Parent-Subsidiary Directive, reference can be made to CJEU, Joined Cases C-283/94, C-291/94 and C-292/94 *Denkavit Internationaal and Others*, ECLI:EU:C:1996:387, points 38–40.

[12] CJEU, Case 80/86 *Kolpinghuis Nijmegen*, ECLI:EU:C:1987:431.

[13] CJEU, Case C-218/01 *Henkel KGaA*, ECLI:EU:C:2004:88, point 60.

[14] CJEU, Case C-212/04 *Adeneler*, ECLI:EU:C:2006:443, point 115.

[15] CJEU, Case C-106/89 *Marleasing*, ECLI:EU:C:1990:395, para 8. See also HTPM van den Hurk, *Europees Gemeenschapsrecht en directe belastingen* (Kluwer 2001) 195.

[16] PJG Kapteyn and P VerLoren van Themaat, *Het recht van de Europese Unie en van de Europese Gemeenschappen* (Kluwer 2003) 438.

[17] CJEU, Case C-397/01 *Pfeiffer*, ECLI:EU:C:2004:584, para 115.

an interpretation *contra legem*[18] or infringes general legal principles.[19] National general principles, such as the principle of legal certainty, can be set aside for giving a directive-consistent interpretation its full effect.[20] To summarise the above, the interpretive obligation is 'strong', but does not require an interpretation of national law that it cannot bear.[21] The obligation of directive-consistent interpretation does not require the judiciary to give retroactive effect to the national provision in scope.[22] This should not be misunderstood: the interpretation of a national provision consistent with an EU directive is not to be confused with denying the benefits of a directive in the event of abusive or fraudulent acts. In the latter situation, courts would not even get to the question of the interpretation of a directive's provision since in abusive situations taxpayers cannot even benefit from any benefits of EU law, ie, access to the directives would be denied. By denying the benefits of a directive in abusive situations,[23] the CJEU appears to give retroactive effect to its case law on the abuse of EU law.[24]

As a result, the implications of the indirect effect of directives are enormous. This implies that national provisions cannot be considered as stand-alone articles, but elements of EU law should be taken into account in the interpretation of national provisions. That is not limited to provisions actually implementing directives, but can be extended to situations where national law predates a directive and was not even intended to implement it,[25] or where it relates to a wholly domestic situation of which the comparable cross-border situation would have been considered to be the implementation of a directive and the Member State concerned wants to apply the same interpretations in both situations.[26]

[18] See, eg, CJEU, Case C-334/92 *Wagner Miret*, ECLI:EU:C:1993:945, para 22. Note that the CJEU decided that settled domestic case law should be set aside by national courts if this national case law is based on an interpretation of national law that is contrary to the objectives of EU law. In that case, national case law cannot be considered '*lex*' in '*contra legem*'. See, in this respect, CJEU, Case C-385/17 *Torsten Hein*, ECLI:EU:C:2018:1018; and APW Duijkersloot, R Ortlep, MJM Verhoeven and RJGM Widdershoven, 'Europees staats- en bestuursrecht' (2019) 46 *Nederlands Tijdschrift voor Bestuursrecht* 236, 264–65. In another case, the CJEU judged that a *contra legem* interpretation would be allowed in favour of the taxpayer. The situation, however, concerned a concretisation of the general non-discrimination principle and the domestic law at issue therefore already infringed primary EU law and fundamental principles as well and, consequently, had to be applied differently. See CJEU, Case C-555/07 *Kücükdeveci*, ECLI:EU:C:2010:21, points 44–56.

[19] Duijkersloot, Ortlep, Verhoeven and Widdershoven (n 18) 264–65.

[20] CJEU, Case C-441/14 *DI*, ECLI:EU:C:2016:278, point 35.

[21] P Craig and G de Búrca, *EU Law: Text, Cases and Materials*, 5th edn (Oxford University Press 2011) 203.

[22] CJEU, Case C-268/06 *Impact*, ECLI:EU:C:2008:223, point 103.

[23] See CJEU, Joined Cases C-116/16 and C-117/16 *Skatteministeriet v T Danmark and Y Denmark Aps*, ECLI:EU:C:2019:135.

[24] See also L De Broe and S Gommers, 'Danish Dynamite: The 26 February 2019 CJEU Judgments in the Danish Beneficial Ownership Cases' (2019) 28 *EC Tax Review* 270, para 3.

[25] See, eg, CJEU, Case C-106/89 *Marleasing* (n 15).

[26] See, eg, CJEU, Case C-28/95 *Leur-Bloem*, ECLI:EU:C:1997:369. That case concerned a domestic merger by exchange of shares. In a cross-border situation, the Tax Merger Directive would have been applicable. During the parliamentary process, the Dutch legislator explicitly indicated that it wanted

III. COMPETENCE IN INTERPRETATIONAL ISSUES

Even though national courts and tax authorities have an obligation to interpret domestic law in conformity with directives, it should be determined which elements can actually be interpreted by national authorities. In that respect, it is important to determine who is competent to interpret a certain provision or term used in a directive.

In that light, several gradations can be distinguished. First, and most importantly, the CJEU indicated in its *VNO* judgment that words or terms that are actually defined in the directive itself have a common understanding that can only be interpreted by the CJEU:

> 9. By the first and second questions, the Hoge Raad asks, in effect, what is the correct interpretation of the expression 'capital goods' appearing in the third indent of the first paragraph of Article 17 of the directive.
>
> 10. It should be noted, in the first place, that the expression at issue forms part of a provision of Community law which does not refer to the law of the Member States for the determining of its meaning and its scope.
>
> 11. It follows that the interpretation, in general terms, of the expression cannot be left to the discretion of each Member State.[27]

Later, this approach, granting interpretive rights especially to the CJEU, was confirmed in several judgments concerning EU Value Added Tax in order to make sure that the concepts following from EU law were interpreted uniformly in order to avoid instances of double taxation or non-taxation which may result from conflicting interpretations by different EU Member States.[28] Such a uniform approach is relevant insofar as concepts used in a directive are relied upon with a view to the attainment of the objective pursued by the directive.[29]

Recently, the CJEU implicitly repeated this reasoning in the field of direct taxation in the so-called *Danish Beneficial Ownership* cases. Under the Interest & Royalties Directive, an intra-EU payment of interest should be exempt from withholding tax if, amongst others, the recipient of the interest qualifies as the 'beneficial owner of the interest'.[30] The concept of 'beneficial ownership', that originates from the OECD Model Tax Convention,[31] is also defined in the Interest & Royalties Directive.[32] The CJEU explicitly judged that the concept

to apply the same rules for domestic mergers. As such, the second instance tax court of Amsterdam considered it necessary to refer the case to the CJEU that allowed the case to be judged even though it concerned a wholly domestic situation.

[27] CJEU, Case 51/76 *VNO*, ECLI:EU:C:1977:12.

[28] See, for instance, CJEU, Case C-73/92 *Commission v Spain*, ECLI:EU:C:1993:891, point 12.

[29] CJEU, Case 252/86 *Bergandi*, ECLI:EU:C:1988:112, point 13.

[30] Council Directive 2003/49/EC (n 4).

[31] See also C Hamra and J Korving, 'Beneficial Ownership Interpreted: To What Extent Are the OECD and the EU on the Same Wavelength?' (2021) 49 *Intertax* 254.

[32] Council Directive 2003/49/EC (n 4) Art 1, para 4.

of 'beneficial ownership' cannot refer to concepts of national law that vary in scope.[33] It immediately added that it is apparent from the Preamble to the Interest & Royalties Directive that the aim of the Directive is that double taxation should be eliminated with respect to interest and royalty payments between associated companies of different Member States and that such payments should be subject to tax once in a single Member State.[34] This remark implies a comparable reasoning as stated above, where the CJEU favoured a uniform interpretation to avoid double taxation or non-taxation within the internal market as a consequence of interpretational differences that go beyond the objective of the directive.

More generally, this CJEU case law needs to be interpreted to provide that concepts used in directives in principle have an EU-wide meaning that requires uniform interpretation by the CJEU if the concept concerned is used in order to achieve the objective of the directive. This would also mean that, as is common in several EU Member States, national interpretations, explanations or remarks made in the parliamentary process would be irrelevant for the interpretation of these directive concepts.

The CJEU's *VNO* judgment mentioned above implies a second category of concepts, ie, provisions in a directive that refer to the law of the Member States for determining its meaning and scope. This would imply that where a concept in a directive explicitly refers to the national law of the Member States, the concept concerned would not be required to be interpreted uniformly. As such, domestic authorities and courts would be free to interpret those concepts under domestic law, without taking into account any EU influences on that concept.[35] The author is, however, not aware of any such example in the field of direct taxation.

A third – and final – category appears to be the grey area between the two categories mentioned above. This concerns concepts included in a directive for which a joint interpretational competence exists for the CJEU and national authorities. Of course, such a joint competence might exist if the directive explicitly provides it, but the author is not aware of any example in the field of direct taxation. Mostly, or maybe always in the field of direct taxation, it would for this specific category concern the interpretation of a concept included in a directive that is not explicitly relevant to achieving the objective of the directive but does not explicitly refer to a division of competence either.[36] In those

[33] CJEU, Joined Cases C-115/16, C-118/16, C-119/16 and C-299/16 *N Luxembourg 1 and others*, ECLI:EU:C:2019:134, point 84.

[34] ibid, point 85.

[35] This essentially follows from CJEU, Case C-468/93 *Gemeente Emmen*, ECLI:EU:C:1996:139, point 25. In that case, it related to the interpretation of the concept of 'building land' under the Sixth VAT Directive that explicitly referred to the laws of the Member States. As such, the Netherlands could apply its own definition of building land, including both improved and unimproved land. However, even if the Directive referred to domestic law interpretations, the Member State concerned should comply with the objective sought by the Directive.

[36] See also, D Weber and J Steenbergen, 'The (Absence of) Member State Autonomy in the Interpretation of DAC6: A Call for EU Guidance' (2021) 30 *EC Tax Review* 254, para 3.

situations, where there is a lack of a clear and uniform definition of the directive's concept in question, there is a certain margin of appreciation for the authorities of the Member States in interpreting the concept.[37] This would also give some leeway to national authorities to come up with their own interpretations in, for instance, the parliamentary process. These national interpretations would remain valid until they are overruled by the CJEU, even if this were to result in a patchwork of interpretations across the EU's internal market. Currently, a (non-tax) case on this issue is pending. In the *Lufthansa Technik AERO Alzey* case, the CJEU is to interpret the concept of 'exceptional circumstances' from Article 23(c) of Regulation 805/2004.[38] As the concept is not explicitly defined, there should be a shared competence for national authorities and the CJEU to interpret the concept. The CJEU has been requested to specify in particular what the interpretational discretion is for national authorities. In the author's opinion, the Lithuanian authorities will have some interpretational space, as 'exceptional circumstances' are not defined by the Regulation. However, in the interpretational process, they should take into account the different methods of interpretation (as explained below).

Of course, within this shared competence, there should be boundaries to the competence of the Member States. When the CJEU ultimately gives a clear interpretation of a concept used, Member States should apply the uniform interpretation as of that moment onwards. Furthermore, the above only relates to the indirect effect of concepts in directives. Therefore, national interpretations can still be overruled by judgments appealing to the direct effect of the provision concerned, including individual concepts used.

IV. INTERPRETATION OF A DIRECTIVE

A. Methods of Interpretation

Irrespective of the answer to the question regarding which authority is competent to interpret a concept from a directive, the CJEU has determined which aspects need to be taken into account upon the interpretation of that concept. The starting point for interpreting a concept or provision is the text of the provision. As early as the *Von Colson* judgment, however, it was stated that the purpose of the directive must be taken into account.[39] Until recently, the CJEU applied the textual, contextual and teleological interpretation method.[40] More recently, the

[37] CJEU, Case C-51/76 *VNO* (n 27) points 16–17.

[38] Pending Case C-393/21, *Lufthansa Technik AERO Alzey*, on Regulation 805/2004 of 21 April 2004 creating a European Enforcement Order for uncontested claims [2004] OJ L143/15.

[39] CJEU, Case 14/83 *Von Colson*, ECLI:EU:C:1984:153, para 26.

[40] See also, K Lenaerts and JA Gutierrez-Fons, 'To Say What the Law of the EU Is: Methods of Interpretation and the European Court of Justice' (2014) 20 *Columbia Journal of European Law* 3.

CJEU decided in its *Wightman* judgment that there are more elements to take into account:

> 47. In that respect, it should be borne in mind that, according to settled case-law of the Court, the interpretation of a provision of EU law requires that account be taken not only of its wording and the objectives it pursues, but also of its context and the provisions of EU law as a whole. The origins of a provision of EU law may also provide information relevant to its interpretation (see, to that effect, judgment of 27 November 2012, Pringle, C-370/12, EU:C:2012:756, paragraph 135; judgments of 3 October 2013, Inuit Tapiriit Kanatami and Others v Parliament and Council, C-583/11 P, EU:C:2013:625, paragraph 50 and the case-law cited, and of 17 March 2016, Parliament v Commission, C-286/14, EU:C:2016:183, paragraph 43).[41]

The interpretation of a provision of national law in accordance with the directive must therefore be based on the text of the provisions of the directive itself, as well as on its purpose,[42] the context[43] and its origins.[44] The CJEU did not determine a hierarchical order of relevance of the accepted interpretation methods. Even though the starting point is the text of the provision, purpose and context cannot, by themselves, create or amend a provision – and thus can only provide help in interpreting the text. In addition, historic interpretation is still rather new, and essentially there is no formal difference concerning the value of all four methods.

By acknowledging the four interpretation methods, there is no difference with the interpretation of many national or international law concepts: in addition to a grammatical method of interpretation, methods of interpretation based on teleology, legal methodology (or legal structure) and legislative history are used to determine the meaning of wording. To that end, reference can also be made to Article 31 of the Vienna Convention on the Law of Treaties (VCLT) that determines that a treaty 'shall be interpreted in good faith in accordance with the ordinary meaning to be given to the terms of the treaty in their context and in the light of its object and purpose'. From this definition, it becomes clear that text, context and purpose need to be taken into account in interpreting a provision from a treaty, such as a tax treaty. Article 32 VLCT accepts preparatory work for a treaty to be useful for interpretational issues as well, but only as a supplementary means of interpretation when the other interpretation methods leave the meaning ambiguous or obscure, or lead to a result which is

[41] CJEU, Case C-621/18 *Wightman*, ECLI:EU:C:2018:999, as confirmed and applied in CJEU, Case C-263/18 *Nederlands Uitgeversverbond*, ECLI:EU:C:2019:1111, and CJEU, Case C-548/18 *BGL BNP Parisbas*, ECLI:EU:C:2019:848.

[42] See also CJEU, Case C-527/18 *Gesamtverband Autoteile-Handel*, ECLI:EU:C:2019:762, paras 35–36.

[43] See also, CJEU, Case C-299/19 *Techbau SpA*, ECLI:EU:C:2020:937; CJEU, Case C-527/18 *Gesamtverband Autoteile-Handel* (n 42) paras 31–34.

[44] See also CJEU, Case C-673/17 *Planet49*, ECLI:EU:C:2019:801, para 56.

manifestly absurd or unreasonable.[45] As EU law can be considered a genus of international (public) law,[46] the CJEU appears to apply concepts and methods that the Member States are familiar with, even without explicitly referencing them, and this acceptance of interpretation methods should also be placed in an EU perspective.[47]

In this chapter, the author will discuss the separate interpretation methods in their order of appearance in the *Wightman* judgment.[48]

B. Text or Grammatical Interpretation

As in 'regular' treaty law,[49] the starting point for interpretation is the actual text of the directive. It goes without saying that the wording chosen by the EU legislator is of relevance in explaining what is meant by certain words or concepts.

Within an EU context, however, we should also take into consideration that all legal texts – such as directives – are available in all EU languages. All language versions are equally valid, meaning that words chosen in a certain language have the same value as in other languages. Even though the internal language of the EU's institutions is French, that language cannot likewise be considered decisive in interpretational disputes. On the other hand, when it can be established that one of the language versions of a certain concept clearly differs from most of

[45] JA Bischoff, 'Interpretation of International Uniform Law' in J Basedow et al (eds), *Max Planck Encyclopedia of European Private Law*, vol II (Oxford University Press 2012).

[46] PJ Slot, 'Annotation to the Wightman Judgment' [2019] *Ars Aequi* 504.

[47] Generally, see K Lenaerts and JA Gutierrez-Fons, *Les méthodes d'interprétation de la Cour de Justice de l'Union européenne* Droit de l'Union européenne, Monographies, 12 (Bruylant 2020).

[48] Besides these interpretation methods, the literature distinguishes a uniform interpretation method and a dynamic interpretation. See KJ Defares, 'Van meelwormen, krekels, sprinkhanen en andere wijzen van uitlegging van Unierecht' (2021) (1–2) *Nederlands tijdschrift voor Europees recht* 16, 17. Under the dynamic approach, provisions of EU law are interpreted in the light of contemporary circumstances, for instance, by taking into account technological developments or a changed societal context the EU legislator was not aware of upon the introduction of the EU legal provision. This dynamical interpretation method has not yet been applied in many cases, let alone in cases concerning direct taxation. Examples of cases of dynamic interpretation are CJEU, Case C-528/16 *Confédération paysanne*, ECLI:EU:C:2018:583; and CJEU Case C-448/14 *Davitas*, ECLI:EU:C:2016:839. The uniform interpretation method requires an autonomous explanation, in which concepts only have a meaning from the perspective of EU law that is necessary for a uniform application of that law. This interpretation method is especially applied for the autonomous interpretation of the core concepts of a directive, eg, 'distribution of profits' and 'withholding tax' under the Parent-Subsidiary Directive. By using autonomous interpretation, the CJEU not only guarantees the uniform application of a directive within the internal market, but also avoids Member States circumventing a directive using domestic interpretations or definitions. See H van den Broek, 'Interpretatiemethoden van het Hof van Justitie in belastingzaken: een kwantitatieve analyse' in R Baas et al (eds), *Rechtspleging en rechtsbescherming. Liber amicorum voor prof dr Leny E de Groot-van Leeuwen (Staat en Recht n 24)* (Wolters Kluwer 2015) 254. See also BP ter Haar, 'Gewezen EU-werknemer behoudt verblijfsrecht bij werkloosheid na twee weken werken' (2020) (3–4) *Nederlands Tijdschrift voor Europees Recht* 117.

[49] See Bischoff (n 45) 983.

the other language versions, the dissenting one should be applied in accordance with the other language versions.[50]

Such a discussion could arise in the context of the Interest & Royalties Directive that, inter alia, contains an obligation to provide a withholding tax exemption between sister companies. The English language version states that 'holdings must involve only companies resident in EU territory'. Especially in the situation of interest and royalty payments between sister companies, this phrase might cause grammatical interpretational issues, as 'holdings' could be interpreted both as 'holding companies', ie, the joint parent company, as well as 'the companies being held', ie, the actual entities involved in paying and receiving. Other language versions are, however, less ambiguous. They refer to *les participations*,[51] *Beteiligungen*,[52] *participaciones*,[53] *partecipazioni*,[54] *deelnemingen*[55] or *innehavet*,[56] indicating that only the latter reading of the term 'holding' has been included in other language versions.[57]

However, as the words of a directive do not usually simply self-define,[58] other interpretational methods often need to be taken into account as well.

C. Purpose or Teleological Interpretation

Besides a textual interpretation, concepts also need to be interpreted in the light of their purpose or objective. It is axiomatic that recourse to the underlying purpose or objective of a legal provision is often crucial to its interpretation, since the words do not just 'self-define'.[59] However, if the text is clear a teleological interpretation cannot lead to an extension of the scope of a directive, as that would result in a contra legem interpretation.[60] As regards the purpose of a directive, the most relevant source can be found in the Preamble to the directive. The *Joint Practical Guide for Drafting EU Legislation* provides further guidance in this regard.[61] It prescribes the information to be included in the preamble: a number of formal reasons and the reasons why the directive was adopted.[62]

[50] More on linguistic interpretations in S Van der Jeught, *Conflicting Language Policies in the EU and its Member States* (Europea Law Publishing 2015).

[51] French language version.

[52] German language version.

[53] Spanish language version.

[54] Italian language version.

[55] Dutch language version.

[56] Swedish language version.

[57] See also J Korving, *Internal Market Neutrality* (Sdu Uitgevers 2019) para 7.4.2.3.

[58] P Craig, 'Pringle: Legal reasoning, text, purpose and teleology' (2013) 20 *Maastricht Journal of European and Comparative Law* 7.

[59] ibid.

[60] Defares (n 48) 16.

[61] *Joint Practical Guide of the European Parliament, the Council and the Commission for persons involved in the drafting of European Union legislation* (2015).

[62] Para 10.1 of the *Joint Practical Guide*.

Anything that does not serve to explain why the provisions of the directive were adopted should be omitted.[63]

These rules apply to all directives. Occasionally, however, an existing directive is amended by a new directive. That new directive has a preamble of its own. As a main rule, the information included in the preamble of the amending directive should meet the same criteria as applicable to an original directive. The *Joint Practical Guide*, however, also provides further clarification on how to deal with the interaction of the preamble of amending directives in relation to the preamble of the original directive that is to be amended:

> 18.11: The recitals to an amending act have to fulfil the same requirements as the recitals to an autonomous act (see Guidelines 10 and 11). However, they have a special purpose in that they are intended only to explain the reasons for the changes made by the amending act: they therefore do not need to repeat the reasons for the act to be amended.
>
> 18.12: It is not good legislative practice to amend the recitals of the act to be amended. Those recitals set out, in a coherent manner, the reasons for the act at the time it was adopted in its original form. Only by means of codification or recast can the initial reasoning and the reasons for the successive amendments be consolidated coherently, with the necessary adaptations.

It can be deduced from this that the preamble to the amending directive of an existing directive, such as ATAD2 – which amends ATAD1 – must fulfil the same conditions as the base directive. However, the statement of the purpose of the amending directive can be limited to the purpose of the amendment. This does not (usually) result in the preamble of the base directive also being amended. Yet the question is whether the preamble to the base directive can still be fully invoked after the element of the base directive referred to in the preamble has been amended by an amending directive. In the author's view, the preamble to the base directive can only be relied on insofar as the directive provisions to which the preamble refers are not substantially amended by the amending directive.

Since the purpose stated in the preamble may be taken into account in determining how a directive provision is to be interpreted, the subsequent question is whether the role of these recitals in the preamble is unlimited. Klimas and Vaiciukaite outline four possible relationships between the preamble recitals and the directive provisions: (i) recitals do not have any (interpretative) effect whatsoever; (ii) the preamble is dominant over the directive provisions; (iii) recitals in the preamble and the directive provisions are equivalent for interpretative purposes; and (iv) recitals are subordinate to the directive provisions.[64] They conclude that the main reason for including recitals in a preamble is political reassurance.[65] In the author's opinion, the recitals in the preamble play an

[63] Para 10.7 of the *Joint Practical Guide*.

[64] T Klimas and J Vaiciukaite, 'The Law of Recitals in European Community Legislation' (2008) 15 *ILSA Journal of International & Comparative Law* 61, 72–73.

[65] ibid 78.

interpretative role. Even though the recitals are not necessarily equivalent to the actual provisions of a directive, they are not fully subordinate to these provisions either. If elements in recitals are mirrored in the actual directive's provisions they can be used (subordinance) and then the interpretational value of the recital is comparable to that of the actual provision (equivalence).

As indicated earlier, the recitals in the preamble can be limited to giving reasons for including a directive provision. The directive provision can then also be interpreted in the light of that objective set out in the preamble.[66] As such, that goes beyond providing political reassurance. Recitals in the preamble cannot be invoked separately; they merely serve to explain a substantive provision.[67] In other words, if the directive provisions themselves do not provide for a particular situation, reliance on the recitals in the preamble cannot independently create such a right. However, it cannot be inferred from this that a textual interpretation of the directive by definition takes precedence over an interpretation according to its object and purpose. It will depend on how far the CJEU believes that it can go towards its desired conclusion through purely textual analysis, and how far it is willing to give voice to the *telos* underlying a particular framework of treaty provisions.[68]

D. Context or Legal Methodology

The third interpretation method is the contextual interpretation method. For a contextual or systematic interpretation, it is aimed to interpret a provision from a directive in such a way that it forms a logical, necessary and smooth part of the whole of which it is a part.[69] The scope of contextual interpretation is to be determined in particular for the interpretation of directive provisions. You could argue that a narrow scope should be taken into account, meaning that only the direct context of the directive's provision – ie, the directive itself – is relevant. An internal contextual interpretation can be relevant, especially to give concepts in a directive a place in the bigger picture of whatever the directive aims for. It is necessary to understand a concept within the context of the instrument to which it actually belongs in order to give it an interpretation within that specific context.

[66] In relation to the comparable discussion on the aim and purpose of a regulation, see pending Case C-393/21 *Lufthansa Technik AERO Alzey GmbH* (n 38), in which the CJEU is asked to explain what can be considered 'exceptional circumstances' in the meaning of Art 23(c) of Regulation No 805/2004. Additionally, the CJEU is asked what the discretion is that the competent authorities of the Member State of enforcement have to interpret the term.

[67] See, for instance, CJEU, Case C-308/97 *Manfredi*, ECLI:EU:C:1998:566.

[68] Craig (n 58) 9–10.

[69] PBN van Os, 'Richtlijnconforme implementatie en interpretatie van nationale wetgeving ter omzetting van een richtlijn, met als casus art 13, lid 17, Wet VPB 1969 ter omzetting van de Antimismatchrichtlijn' (2018) 5 *NTFR-Artikelen* 10.

Interpretation, however, is not limited to taking into account an 'internal context' of the directive concerned. To start with, the *Oxford Dictionary* defines 'context' as 'the situation or set of circumstances in which something happens and that helps you to understand it'.[70] This appears to envisage a much broader perspective than merely the relatively small whole of which the provision is part.

In its *Cilfit* judgment, the CJEU accepted and explained the contextual interpretation method:

> Finally, every provision of Community law must be placed in its context and interpreted in the light of the provisions of Community law as a whole, regard being had to the objectives thereof and to its state of evolution at the date on which the provision in question is to be applied.[71]

In the author's opinion, the CJEU implied in *Cilfit* that context is broader than the text of the directive of which the concept to be interpreted is a part, as the CJEU refers to an interpretation in the light of the provisions of 'EU law as a whole'. Consequently, a broader legal framework can be taken into account in order to determine the correct interpretation of a directive's provision in a legal context, ie, by placing a directive's provision in a broader framework of laws and other legal sources.[72] This 'external context', in which other elements of the broader legal picture are taken into consideration as well, was also accepted by the CJEU.[73] Previously, in interpreting directive provisions in their context, the CJEU considered relevant the way in which these provisions related to fundamental freedoms,[74] the system and structure of the directive itself,[75] bilateral tax treaties,[76] and other directives.[77]

It can be concluded that all elements of both EU law and tax treaty law can be taken into account for an external contextual interpretation of a provision in an EU tax directive. The example of the relation with provisions in other directives is exemplary. The *Punch Graphix* case related to the effects of the Parent-Subsidiary Directive in case of a liquidation. That directive does not include a definition of the concept of 'liquidation', but the CJEU referred to the definition of 'merger' as used in the Tax Merger Directive that dates back to the same day as the introduction of the Parent-Subsidiary Directive. According to the CJEU, both directives, governing different types of transnational cooperation

[70] See: www.oxfordlearnersdictionaries.com/definition/academic/context).

[71] CJEU, Case 283/81 *CILFIT*, ECLI:EU:C:1982:335, point 20.

[72] Defares (n 48) 16.

[73] van Os (n 69).

[74] CJEU, Case C-168/01 *Bosal Holdings*, ECLI:EU:C:2003:479, point 26.

[75] CJEU, Case C-27/07 *Banque Fédérative du Crédit Mutuel*, ECLI:EU:C:2008:195, point 22; and CJEU, Case C-247/08 *Gaz de France*, ECLI:EU:C:2009:600, point 26.

[76] CJEU, Case C-338/08 *Ferrero*, ECLI:EU:C:2010:364, point 37.

[77] CJEU, Case C-371/11 *Punch Graphix*, ECLI:EU:C:2012:647, point 35. See also, van den Broek (n 48) 251.

between companies, constitute, according to the EU legislature's plan, a whole, in that they complement each other.[78]

The above is also in line with the rules on contextual interpretation as included in Article 31(3) VCLT. That paragraph enlarges the scope of materials to be used in contextual interpretation to: (a) specific (even informal) agreements the parties concluded subsequently with regard to the treaty; (b) to the subsequent practice in the application of the treaty; and (c) any relevant rules of international law applicable in the relations between the parties.[79] Also from international practice, it can be understood that a broad contextual perspective exists concerning the interpretation of – in that case – provisions in bilateral agreements. As indicated above, a comparable reasoning applies to secondary EU law. The starting point is an individual directive's provision. Besides the textual analysis, a contextual interpretation can help gain an understanding of the concept of that individual provision. That does not necessarily mean that the wording of concepts in different contexts always needs to be interpreted identically as well. The Court of the European Free Trade Association indicated that the provision of a directive within the context of the European Economic Area (EEA) needed to have a broader interpretation than the CJEU had given to that provision in an EU context,[80] potentially in order to safeguard homogeneity within the EEA's legal order.[81] The example illustrates the relevance of context of a directive's provisions, both in relation to the instrument and the entire legal order of which it is a part.

E. Origins or Historical Interpretation

A fourth interpretation method relates to a historic interpretation. This method, that some EU Member States can allow for the interpretation of national legal provisions, was only recently accepted for the interpretation of EU law. In its *Pringle* judgment,[82] the CJEU accepted for the first time that the preparatory work of the Treaties can be taken into consideration as a means of interpretation.[83] Later, the historical interpretation method was confirmed as interpretation method in the *Wightman* judgment.[84]

The *Pringle* case related to the relation between the Treaty on the European Stability Mechanism (ESM) and primary EU law. The ESM framework was

[78] CJEU, Case C-371/11 *Punch Graphix* (n 77) point 35.

[79] Bischoff (n 45) 984.

[80] EFTA Court, 27 June 2014, E-26/13 *Gunnarsson*.

[81] E Ros, 'Hoe het EVA-hof in een fiscaal arrest een bijzondere symbiose tussen context, homogeniteit en effectiviteit tot stand bracht' (2019) 251 *WFR* 1528.

[82] CJEU, Case C-370/12 *Pringle*, ECLI:EU:C:2012:756.

[83] DU Galetta and J Ziller, 'The Bundesverfassungsgericht's Glaring and Deliberate Breaches of EU Law Based on "Unintelligible" and "Arbitrary" Grounds' (2021) 37 *European Public Law* 633.

[84] CJEU, Case C-621/18 *Wightman* (n 41).

finally agreed after major political discussions.[85] For this research, an especially relevant question is whether the ESM Treaty is in breach of the 'no bail-out clause' in Article 125 of the TFEU.[86] The first paragraph of that Article reads as follows:

> The Union shall not be liable for or assume the commitments of central governments, regional, local or other public authorities, other bodies governed by public law, or public undertakings of any Member State, without prejudice to mutual financial guarantees for the joint execution of a specific project. A Member State shall not be liable for or assume the commitments of central governments, regional, local or other public authorities, other bodies governed by public law, or public undertakings of another Member State, without prejudice to mutual financial guarantees for the joint execution of a specific project.

Essentially, the no bail-out clause indicates that the EU is not liable for financial commitment by individual Member States, and the same goes for Member States not being liable for such obligations by other Member States. Under the ESM, however, some financial assistance between Member States would be possible. *Pringle* took the position that as a result thereof, the ESM Treaty infringed Article 125 TFEU. The CJEU did not agree and stated that it is apparent that Article 125 TFEU is not intended to *prohibit* either the EU or the Member States from granting any form of financial assistance at all to another Member State.[87] The EU and its Member States are simply not liable for each other's commitments. Besides referring to textual, contextual and teleological arguments, the CJEU also referred to a historical argument:

> 134. To that end, it must be recalled that the origin of the prohibition stated in Article 125 TFEU is to be found in Article 104b of the EC Treaty (which became Article 103 EC), which was inserted in the EC Treaty by the Treaty of Maastricht.
>
> 135. It is apparent from the preparatory work relating to the Treaty of Maastricht that the aim of Article 125 TFEU is to ensure that the Member States follow a sound budgetary policy (see Draft treaty amending the Treaty establishing the European Economic Community with a view to achieving economic and monetary union, Bulletin of the European Communities, Supplement 2/91, pp 24 and 54). The prohibition laid down in Article 125 TFEU ensures that the Member States remain subject to the logic of the market when they enter into debt, since that ought to prompt them to maintain budgetary discipline. Compliance with such discipline contributes at Union level to the attainment of a higher objective, namely maintaining the financial stability of the monetary union.[88]

As this was only the first time that the CJEU actually referred to historical arguments, we had to wait and see whether the CJEU would confirm its case law

[85] For an overview of the historical relations before the ESM Treaty, see Galetta and Ziller (n 83).
[86] CJEU, Case C-370/12 *Pringle* (n 82) point 129.
[87] ibid, point 130.
[88] ibid, points 134–35.

and whether a historical interpretation could be used more often in interpretational discussions. As the CJEU confirmed the existence and relevance of the historical interpretation method in the *Wightman* case,[89] it seems acceptable to apply the use of historic arguments more often in interpretational discussions. The *Wightman* case concerned the United Kingdom's notification of withdrawal from the EU under Article 50 of the Treaty on European Union (TEU), and especially the question whether, when and how that notification could be unilaterally revoked.[90] In relation to the historic arguments, the CJEU judged:

> 68. The origins of Article 50 TEU also support an interpretation of that provision as meaning that a Member State is entitled to revoke unilaterally the notification of its intention to withdraw from the European Union. That article largely adopts the wording of a withdrawal clause first set out in the draft Treaty establishing a Constitution for Europe. Although, during the drafting of that clause, amendments had been proposed to allow the expulsion of a Member State, to avoid the risk of abuse during the withdrawal procedure or to make the withdrawal decision more difficult, those amendments were all rejected on the ground, expressly set out in the comments on the draft, that the voluntary and unilateral nature of the withdrawal decision should be ensured.
>
> 69. It follows from the foregoing that the notification by a Member State of its intention to withdraw does not lead inevitably to the withdrawal of that Member State from the European Union. On the contrary, a Member State that has reversed its decision to withdraw from the European Union is entitled to revoke that notification for as long as a withdrawal agreement concluded between that Member State and the European Union has not entered into force or, if no such agreement has been concluded, for as long as the two-year period laid down in Article 50(3) TEU, possibly extended in accordance with that provision, has not expired.
>
> 70. That conclusion is corroborated by the provisions of the Vienna Convention on the Law of Treaties, which was taken into account in the preparatory work for the Treaty establishing a Constitution for Europe.
>
> 71. In the event that a treaty authorises withdrawal under its provisions, Article 68 of that convention specifies inter alia, in clear and unconditional terms, that a notification of withdrawal, as provided for in Article 65 or 67 thereof, may be revoked at any time before it takes effect.[91]

Consequently, the CJEU again referred to historic documents and the origin of Article 50 TEU, even though the original source, the Constitution for Europe, had never entered into effect. It even went further back in time by also taking into account one of the fundamental sources that was used for the Constitution for Europe, ie, the VCLT. From its argumentation it becomes clear that historic sources can help in the interpretation of concepts from primary and secondary EU law.

[89] CJEU, Case C-621/18 *Wightman* (n 41) point 47.
[90] ibid, point 10.
[91] ibid, points 68–71.

What is still to be determined is which historic sources can actually be taken into account for interpretational purposes. Thus far, the CJEU has limited the historic sources used to documents that were available in a very public source, the *Bulletin of the European Communities*.[92] This is, however, still rather limited. Many other historic sources could also provide insights as to why certain concepts or words were used as is, giving them interpretational value. Maybe the desire not to take into account all historical documents comes from some anxiety in the negotiating processes of EU law. Apparently, the founding fathers were afraid that reading strongly worded debates among negotiators on controversial treaty provisions could revive ghosts from the past.[93] After all, EU secondary legislation often represents the result of compromises.[94] Even when the records of later negotiations were perhaps less sketchy and less protected against publicity, the CJEU nevertheless did not show any interest in going back to the historical record of the conferences of Maastricht, Amsterdam and Nice.[95] This reserve has now changed.

Thus far, however, the use of historical sources is limited to publicly available information. Therefore, we need to wait and see whether the CJEU will now also take into account preparatory documents or Working Party papers for interpretational purposes. In the field of direct taxation, directives lack an extensive parliamentary history. Since these preparatory documents are not part of any parliamentary process, but are actually side-steps from the process, it could be argued that these preparatory documents cannot be used as a separate source for historical interpretation or for filling legislative lacunes, but only for the clarification of text, context or purpose of a directive if these are unclear or ambiguous.[96] Prior to the judgments in *Pringle* and *Wightman*, the CJEU in direct tax cases judged that 'expressions of intent on the part of Member States in the Council have no legal status if they are not actually expressed in the legislation',[97] and

> declarations recorded in Council minutes in the course of preparatory work leading to the adoption of a directive cannot be used for the purpose of interpreting that directive where no reference is made to the content of the declaration in the wording of the provision in question, and, moreover, such declarations have no legal significance.[98]

[92] PJ Kuijper, 'International Law in the Case Law of the Court of Justice: Recent Trends' (2013) 41 *Legal Issues of Economic Integration* 1, 4.

[93] ibid 3.

[94] H Rösler, 'Interpretation of EU Law' in J Basedow et al (eds), *Max Planck Encyclopedia of European Private Law*, vol II (Oxford University Press 2012) 979.

[95] Kuijper (n 92) 3.

[96] van Os (n 69). See also, van den Hurk (n 15) 275.

[97] CJEU, Joined Cases C-283/94, C-291/94 and C-292/94 *Denkavit Internationaal and Others* (n 11) point 29.

[98] CJEU, Case C-375/98 *Epson Europe*, ECLI:EU:C:2000:302, point 26.

The judgments in *Pringle* and *Wightman*, however, provide some more interpretational light in the application of historical sources. In doing so, the CJEU appears – at least in those two judgments – to have moved away from the more restrictive use of historical sources as preferred by Article 32 VCLT. By its recent judgments, the CJEU seems more inclined to resort to historical interpretation, if it can confirm and bolster the interpretation which seems appropriate according to text and context, object and purpose taken together have collectively yielded a plausible (but perhaps not yet wholly convincing) interpretation.[99]

As such, it is also important to become familiar with historic sources for EU (Direct) Tax Directives. The actual parliamentary documents are to a large extent publicly available. Other underlying documents from preparatory bodies of the European Commission, the European Council or the European Parliament were not, which could have been the reason why references to these documents were not accepted in court.[100] Nowadays, however, they can be requested from the General Secretariat of the European Commission, for instance, by submitting a public access to government information request.[101] The Working Party documents to be requested may contribute to gaining an insight into the deliberations preceding the creation of the final directive, and may thus be relevant for interpreting the provisions of the directive from a historic – but also from a contextual or teleological – perspective.[102] The Dutch Supreme Court has already indicated that if an unpublished general policy was requested and granted under the Dutch Freedom of Information Act (Wet Openbaarheid van Bestuur), such internal documents could be relied on in court.[103] By analogy, the CJEU could decide the same for documents to which public access was granted under EU Regulation 1049/2001. However, some effort is still required to obtain these documents.

The relevance of historical documents for the interpretation of EU Tax Directives is probably here to stay. Even though the author does not expect historical interpretation to fill legislative lacunes, it could help in interpreting concepts and rules and, potentially, provide for an even better outcome of judgments where other interpretational methods do not suffice on their own. Once those documents are publicly available, the CJEU should also take them into account for interpretational purposes. This would, however, require more transparency towards preparatory documents. Sometimes certain Working Party documents are made public. As a consequence, the public may become aware of documents including arguments, interpretations, choices or agreements among the Member States in the legislative process, even though these documents were

[99] Kuijper (n 92) 4–5.
[100] van den Broek (n 48) 257.
[101] Pursuant to Regulation 1049/2001.
[102] However, the author is not aware of CJEU case law that gives any legal status to these documents.
[103] HR 9 April 2021, Case 19/03791, ECLI:NL:HR:2021:439; and HR 11 June 2021, Case 20/00892, ECLI:NL:HR:2021:778.

not necessarily supposed to be made public. Even though these documents are mainly leaked and not formally published in the *Official Journal*, the positions and interpretations arising from them should in my opinion be admissible in court as well.[104] Therefore, the author would argue in favour of the publication of more preparatory documents and not limiting these to be provided upon request. After all, increased transparency is required from taxpayers towards Member States' authorities, but this should not be a one-way street.

F. Interim Conclusion

Interpretation in conformity with the directive is intended to interpret a provision of national law (which may be in conflict with the directive on the basis of which the provision was transposed into national law) in such a way that the national provision can be applied as prescribed and intended in the directive without amendment. In doing so, consideration should be given not only to the text of the directive, but also to its purpose, context and history. The preamble can provide guidance on the purpose of the directive, albeit that recitals to the preamble are not independent provisions which can be relied upon. In a contextual interpretation, the CJEU should not limit itself to the context in the directive concerned but should extend the contextual scope to other directives or legal surroundings. The historical interpretation method is still rather new and requires case law to define, or redefine, its scope of application. In the opinion of the author, the time is also right to refer to preparatory documents from Working Parties in order to interpret concepts from a directive, especially where that would not lead to new rules without a basis in the directive itself and would only interpret the existing content.

V. APPLICATION OF INTERPRETATION METHODS TO CONCEPTS IN TAX DIRECTIVES

A. Introduction

Having now described the theoretical framework regarding interpretation methods, the author will illustrate the above in relation to two specific recent developments affecting direct taxation to some extent. First, an interpretational issue in relation to the anti-hybrid rules in the Anti-Tax Avoidance Directive will be addressed, especially where it relates to the scope of ATAD2. This will be followed by a discussion on the concept of 'payment' in hallmark C1 of the fifth amendment to the Directive on Administrative Cooperation.

[104] See also, van den Broek (n 48) 258.

B. The Anti-Tax Avoidance Directive

i. Introduction

The purpose of the amendment to the Anti-Tax Avoidance Directive (ATAD) was to combat hybrid mismatches. Essentially, the original Directive only resolved matters of double deductions or deductions without inclusions in intra-EU situations. The scope of ATAD was extended through its amending directive, by including hybrid mismatches in third-country situations as well. As the EU does not have legislative powers in those third countries, ATAD2's solution was found in a primary and a secondary rule.[105] The latter would effectively only apply if the primary rule were to require a third country to deny a deduction or include income.

In implementing ATAD2 in the Netherlands, some potential overkill could arise. This can be illustrated by the following example:[106]

> US parent company M holds all the shares in a Dutch bv, ie a Dutch limited liability company. The company manufactures goods for M, incurring costs of 100 in the process. M pays the company an annual fee of 110 (to be considered at arm's length) for this. M sells the goods which the bv manufactures on the US domestic market for 120.
>
> The Netherlands taxes the bv, without application of the ATAD2 correction, for a profit of 110 -/- 100 = 10. Without the application of the check-the-box system, the US would also consider the bv as independently liable to pay tax and would only tax M for its profit of 120 -/- 110 = 10. In total, the Group result of 20 would only be taxed once: 10 in the Netherlands and 10 in the US. This changes if the US considers the bv to be a disregarded entity under the check-the-box system. In that situation, the US would consider the bv to be transparent for tax purposes. As a result, the bv's result will also be taxed at the level of M. M is taxed for 120 -/- 100 = 20. Without the ATAD2 correction, the bv is still taxed for 10 in the Netherlands, so 30 is taxed in aggregate. That is 10 more than the Group result of 20, because the bv's profit of 10 is taxed in both the Netherlands and the US. Double taxation occurs as a result of the choice to qualify the Dutch bv as tax transparent.[107] This double taxation may be cancelled out in whole or in part since M may, under certain conditions, offset the corporate income tax paid by the bv against the US corporate income tax. However, this does not alter the fact that the choice for the check-the-box system leads in principle to double taxation.

[105] Interestingly enough, the European Commission initially wanted to counter hybrid mismatches by using a system of mutual recognition. Later, however, the Member States suggested the application of the primary and secondary rule following the OECD's suggestions under BEPS Action 2. See WPTQ on Hybrid Mismatches, Room Document #2 of 4 March 2016, Ares(2016)3253800.

[106] See PGH Albert, GK Fibbe and LR Jacobs, 'Overkill bij ATAD2: wat gaat de Hoge Raad of staatssecretaris doen?' (2021) 14 *MBB*. See also WR Kooiman and JJAM Korving, 'Hybride interpretatie' (2021) 18 *MBB*.

[107] The author realises that tax advantages may also arise in more complex group structures. Due to the abstract nature of the case, he will not discuss this here.

However, as a result of the Dutch implementation of the ATAD2 rules, the cost deduction in the Netherlands would be disallowed, because the bv incurs costs that are deductible for corporate income tax purposes in the Netherlands and, due to the tax transparency, in the United States. Due to the tax transparency of the bv, the minus and plus levels balance each other out at the level of the parent company, so that the remuneration as such is not reflected in the tax base of the latter. This would be the reason for not qualifying the income of the bv as dual inclusion income and, hence, not allowing a deduction, even though it is actually taxed twice.[108]

From an interpretational perspective, the above example raises the question of whether the Dutch ATAD2 implementing provisions could be interpreted in such a way that they do not apply to a situation where the hybrid mismatch causes double taxation. In addition, it could be argued that the concept of 'dual inclusion income' should have a broader interpretation than the one made by the Dutch legislator. Both elements will be discussed below.

ii. The Limited Scope of the ATAD2

The first question is whether the limitation on deductions for double deduction applies in a situation resulting in double taxation. Article 9(1)(b) of the Directive stipulates that the deduction is denied in the payer's Member State insofar as the hybrid mismatch results in a double deduction and the deduction is not denied in the investor jurisdiction. In the passage below, the author interprets whether that provision would mean that situations leading to double taxation should be out of scope.

In relation to a textual interpretation, the wording of the provision does not indicate that the deduction limitation would not apply to the scenario in which the hybrid mismatch leads to double taxation. Moreover, the text of the Directive is, in any case, silent on the scope of the deduction restrictions. In itself, the text is undecisive. When the objective is taken into account, it becomes clear from the Preamble to ATAD2 that the purpose of that Directive is to address tax avoidance arising from hybrid mismatches. This is still implicit in the references to ATAD1 and the BEPS Action Report 2, where tax avoidance is constantly mentioned. However, in the Preamble to ATAD2 it is explicated that 'in order to ensure proportionality, it is necessary to address only the cases where there is a substantial risk of avoiding taxation through the use of hybrid mismatches'.[109] In the author's opinion, the reference to 'avoiding taxation' can be interpreted as lacking taxation and not, as in the example, that it is to be applicable to

[108] See also *Parliamentary Documents II* 2018/19, 35 241, 3, 64.
[109] Preamble to Directive 2017/952, point 12.

situations leading to double taxation. As such, applying a deduction limitation on top of that is diametrically opposed to the objective of ATAD2.

Under a contextual interpretation, points 5, 23, 25 and 30 of the Preamble to ATAD2 show that the Directive aims to neutralise the effect of hybrid mismatches. The principle of neutrality also fits within EU law as a whole. For example, Recital 5 of the Preamble to ATAD1 considers that not only tax avoidance practices should be countered, but that other market obstacles, such as double taxation, should also be avoided.[110] From a neutral point of view, a situation of double taxation should actually be remedied, but as the Directive only tackles one side (double non-taxation) it should certainly not be aggravated, meaning that this contextual element can only be given a certain interpretative meaning but no legal force as an argument by itself.

A historical analysis is interesting. ATAD2 has its origins in the Organisation for Economic Co-operation and Development (OECD) report on BEPS Action 2.[111] Previously in discussions on the introduction of an anti-hybrid mismatch provision in ATAD1, the Member States explicitly referred to aligning the EU proposal with the OECD's BEPS Action 2.[112] In ATAD2's Preamble, the BEPS Action 2 report is also explicitly identified as a source of interpretation.[113] The scope of the OECD report becomes immediately clear in its first sentence: 'Hybrid mismatch arrangements exploit differences in the tax treatment of an entity or instrument under the laws of two of more jurisdictions to achieve double non-taxation, including long-term deferral'. This concerns hybrid mismatches that lead to double non-taxation. Hence, the origins of the case also advocate a limited interpretation in which Article 9(1)(b) cannot be applied to a hybrid mismatch that actually leads to double taxation.

Taking into account the above, it could be argued that, even though a textual analysis would not directly limit hybrid mismatch rules under ATAD2 to situations not leading to double taxation, the purpose, context and origins of ATAD2 argue in favour of the limited interpretation that Article 9(1)(b) does not apply in situations where a difference of qualification leads to double taxation.

[110] Since the purpose of avoiding double taxation, as observed in Recital 5 of the Preamble to ATAD1, is not fundamentally altered by the extension of the anti-hybrid mismatch provisions in ATAD2, the author finds it plausible that this recital from the base directive may also be used in the interpretation.

[111] OECD, *Neutralising the Effects of Hybrid Mismatch Arrangements, Final Report on BEPS Action 2* (5 October 2015).

[112] See, for instance, WPTQ on the Anti-Tax Avoidance Directive, Room Document #1 of 6 April 2016, Ares(2016)3255475, 22–24; and, WPTQ on the Anti-Tax Avoidance Directive, Room Document #2 of 4 May 2016, Ares(2016)3267631, 4–5. Irrespectively, in the drafting process the Slovak presidency indicated that 'the definitions and rules in ATAD2 should be described more accurately. A Directive, as a self-standing legislative instrument, should be sufficiently clear and precise by itself without making the consultation of any other instrument (ie the OECD report on Action 2) a necessary step'; see WK 1181/2016 INIT of 23 November 2016, 2.

[113] Preamble to Directive 2017/952, point 28. The desire of ATAD2 to be compliant with the OECD BEPS Action 2 report was also reflected in preparatory documents, such as WK 1501/2016 INIT of 1 December 2016, 1–2; and, WK 875/2016 INIT of 16 November 2016, 5–6.

iii. Alternative 2: Dual Inclusion Income Exists

If the arguments described above are weighed in such a way that a strict interpretation prevails over an interpretation according to purpose and scope, the subsequent question would be whether there is dual inclusion income within the meaning of ATAD2. If the income of the Dutch bv in the example can be considered to be double taxed, the deduction limitation could still not be applied.

From an interpretational perspective, the actual text of ATAD2 will be taken into consideration first. Dual inclusion income is defined in ATAD2 as any item of income that is included under the laws of both jurisdictions where the mismatch outcome has arisen. This wording can be read as meaning that it is not simply a matter of double taxation, but that the item of income as such must be included in the basis of another jurisdiction (legal interpretation). This is not the case in the above example. In addition to this legal interpretation, it is possible to read the wording in such a way that it is about the income effectively being picked up in both jurisdictions (economic interpretation). In the example, the income of the Dutch bv is also included at the level of the parent company in the United States, albeit that the income of the Dutch bv and the corresponding deduction at the level of the parent company cancel each other out.

From a teleological perspective, it is clear that the purpose of the deduction for dual inclusion income is to avoid a situation where the deduction of costs is denied, while the income is taxed twice. This is also in line with the aforementioned purpose of avoiding double taxation in Recital 5 of the Preamble to ATAD1. In view of this purpose, when interpreting the concept of 'dual inclusion income' in conformity with the Directive, it would not be reasonable to distinguish between income that is included in the tax base in the other jurisdiction (legal interpretation) and income that is not recognised as such in the other jurisdiction, but is in fact taxed twice (economic interpretation).

The system of the Directive shows that ATAD2 only applies insofar as a hybrid mismatch exists (see also Recital 29 of the Preamble) and insofar as income is not double taxed at the same time. In view of this 'insofar approach', it would be logical from a contextual perspective to also allow deductions if the income originates from the entity with which the hybrid mismatch exists. The fact that the income is not, per se, legally taxed in the other jurisdiction in such a case does not prevent double taxation.

Again, it is important that the OECD report on BEPS Action 2 is used as a source of historical interpretation as ATAD2 is clearly inspired by that report. The report does not explicitly dedicate a passage to a situation such as the one in the above-mentioned example. Even though it does discuss the interpretation of the concept of 'dual inclusion income', the passages on this subject are rather ambiguous.[114] Yet, the purpose of avoiding double taxation is mentioned

[114] Illustratively: in para 125 of the report it is stated that, in principle, it should be determined juridically whether income is included dually, while in paragraph 137, the emphasis is on the effect of the arrangement that tends towards a more economical reading.

at various points in the report. An interpretation of ATAD2 that prevents double taxation as far as possible would be in line with this line of reasoning. This is an argument in favour of a broad interpretation of the concept of 'dual inclusion income'.

Should it be concluded that ATAD2 applies to the example under section V.B.i, the different methods of interpretation provide arguments for a broad interpretation of the concept of 'dual inclusion income'. This broad interpretation implies that the income that also originates from the entity with which the hybrid mismatch exists, qualifies as dual inclusion income. This interpretation would also be applicable in situations where the hybrid mismatch does not actually lead to double taxation.

By including the term 'dual inclusion income' in ATAD2, this concept has become a term that requires an EU law context and interpretation. As such, little significance should be given to national positions taken in the parliamentary process.[115] The concept can only be interpreted by the CJEU under EU law.

C. The Directive on Administrative Cooperation

i. Introduction

The Directive on Administrative Cooperation (DAC) has been amended several times. One of the amendments was made by the Directive on mandatory automatic exchange of information in the field of taxation in relation to reportable cross-border arrangements.[116] This fifth amendment, and sixth version, is therefore referred to as DAC6.[117]

DAC6 builds on OECD BEPS Action 12 on Mandatory Disclosure Rules and is aimed at exchanging information on potentially aggressive tax practices. To that end, intermediaries, such as tax advisers and lawyers, need to disclose information on reportable cross-border arrangements within 30 days after the tax advice is made available for implementation, is ready for implementation

[115] Even though the State Secretary for Finance considers the economic interpretation following a teleological, contextual and historic reading of the concept impossible, he promised to contact the European Commission in order to discuss this effect. See *Parliamentary Documents I* 2019/20, 35 241, C, 16; and, *Parliamentary Documents I* 2019/20, 35 241, E, 13. In the end, however, he took the position that there was insufficient interpretative space under ATAD2 to avoid double taxation unilaterally. He hid behind remarks from the European Commission, even though the European Commission actually acknowledged that, according to them, ATAD2 would leave sufficient space to resolve double taxation issues unilaterally; *Parliamentary Documents I* 2019/20, 35 241, U, 2. Ultimately, MP Idsinga proposed an amendment to Dutch law in order to abolish the overkill as explained above, referring to a publication by the author of this contribution; *Parliamentary Documents II* 2021/22, 35 931, 6.

[116] Council Directive 2018/822 (n 9) 1–13.

[117] Subsequent amendments to the DAC are foreseen in relation to the exchange of information on online platforms, cryptocurrencies and shell entities.

or the first step of implementation has been made, whichever occurs first. If no intermediary is involved or the intermediary can appeal to legal professional privilege, the reporting obligation may shift to the relevant taxpayer.

Tax advice needs to be qualified as a reportable cross-border arrangement in order to be disclosed. The concept of arrangement is broad and should cover almost all transactions, instruments or constructions. Whether that arrangement is cross-border is defined in DAC6.[118] A cross-border arrangement is reportable if it qualifies within the scope of one of the hallmarks in Annex IV to the Directive. The hallmarks have deliberately been formulated broadly to avoid evasive planning around overly tight definitions.[119] In order to avoid over-reporting, the creation of a negative hallmark was proposed during the negotiation process that would constitute an exemption from reporting the schemes that are, for example, already well known to tax authorities or that are based on the use for statutory exemptions and reliefs in a routine fashion for bona fide purposes.[120] This negative hallmark was never included in DAC6.[121]

DAC6 contains a large number of concepts. Many EU Member States have implemented DAC6 by referring directly to concepts or definitions as used in DAC6 itself. As such, directive-consistent interpretation is explicitly relevant to this directive. Before addressing one specific example, ie, the concept of 'payment' in hallmark C1,[122] it is important to address the fact that the hallmarks are an important element for intermediaries and taxpayers in order to understand in which situations they need to disclose information. However, the hallmarks are not essential for the fundamental effect of DAC6. As such, the interpretation of concepts and understandings included in the hallmarks is still to some extent a joint competence of the CJEU and the individual Member States. In the case of a dispute, however, the CJEU has the final say.[123]

ii. 'Payment'

Hallmark C1 requires the reporting of deductible cross-border payments made between two or more associated enterprises, where the payment receives a

[118] Art 3, para 18 of Directive 2011/16.

[119] European Commission, Questions and Answers on new tax transparency rules for intermediaries (21 June 2017), available at europa.eu/rapid/press-release_MEMO-17-1677_en.htm. In this Q&A document, the European Commission indicates the following: 'They [the hallmarks] are as wide-ranging as possible to avoid any loopholes or omissions that could be exploited by aggressive tax planners'.

[120] WK 12943/2017 INIT of 10 November 2017, 2.

[121] More extensively on the introduction and effects of DAC6, see J Korving and J Verbaarschot, 'Mandatory Disclosure in the Netherlands – To Disclose or Not to Disclose: That Is the Question' (2019) 59 *European Taxation* 461; and J Korving, 'A Guide to the Netherlands DAC6 Guidelines' (2021) 61 *European Taxation* 12.

[122] The author notes that almost every concept used in the hallmarks, as well as in the main body of DAC6, could have been used as an example. The author just had to make a choice.

[123] See also, Weber and Steenbergen (n 36).

beneficial treatment at recipient level.[124] This raises the question of how the concept of 'payment' is to be interpreted from a directive perspective, especially whether a 'payment' would only include actual transfers of means or could also include deemed payments. The author will answer the question from an interpretative perspective, taking into account the four interpretational methods as indicated above.

The grammatical interpretation would be the starting point. However, purely from a textual perspective, there are no indications of a broad or narrow interpretation of the concept of 'payment'.

A teleological approach would probably favour a broad approach, including deemed payments in the scope of 'payment'. The main objective of DAC6 is to ensure the proper functioning of the internal market and to prevent loopholes in the proposed framework of rules.[125] The EU legislator added that:

> Aggressive tax-planning arrangements have evolved over the years to become increasingly more complex and are always subject to constant modifications and adjustments as a reaction to defensive countermeasures by the tax authorities. Taking this into consideration, it would be more effective to endeavour to capture potentially aggressive tax-planning arrangements through the compiling of a list of the features and elements of transactions that present a strong indication of tax avoidance or abuse rather than to define the concept of aggressive tax planning.[126]

From this statement, it becomes clear that the EU legislator did not intend to take a narrow approach, but that it wanted to keep some interpretational space in order to apply the hallmarks in an ever-changing tax landscape. Consequently, the hallmarks would not require updating on a regular basis, but would need to be formulated broadly covering future situations as well.

The contextual interpretation method is not decisive. As DAC6, or actually DAC as a whole, does not directly relate to tax matters but merely to the exchange of information on tax issues, a content-wise interpretation of concepts is hard to find in the context of this set of administrative rules. On the other hand, within this context, a broad interpretation would not necessarily be problematic as it is to be dealt with from the perspective of mutual assistance. In a broader context, taking into account OECD materials, the outcome would still be ambivalent. On the one hand, the report on BEPS Action 2 includes the following definition of a payment, excluding deemed payments:

> Payment includes any amount capable of being paid including (but not limited to) a distribution, credit, debit, accrual of money but it does not extend to payments that are only deemed to be made for tax purposes and that do not involve the creation of economic rights between parties.[127]

[124] The beneficial treatment can exist in the fact that the recipient (a) is not a tax resident in any jurisdiction, (b) is tax resident in a non-cooperative jurisdiction or in a jurisdiction with (hardly) any corporate income tax, (c) can apply a full exemption or (d) can apply a preferential regime.

[125] Preamble to Directive 2018/822 (n 9) point 8.

[126] ibid, point 9.

[127] OECD, *Neutralising the Effects of Hybrid Mismatch Arrangements*, Final Report on BEPS Action 2 (n 112); OECD/G20, Base Erosion and Profit Shifting Project (OECD 2015) 123.

Contrary to that, the concept of 'paid' is also used in the OECD Model Tax Convention, for instance, for payments that are traditionally considered as deductible in the source state, such as interest and royalties. In relation to interest, the Commentary to the OECD Model Tax Convention explains that the term 'paid' has a very wide meaning, since the concept of payment means the fulfilment of the obligation to place funds at the disposal of the creditor in the manner required by contract or by custom. Even though a narrow interpretation, excluding notional or deemed interest, would be possible, a broader interpretation in the light of the need for internal consistency of the distributive norms and the objective of the OECD Model Tax Convention, including deemed interest, is preferable and more convincing.[128] As a result, the contextual interpretation appears to favour a broad interpretation of the concept of 'payment' as well.

Lastly, a historical analysis might also shed some light on the matter. DAC6 was clearly inspired by OECD BEPS Action 12 on Mandatory Disclosure Rules.[129] In drafting the hallmarks, the Commission explained in relation to hallmark C1 that the OECD Recommendation regarding cross-border schemes is to develop hallmarks that focus on BEPS-related risks and that are sufficiently wide to capture different and innovative tax planning techniques.[130] Hallmark C1 is based on elements of the OECD BEPS Action 12 report and pre-existing hallmarks under Portuguese law,[131] which in turn were based on the UK regime.[132] References to Portuguese and UK law, however, do not relate to the concept of 'payment'.[133] Referring to the OECD BEPS Action 12 Report, where it explains the broad interpretation of a 'transaction', an analogously broad interpretation of the concept of 'payment' would be reasonable:

> The definition of transaction should also capture notional or deemed transactions that are recognised for tax purposes in the counterparty jurisdiction even if such transactions are not treated as having any economic or tax consequences in the reporting jurisdiction.

Taking into account the above, the concept of 'payment' within hallmark C1 would have a broad interpretation, including deemed payments of interest. This means that some EU Member States, applying the narrow approach, would technically not interpret the concept appropriately. However, as explained above and in relation to the interpretation of hallmarks, the CJEU would indeed have the final say but national interpretations can coexist until that moment,

[128] See W Haslehner, 'Article 11: Interest' in E Reimer and A Rust (eds), *Klaus Vogel on Double Taxation* Conventions, vol I, 4th edn (Kluwer Law International 2015) 904–05.

[129] Preamble to Directive 2018/822 (n 9) point 4.

[130] WK 9981/2017 INIT of 21 September 2017, 5.

[131] ibid.

[132] 2017/0138 (CNS), 10582/17 ADD2 of 22 June 2017, 12.

[133] Under Portuguese law, it was the effect of the scheme that triggered national disclosure rules, eg, a company enjoying a certain benefit because a listed jurisdiction was involved or foreign taxes were paid, were too low from a Portuguese tax perspective. See Portuguese Ministry of Finance and Public Administration Decree-Law no 29/2008. The UK DOTAS system, as a predecessor to DAC6, also did not depend on there being a payment.

since the narrow approach does not immediately have to be changed. It would, for instance, be up to the European Commission to take action against a potentially improper application of the hallmark.

VI. CONCLUDING REMARKS

The theory behind directive-consistent interpretation is old. Nevertheless, in the field of direct taxation, it is still hardly debated. The topic is, however, very important as most harmonisation on direct tax issues has taken the form of a directive. The author does not expect that to change in the near future. Also, taking into account that Member States, probably in order to avoid infringement procedures over the incorrect implementation of directives, implement directives almost by copying the text of directives into national law or by directly referring to provisions of directives, makes a good understanding of how the provisions of directives – and EU law in general – need to be interpreted relevant.

The CJEU have already acknowledged the relevance of textual analysis. It is the starting point for interpretational discussions in an EU context. If the text of a provision is not fully clear, the objective of the rule and its context could provide for more guidance on how a provision was to be interpreted. Recently, the CJEU finally accepted the relevance of legal history for interpretational purposes. To that end, it has to be stated that it only allowed relevant historic materials that were publicly available, for instance, because the document was published in one of the EU's official journals. The author would call on the EU institutions to also publish more background documentation and information for interpretative purposes. Naturally, those documents should not be edited or limited as, for instance, Member States are reluctant to publish how they consider a provision is to be interpreted.

The relevance of interpretation in line with a directive was illustrated by two practical examples, relating to two recent EU directives that are closely linked to direct taxation. The author could actually fill an entire contribution merely by addressing examples of either of those directives. Much is still to be discovered. Looking ahead, new directives on direct taxation already await to be interpreted. However, the more important a provision is to the core of the instrument, the more the CJEU is entitled to say. But as interpretation also requires the weighing of arguments, in the end the judges will decide.[134]

[134] Free to ABBA, 'The Winner Takes It All', 1980 (credits: B Andersson, B Ulvaeus and M Tretow).

12

Legal Standards and EU Tax Law

STEFAN OLSSON*

I. INTRODUCTION

A 'European Union (EU) tax law' is often spoken about. However, as is well known to anybody with an interest in tax law, there is no EU tax law in the sense of a complete tax system, at least if you disregard the Value Added Tax, VAT. There is merely the influence of EU legal sources on national tax law. As all EU law, the influence on national tax law can in principle be divided into two parts. First, all national legislation must fulfil the demands of EU primary law, including the fundamental freedoms. Second, national law must be adapted to comply with the demands of secondary EU law, such as directives. As stated by Terra and Wattel more than 20 years ago, a certain degree of tax harmonisation is necessary for the establishment and functioning of the internal market.[1]

EU directives have in turn two different characteristics. Regarding indirect taxation, and especially VAT, EU law has set up a more or less complete tax system, which is in force in all EU Member States. In the field of direct taxation, however, only small parts of the national tax systems are governed by directives, and mainly concern corporate taxation. The reason behind the state of things is of course quite easy to explain. VAT has proved to be a tax that is easy to 'sell' to politicians and has been adopted not only by the EU Member States, but also by many other countries around the world. Direct taxation, and especially corporate taxation, on the other hand, is safeguarded by national governments and even limited harmonisation efforts, such as the proposed Common Consolidated Corporate Tax Base (CCCTB), have proved very difficult to implement politically. In this context, it is almost surprising to see the implementation of new EU law as a result of the Base Erosion and Profit Shifting project (BEPS).[2]

* Professor of Tax Law, Karlstad Business School.

[1] B Terra and P Wattel (eds), *European Tax Law*, 3rd edn (FED 2001).

[2] Council Directive (EU) 2016/1164 of 12 July 2016 laying down rules against tax avoidance practices that directly affect the functioning of the internal market [2016] OJ L193/1 is one example.

These efforts do, however, focus on specific issues, like combating tax fraud and tax evasion. Nevertheless, it seems to be easier for the Member States to accept harmonised rules, which strengthen the States' positions at the expense of the taxpayer. More generally aimed efforts of harmonisation, such as the Parent-Subsidiary Directive (current version 2011/96/EU), which aims to eliminate double taxation between parent companies and subsidiaries, has proven to be more difficult to adopt. The original directive was first proposed in 1969, but could not be adopted until 1990.

EU direct law harmonisation can therefore not be seen as a complete tax system, but rather as a 'smorgasbord' of different tastes, but with the difference that the Member States do not have the option to choose among the dishes. However, not only directives that can be considered as pure tax law may affect the national tax systems. For example, it is obvious that EU legislative acts in such areas as corporate and accounting law may influence national tax law. The focus of this contribution is not, however, on how these parts of EU law may affect tax law, but primarily how norms produced by actors other than the EU nevertheless have effect as binding rules when applied in EU Member States.

The aim and purpose of this contribution is to describe and analyse the concept of legal standards, especially the International Accounting Standards (IAS) and the International Financial Reporting Standards (IFRS), and their impact on tax law. A comparison is also made with the similar International Standards of Auditing (ISA), that govern auditing in EU Member States and therefore will have an influence on both corporate law and tax law.

The outline of this contribution is as follows: we depart from the notion of the legal standard from a Nordic perspective. Legal standards in Sweden often are labelled as 'good practices' of different forms. Thereafter, the legal standard of General Acceptable Accounting Practices (GAAP) will be described from an international perspective. The connection between accounting and tax law and the impact international accounting standards have on tax law are subsequently described. A comparison is also made with the similar international auditing standards and their role in EU law.

II. LEGAL STANDARDS

A legal standard, in the way it has been acknowledged in Nordic legal science, is a standard that is in some way produced outside the legal system, but referred to in legislation.[3] The Nordic notion of a legal standard often departs from the Norwegian professor Ragnar Knoph's posthumously published work from 1939.[4] In a broader international perspective, it seems that a legal standard

[3] See S Strömholm, *Rätt, rättskällor och rättstillämpning*, 5th edn (Norstedts Juridik 1996) 252.
[4] R Knoph, *Rettslige standarder: Saerlig grunnlovens* § 97 (Grøndahl & Søn 1939).

may be any kind of norm that is unclear and has to be completed with judiciary decision in order to become applicable.[5] A legal standard in this sense can be described as the opposite of a clear legal rule. In this contribution, a narrower notion of a legal standard will be used. Knoph first compared the legal standard to the general clause, with the approach that the legal standard was mainly derived from Anglo-American legal systems, while the general clause is supposed to be a German legal notion.[6] He concludes that the two notions are closely related, but not identical. According to Knoph, the general clause is usually applicable to a number of different situations and is intended to supplement or even amend the results of other more specific legal rules. The legal standard may supplement the written legal norms, but is not intended to override a clear and specific rule.

Another track pursued by Knoph was the question of whether a legal standard in fact was the same as a legal principle. However, there is no clear definition of a legal principle. A principle may have its importance on a *law-making level*.[7] This kind of principle sets the boundaries for the competence to create a specific legal act, such as the principle of legality. Another principle may have its primary use on an *act of application of law level*, such as the principle of *legal certainty*. This distinction does not, however, say anything about what comprises a legal principle. A legal principle is often understood as some kind of meta principle, which is not enacted, but is nonetheless supposed to be valid. The Dworkian conception of principles as a type of 'trump', that overrides existing legal acts, is an example of this form of definition of a legal principle. Alexander Peczenik has stated that a legal principle is valid if it is ethically acceptable and motivates the content of legal acts, preparatory works and case law. These kinds of legal principles therefore appear as *value principles*. It is, however, not difficult to find legal principles that can hardly be described as value principles. Classical principles of interpretation, used in Swedish and other legal systems, as *lex specialis* and *lex posterior*, are examples of this.

Legal principles can also be divided into general and special principles. General principles, such as the interpretation principles mentioned above, are applicable throughout the legal system, while special principles are applicable only in specific legal fields. Tax law principles naturally belong to the second category. Further, principles can be divided between those that are written down in statutes,[8] and those that are unwritten but still supposed to be valid in the

[5] HB Schaefer, 'Legal Rules and Standards' in CK Rowley and F Schneider (eds), *Encyclopedia of Public Choice* (Kluwer 2004).

[6] Knoph (n 4) 3.

[7] S Bergström, *Förutsebarhet: En studie av regeringsrättens rättstillämpning* (Iustus Förlag 1987) 15; and S Olsson, *Författningsprövning i skatterätten* (Iustus Förlag 2006) 58–59.

[8] eg, the *principle of contingency* in ch 44 § 21 Swedish Income Tax Act.

legal system, for example, through case law.[9] Many legal principles are in any case quite vague, and not suitable as a tool to solve actual legal problems.[10] This also seems to have been the position of Knoph.[11] Even if a legal principle might appear in a legal standard, the two are not the same legal concept.

Knoph also analysed whether a legal standard would be the equivalent of a form penalty. Such a penalty is contained in a criminal law statute, which refers to another statute in order to define the criminal action. In the Swedish legal system, form penalties are usually found in what has been labelled as *special criminal law*. Examples in Swedish law are the Swedish Companies Act and the Energy Taxation Act.[12] Form penalties seem, however, to refer only to public law sources, while the legal standards are usually considered to be civil or private law. Therefore, the legal standards do not seem to be equivalent to a form penalty.

The legal standard may be described as a kind of benchmark, which must be achieved by courts and other practitioners.[13] Instead, as shown in this contribution, legal standards often take on the character of a written regulation, but in contrast to an official legal act, they have not been enacted by Parliament but are instead enacted by a private law body. It is therefore primarily the second definition that is used in this contribution for the notion of a legal standard.

III. GOOD PRACTICE

Legal standards are in Swedish law often referred to as a 'good practice' in some specific field, for example, 'good accounting practices',[14] 'good estate agent practices' or 'good lawyer practices'. The content of and the way to determine the 'good practice' is, however, quite different depending on the form of 'good practice'. Further, the extent to which they are subject to sanctions, from a court or from some other kind of public or private body, differs between different forms of 'good practices'.

Good accounting practices depends, as will be described below, to a large extent on national or international standard setters. The same could be said about *good auditing practices* and *good auditor practices*. The legal standard for auditing will also be described and discussed below. In contrast, *good estate agency practices* do not rely on any published standards, but are established

[9] eg, the principle that a transaction concerning real estate should be considered to be either a sale or a gift, but never both. This is different from, for example, a transaction of shares, which can be considered to be both in a sale and a gift, see RÅ 1943 ref 9.

[10] M Dahlberg, 'Om principer vid tolkningen av skattelag' [2004] *Skattenytt* 664.

[11] Knoph (n 4) 5.

[12] Ch 30 Swedish Companies Act (2005:551); ch 10 Energy Taxation Act (1994:1776).

[13] This is how the legal standard is conceived by M Knutsson, C Norberg and P Thorell, *Redovisningsfrågor i skattepraxis*, 3rd edn (Iustus 2012) 34–36.

[14] Also referred to as 'Generally Accepted Accounting Practices', GAAP.

exclusively by the governmental body the Swedish Board of Supervision of Estate Agents (Fastighetsmäklarinspektionen).[15] In a similar way, *good lawyer practices* depend to a large extent on decisions made by the disciplinary board of the Swedish Bar Association (Svenska Advokatsamfundet). These decisions are supplemented by guiding statements on good lawyer practices issued by the board of the Bar Association. These guiding statements are, however, seldom longer than one page and on average not more than one statement is published every year.

The variations in good practices described above must be seen as examples. From a Swedish perspective, private law bodies that produce and uphold good practices, usually concerning their member companies, are not uncommon. This is particularly common in the marketing law area, but also exists in capital markets. When a specific branch voluntarily adopts a common good practice and an organisation to control or sanction departures from good practice it is usually labelled as *self-regulation*. There is also a tendency in different professional occupations to produce good practices and preferably some kind of authorisation system for their own profession, in order to strengthen the reputation and salaries in that profession. These tendencies implicate a growing importance of legal standards, in contrast to public regulation at the national or EU level.

IV. GENERALLY ACCEPTED ACCOUNTING PRINCIPLES

Accounting standards can be produced both by public or private bodies. In Sweden, good accounting practices or *generally accepted accounting principles* are defined by the governmental authority the Swedish Accounting Standards Board (Bokföringsnämnden) as far as non-listed companies are concerned. Internationally, accounting standards are produced by the private organisation International Accounting Standards Board (IASB). In the perspective presented in this contribution, it is the international standards that are of paramount interest.

The international accounting principles were originally produced by the International Accounting Standards Committee (IASC), founded in London in 1973. The Committee was constructed as an expert organisation, run by auditors. Criticism of the domination of the audit profession on the standard setting led to a reorganisation of the IASC and the establishment of the International Accounting Standards Board in 2001. The IASB, in contrast to the IASC, represents different parties and is not solely connected to the auditors. The Board comprises of 12 members, representing a mixture of auditors, standard setters, users and academics.

[15] Except the few cases where a decision made in an inspection against an estate agent is challenged in court and later amended by the court.

Behind the IASB is the IFRS Foundation, with its seat in Delaware in the United States. The Foundation is led by 22 trustees, who are appointed from around the world according to a specific scheme. The American and European influence is still dominant, although the international standards are not applied by American enterprises.[16] The members of the Standards Board are appointed by the trustees for a period of five years and may be re-elected once. Supporting the trustees is the Advisory Council, with 50 members representing authorities, organisations and auditing firms around the world.

Since the reorganisation of standard setting, the process has acquired a rather high degree of transparency. Draft papers, labelled as exposure drafts, are published and comments and opinions on the drafts are both welcomed and published on the website. Comment letters on the drafts are issued by public authorities, accounting organisations, auditing firms, business companies and even by auditors and accounting experts themselves.

The published standards of the IASB are labelled International Financial Reporting Standards (IFRS). Up to the present, 17 IFRS standards have been published. A further 24 older International Accounting Standards (IAS), produced by the IASC, are still valid. The standards are produced in a seemingly ad hoc scheme, in which different accounting issues are treated, apparently in an order according to when the issues aroused attention. In that way, the IAS/IFRS standards cannot be seen as a complete regulatory system, since the IASB is always in the process of rewriting or amending existing standards, or creating new standards regarding accounting issues that have not been covered by existing standards.

A phenomenon that seems to be common, both for international and national standard setters, is that generally applicable standards are supplemented with clarifications or interpretations in more detailed matters. Regarding the IASB, these interpretations were originally written by a Standards Interpretations Committee and both the interpretations and the Committee were labelled SIC.[17] Since 2004, the interpretations have been called IFRIC produced by the IFRS Interpretations Committee, consisting of 15 members. Fifteen IFRIC interpretations have been published as valid by IASB.

V. INTERNATIONAL ACCOUNTING STANDARDS AND EU LAW

At the turn of the last century, there was growing concern in the EU regarding the growth of business in comparison with primarily North America and South East Asia.[18] The Commission identified the division of the financial

[16] According to US GAAP, the standards of FASB are applied.
[17] Today, five of these older interpretations are still valid.
[18] The Lisbon European Council of 23 and 24 March 2000.

markets within the EU along national borders as being part of the problem.[19] A way to improve the markets, and progress towards a unified EU financial market, would be to adopt a common accounting standard for the preparation and setting up of the consolidated statements in listed corporations in EU Member States.[20]

The harmonisation of accounting rules at the EU level had until then only been conducted in the form of directives that had to be implemented in national law.[21] Although the then applicable accounting directives had been criticised as being too detailed, they were at the same time considered far too vague to be acceptable for the companies on the international capital market.[22] According to the Commission, this form of harmonisation would be too slow and difficult to achieve the goal of a rapid improvement of the financial market. Furthermore, the EU law principles of subsidiarity and proportionality weighed against more new regulation at the EU level. It was also deemed necessary that the standards adopted could easily be changed in order to be sure to keep them up to date as regards the development of international accounting practices.

Instead of creating new EU accounting directives, the Commission's solution was the adoption of an EU regulation, directly applicable in the Member States. The technique of using regulations in a field that has traditionally been harmonised through EU directives has also occurred later, for example, in the field of VAT. However, when it was introduced in the early 2000s it was described as 'revolutionary'.[23]

Through IAS Regulation 1606/2002, an already existing accounting standard could be adopted as part of EU law.[24] At that time, European companies that were listed on the New York Stock Exchange had to set up their consolidated statements according to US GAAP, the Financial Accounting Standards Board (FASB) standards, while the IAS standards were mainly used in Europe. In Sweden at this time, listed companies followed the standards set by the private accounting body Redovisningsrådet. These standards were to a large extent mere translations into Swedish of the then existing IAS standards. The international accounting standards were therefore known to European companies.

The choice was then made to incorporate the international IAS accounting standards into EU law. If the IAS standards have been criticised for being too complicated for practical use in companies, the US GAAP, which would be the only alternative solution, is known to be even more comprehensive.

[19] The Commission's Financial Services Action Plan.

[20] Preamble no 6, reg 1606/2002.

[21] See ch 7.

[22] See K van Hulle, 'From Accounting Directives to International Accounting Standards' in C Leuz, D Pfaff and A Hopwood (eds), *Economics and Politics of Accounting: International Perspectives on Research Trends* (Oxford University Press 2004) 355–57.

[23] van Hulle, ibid, 363.

[24] Regulation (EC) No 1606/2002 of the European Parliament and of the Council of 19 July 2002 on the application of international accounting standards [2002] OJ L243/1.

On 19 July 2002, Regulation 1606/2002 on the application of international accounting standards was adopted. It is a fairly short legal act, compromising less than three full pages, excluding the Preamble. On the other hand, the IAS Regulation is complemented with another regulation, containing all international accounting standards that have been accepted as parts of EU law. This regulation is frequently updated and has currently 1213(!) pages.[25]

It is stated in the regulation that:

> It is important for the competitiveness of Community capital markets to achieve convergence of the standards used in Europe for preparing financial statements, with international accounting standards that can be used globally, for cross-border transactions or listing anywhere in the world.[26]

The Preamble also makes clear that the international standards are acceptable as a part of EU law only if they are compatible with the basic requirements of the then valid accounting directives, if the standards' 'application results in a true and fair view of the financial position and performance of an enterprise'.[27] In order to ascertain the compatibility of the international standards, a special mechanism for the implementation of the standards into EU law was created. As an overall rule, the Commission has the power to decide on the applicability of international accounting standards within the Community.[28] Also according to the regulation, the Commission should be supported by an accounting regulatory committee.[29] A task of the committee would be to provide support and expertise for the Commission to adopt proposed new international standards and proposed changes to existing standards. It would also

> be a means to deliberate, reflect and exchange information on international accounting standards among the main parties concerned, in particular national accounting standard setters, supervisors in the fields of securities, banking and insurance, central banks including the European Central Bank (ECB), the accounting profession and users and preparers of accounts.[30]

The committee that would fulfil these tasks was called the European Financial Reporting Advisory Group (EFRAG). The group is a private body and was created in 2001, as a result of the IAS Regulation. The members of the association are eight European stakeholder organisations, representing,

[25] Commission Regulation (EC) No 1126/2008 of 3 November 2008 adopting certain international accounting standards in accordance with Regulation (EC) No 1606/2002 of the European Parliament and of the Council [2008] OJ L320/1.

[26] Regulation (EC) No 1606/2002, Preamble no 5.

[27] Regulation (EC) 1606/2002, Preamble no 9.

[28] Art 3, Regulation (EC) 1606/2002.

[29] Art 6, Regulation (EC) 1606/2002.

[30] Regulation (EC) 1606/2002, Preamble no 11.

for example, business, banking and insurance branches, and nine national standard setting organisations. Sweden is represented by the Association for Generally Accepted Practice in the Securities Market (Föreningen för god sed på värdepappersmarknaden).

With the IAS Regulation, it was decided that as from 2005, consolidated accounts of publicly traded companies should be prepared according to the international accounting standards IAS and IFRS, that had been accepted by the Commission as part of EU law. According to the Regulation, it is also optional for Member States to allow or demand that the annual statements of the publicly traded companies, and even non-listed companies, should be set up according to the international standards.

VI. INTERNATIONAL ACCOUNTING STANDARDS AND NATIONAL ACCOUNTING AND TAX LAW

From a Swedish perspective, the complete IAS/IFRS standards (also known as full IFRS) are never applicable when setting up the annual statement in a limited company. Regarding publicly traded companies, the annual statement should be set up according to RFR 2, a standard set up by the Council for Swedish Financial Reporting (Rådet för Finansiell Rapportering). The Council is a private body, devoted to complementary accounting standards for listed companies. The principal idea behind RFR 2 is that the annual accounts in publicly traded companies should, as far as possible, be set up according to the IAS/IFRS standards, except when the international standards violate Swedish law, foremost the Annual Accounts Act (årsredovisningslagen). Reporting according to RFR 2, when parts of the international standards are not applicable in the annual statement, is labelled 'IFRS limited by law' (*lagbegränsad IFRS*). This limitation is of great importance for Swedish business taxation since RFR 2 hinders the application of the fair value of assets in the annual statements and further in the business income tax return.

The impact of international standards on national tax law will of course differ between the EU Member States since each country has its own tax law and the influence from accounting on business taxation also differs from one Member State to another. From a Swedish perspective, the connection between accounting and business taxation has traditionally been close. As a main principle, taxable income and deductible expenses should be declared the year that they are assigned according to Swedish GAAP.[31] The exceptions from this principle are extensive and mainly concern the periodisation of different kinds of costs, inventory, stock, buildings etc. This means that in Swedish tax law, it is primarily regarding income that the Swedish GAAP will determine to which taxation year a specific transaction will be assigned.

[31] Ch 14 § 2 Income Tax Act (1999:1229).

In Sweden, the accounting norms produced by the governmental authority, the Bokföringsnämnden, are therefore of great importance in calculating the taxable profit or loss in a non-listed limited company.[32] In the same way, the main part of the international accounting standards are directly applicable in establishing profit or loss in a listed Swedish company and will in that respect affect the calculation of tax in those companies.[33] As already stated above, the accounting standards that endorse assessment at fair value for different kinds of assets will not be used while setting up the annual statement in listed companies. An exception applies to the valuation of financial statements and tax returns.[34]

The exact content of the Swedish GAAP may therefore differ depending on the size of the actual company. The Swedish GAAP of today is much more than just 'generally accepted accounting principles'. Regarding non-listed companies, the Swedish Accounting Standards Board produces accounting standards that appear as complete regulations for companies of different sizes. If physical persons are overlooked, limited non-listed companies are divided into *smaller* and *larger* companies, both in the Annual Accounts Act and in Swedish GAAP. Accounting rules for smaller companies are simplified, while the regulations applicable for larger companies are influenced by the international standard 'IFRS for SMEs', produced by the IASB.

VII. A TRUE AND FAIR VIEW IN THE ACCOUNTING DIRECTIVE

Regarding non-listed companies in EU Member States, Accounting Directive 2013/34/EU is the main source for the harmonisation of the national accounting rules. The Directive superseded the older fourth (78/660/EEC) and seventh (83/349/EEC) company directives. Although efforts have been made to modernise them, these directives have long been considered outdated, especially as compared to the IFRS standards. The purpose of the Accounting Directive has, however, not been a paradigmatic change of the fundamental accounting principles for non-listed companies, but has rather simplified the accounting rules for small and medium-sized enterprises.

The EU Accounting Directive refers to the notion of 'a true and fair view' of the company's assets, liabilities, financial position and profit or loss.[35] The notion was originally incorporated into EU law from British accounting law.[36] In the UK, the notion has been a part of the Companies Act since 1947 and has a strong connection to British self-regulation in the accounting field.[37] It will

[32] Ch 14 § 2 Income Tax Act.
[33] According to the standard RFR 2, issued by Council for Swedish Financial Reporting.
[34] Ch 4 §§ 14 a–14 e Annual Accounts Act, ch 17 §§ 19–21 Income Tax Act.
[35] Art 4. 3 p. 2013/34/EU.
[36] P Thorell, *Redovisning och juridik* (Iustus 2008) 26–27.
[37] ibid 43 and 56.

be interesting to see after Brexit whether EU accounting law will in the future be dependent on a legal notion that derives from a country that is no longer a Member State.

From a Swedish perspective, it has been discussed whether a true and fair view is a legal standard or not in Swedish accounting, but the conclusion seems to be that it is not.[38] It would seem that the notion has not been referred to by Swedish administrative courts. It is, however, obvious that the EU law notion of a true and fair view has an impact on national tax law in different Member States. Of the very few European Court of Justice (ECJ) decisions regarding the notion, several of them have been national tax cases where the national courts have requested a preliminary ruling from the ECJ. As pointed out by the ECJ, the Accounting Directive has not been designed to lay down the conditions where the annual accounts may serve as a basis for the assessment of tax.[39] It is, however, not excluded that the annual accounts are used for this purpose in the Member States. Further, it is stated that the Directive is not intended to regulate in detail all accounting questions which depend on specific facts.[40] The Directive only aims to draw up general principles that must be recognised in the Member States when setting up annual accounts. The principle of a true and fair view has nonetheless been tried by the ECJ in some cases.

In *DE + ES Bauunternehmung Gmbh v Finanzamt Bergheim*, the Court found that the fourth Company Directive

> requires provision to be made for potential liabilities under warranties, such as those in question in the main proceedings, as obligations arising in law before the date of the balance sheet but whose effects will not become apparent until after that date.[41]

As no harmonised rules had been adopted concerning how to calculate such liabilities, national rules could be used insofar as the annual accounts give a true and fair view of the company's assets, financial position and the profit or loss of the company, and that the provisions do not exceed in amount the sums which are necessary.

BIAO v Finanzamt für Grossunternehmen in Hamburg concerned a German branch of a French bank, that had 'sub-participated' in a loan between two other banks.[42] The German branch feared a loss as a result of the participation in the loan agreement and made a cover for the possible loss on the balance sheet. According to the ECJ, the Accounting Directive did not preclude such a

[38] See J Bjuvberg, *Redovisningens betydelse för beskattningen* (MercurIUS 2006) 177–79; M Knutsson, C Norberg and P Thorell, *Redovisningsfrågor i skattepraxis*, 3rd edn (Iustus 2012) 35.

[39] Case C-306/99 *BIAO v Finanzamt für Grossunternehmen in Hamburg* [2003] ECR I-0001, ECLI:EU:C:2003:3, para 70.

[40] ibid para 76.

[41] Case C-275/97 *DE + ES Bauunternehmung Gmbh v Finanzamt Bergheim* [1999] ECR I-05331, ECLI:EU:C:1999:406.

[42] Case C-306/99 *BIAO* (n 39).

provision, as long as the loss or debt in question could be characterised as 'likely or certain' at the balance-sheet date. The Court also stated that

> in order to ensure compliance with the principle of prudence and the principle that a true and fair view of the assets and liabilities be given, the most appropriate method of valuation might be to carry out a globalised assessment of all the relevant factors.

The Court stated in *État belge v GIMLE SA* that it was not acceptable according to the principle of a true and fair view to deviate from more detailed rules of valuation in the then valid fourth directive, in favour of a valuation at fair value.[43]

In the combined cases *Immo Chiaradia SPRL* and *Docteur De Bruyne SPRL v État belge* the Court concluded that the principle of a true and fair view is not

> precluding an accounting method according to which a company issuing a share option may recognise as income the grant date price of that option in the course of the accounting year in which that option is exercised or at the end of its period of validity.[44]

It is quite clear from the above-described cases that the Court has not found that its task is to interpret what the principle of a true and fair view really means in the specific cases. The Court has merely found that the principle does not preclude national accounting rules, as far as they are compatible with the principle. Furthermore, the principle does not support the deviation of the more detailed rules in the Accounting Directive. In the way it has been referred to by the Court, the principle appears to be more a benchmark in the sense described above, than a detailed standard that gives specific answers in different situations. As a result of this fact, if the impact on national accounting law is limited, then the impact on national tax law will be equally limited.

VIII. INTERNATIONAL AUDITING STANDARDS

The standardised international auditing norms have a somewhat similar history to international accounting standards. Originally, the standards were produced by the International Auditing Practice Committee, founded in 1978. In 2002, the organisation was reconstructed as the International Auditing and Assurance Standards Board (IAASB). The Board is run by the International Federation of Accountants.[45] It consists of 18 members, who are auditors or

[43] Case C-322/12 *État belge v GIMLE SA*, ECLI:EU:C:2013:632.

[44] Case C-444/16 C-445/16 *Immo Chiaradia SPRL and Docteur De Bruyne SPRL v État belge*, ECLI:EU:C:2017:465.

[45] It should be noted that the words *accountant* and *auditor* are often used in a similar way internationally to describe a person that performs an audit.

academics from different parts of the world, each supported by a technical adviser. The IAASB produces the ISA, but the activities of the auditors are also governed by an overall ethical framework, the Code of Ethics for Professional Accountants, produced by a different body, the International Ethics Standards Board for Accountants.

The ISA Standards have been implemented to form part of EU law. According to Article 26 of Directive 2006/43/EC (the Auditing Directive), 'Member States shall require statutory auditors and audit firms to carry out statutory audits in compliance with international auditing standards adopted by the Commission'. The same Article states that the international auditing standards mentioned are ISA and other standards produced by the IAASB. These international standards are therefore to be seen as compulsory regarding the auditing of both listed and non-listed companies in the EU. It also follows from the Directive that the Member States may apply national standards, as long as they do not cover the same subject matters as an international standard already adopted by the Commission as part of EU law.

Similar to the IAS Regulation, the Auditing Directive prescribes a special mechanism for the Commission to adopt the international standards while safeguarding the quality and acceptability of the standards. Apart from certain requirements that must be reached by the standards,[46] the Commission is assisted by a special committee.[47]

The power of the Commission to implement the international auditing standards as part of EU law is repeated in Regulation 537/2014, which is specially aimed at the auditing of public-interest entities.[48] In the Regulation, the framework is set for the above-mentioned assisting committee, which has been labelled the Committee of European Auditing Oversight Bodies (CEAOB).[49] The Board members are national supervising authorities, such as, for example, the Swedish Inspectorate of Auditors (Revisorsinspektionen). Also, the European Securities and Markets Authority is a member of the Board, but does not have the right to vote. Further, the EEA members, Iceland, Lichtenstein and Norway, are represented on the board without being members.

Despite the similar legal constructions for the adoption by the Commission of the international accounting and auditing standards, there is a major difference in the composition of the committees that are intended to assist the Commission in the adoption of the standards. The EFRAG consists of private law bodies like European stakeholder organisations and national standard setters, while the

[46] Directive 2006/43/EC of the European Parliament and of the Council of 17 May 2006 on statutory audits of annual accounts and consolidated accounts, amending Council Directives 78/660/EEC and 83/349/EEC and repealing Council Directive 84/253/EEC [2006] OJ L157/87, Art 26(3).

[47] ibid Art 48(1).

[48] Regulation (EU) No 537/2014 of the European Parliament and of the Council of 16 April 2014 on specific requirements regarding statutory audit of public-interest entities and repealing Commission Decision 2005/909/EC, Art 9.

[49] ibid Art 30.

CEAOB mainly has national supervisory authorities as members. An explanation for this difference lies in the different interests in accounting and auditing. The group statements are mainly intended for businesses and investors, while the auditors are subject to public supervision, and if they have acted incorrectly, may be subject to public sanctions. The public interest is more obvious regarding the standards governing auditing than the accounting standards.

IX. IFRS AND CCCTB

The process of establishing a Common Consolidated Corporate Tax Base (CCCTB) has been on and off, mainly off, for a number of years. Initially, it was discussed whether the corporate tax base could be based on IFRS financial reporting. A coordination between financial and fiscal accounting would of course lead to benefits for both businesses and tax authorities. However, even at an early point the Commission pointed out the problems with such a solution. It might sound like a good idea to let the common tax base follow the future development of the IFRS standards.[50] However, several Member States do not accept the IFRS standards when setting up the annual statements of companies, as is the case in Sweden, where full IFRS is not allowed even in the annual statements of listed companies. There might also be parts of the international standards that are not suitable for taxation. If there were a link in EU law between financial and tax accounting, the latter would probably have to depend more on national GAAP in the different Member States rather than the international accounting standards.

Therefore, in the original 2011 proposal for the CCCTB it was expressively stated that the corporate tax base rules were valid without prejudice to the then existing fourth and seventh Company Directives or IAS Regulation 1606/2002.[51] The proposal contained a set-up of special tax accounting rules, which if they had been implemented, would have meant a complete separation of financial and tax accounting. The set of rules were supposed to be optional for all companies.

Since the 2011 proposal for a CCCTB was never realised and the process was halted, the Commission made a new approach in 2016. The new approach consisted of two proposed directives. The proposal was thus divided into one directive, concerning the common corporate tax base, and another regarding the consolidation for tax purposes. In the latter mentioned proposed directive, no reference was made to the IFRS standards. The proposed directive on a common tax base was meant to be mandatory for companies that belonged

[50] CCCTB/WP057 Brussels (26 July 2007).

[51] European Commission, 'Proposal for a Council Directive on a Common Consolidated Corporate Tax Base (CCCTB)' COM(2011) 121 final.

to a consolidated group for financial accounting purposes, with a consolidated turnover of at least €750,000.000(!)[52] It was further stated that a 'consolidated group for financial accounting purposes' should be defined as 'all entities that are fully included in consolidated financial statements drawn up in accordance with the International Financial Reporting Standards or a national financial reporting system'.[53] Subsequently, the 2016 proposal also relied on separate tax accounting, set up independently of the accounting standards used in the financial statement of the company. It has so far proved to be as politically difficult to implement the 2016 proposal as the forerunner from 2011. Therefore, in May 2021 the Commission withdrew the proposal and instead launched a similar proposal named Business in Europe: Framework for Income Taxation (BEFIT). The BEFIT proposal will be put forward in 2023 at the earliest.

X. CONCLUDING REMARKS

In this contribution, the notion of the legal standard and its influence on tax law has been analysed. The departing point has been the Nordic understanding of the notion, as expressed by Knoph and Strömholm, as a standard produced outside the legal system, but referred to by the legislation. It has also been concluded that a legal standard could have quite a different appearance, as a more or less complete written set of standards or a mere benchmark, which has to be observed by courts and practitioners.

From a tax law perspective, there are primarily two legal standards that may affect the taxation. These two are also extreme examples of legal standards. First, the international accounting standards IAS/IFRS are produced by a private body, IASB. They are accepted as part of EU law through a special mechanism, with a private law body, the EFRAG, examining the standards before the formal decision of the Commission. The international accounting standards appear as an almost complete set of standards, intended to govern exclusively group accounting and are used by all listed companies both in the EU and the rest of the world, except in the United States. Whether these standards will affect the taxation in different EU Member States depends on the extent to which they are applicable also when setting up the annual accounts in the company belonging to such groups and regarding what at level there is a connection between accounting and taxation in the specific country.

As another extreme, there is the principle of a true and fair view in the Accounting Directive. The principle is acknowledged as a legal standard in EU law, but not in national Swedish accounting law. The actual wording of the

[52] European Commission, 'Proposal for a Council Directive on a Common Consolidated Corporate Tax Base (CCCTB)' COM(2016) 683 final, Art 2(1)(c).

[53] European Commission, 'Proposal for a Council Directive on a Common Corporate Tax Base' COM(2016) 685 final, Art 4(10) p.

principle has been implemented from British accounting law. There is, however, a lack of definition of the principle in EU law. According to the case law of the ECJ, it is obvious that from an EU law perspective, the principle does not have a specific content, but mainly serves as a benchmark that has to be acknowledged in national accounting law.

It has also been described in this contribution that the implementation of international auditing standards in EU law is similar to the implementation of international accounting standards. There is, however, a difference in the fact that the international auditing standards concern all listed and non-listed companies in the EU that are subject to auditing. The auditing standards will have less impact on national taxation in a regulatory way, since they do not govern the composition of annual accounts. However, in practice they are of importance, as long as there is a connection between accounting and taxation, since the auditors themselves govern the correct application of the international or national accounting norms.

Further, it has been concluded in this contribution that a possible future establishment of the BEFIT proposal will probably result in a completely new set of tax law rules that will govern the gain and loss calculation for tax purposes in the companies subject to BEFIT. International or national accounting standards will not affect the taxation of these companies.

What are the consequences of the influence from international, private body standard setters on the national power to tax in the EU Member States? The actual influence of the international accounting standards will, as stated above, differ between Member States, regarding the extent to which there is a close connection between accounting and corporate taxation. Similarly, the influence of the international auditing standards will consequently differ regarding to the extent to which annual accounting is subject to auditing and further, to the extent to which it is the basis for taxation of the company.

As shown above, there is a democratic control of the incorporation of the international standards into EU law, conducted by the Commission. Every new standard or amendment to an existing standard has to be accepted by the Commission. In fact, the actual assessment of the new standards is outsourced to a private law body, the EFRAG, regarding accounting standards, and to a committee, the CEAOB, assessing the auditing standards. However, few deviations from the standards issued by IASB have been made by the EFRAG. The international accounting standards are applied, at least when setting up the consolidated group statements in listed companies, in most countries around the world except the United States. Therefore, it is unlikely that the EFRAG will propose a deviation from the standards issued by the IASB, unless there is a serious ground for doing so. In the interests not of a European, but almost of a global harmonisation, a deviation from both the accounting and auditing standards will be unlikely. In that respect, the international standard setters have a substantial influence over accounting and auditing in the EU Member States. But the national power to tax is safeguarded in other ways. Instead of the consolidated statements in a group, the annual statement of the specific company is the basis for taxation in most countries where there is a connection between accounting and taxation. In Sweden, for example, the safeguarding of the national tax system is conducted in two ways. First, international accounting standards are only compulsory in the group accounting of listed companies. Second, as mentioned above, the annual statements in companies belonging to a listed group are set up according to 'IFRS limited by law', produced by the RFR. The standard RFR 2 prescribes that the international accounting standards should be applied when setting up the annual statement in a company within a listed group, insofar as they do not violate Swedish accounting law. The supposedly negative effects on taxation of applying the international accounting standards are in that way prevented. The content of RFR 2 and the application of the standard by Swedish listed companies have therefore successfully preserved the Swedish tax system from the influence of non-Swedish, private body standard setters.

13

Is the OECD Able to Exert Influence on the Essence of OECD-Inspired EU Secondary Law?

STEFANIE GERINGER*

I. INTRODUCTION

ORIGINATING IN *BERLIOZ*,[1] the European Court of Justice (ECJ) has developed a new argumentative pattern when it interprets European Union (EU) secondary law inspired by the work of the Organisation for Economic Co-operation and Development (OECD).[2] The Court has hence extended its assessment procedure, which now reflects a two-tier structure. Its traditional approach to apply an autonomous interpretation of EU secondary law provisions has been paralleled by references to related OECD documents. For this purpose, the Court has endorsed a dynamic interpretation of the OECD's Model Tax Convention on Income and on Capital (MTC)[3] and the accompanying Commentary. This development has been addressed to some

* Dr Stefanie Geringer is a researcher in the Department of Tax Law at the University of Vienna and a tax adviser at BDO Austria. An earlier version of this contribution was presented at 'The Power to Tax in Europe' Swedish Network for European Legal Studies (SNELS) conference (Stockholm, 25–26 November 2021). The author is grateful to Rick Krever, Werner Haslehner and Moritz Scherleitner for their invaluable remarks and related discussions. The usual disclaimer applies.

[1] Case C-682/15 *Berlioz Investment Fund*, ECLI:EU:C:2017:373.

[2] For the sake of completeness, it should be mentioned that ECJ case law encompasses a noticeable body of decisions in which the relevance of the OECD MTC and its Commentary was discussed in the context of EU primary law. These judgments (and particularly the Court's ambiguous stance on this issue) are, however, not covered by the aim of this contribution.

[3] The currently relevant condensed version was published on 18 December 2017 and is accessible via the OECD's webpage: www.oecd.org/ctp/model-tax-convention-on-income-and-on-capital-full-version-9a5b369e-en.htm. Inasmuch as they are not explicitly made to other versions of the OECD MTC Commentary, references in this contribution are meant to relate to the condensed version of 2017.

extent in related research.[4] A comprehensive analysis of the relevant case law, including particularly the recent decision in *État luxembourgeois*,[5] has, however, not been conducted yet. The significance of such an assessment is particularly clear against the background that a dynamic use of the OECD MTC and its Commentary might allow the OECD, an intergovernmental network that is legitimised by neither the EU nor domestic lawmakers,[6] to influence the meaning of OECD-induced secondary law provisions. Undisputedly, this would have tremendous effects on the current state of power to tax in Europe.

This contribution attempts to close this gap in scholarly literature. First, the state of opinion regarding the use of a static or dynamic interpretation of the OECD MTC Commentary in interpreting double tax conventions (DTCs) is explored (section II). Such an assessment is relevant for the purposes of this contribution considering that the discourse on the use of a dynamic understanding originates from international tax law. Hence, it can be considered to inform discussions relating to the ECJ case law on OECD-inspired concepts of EU secondary law. In this context, it is shown that the legitimacy of a dynamic approach is (already) highly disputed at the tax treaty level. This is followed by a section providing an overview of the ECJ's decisions in *Berlioz*, *N Luxembourg 1 and Others*[7] and *État luxembourgeois* (section III), which forms the basis for the subsequent evaluation of the Court's new argumentative pattern (section IV). Accordingly, the presentation of the relevant case law is limited to the argument regarding a potential (dynamic) relevance of the OECD MTC and its Commentary in both the Advocates General (AG) Opinions and the Court's reasoning. The ECJ's new approach to apply a dynamic interpretation of the OECD MTC Commentary for the purpose of interpreting OECD-induced concepts in EU secondary law is then assessed from two different angles. Hence, the assessment covers an investigation into the doctrinal consistency of the Court's arguments as well as a discussion of the implications of a dynamic use of the OECD MTC Commentary for democratic representation and legitimacy. It is demonstrated that the Court has not overturned its traditional approach, but merely extended it by way of contextualising its findings from an autonomous

[4] eg, M Lang, 'Double Taxation Conventions in the Case Law of the CJEU' (2018) 46 *Intertax* 181, 185–86; L De Broe and S Gommers, 'Danish Dynamite: The 26 February 2019 CJEU Judgments in the Danish Beneficial Ownership Cases' (2019) 28 *EC Tax Review* 270, 292; J Englisch, 'The Danish tax avoidance cases: New milestones in the Court's anti-abuse doctrine' (2020) 57 *Common Market Law Review* 503, 518; W Schön, 'Interpreting European Law in the Light of the OECD/G20 Base Erosion and Profit Shifting Action Plan' (2020) 74 *Bulletin for International Taxation* 286, 292 and 294; C Hamra and J Korving, 'Beneficial Ownership Interpreted, To What Extent Are the OECD and the EU on the Same Wavelength?' (2021) 49 *Intertax* 254, 269; R Danon et al, 'The Prohibition of Abuse of Rights After the ECJ Danish Cases' (2021) 49 *Intertax* 482, 508.

[5] Case C-437/19 État luxembourgeois (Informations sur un groupe de contribuables), ECLI:EU:C:2021:953.

[6] See in detail section IV.B.

[7] Joined Cases C-115/16, C-118/16, C-119/16 and C-299/16 *N Luxembourg 1 and Others v Skatteministeriet*, ECLI:EU:C:2019:134.

interpretation with related OECD documents. This new argumentative pattern can thus not produce the problematic effects on established democratic structures that would inform an exclusive reliance on a dynamic interpretation of the OECD MTC and its Commentary. It is shown that the Court's stance can nevertheless be found to entail doctrinal flaws due to the fact that these additional references do not add substantial value; a dynamic interpretation is unnecessarily applied; and most importantly, the permissibility of a dynamic interpretation is not demonstrated. The chapter closes with a summary of the key findings and an answer to the question in the title of this contribution (section V).

II. THE ARGUMENT ON A POTENTIALLY DYNAMIC RELEVANCE OF THE OECD MTC COMMENTARY IN THE TREATY CONTEXT

The vast majority of the roughly 3,000 DTCs currently in effect[8] were devised using the OECD MTC as a negotiation base. This assertion holds particularly true for DTCs signed between the EU Member States.[9] In tax scholarship, it is broadly acknowledged that the version of the OECD MTC Commentary relevant at the time of signing a bilateral tax treaty can prove valuable for interpretation purposes inasmuch as treaties follow the OECD model (static approach).[10] Due to their reliance on the model provisions, it can be reasonably assumed that the negotiation partners considered the Commentary a viable source of inspiration in the interpretive process.

By contrast, it is debated whether later changes to the OECD MTC Commentary should be taken into account (dynamic or ambulatory approach).[11] These discussions are nurtured by the fact that the DTCs themselves, as well

[8] eg, Y Brauner, 'What the BEPS?' (2014) 16 *Florida Tax Review*, 55, 61; I Grinberg, 'The New International Tax Diplomacy' (2016) 104 *Georgetown Law Journal* 1137, 1141; RS Avi-Yonah, *International Tax Law*, 2nd edn (Edward Elgar Publishing 2019) 3.

[9] J Heinrich and H Moritz, 'Interpretation of Tax Treaties' (2000) 40 *European Taxation* 142, 148; M Lang, 'Tax Treaty Policy' in K Andersson, E Eberhartinger and L Oxelheim (eds), *National Tax Policy in Europe: To Be or Not to Be?* (Springer 2007) 206.

[10] eg, HJ Ault, 'The Role of the OECD Commentaries in the Interpretation of Tax Treaties' (1994) 22 *Intertax* 144, 146–47; K Vogel, 'The Influence of the OECD Commentaries on Treaty Interpretation' (2000) 54 *Bulletin for International Fiscal Documentation* 612, 615; JF Avery Jones, 'The Effect of Changes in the OECD Commentaries after a Treaty is Concluded' (2002) 56 *Bulletin for International Fiscal Documentation* 102, 102–03; P Wattel and O Marres, 'The Legal Status of the OECD Commentary and Static or Ambulatory Interpretation of Tax Treaties' (2003) 43 *European Taxation* 222, 224; DA Ward, 'The Role of the Commentaries on the OECD Model in the Tax Treaty Interpretation Process' (2006) 60 *Bulletin for International Fiscal Documentation* 97, 99; M Lang and F Brugger, 'The role of the OECD Commentary in tax treaty interpretation' (2008) 23 *Australian Tax Forum* 95, 100–01; K Vogel and A Rust, 'Introduction' in E Reimer and A Rust (eds), *Klaus Vogel on Double Taxation Conventions*, vol I, 4th edn (Kluwer Law International 2015) para 104.

[11] eg, Danon et al, 'The Prohibition of Abuse of Rights After the ECJ Danish Cases' (n 4) 509; U Linderfalk and M Hilling, 'The Use of OECD Commentaries as Interpretative Aids – The Static/Ambulatory–Approaches Debate Considered from the Perspective of International Law' (2015) 2 *Nordic Tax Journal* 34.

as the related protocols, usually remain silent on this matter.[12] Although the OECD endorsed the application of a dynamic approach in as early as 1997,[13] it ought to be borne in mind that statements by the OECD bodies cannot assert a legal obligation upon the contracting partners.[14]

Both positions incorporate certain advantages.[15] The following arguments are a particularly good defence of the static approach to the OECD MTC Commentary:

- It serves legal certainty.
- It complies with the requirements of national constitutional laws, in particular the principle of separation of powers.
- It ensures a uniform application in the contracting states irrespective of changes to the OECD MTC Commentary.
- It can be reasonably held to reflect the contracting parties' intentions.

However, there are also reasonable arguments for the use of a dynamic understanding in the interpretation of model-inspired treaty provisions:

- It allows for considering changes in the political, economic, legal and societal environments as well as technological advances.[16]

[12] A noticeable deviation from this general practice can be identified in the Austrian tax treaty policy. Since the 1990s, Austria has been eager to implement interpretation clauses in its bilateral tax treaties which declare that '[t]he Commentary – *as it may be revised from time to time* – constitutes a means of interpretation in the sense of the Vienna Convention of 23 May 1969 on the Law of Treaties' (eg, Protocol to the Convention between the Republic of Austria and Bosnia and Herzegovina for the Avoidance of Double Taxation with Respect to Taxes on Income and on Property, BGBl. III 2011/168, para 1 (emphasis added)). See also Heinrich and Moritz (n 9) 149; Ward (n 10) 100, fn 19; T Dubut, 'The Court of Justice and the OECD Model Tax Conventions or the Uncertainties of the Distinction between Hard Law, Soft Law, and No Law in the European Case Law' (2012) 40 *Intertax* 2, 9, fn 70. This approach has, however, been criticised on the grounds of constitutional concerns; eg, M Lang, 'Later Commentaries of the OECD Committee on Fiscal Affairs, Not to Affect the Interpretation of Previously Concluded Tax Treaties' (1997) 25 *Intertax* 7, 8.

[13] Compare OECD, 'Recommendation of the Council OECD Legal Instruments concerning the Model Tax Convention on Income and on Capital' [1997] OECD/LEGAL/0292: 'RECOMMENDS the Governments of Member countries: … That their tax administrations follow the Commentaries on the Articles of the Model Tax Convention, as modified from time to time, when applying and interpreting the provisions of their bilateral tax conventions that are based on these Articles' (emphasis omitted).

[14] In the same vein, Lang and Brugger (n 10) 102.

[15] Due to limitations in the scope of this contribution, the arguments made in favour of a static or dynamic understanding of the OECD MTC Commentary are only roughly outlined below, which should suffice for the purpose of this assessment. For more elaborated analyses, see, eg, Avery Jones (n 10) 103–04; Lang, 'Later Commentaries of the OECD Committee on Fiscal Affairs' (n 12) 8; Lang and Brugger (n 10) 107; Linderfalk and Hilling (n 11) 54–55; Vogel (n 10) 615; Ward (n 10) 99; Wattel and Marres (n 10) 222–23; M Lang, 'Can law regulate its own interpretation? Relevance and meaning of Articles 31–33 of the Vienna Convention on the Law of Treaties (VCLT) and Article 3 para 2 of the Model Convention of the Organisation for Economic Co-Operation and Development (OECD MC) for the interpretation of double-taxation conventions' in Y Brauner (ed), *Research Handbook on International Taxation* (Edward Elgar Publishing 2020) 182.

[16] Which seems all the more relevant when the DTCs' usual life span (10–20 years) is taken into account.

- It is capable of meeting legitimate expectations of taxpayers.
- It does justice to the principle of equality because model-inspired treaty provisions are uniformly applied no matter when the relevant treaty was signed.

The merits of both sides of the argument are reflected in the highly divergent case law in the EU Member States and beyond.[17]

III. THE USE OF A DYNAMIC UNDERSTANDING OF THE OECD MTC COMMENTARY IN ECJ CASE LAW ON OECD-INSPIRED CONCEPTS IN EU SECONDARY LAW

A. *Berlioz* (C-682/15)

Berlioz Investment Fund SA (hereafter Berlioz), a Luxembourg corporation, received dividends from a French subsidiary that were exempt from withholding taxation.[18] The French tax authorities forwarded an information request to the Luxembourg tax administration pursuant to the Directive on Administrative Cooperation (DAC)[19] so as to be able to verify that the requirements for an exemption from withholding taxation were met. In accordance with the domestic transposition provisions, the Luxembourg tax administration directed Berlioz to forward the relevant information. Berlioz only partly complied with this request, arguing that some of the information requested could not be considered foreseeably relevant within the meaning of the DAC.[20] In response to its refusal to provide the information requested, the Luxembourg tax administration imposed the highest possible fine (€250,000)[21] on Berlioz. The Administrative Tribunal, which decided on the corporation's action against this decision, reduced the fine to €150,000. However, it found the measure to be fundamentally appropriate, and hence refused annulment.[22] Berlioz then lodged an appeal before the Luxembourg Administrative Court and considered the refusal to assess the lawfulness of the information order as a breach of its right to an effective remedy in the sense of Article 6, paragraph 1 of the European Convention for the Protection of Human Rights and Fundamental

[17] For an overview of the case laws in selected countries, see, eg, Wattel and Marres (n 10) 229–32.

[18] Case C-682/15 *Berlioz Investment Fund* (n 1) para 21.

[19] Council Directive 2011/16/EU of 15 February 2011 on administrative cooperation in the field of taxation and repealing Directive 77/799/EEC [2011] OJ L64/1 (DAC).

[20] Case C-682/15 *Berlioz Investment Fund* (n 1) paras 22–24.

[21] According to the provisions in the Luxembourg domestic law cited in this judgment, an administrative fine on the holder of the information in the case of non-provision can be set at a maximum of €250,000; Case C-682/15 *Berlioz Investment Fund* (n 1) para 19.

[22] Case C-682/15 *Berlioz Investment Fund* (n 1) paras 25–27.

Freedoms (ECHR).[23] Apart from questions relating to the compatibility of Luxembourg law with EU fundamental rights,[24] the Administrative Court asked whether the notion of foreseeable relevance ought to be understood as a condition for a legitimate request under the DAC regime, as well as for a related information order issued to a third party. In this context, the domestic court specifically pointed to the parallels between the DAC and the OECD MTC with regard to the foreseeable relevance criterion.[25]

In his Opinion, AG Wathelet kept his observations on this question rather short and strictly adhered to the request of the national court. He derived from a textual (and arguably also a contextual) interpretation of Article 1, paragraph 1 and Article 5 of the DAC that the foreseeable relevance ought to be regarded as a condition for any request based on this directive. It subsequently determines the boundaries for legitimate information orders by the requesting authority.[26]

The ECJ largely followed the AG's arguments. It accordingly found that the foreseeable relevance ought to be considered 'a necessary characteristic of the requested information'[27] and hence 'a condition of the request relating to that information'.[28] This assertion would have already answered the preliminary question posed by the Luxembourg Administrative Court. However, the Court decided to delve further into the essence of the foreseeable relevance criterion and thereby to go beyond the AG's considerations.

In this context, the ECJ first referred to Recital 9 of the DAC according to which the foreseeable relevance criterion should be understood in the widest possible extent. Only 'fishing expeditions' and requests that could be considered irrelevant for the underlying tax assessment are excluded from the scope of the Directive.[29]

The Court then turned to a discussion of the relationship between the DAC and Article 26 of the OECD MTC. It found the foreseeable relevance criterion in the Directive to reflect that which is used in Article 26 of the OECD MTC based on two arguments. First, it identified similarities between the concepts employed. Second, it pointed to the Explanatory Memorandum to the

[23] Case C-682/15 *Berlioz Investment Fund* (n 1) para 28. The Administrative Court that forwarded the questions to the ECJ for a preliminary ruling moreover considered Art 47 of the European Charter of Human Rights (hereafter Charter), which is substantially identical to Art 6, para 1 ECHR, to be relevant. The ECJ discussed the related questions exclusively in light of Art 47 Charter. See particularly Case C-682/15 *Berlioz Investment Fund* (n 1) paras 29 and 54.

[24] Which, in light of the aim of this contribution, are not further discussed in the following.

[25] Case C-682/15 *Berlioz Investment Fund* (n 1) para 31 (fourth question).

[26] Case C-682/15 *Berlioz Investment Fund*, Opinion of AG Wathelet delivered on 10 January 2017, ECLI:EU:C:2017:2, paras 118–22.

[27] Case C-682/15 *Berlioz Investment Fund* (n 1) para 63.

[28] ibid.

[29] ibid para 66.

Directive Proposal of 2009 where the OECD MTC was mentioned as a source of inspiration.[30]

These findings formed the basis for the Court's approach to use statements from the 2012 update to the OECD MTC Commentary in order to support its initial findings based on Recital 9 of the DAC:

> According to the commentary on that article adopted by the OECD Council on 17 July 2012, Contracting States are not at liberty 'to engage in fishing expeditions', nor to request information that is unlikely to be relevant to the tax affairs of a given taxpayer. On the contrary, there must be a reasonable possibility that the requested information will be relevant.[31]

Building on these preliminary conclusions, the Court recognised both the requesting authority's obligation to assess the foreseeable relevance of the information requested, and the third party's entitlement to contest the legality of the information order.[32]

B. *N Luxembourg 1 and Others* (Joined Cases C-115/16, C-118/16, C-119/16 and C-299/16)

All cases joined in *N Luxembourg 1 and Others* centred on interest payments paid by Danish corporations to associated companies in either Luxembourg or Sweden. Assessments of the Danish tax authorities revealed that the underlying agreements had been broadly paralleled by obligations of the recipients to pay interest to their parent companies.[33] The latter were found to be overwhelmingly residents of third countries in the majority of the cases.[34] The interposed companies displayed very little, or in some years even zero, taxable income in

[30] ibid para 67. For the references in question, see European Commission, 'Proposal for a Council Directive on administrative cooperation in the field of taxation' COM(2009) 29 final, 6–7 (DAC Proposal).

[31] Case C-682/15 *Berlioz Investment Fund* (n 1) para 67.

[32] ibid paras 70–74.

[33] In Case C-115/16, the interest rates amounted to 10% and 9.96875% respectively, and in Case C-299/16 to 9.875% and 9% respectively. By contrast, the interest rates were found to be identical in the situations underlying Cases C-118/16 and C-119/16. The debt amounts were identical in the agreement between the Danish corporation and the first recipient and the agreement between the first recipient and the second recipient in all four cases; Joined Cases C-115/16, C-118/16, C-119/16 and C-299/16 *N Luxembourg 1 and Others* (n 7) paras 35, 53, 61 and 68–69.

[34] Joined Cases C-115/16, C-118/16, C-119/16 and C-299/16 *N Luxembourg 1 and Others* (n 7) paras 30, 58 and 66. In Case C-118/16, the parent company was owned by a Luxembourg SICAR which the Danish tax authorities considered to be a transparent entity under Danish law. The Danish corporation was apparently unable to produce documentation showing that a majority of the investors in the SICAR were residents of other EU Member States; Joined Cases C-115/16, C-118/16, C-119/16 and C-299/16 *N Luxembourg 1 and Others*, ibid, para 55.

three of the four cases.[35] In three of the four cases, the intermediary companies' activities were also effectively restricted to the mere holding of the shares in the Danish corporations and the obligations stemming from the debt agreements.[36] The intermediaries in the *N Luxembourg 1* case (C-115/16) apparently had limited economic substance due to minimum personnel capacities, comparably miniscule other expenditures and a joint postal address for both the first and second recipients.[37] By contrast, the interposed company in the *Z Denmark* case (C-299/16) was engaged with product registration and various administrative tasks, had 10 employees and leased part of the offices at the headquarters of its Swedish parent company (arguably another intermediary). Its other income was, however, similarly found to be comparably neglectable in the relevant years.[38] These structures were all established after a new withholding taxation regime had been adopted in Denmark.[39] The Danish tax authorities did not recognise the recipient entities as the beneficial owners of the interest payments pursuant to Article 1, paragraph 4 of Council Directive 2003/49/EC (IRD)[40] in each of the four cases. Consequently, relief from withholding taxation was denied.[41] Among other things, the Danish courts in charge of the appeal proceedings asked the ECJ for a preliminary ruling concerning the essence of the IRD's beneficial ownership concept. They particularly requested whether it should be interpreted in accordance with the corresponding concept in Article 11 of the OECD MTC 1977.[42]

AG Kokott began the assessments in all of her Opinions by arguing that the beneficial ownership concept in the IRD basically referred to the legal owner, hence the person entitled under civil law to demand payment of the interest.[43] From the examples enumerated in Article 1, paragraph 4 of the IRD,

[35] Joined Cases C-115/16, C-118/16, C-119/16 and C-299/16 *N Luxembourg 1 and Others* (n 7) paras 53, 61 and 71. Regarding the situation underlying Case C-115/16, the statements that are included in the ECJ's decision only describe a significantly limited presence of substance and economic activity in the Luxembourg intermediaries; Joined Cases C-115/16, C-118/16, C-119/16 and C-299/16 *N Luxembourg 1 and Others*, ibid, paras 36–40.

[36] Joined Cases C-115/16, C-118/16, C-119/16 and C-299/16 *N Luxembourg 1 and Others* (n 7) paras 39, 61 and 71.

[37] ibid paras 36–38 and 40.

[38] ibid paras 52–53.

[39] ibid paras 33–34, 46, 50, 58, 61, 65 and 67–70.

[40] Council Directive 2003/49/EC of 3 June 2003 on a common system of taxation applicable to interest and royalty payments made between associated companies of different Member States [2003] OJ L157/49 (IRD).

[41] Joined Cases C-115/16, C-118/16, C-119/16 and C-299/16 *N Luxembourg 1 and Others* (n 7) paras 41, 55, 60 and 73.

[42] ibid paras 45, 57, 63 and 79.

[43] The AG delivered a single Opinion for each of the four cases. However, her reasoning relating to the IRD's beneficial ownership concept can be found to be virtually identical. It thus makes sense to discuss her arguments in the four Opinions jointly in the subsequent assessment. For the sake of simplicity, the Opinion of AG Kokott in *N Luxembourg 1* (Case C-115/16) is representatively referred to in the following section.

she deduced that an interest recipient could be considered the beneficial owner if this person collected the interest in their own name and on their own account (ie, for their own benefit in the language of the Directive). Arguably, the AG considered the legal owner to be the beneficial owner inasmuch as both the legal and economic ownership were attributed to the same person; otherwise, substance over form should prevail.[44] She left it to the domestic courts to examine whether the structures in the individual cases spoke for the existence of a (hidden) trust relationship. She nevertheless identified several indicia that she considered relevant for purposes of such an assessment.[45]

After having carved out the essence of the IRD's beneficial ownership concept, the AG further discussed its relationship with Article 11 of the OECD MTC 1977. In her Opinion, the Directive's beneficial ownership concept ought to be interpreted autonomously and independently of Article 11 of the OECD MTC 1977 or subsequent versions of the model. Accordingly, she refused to attach value to the OECD MTC Commentary in the interpretive process. The Commentary could hence not directly affect the interpretation of EU law, even if the terms used were identical. To bolster her argument, the AG first referred to the Commentary's quality as a soft law (hence not legally binding) instrument. She additionally pointed to the fact that the Commentary merely reflected the legal opinions of the people who worked on the OECD MTC, but not the views of parliamentary legislators or the EU lawmakers. The use of the OECD MTC and the Commentary as a source of inspiration was nevertheless found to be legitimate inasmuch as it was indicated by the wording and the history of the respective Directive.[46] In these situations, only the OECD MTC and its Commentary that were available at the time of adoption could be considered appropriate means. Taking subsequent versions of the OECD MTC and the Commentary into account would, however, empower 'the OECD member countries … to decide on the interpretation of an EU directive'.[47] This notwithstanding, the AG acknowledged that the beneficial ownership concepts of the IRD and the OECD MTC, read in light of the more recent versions of the Commentary, appeared to take a similar approach.[48]

The ECJ arguably came to the same conclusion as AG Kokott (hence, the supremacy of an economic approach). However, it did so in a significantly different manner. The judges did not concern themselves with a discussion of the relevance of a legal or an economic understanding in their argument. By

[44] eg, Case C-115/16 N *Luxembourg 1*, Opinion of AG Kokott delivered on 1 March 2018, ECLI:EU:C:2018:143, para 47.

[45] In detail, eg, Case C-115/16 N *Luxembourg 1*, Opinion of AG Kokott (n 44) paras 43–45.

[46] ibid paras 49–52.

[47] ibid para 53.

[48] ibid para 54.

contrast, they immediately found that the idea of beneficial ownership referred to the entity that economically benefits from the interest and hence 'has the power freely to determine the use to which it is put'.[49] This assertion was based on a comparative analysis of the 23 language versions of the IRD[50] which demonstrated the use of semantically diverging expressions in these documents and hence the defects of a strictly formal understanding of the IRD's beneficial ownership concept.[51]

The ECJ's argument, moreover, diverged from the AG's Opinions regarding the relevance attributed to the OECD MTC and its Commentary. In a similar vein as in *Berlioz*,[52] the Court referred to the OECD MTC Commentary to support its interpretive result stemming from an analogous interpretation of Article 1, paragraph 1 of the IRD.[53] The legitimacy to consider OECD work in the interpretive process was derived from statements in the Explanatory Memorandum to the Directive draft of 1998 which acknowledged the role of the OECD MTC 1996 in the IRD's drafting.[54] Against this backdrop, the Court considered 'that model, and the successive amendments of that model and of the commentaries relating thereto [to be], therefore, relevant when interpreting Directive 2003/49'.[55] The judges did not share the applicants' concerns regarding the lack of democratic legitimacy in the context of an interpretation that took the OECD MTC and its Commentary into account. Instead, they argued that

> such an interpretation, even if it draws on the OECD's documents, has its basis, as is clear from paragraphs 85 to 90 above, in the directive itself and in its legislative history reflecting the democratic process of the European Union.[56]

Based on these findings, the development of the OECD MTC and its Commentary was found to support the ECJ's earlier conclusion that conduit companies cannot

[49] Joined Cases C-115/16, C-118/16, C-119/16 and C-299/16 *N Luxembourg 1 and Others* (n 7) para 89.

[50] A Gaelic version is apparently not (yet) available; see also: eur-lex.europa.eu/legal-content/EN/TXT/?uri=CELEX%3A02003L0049-20130701.

[51] Joined Cases C-115/16, C-118/16, C-119/16 and C-299/16 *N Luxembourg 1 and Others* (n 7) para 89.

[52] See section III.A.

[53] Joined Cases C-115/16, C-118/16, C-119/16 and C-299/16 *N Luxembourg 1 and Others* (n 7) para 92.

[54] For the references in question, see European Commission, 'Proposal for a Council Directive on a common system of taxation applicable to interest and royalty payments made between associated companies of different Member States' COM(1998) 67 final, 6 and 8 (IRD Proposal).

[55] Joined Cases C-115/16, C-118/16, C-119/16 and C-299/16 *N Luxembourg 1 and Others* (n 7) para 90.

[56] Joined Cases C-115/16, C-118/16, C-119/16 and C-299/16 *N Luxembourg 1 and Others* (n 7) para 91. See, however, A Cordewener 'The Interest and Royalty Directive' in PJ Wattel, O Marres and H Vermeulen (eds), *Terra/Wattel – European Tax Law*, vol I, 7th edn (Kluwer Law International 2019) 404 (arguing in the context of the question of whether subsequent amendments must be taken into account that '[i]t is hard to imagine that the CJEU would feel tempted to venture into these realms').

be considered to be covered by the scope of the Directive's beneficial ownership concept.[57]

C. *État luxembourgeois* (C-437/19)

The ECJ had the opportunity to shed further light on the essence of the DAC's foreseeable relevance criterion in *État luxembourgeois*. This case shares another characteristic with the decision in *Berlioz*: it also concerned an information request by France to Luxembourg under the DAC regime.

Both a French and a Luxembourg company, the latter being the indirect parent company of the former, owned immovable property in France. According to French law, natural persons that directly or indirectly owned immovable property in France were obliged to declare that property. This obligation was apparently not met in the situations at issue. Hence, the French tax authorities asked the Luxembourg tax authorities to ascertain the identity of the shareholders and beneficial owners of the Luxembourg company (which, considering the group's structure, naturally had to be identical to the natural persons behind the French company). The Luxembourg tax authorities forwarded a related order to the Luxembourg company, but the corporation refused to provide the information requested. Accordingly, an administrative fine was imposed.[58] The Administrative Court allowed an appeal of the Luxembourg company and annulled the decision of the Director of the Direct Taxation Administration. It argued that the French request was manifestly devoid of any foreseeable relevance, as doubts remained concerning the identity of the taxpayer to whom that request related. This assertion was based on the fact that the French company was mentioned in the request although the French tax authorities asked for information on the identity of the beneficial owners of the Luxembourg company. This judgment was then contested by the Luxembourg State and brought to the Higher Administrative Court. The Higher Administrative Court did not share the Administrative Court's opinion regarding the alleged contradiction between the identity of the taxpayer as stated in the information order and the tax purpose pursued. However, it considered the fact that these taxpayers were not identified individually and by

[57] Moreover, the Court considered its findings to be supported by the Nordic Tax Convention that was applicable in two of the four cases (see the statements in question in Joined Cases C-115/16, C-118/16, C-119/16 and C-299/16 *N Luxembourg 1 and Others* (n 7) paras 55 and 60–61), and simultaneously drew upon the OECD MTC's definition; Joined Cases C-115/16, C-118/16, C-119/16 and C-299/16 *N Luxembourg 1 and Others*, ibid, paras 92–93.

[58] Case C-437/19 *État luxembourgeois* (n 5) paras 16–18 and 20. The Luxembourg company additionally brought a formal administrative appeal against that order which was still pending before the Luxembourg Administrative Court at the time of the ECJ's decision; Case C-437/19 *État luxembourgeois*, ibid, para 19.

name, but only referred to as a group of people who were designated as a whole on the basis of common criteria, potentially problematic.[59] Referring to the findings in *Berlioz*,[60] the Higher Administrative Court acknowledged the possibility of justifying group requests on the basis of an interpretation for which purposes a dynamic understanding of the OECD MTC Commentary was applied. It was nevertheless not convinced that such an interpretation could be reconciled with the concept of identity in Article 20, paragraph 2(a) of the DAC. Hence, the Higher Administrative Court decided to refer this question, among others,[61] to the ECJ.[62]

In her assessment of the foreseeable relevance criterion, AG Kokott first drew towards an analysis of the wording, the regulatory context and the purpose of the DAC. She accordingly highlighted that the scope of the Directive was not limited to information requests concerning individual taxpayers that were identified by name, or conversely, did not exclude requests concerning a group of taxpayers. She found this assertion to be supported by Recital 9 of the DAC where it was clarified that the standard of foreseeable relevance was intended to provide for the widest possible exchange of information in tax matters. Similarly, the term 'identity' in Article 20, paragraph 2(a) of the DAC could not be understood as exclusively referring to identification by name. It should indeed have covered all the characteristics or attributes that distinguished one person from another and likewise precluded any confusion.[63]

According to AG Kokott's findings, this broad interpretation was moreover indicated by the spirit and purpose of the foreseeable relevance criterion. Generally disallowing information requests concerning a group of taxpayers would run counter to the Directive's goal of safeguarding the effectiveness of the exchange of information in tax matters between the Member States. Given the comparably higher risk of 'fishing expeditions' in the context of group requests, these enquiries ought, however, to meet three criteria:

- The description of the relevant group of taxpayers must be specific and detailed enough to allow for unequivocal identification.
- The requesting state has to include information on the tax purpose for which the information is sought (ie, the tax obligations and the facts of the case). This requirement is meant to put the requested state in a position in which it is able to assess the request's plausibility in light of the foreseeable relevance criterion.

[59] Case C-437/19 *État luxembourgeois* (n 5) paras 21–29.

[60] See section III.A.

[61] In light of the aim of this contribution, the questions relating to EU fundamental rights are not discussed in the following.

[62] Case C-437/19 *État luxembourgeois* (n 5) paras 30–31 and 36 (first and second questions).

[63] Case C-437/19 *État luxembourgeois (Informations sur un groupe de contribuables)*, Opinion of AG Kokott delivered on 3 June 2021, ECLI:EU:C:2021:450, paras 39–49.

- Therefore, the requesting state must also demonstrate that it can be reasonably assumed that these taxpayers did not comply with their tax obligations.[64]

The AG considered these conditions to be fulfilled in the present case. Nevertheless, she left it to the domestic courts to decide on this matter (on the basis of an overall assessment).[65]

In a next step, AG Kokott contextualised her findings from an autonomous interpretation of the DAC with the Commentary on Article 26 of the OECD MTC and found her results to be confirmed by the statements in the revised version.[66] She began her argument by stressing the Commentaries' status as mere soft law instruments in a similar vein as in her Opinions in the *N Luxembourg 1 and Others* cases.[67] However, she further acknowledged that 'the authors of those commentaries reach[ed] the correct conclusion'.[68] Arguably, the AG thereby aimed to attribute to the Commentary a similar relevance as opinions in scholarly literature.[69]

The ECJ broadly followed AG Kokott's argument. The provision of the taxpayer's identity was hence considered vital for the purposes of the review by the requested authority regarding the foreseeable relevance of the information requested.[70] In agreement with its long-standing case law,[71] the Court endorsed an autonomous interpretation of the term 'identity of the person under examination or investigation', which ought to be conducted in light of the wording, the context and the objectives pursued. For their related findings, the judges widely relied on AG Kokott's arguments to conclude that a broad interpretation is indicated against the background of the Directive's aims. Accordingly, this concept ought to be understood as referring to all qualities or characteristics that enable an identification of the person(s) under examination or investigation. The Court further confirmed the requirements for legitimate group requests that had been enunciated in the AG's Opinion.[72]

The autonomous interpretation of the DAC was again[73] contextualised with statements in the Commentary on Article 26 of the OECD MTC. The ECJ

[64] ibid paras 50–63.
[65] ibid para 63.
[66] ibid paras 66–70.
[67] See section III.B.
[68] Case C-437/19 *État luxembourgeois*, Opinion of AG Kokott (n 63) para 67.
[69] In addition, AG Kokott found that her interpretation did not conflict with the recent amendments to the DAC through which, inter alia, a specific provision on group requests was introduced. She based her argument on the fact that this provision had been implemented solely for reasons of legal certainty and legal clarity; Case C-437/19 *État luxembourgeois*, Opinion of AG Kokott (n 63) paras 71–73.
[70] Case C-437/19 *État luxembourgeois* (n 5) para 44.
[71] In the area of direct tax law see, eg, Case C-58/01 *Océ van der Grinten*, ECLI:EU:C:2003:495, para 46.
[72] Case C-437/19 *État luxembourgeois* (n 5) paras 40–68.
[73] See sections III.A and III.B.

shared AG Kokott's Opinion that the EU-based findings correspond with the views expressed in the 2012 update.[74]

IV. ASSESSMENT OF THE ECJ'S METHODOLOGY TO APPLY A DYNAMIC UNDERSTANDING OF THE OECD MTC COMMENTARY

A. Assessment Through the Lens of Legal Doctrine

The Court's approach in *Berlioz*, *N Luxembourg 1 and Others* and *État luxembourgeois* appears to have initiated a new era in the case law devoted to the interpretation of secondary EU law. In *Cobelfret*,[75] the judges made clear only a few years ago that

> in the absence of an express indication to the contrary, a Community act such as Directive 90/435 must be interpreted in the context of the sources of Community law and of the Community legal order itself … It is only in the absence of unifying or harmonising Community measures that it is for the Member States, which retain the power to define, by treaty or unilaterally, the criteria for allocating their powers of taxation, particularly with a view to eliminating double taxation, to take the measures necessary to that end by applying, in particular, the apportionment criteria followed in international tax practice, including the model conventions drawn up by the OECD … That is not the situation in the present case.[76]

Nevertheless, the ECJ's new argumentative pattern cannot be found to have overturned the established doctrine. A comparative analysis of the arguments in the three decisions elucidates that the Court has merely extended its assessment routine, which now reflects a two-pronged approach:

- In a first step, the Court performs an autonomous interpretation of OECD-inspired concepts of EU secondary law in light of the wording, the context and the objectives pursued.[77] This part of the analysis resonates with the Court's traditional approach.
- In a second step, the results derived from an autonomous interpretation are contextualised with related statements in the OECD MTC Commentary. This comparison is conducted only to confirm the findings from the first step of the assessment.[78]

[74] Case C-437/19 *État luxembourgeois* (n 5) paras 69–71.

[75] Case C-138/07 *Cobelfret*, ECLI:EU:C:2009:82.

[76] ibid paras 56–57.

[77] Case C-682/15 *Berlioz Investment Fund* (n 1) para 66; Joined Cases C-115/16, C-118/16, C-119/16 and C-299/16 *N Luxembourg 1 and Others* (n 7) paras 88–89; Case C-437/19 *État luxembourgeois* (n 5) paras 49–62.

[78] Such an understanding is inferred from the language used in these decisions; eg, Case C-437/19 *État luxembourgeois* (n 5) para 69: 'Lastly, it should be added that that interpretation … corresponds to'.

The identified characteristics of the Court's new approach do not support some of the concerns expressed in the aftermath of the *N Luxembourg 1 and Others* judgment. Hence, the interpretation in the OECD Commentary has not become 'legally binding through the [directives]' to the effect that 'the OECD has de facto legislative powers within the EU because it influences the interpretation of [these] concept[s]'.[79]

This does not mean, however, that the ECJ's reasoning could not be considered problematic on other grounds. The Court memorably illustrated in each of the three decisions that a robust interpretive result can be reached solely on the basis of EU legal sources (which would have further safeguarded coherency in its case law). Conversely, it failed to explain what value is added by additional references to statements in the OECD MTC Commentary (regardless of the version used). The criticism is hence directed at the Court's omission of the necessary steps in the building of a sound argument in this context.

That notwithstanding, it appears plausible to consider the OECD MTC and its Commentary as an auxiliary source of inspiration particularly in the cases of the DAC's foreseeable relevance criterion and the IRD's beneficial ownership concept against the background of their historical development.

For purposes of the DAC, the Court pointed to statements in the Explanatory Memorandum to the 2009 Proposal that stress the significance of the OECD MTC in the Directive's legal framing.[80] Although no reference was made to the foreseeable relevance concept in Article 26 of the OECD MTC,[81] it can be reasonably argued that this criterion was 'borrowed' from the model treaty. This notion is inferred from Recital 9 of the DAC which is framed in terms that virtually correspond to the wording in the OECD MTC Commentary.[82] Contextualising the DAC's foreseeable relevance criterion with the OECD MTC and its Commentary hence makes sense.[83]

[79] De Broe and Gommers (n 4) 292–93 (the language was adapted for purposes of this assessment against the background that the original argument was limited to the beneficial ownership requirement in the IRD).

[80] References were made to the Joint Council of Europe/OECD Convention on Mutual Administrative Assistance in Tax Matters in the context of Art 2, to the 2002 OECD Model agreement on exchange of information in tax matters (TIEA model) in the context of Art 7, paras 5 and 6, and to Art 26, paras 4 and 5 OECD MTC in the context of Art 17; DAC Proposal, 6–7.

[81] The foreseeable relevance concept was first introduced in the OECD's TIEA model and later transplanted into Art 26 OECD MTC with the 2005 update; OECD MTC Commentary 2005, Art 26, paras 4 and 4.1.

[82] Recital 9 DAC diverges from the statements in the OECD MTC Commentary 2005 (ibid, Art 26, para 5) only inasmuch as reference is made to the 'Member States' instead of the 'contracting partners'. Beyond these terminological deviations that are inherent to the system, their essence can thus be found to be identical.

[83] In a similar vein, Lang, 'Double Taxation Conventions in the Case Law of the CJEU' (n 4) 186: 'The rule of Article 26 OECD MC was obviously the inspiration for the provision of the directive. Therefore, it is definitely justified as part of historical interpretation that the CJEU reverts to the work of the OECD, since it served as the basis for the provision of the Directive'.

The specific references to statements in the updated Commentary of 2012 both in *Berlioz* and *État luxembourgeois*[84] deserve nonetheless a closer examination. The foreseeable relevance concept was introduced in the OECD MTC in 2005,[85] and the Commentary has held ever since that

> [t]he standard of 'foreseeable relevance' is intended to provide for exchange of information in tax matters to the widest possible extent and, at the same time, to clarify that Contracting States are not at liberty to engage in 'fishing expeditions' or to request information that is unlikely to be relevant to the tax affairs of a given taxpayer.[86]

In the *Berlioz* case, the Court could have thus moved on solid doctrinal ground if it had simply referred to the findings in the Commentary on Article 26 of the OECD MTC as adopted in 2005. This version should have been known to the EU lawmakers at the time of the DAC's drafting and could hence be reasonably considered to have inspired the Directive's design. Naturally, this finding cannot hold true for the updated Commentary of 2012 that was adopted after the DAC's introduction.[87]

The Court's reliance on the 2012 version can therefore be challenged for at least two reasons:

- The use of a dynamic understanding of the OECD MTC Commentary does not add any value compared with an interpretation in light of the 2005 version that was arguably known to the EU lawmakers at the time of the drafting of the DAC. Hence, it can be found to have been applied unnecessarily.
- Neither the explanatory statements nor the DAC itself demonstrate the legitimacy of a dynamic interpretation.[88] However, the Court did not provide

[84] Case C-682/15 *Berlioz Investment Fund* (n 1) para 67; Case C-437/19 *État luxembourgeois* (n 5) para 69. See also sections III.A and III.C.

[85] See also X Oberson in R Danon, D Gutmann, X Oberson and P Pistone (eds), *Modèle de Convention fiscale OCDE concernant le revenue et la fortune – Commentaire* (Helbing Lichtenhahn 2014) Art 26 para 35; AP Dourado in E Reimer and A Rust (eds), *Klaus Vogel on Double Taxation Conventions*, vol I, 4th edn (Kluwer Law International 2015) Art 26 para 168; S Hemels, 'Administrative Cooperation in the Assessment and Recovery of Direct Tax Claims' in PJ Wattel, O Marres and H Vermeulen (eds), *Terra/Wattel – European Tax Law*, vol I, 7th edn (Kluwer Law International 2019) 554.

[86] OECD MTC Commentary 2005, Art 26, para 5.

[87] The DAC was adopted by the Council on 15 February 2011 and published in the *Official Journal* of the European Union on 11 March 2011. See also Lang, 'Double Taxation Conventions in the Case Law of the CJEU' (n 4) 186: 'One can hardly claim that the authors of the Directive had already predicted these later developments'.

[88] See, however, Recital 13 of Council Directive 2014/107/EU of 9 December 2014 amending Directive 2011/16/EU as regards mandatory automatic exchange of information in the field of taxation [2014] OJ L359/1: 'In implementing this Directive, Member States should use the Commentaries on the Model Competent Authority Agreement and Common Reporting Standard, developed by the OECD, as a source of illustration or interpretation and in order to ensure consistency in application across Member States. Union action in this area should continue to *take particular account of future developments at OECD level*' (emphasis added).

> an explanation as to why such an approach should nevertheless be permissible. The absence of a justification is even more remarkable considering that the legitimacy of a dynamic use of the OECD MTC Commentary is already highly disputed for its traditional legal environment (ie, double tax treaties).[89] This circumstance arguably increases the need for a sound argument to nevertheless apply this method (also) in the EU context.

To some extent, these observations are analogously applicable to the Court's reasoning in *État luxembourgeois*. The concept of group requests was discussed for the first time in the 2012 update of the Commentary on Article 26 of the OECD MTC. However, the ECJ's argument in the context of an autonomous interpretation is based on ideas expressed in Recital 9 of the DAC which, as was already mentioned above, is worded in an almost identical way as the related paragraphs in the OECD MTC Commentary of 2005. It can be inferred from the explanatory remarks in the 2012 update[90] that the addition of language in respect of group requests was aimed at further clarifying the essence of the foreseeable relevance concept.[91] In order to provide a doctrinally convincing argument, it would have thus been up to the Court to trace these developments at the OECD level and demonstrate that the findings in the 2012 update were grounded in the 2005 Commentary.[92] In a similar vein as in *Berlioz*, the ECJ did not, however, forward any justification for the use of a dynamic understanding of the Commentary on Article 26 of the OECD MTC.

For the purpose of the IRD, the ECJ similarly held that the EU lawmakers' reliance on established OECD concepts due to the IRD's legal design could be derived from the Explanatory Memorandum to the 1998 Proposal.[93] Although the related references do not cover the beneficial ownership requirement, a historical interpretation should nevertheless be capable of constructing the necessary nexus. The Court's stance on the principal relevance of the OECD MTC and its Commentary hence appears likewise comprehensible.[94]

[89] See section II.

[90] OECD MTC Commentary, Art 26, para 4.4.

[91] In the same vein, Oberson (n 85) para 48; AC Valdés Zauner, 'Exchange of Information through Group Requests' in O-C Günther and N Tüchler (eds), *Exchange of Information for Tax Purposes* (Linde 2013) 501; F Debelva and N Diepvens, 'Exchange of Information. An Analysis of the Scope of Article 26 OECD Model and its Requirements: In Search for an Efficient but Balanced Procedure' (2016) 44 *Intertax* 298, 303.

[92] S Geringer, 'Gruppenanfragen im Kontext des DAC-Regimes: Die Rs *État luxembourgeois*' (2022) 32 *Steuer und Wirtschaft International* 296, 302–03.

[93] References were made to the definitions of the terms 'interest' and 'royalties' in the context of Art 2, as well as to the specific anti-abuse clauses regarding interest and royalty payments between related parties in the context of Art 5 (Art 4, para 2 in the IRD's final version); IRD Proposal, 6 and 8.

[94] In the same vein, Englisch (n 4) 525; Schön (n 4) 292. More strongly, De Broe and Gommers (n 4) 288–89: 'Although not explicitly mentioned in the 1998 proposal nor in the recitals to the IRD, the European Commission has without any doubt found inspiration with the OECD's BO concept'.

The argumentative base for this assumption is, however, arguably thinner than in the context of the DAC's foreseeable relevance criterion. This assertion is informed by the fact that the provisions on the beneficial ownership concept in the IRD diverge noticeably from the wording of Article 11, paragraph 4 and Article 12, paragraph 3 of the OECD MTC respectively.[95] Hence, the IRD's beneficial ownership concept could be reasonably considered to have evolved beyond its inspirational source (at least to a certain extent).[96]

Another notable parallel with the *Berlioz* and *État luxembourgeois* judgments can be identified in that the Court's reasoning regarding related OECD work in *N Luxembourg 1 and Others* could have been similarly put on a more robust argumentative basis. The statements in one of the paragraphs in the OECD MTC Commentary 2003 that informed the Court's opinion were bolstered by means of a reference to the report of the OECD's Committee on Fiscal Affairs on 'Double Tax Conventions and the Use of Conduit Companies' from 1986.[97] This report elucidated, inter alia, the essence of the OECD MTC's beneficial ownership concept, and accordingly found that

> Articles 10 to 12 of the OECD Model deny the limitation of tax in the State of source on dividends, interest and royalties if the conduit company is not its 'beneficial owner'. Thus the limitation is not available when, economically, it would benefit a person not entitled to it who interposed the conduit company as intermediary between himself and the payer of the income.[98]

[95] Art 1, para 4 IRD includes a definition of the term 'beneficial owner' for purposes of the companies covered by the Directive. Hence, a company that 'receives those payments for its own benefit and not as an intermediary, such as an agent, trustee or authorised signatory, for some other person', is considered to be the beneficial owner. Conversely, Art 11 OECD MTC remains silent on this matter, and further guidance is only provided by the OECD MTC Commentary. Moreover, a second definition tailored to permanent establishments is embedded in Art 1, para 5, IRD. In contrast to Art 1, para 4 IRD, it additionally requires that the interest and royalty payments are effectively connected with the relevant permanent establishment and subject to tax in the state in which the permanent establishment is situated.

[96] Concurring I Lazarov, '(Un)Tangling Tax Avoidance Under the Interest and Royalties Directive: the Opinion of AG Kokott in N Luxembourg 1' (2018) 46 *Intertax* 873, 878. Moreover in favour of an autonomous EU concept, eg, De Broe and Gommers (n 4) 289; Hamra and Korving (n 4) 269 and 272; L Hinnekens, 'European Commission introduces beneficial ownership in latest tax directives proposals adding to the confusion with regard to its meaning' (2000) 9 *EC Tax Review* 43, 44; K Eicker and F Aramini, 'Overview on the recent developments of the EC Directive on Withholding Taxes on Royalty and Interest Payments' (2004) 13 *EC Tax Review* 134, 135; M Greggi, 'Taxation of Royalties in an EU Framework' (2007) 46 *Tax Notes International* 1149, 1159; J Lopez Rodriguez and G Kofler, 'Beneficial Ownership and EU Law' in M Lang, P Pistone, J Schuch, C Staringer and A Storck (eds), *Beneficial Ownership: Recent Trends* (IBFD 2013) 236; A Meindl-Ringler, *Beneficial Ownership in International Tax Law*, Series on International Taxation, vol 58 (Kluwer Law International 2016) 300.

[97] OECD MTC Commentary 2003, Art 10, para 12.1.

[98] OECD, 'Double Tax Conventions and the Use of Conduit Companies' (OECD 1987) para 14 (b). Compare moreover RJ Danon, 'The PPT in Post-BEPS Tax Treaty Law: It Is a GAAR but Just a GAAR!' (2020) 74 *Bulletin for International Taxation* 242, 248 (referring to the ECJ's enumeration of indicia for the purpose of identifying abusive arrangements in the context of conduit companies as 'very much in line with the 1986 OECD Conduit Report').

The findings in the report seem to have been broadly transferred to the OECD MTC Commentary through the 2003 update.[99] Hence, the ECJ's argument would have proven more convincing if references had been made to the 1986 report, which the EU lawmakers had arguably been familiar with by the time the IRD was drafted.[100]

The Court's reasoning in *N Luxembourg 1 and Others* diverges from its line of argument in both *Berlioz* and *État luxembourgeois* inasmuch as the acceptance and application of a dynamic understanding of the OECD MTC Commentary are expressly confirmed.[101] In a similar vein, the ECJ did not explain, however, why it can be deemed feasible to consider 'the successive amendments of that model and of the commentaries relating thereto'[102] in the interpretive process even though neither the IRD itself nor the preparatory work provide any such indications.[103]

B. Assessment Through the Lens of Democratic Legitimacy

The issue of democratic legitimacy permeating a dynamic understanding of the OECD MTC Commentary was not addressed either in *Berlioz* or in *État luxembourgeois*. The following observations are hence exclusively devoted to the Court's statements in *N Luxembourg 1 and Others*.

In response to related concerns that the taxpayers expressed in the main proceedings,[104] the ECJ resorted to the plain statement that 'such an interpretation, even if it draws on the OECD's documents, has its basis … in the directive itself and in its legislative history reflecting the democratic process of the European Union'.[105] This reasoning is fundamentally flawed. As was argued above,[106] neither the IRD itself nor the *travaux préparatoires* indicate that the

[99] Englisch (n 4) 526; L De Broe, *International Tax Planning and Prevention of Abuse*, IBFD Doctoral Series, vol 14 (IBFD 2008) 665.

[100] At least, there is a realistic chance that they considered the 1986 report, which cannot be said in the same manner about the 2003 update. See also Englisch (n 4) 527, fn 82: 'As regards the commentary to the 2003 OECD Model Tax Convention in particular, it was endorsed by the OECD Council already on 28 Jan, ie before the formal adoption of the Interest and Royalties Directive by the EC Council on 3 June 2003. The 2003 commentary might thus even still have informed the deliberations in Council, even though the last discussions within the Council before reaching political agreement took place in Dec 2002'.

[101] Joined Cases C-115/16, C-118/16, C-119/16 and C-299/16 *N Luxembourg 1 and Others* (n 7) para 90. See also Danon et al, 'The Prohibition of Abuse of Rights After the ECJ Danish Cases' (n 4) 508; De Broe and Gommers (n 4) 293; Englisch (n 4) 518; Schön (n 4) 295, fn 103.

[102] Joined Cases C-115/16, C-118/16, C-119/16 and C-299/16 *N Luxembourg 1 and Others* (n 7) para 90.

[103] eg, De Broe and Gommers (n 4) 293; Englisch (n 4) 525–26.

[104] See also section III.B.

[105] Joined Cases C-115/16, C-118/16, C-119/16 and C-299/16 *N Luxembourg 1 and Others* (n 7) para 91.

[106] See section IV.A.

EU lawmakers endorsed a reading of OECD-induced concepts in light of a dynamic interpretation of the OECD MTC and its Commentary.

Beyond that, the Court's indifferent attitude regarding the issue of potentially insufficient democratic legitimacy is striking at first sight.[107] In this context, it should be recalled that all directives in the field of direct taxation[108] have so far been adopted on the basis of Article 115 of the Treaty on the Functioning of the European Union (TFEU).[109] This competence norm requires unanimity among the Member States' representatives[110] in the Council of the European Union.[111] The EU's law-making process could similarly be criticised from a democratic perspective due to the fact that the European Parliament (hence, the EU body in which the EU citizens are directly represented) is merely attributed a consultative role in the specific legislative procedure.[112] Nevertheless, it can at least be argued that the members of the Member States governments are directly or indirectly[113] legitimised by the peoples of the Member States. Accordingly, not only the Member States' decision-making power regarding the pace of integration at the EU level, but also democratic legitimacy is to some degree preserved. This assertion holds all the more true if it is borne in mind that these processes were approved in accordance with the requirements

[107] Concurring De Broe and Gommers (n 4) 293; Englisch (n 4) 525.

[108] Considering both substantive and procedural directives, five directives in addition to the DAC and the IRD are relevant as of writing: Council Directive 2009/133/EC of 19 October 2009 on the common system of taxation applicable to mergers, divisions, partial divisions, transfers of assets and exchanges of shares concerning companies of different Member States and to the transfer of the registered office of an SE or SCE between Member States (codified version) [2009] OJ L310/34; Council Directive 2010/24/EU of 16 March 2010 concerning mutual assistance for the recovery of claims relating to taxes, duties and other measures [2010] OJ L84/1; Council Directive 2011/96/EU of 30 November 2011 on the common system of taxation applicable in the case of parent companies and subsidiaries of different Member States (recast) [2011] OJ L345/8; Council Directive (EU) 2016/1164 of 12 July 2016 laying down rules against tax avoidance practices that directly affect the functioning of the internal market [2016] OJ L193/1; Council Directive (EU) 2017/1852 of 10 October 2017 on tax dispute resolution mechanisms in the European Union [2017] OJ L265/1.

[109] Treaty on the Functioning of the European Union (consolidated version) [2012] OJ C 326 (TFEU).

[110] Compare Art 16, para 2 of the Treaty on European Union (consolidated version) [2012] OJ C 326 (TEU): 'The Council shall consist of a representative of each Member State at ministerial level, who may commit the government of the Member State in question and cast its vote'.

[111] See, therefore, Art 115 TFEU: 'the Council shall, *acting unanimously* in accordance with a special legislative procedure and after consulting the European Parliament and the Economic and Social Committee' (emphasis added).

[112] For a particularly critical stance in the context of OECD BEPS Action Plan's adoption, see Schön (n 4) 302: 'Any consensus found at the level of … the European institutions is nothing more than an agreement between Member States acting as a 'cartel' of fiscal authorities, aligning their policies to fight a common antagonist'.

[113] In the case that the national governments ought to be confirmed by the parliaments (ie, the national bodies in which the Member States' citizens are directly represented), according to the requirements of the national constitutional laws.

of the Member States' constitutional laws in the course of the adoption of the EU Treaties.

A similar argument cannot be made as regards the decision-making processes at the OECD level. Apart from being considered opaque,[114] they can be found to exclusively involve representatives from national tax authorities that are not subject to any legislative control.[115] Attributing relevance to amendments to the OECD MTC and its Commentary concerning OECD-inspired concepts in EU secondary law could accordingly translate into the OECD bodies having a direct impact on the essence of EU law.[116] Such an approach would likely stand in fundamental conflict with the requirements of both the EU[117] and domestic constitutional systems.

Arguably, the issues arising from a dynamic understanding of the OECD MTC and its Commentary could produce even more dire consequences in the EU context. This assertion stems from the fact that, as of writing, five of the 27 Member States are not members of the OECD.[118] Taxpayers in these countries would accordingly be confronted with a situation in which legally non-binding decisions of an intergovernmental network could influence their tax liability even though no (governmental) representatives of their countries are able to engage in the related decision-making processes.

It has already been revealed in the assessment relating to the doctrinal aspects of the Court's new argumentative pattern[119] that the ECJ has used a (dynamic) reference to the OECD MTC and its Commentary merely to bolster the interpretive result from an autonomous interpretation of the relevant EU secondary law provisions. The application of a dynamic understanding in its current manner should hence not be capable of producing the problematic effects discussed above. This might explain why the Court has seemingly demonstrated no sensitivity regarding the potentially wide-reaching effects of a dynamic use of the OECD MTC and its Commentary in its reasoning.[120]

[114] eg, A Christians, 'Sovereignty, Taxation, and Social Contract' (2009) 18 *Minnesota Journal of International Law* 99, 112–13; T Diniz Magalhães and I Ozai, 'A Different Unified Approach to Global Tax Policy: Addressing the Challenges of Underdevelopment' (2021) 4 *Nordic Journal on Law and Society* 1, 14–15.

[115] eg, De Broe and Gommers (n 4) 293.

[116] Depending on how the OECD work is effectively implemented in the interpretive process (ie, as the basis of the argument or merely to support the findings from an autonomous interpretation of EU law; see below).

[117] In a similar vein, see J Wouters and M Vidal, 'An International Lawyer's Perspective on the ECJ's Case Law Concerning the OECD Model Tax Convention and its Commentaries' in L Hinnekens and P Hinnekens (eds), *A Vision of Taxes within and outside European Borders: Festschrift in Honor of Prof Dr Frans Vanistendael* (Kluwer Law International 2008) 1003.

[118] This concerns Bulgaria, Croatia, Cyprus, Malta and Romania: www.oecd.org/about/.

[119] See section IV.A.

[120] For a similar less critical (yet undifferentiated) stance, see J López Rodríguez, 'Some Thoughts to Understand the Court of Justice Recent Case-Law in the Danmark Cases on Tax Abuse' (2020) 29 *EC Tax Review* 71, 81–82.

V. CONCLUSIONS

In its decisions in *Berlioz*, *N Luxembourg 1 and Others* and *État luxembourgeois*, the ECJ has developed a new argumentative pattern for purposes of the interpretation of OECD-inspired concepts of EU secondary law provisions, which is characterised by a two-tier structure. Accordingly, the reasoning has been based on an autonomous interpretation of the relevant EU secondary law provisions in light of the wording, the context and the objectives pursued. The findings stemming from an EU-based interpretation were then bolstered by statements in related OECD work. This has included the use of a dynamic understanding of the OECD MTC and its Commentary. The legitimacy of a dynamic interpretation is already highly disputed in a tax treaty context. Its application in the recent ECJ case law appears similarly flawed and potentially problematic. Most notably, the use of a dynamic interpretation of the OECD MTC and its Commentary could have a noticeable impact on the current state of power to tax in Europe.

From a doctrinal perspective, the Court's lines of argument in the three decisions share remarkable similarities. The judges did not overturn their previous methods, but merely extended their assessment to apply a two-pronged approach. The lack of value added by additional references to the OECD MTC and its Commentary can be identified as a first criticism. Another defect in the Court's argument relates to the fact that it partially unnecessarily relied on a dynamic interpretation of the OECD MTC and its Commentary. Hence, the ECJ could have used OECD documents that had been available at the time of the drafting of the respective directives, and had thus arguably been known to the EU lawmakers. The arguably most severe flaw in the Court's reasoning might yet be found in the absence of an explanation regarding the fundamental legitimacy of applying a dynamic understanding to the OECD MTC and its Commentary. The need to justify such an approach appears to be underlined against the background that neither the directives nor the related preparatory work suggest the relevance and permissibility of a dynamic understanding of the OECD MTC and its Commentary.

From a democratic perspective, the judges' rather indifferent response to the legitimate concern of a potentially insufficient democratic legitimacy in *N Luxembourg 1 and Others* is striking. A dynamic understanding of the OECD MTC and its Commentary is capable of shifting legislative powers to an intergovernmental network that has not been legitimised by the peoples of the Member States to take appropriate measures. This would be in evident conflict with both the EU and national constitutional regimes. Because not all EU Member States are also members of the OECD, such a development would arguably prove even more problematic in the specific EU context. However, the ECJ has applied a dynamic understanding merely to support the interpretive result stemming from an autonomous interpretation of EU law. The aforementioned serious effects should therefore not materialise in the course of a dynamic interpretation of the OECD MTC and its Commentary as it is used by the Court. This could explain the judges' seemingly relaxed attitude in the *N Luxembourg 1 and Others* judgment.

In light of the findings in the preceding sections, the question raised in the title of this contribution should be answered in the negative. Hence, the ECJ's new argumentative pattern does not have the capacity to permit the OECD to take influence on the meaning of OECD-inspired secondary law provisions, and thereby to shift the stakes of taxation powers in Europe. It is nevertheless hoped that the Court will advance its arguments in the context of an interpretation of OECD-inspired concepts in EU secondary law provisions on a more robust doctrinal foundation in the future.

Index

www.ingramcontent.com/pod-product-compliance
Ingram Content Group UK Ltd.
Pitfield, Milton Keynes, MK11 3LW, UK
UKHW020248290926
15470UKWH00002B/802

9 781509 964017